HUMAN RIGHTS IN THE **MAYA REGION**

HUMAN RIGHTS
IN THE **MAYA REGION**

Global Politics, Cultural Contentions,

and Moral Engagements

EDITED BY PEDRO PITARCH,

SHANNON SPEED, AND

XOCHITL LEYVA SOLANO

Duke University Press   Durham and London   2008

© 2008 Duke University Press

All rights reserved

Designed by Heather Hensley

Typeset in Minion Pro by Keystone Typesetting, Inc.

Library of Congress Cataloging-in-Publication Data appear
on the last printed page of this book.

Contents

Abbreviations

ADR, alternative dispute resolution

AIDPI, Accord on the Identity and Rights of Indigenous People

ASIES, Research and Social Sciences Association

CAJ, justice administration center

CALDH, Center for Legal Action and Human Rights

CDHFBC, Fray Bartolomé de Las Casas Human Rights Center

CDLI, Committee for the Defense of Indigenous Liberty

CEDAW, United Nations Convention for the Elimination of All Forms of Discrimination against Women

CEDH, State Human Rights Commission

CEDIAC, Center for Indigenous Rights

CEH, Commission for Historical Clarification

CERJ, Runujel Junam Counsel of Ethnic Communities

CMDPDH, Mexican Commission for the Defence and Promotion of Human Rights

CNDH, National Human Rights Commission

COAO, Coalition of Autonomous Organizations of Ocosingo

COCOPA, Peace and Harmony Commission

CODAIF, Diocesan Committee on Aid to Border Immigrants

CODHEY, Human Rights Commission of Yucatán

CODIMUJ, Diocesan Coordination of Women

CONAPO, National Council of Population and Housing

CONAVIGUA, National Committee of Guatemalan Widows

CONIC, National Indigenous and Campesino Coalition

CONPAZ, Coordination of Nongovernmental Organizations for Peace

CPP, Penal Procedures Code

CPR, Communities of Population in Resistance

CRC, United Nations Convention on the Rights of the Child

CRIACH, Counsel of Indigenous Representatives of the Chiapas Highlands

CUC, Committee for Peasant Unity

DEMI, Office for the Defense of Indigenous Women

EGP, Guerrilla Army of the Poor

EZLN, Zapatista Army of National Liberation

FAFG, Guatemalan Forensic Anthropology Foundation

FIDH, International Federation for the Rights of Man

FIS, Fund for Social Investment

FGL, Local Guerrilla Force

FRG, Guatemalan Republican Front

FRI, Immediate Response Force

GAM, Mutual Support Group

GANA, Grand National Alliance (Guatemala)

IACHR, Inter-American Court of Human Rights

IDB, Inter-American Development Bank

IDIES, Institute of Economic and Social Research

IFAD, International Fund for Agricultural Development

IIDH, Inter-American Institute of Human Rights

ILO, International Labor Organization

INAB, National Forestry Agency

INGUAT, Guatemalan Institute of Tourism

INMECAFE, Mexican Coffee Institute

MINEDUC, Department of Education (Guatemala)

MINUGUA, United Nations Verification Mission in Guatemala

MIRA, Anti-Zapatista Indigenous Revolutionary Movement

NAFTA, North American Free Trade Agreement

OAS, Organization of American States

PAC, Civil Self-Defense Patrols

PAN, National Action Party (Mexico)

PAN, National Progress Party (Guatemala)

PDH, Human Rights Ombudsman

PNC, National Civil Police (Guatemala)

PRD, Revolutionary Democratic Party (Mexico)

PRI, Revolutionary Institutional Party (Mexico)

REMHI, Interdiocesene Project for the Recuperation of Historical Memory

SEGEPLAN, Planning and Programming Secretariat of the Presidency

SIPAZ, International Service for Peace

UCJ, Earth Tree Water

UNDP, United Nations Development Programme

UNESCO, United Nations Educational, Scientific and Cultural Organization

URNG, Revolutionary National Unity of Guatemala

USAID, United States Agency for International Development

YUCATÁN

Gulf of Mexico

QUINTANA ROO

CAMPECHE

MEXICO

TABASCO

OAXACA

CHIAPAS

BELIZE

Caribbean Sea

GUATEMALA

HONDURAS

EL SALVADOR

Pacific Ocean

NICARAGUA

Human Rights and the Maya Region

In recent years, in a process many have come to refer to as globalization, the model of neoliberal democracy has spread throughout Latin America. Concurrently, human rights have become a concern of both states and their populations, and they have emerged as a key discourse in the renegotiation of the relationship between states and indigenous people, who regularly deploy human rights discourse to legitimate their positions and to pursue their goals. Perhaps nowhere is this clearer than in the Maya regions of Chiapas and Guatemala, where in the past two decades indigenous social movements have been engaged in an ongoing negotiation with the state and where the presence of multinational actors has brought human rights to notable prominence. But the question of how indigenous peoples are understanding, appropriating, and engaging with the nonlocal discourse of human rights, as well as the effects of its increased presence on indigenous identities and cultures, have not been sufficiently studied or understood.

The contributors to this volume explore the experience of the Maya region to shed light on broader questions about human rights and indigenous peoples today. As a diverse group of academics, activists, and indigenous people with long experience in Mexico and Central America, they bring a variety of perspectives to discussions centered around three interrelated questions: What is the relationship between globalized discourses such as human rights and local cultures? How are human rights working within the neoliberal state? In what ways do local appropriations of human rights discourse and the spaces opened by human rights discourse and its practices offer new possibilities for struggle, particularly for antiracist, anti-neoliberal, or other countersystemic struggles? Before situating ourselves within the parameters of these debates, we want to delineate the region studied and clarify why it is relevant to these questions.

The Maya Region

What constitutes the Maya region has been largely a subject of academic debate. Some definitions of the Maya region focus on notions of history, others on sociolinguistics, and still others on territory. For example, Alain Breton and Jacques Arnauld (1995: 10) affirm that with the "generic appellative of 'Mayas,' different groups of common origin and related languages have for centuries occupied the territorial extension that covers the south of Mexico (the states of Campeche, Quintana Roo, Tabasco, Yucatan, and Chiapas), Guatemala, Belize and western Honduras." This territorial extension has been called the "Maya area" or "Maya region" (Mesa Redonda 1984; see map). Some conceptualizations of the region emphasize a sense of cultural continuity or cultural change. They may differentiate the "historic Maya Area" from the "current Maya Area" (Breton and Arnauld 1994: 21–22) or suggest a prehispanic, colonial, and modern Maya region (Valdés 2003: 15). Further, the concept of the Maya region overlaps but does not directly coincide with that of Mesoamerica as defined by Paul Kirchhoff (1960).[1] While Kirchhoff identified a linguistic-cultural group he calls "Maya-Zoque" or "Macro-Maya" within the cultural macro-area of Mesoamerica, the original definition he assigned to Mesoamerica—what we could call the historic Mesoamerica—does not coincide with the one it is given today by its many diverse actors (Fábregas 2000: 145). Notions such as "Mesoamerica"—and the "Maya region"—have to be understood today based on their present context and taking into account not only the given demographic, economic, political, religious, and cultural changes they have undergone but also the interests at play in particular moments of the resignification (Fábregas 2000).

Whether or not indigenous individuals and communities understand themselves as Maya or as inhabiting a Maya region varies greatly. For a variety of social and historical reasons, some of which are discussed at greater length below, many indigenous peoples are more inclined to identify based on community, subregional, or language criteria. For example, in the Chiapas highlands, one might identify as "Pedrano" (from the municipality of San Pedro Chenalhó) or as "Tzotzil" (the Mayan language spoken there). Many indigenous people, particularly in Mexico, may identify themselves as peasants rather than as Indians. And we would venture to say that almost all would be more likely to identify themselves as "Chiapanecos" or "Mexicanos" than to link themselves to a Maya region. Indeed, outside academic circles, the concept of a Maya region has been most actively circulated by government tourism agencies promoting the "Ruta Maya." In Guatemala over the course of the 1990s, the Maya movement adopted a pan-Mayan identity (see Warren 1998) and consequently the concepts of Maya, Mayaness (Mayanidad) or Mayanization (Mayanización) have greater prominence in that country (Carmack 1988; Cojtí Cuxil 1997; Wilson 1995; Schackt 2002; Bastos and Camus 2003; Zapeta García 2005; *Memoria de los conversatorios* 2006; Mendizábal 2007) than in Mexico. Nevertheless, regional and local identifications continue to be important, even primary, for many indigenous communities. Indigenous rights movements in Chiapas, including the largely indigenous-based Ejercito Zapatista de Liberación Nacional (Zapatista Army of National Liberation, EZLN), have not asserted a Mayan identity, opting instead for a broader "indigenous" positioning. The coherence of the Maya region, for us, lies more in the series of historical, sociocultural, and political dynamics shared by much of Guatemala and the Mexican state of Chiapas than in a generalized and homogeneous understanding of the region as such by the current Mayan people who reside there.[2]

But academic discussions of the Maya region have paralleled the political dynamics lived by indigenous people in the region. For example, in the past two decades, Mayistas have perhaps most engaged in thinking about the Maya region in a collective, systematic, and multidisciplinary manner.[3] The chronicles of their colloquia and congresses since 1985 reflect these scholars' evolving interest in Mayan issues, including increasingly linking them with human rights and indigenous rights. The papers presented in roundtable sessions on Mayan rights reflected the broader political environment of the late 1980s, which included the massive flight of indigenous refugees from the Guatemalan military's scorched-earth campaign and the violent repression of social organizations in Chiapas.[4] By 1992, human rights had again appeared as a central topic, now tied to the call for rights to indigenous self-determination and autonomy in Latin America (Díaz-Polanco 1996; De la Peña 1998; Assies, van der Haar, and Hoekema 1999; Bengoa 2000; Stavenhagen this volume).[5] These roundtable discussions about Mayans' human rights were oriented exclusively to Guatemala and the Mexican state of Chiapas (excluding other concentrations of Mayas), due in all likelihood to the fact that in Chiapas and Guatemala the discourse and the contemporary practice of human rights were emerging in the context of war and state repression.

Human and Indigenous Rights in Chiapas and Guatemala

Several factors make it fruitful to think and write comparatively about human rights in Chiapas and Guatemala. First, both areas are characterized by immense socioeconomic inequalities and by the existence of large indigenous populations that are primarily of Mayan origin, who live in conditions of marginalization and exclusion, and who are permanent victims of discrimination, racism, and structural violence.[6] Also, there are politicized and organized indigenous populations in both regions that perceive human rights as an axis of social, political, and cultural struggle (Alejos 1992–94; Kovic, Sanford, Ekern, Otzoy, Speed and Reyes, Speed and Leyva Solano this volume). In both places these organized struggles confront nation-states that are reconfiguring in light of new "neoliberal multicultural" politics (Hale 2002; see also Bastos 2001, 2004; Hale 2006b; Díaz-Polanco 2006; Sieder, Stavenhagen, and Carmack this volume). These are thus significant shared social conditions in which the doctrine of human rights is interpreted and resignified by the broad Mayan populations of Chiapas and Guatemala. Since today's structural conditions are products of historical processes, a brief examination of them will add elements to the understanding of the current human rights situation in both entities.

J. E. Rolando Ordóñez asserts that Chiapas and Guatemala can be thought of comparatively because they have the same Mesoamerican Mayan roots, share the experience of the Spanish conquest, and above all belonged to the same political-administrative entity in colonial times.[7] In the colonial era the territory subject to the jurisdiction of the Audiencia of Guatemala stretched from the current border that separates the Mexican states of Chiapas and Oaxaca in the north to nearly as far south as the current border between Costa Rica and Panama. It included the cities of San Cristóbal de Las Casas and Tuxtla, as well as the Soconusco region (located in present-day Chiapas) (Solórzano 1993: 14). The Audiencia of Guatemala was part of the Mexican viceroyalty but enjoyed great autonomy because it answered to the Council of the Indies. This gave its governing elite great power, which provoked tensions among the political classes on both sides (the Mexican and the Guatemalan), but also lead to strategic alliances. For example in 1821, Guatemalan political factions hurried to declare their independence from Spain to avoid an armed confrontation with the Mexican troops. At the same time, one of these factions announced the annexation of the Central American provinces to the Mexican empire of Agustín de Iturbide. This annexation lasted only one year because of Iturbide's fall, and "rapidly the councils of the Central American cities declared the absolute independence of Central-America . . . on July 1 of 1823" (Solórzano 1993: 68). At that moment Chiapas became a sovereign country governed by a sovereign assembly that signed the Free Chiapas Plan, which had the objective of "democratically" deciding its political destiny through a plebiscite.[8] This plebiscite took place in 1824, and the majority favored the annexation of Chiapas to Mexico.[9]

But even though the nineteenth century marked the moment of formal separation between Chiapas and Guatemala, it was reinforced by the Mexican Revolution at the beginning of the twentieth century, which moved the Guatemalan oligarchy and military elites further and further away from the Mexican political class. In fact, the social ideas spread by this revolution set the most important seal of differences between Chiapas and Guatemala: the agrarian reform that led to the creation of the collective property called the ejido. Its existence did not prevent decades of agrarian struggle in Mexico, but made it possible that by 1994, even in marginal border states such as Chiapas, 52.58 percent of the cultivable surface was in the hands of *ejidatarios* or *comuneros* (collective landholders) and that only 24.63 percent belonged to private landowners (Villafuerte et al. 1999: 123). This differed tremendously from Guatemala where in the same years less than 3 percent of the population owned 70 percent of the arable land,[10] and 1.5 percent of the rural properties occupied 63 percent of the area dedicated to agriculture (Sieder 2001: 63; Bastos and Camus 2003: 13).

The postrevolutionary agrarian policy went in tandem with a corporatist, clientelist, authoritarian, and assimilationist *indigenista* politics. This form of governance differed significantly from forms of governance and state discourse in Guatemala, where an exclusionary Guatemalan state employed politics of extermination instead of integration and was highly militarized within the anticommunist framework of the Cold War. Guatemala has been characterized by having a relatively weak state and by the perpetuation of a strong ethnic division between indigenous and nonindigenous (Ladinos).[11] This state committed flagrant human rights violations against the Mayan communities during the genocidal repression of the 1980s commonly known as La Violencia (see Zur 1998; Warren 1998; Sanford 2003). Mexico, by contrast, was characterized by a relatively strong state that addressed the "problem" of the indigenous population with assimilation tactics whose purpose was to "modernize" the indigenous peoples. The emergent ideology of *mestizaje* incorporated indigenous people as part of the national past by positing that the Mexican population was a racial mix between Spaniards and Indians that constituted a "cosmic race" (Vasconcelos 1997).[12] The corporatist politics of the Mexican state worked to include the indigenous population into its project and to ensure their support and their vote for the party in power. However, whenever corporatist approaches failed, the Mexican state would turn to repression and to human rights violations against the masses, primarily the poor and rural indigenous population (HRW 1997; PHR 1994; AI 1986).

As we have mentioned, from the 1980s until the Zapatista uprising of 1994, the discourse of human rights in Chiapas was closely linked to the process of the Guatemalan refugees and the debate about the "right to refuge" of the Mayas arriving in Chiapas as a consequence of the Guatemalan government's scorched-earth campaign (see Foro de Reflexión 1990; Camey Rodríguez 1992; Castañeda 1992; Ruiz García 1992; Freyermuth and Hernández 1992; Castro Soto 1994; Kauffer 1998). This happened just as Chiapas went through one of its most intense periods of political repression, one waged against independent peasant movements that took over land and estates and allied with the parties and confederations opposing the then-ruling party (Institutional Revolutionary Party, PRI). Thus the Guatemalan refugee crisis combined with the political-religious communitarian (see Fernández 1995; CNDH 1995; Kovic 2005) and the agrarian-regional struggles against abuses of power by the government, by caciques, and by large landowners (see CNPA and FNCR 1981; Albores and González 1983; CLCH 1986; Burguete Cal y Mayor 1989, 1994; De la Cruz and Pérez 1993; Gómez and Kovic 1994; SERPAJ 1995) to create a setting ripe for the development of human rights discourse and practice. At this time, the primary promoters of human rights were the diocese of San Cristóbal, local nongovernmental organizations (García Aguilar 1998), and the militants of the leftist movements (see Burguete Cal y Mayor 1989, 1994; Kovic, Speed and Reyes this volume).

The discourse of human rights had thus already made its entrance in various parts of the Maya region when the EZLN launched its armed movement against the Mexican government on the eve of the North American Free Trade Agreement (NAFTA). The Zapatista uprising, a predominantly Mayan insurgency, brought human rights even more strongly to the fore. With the political-military conflict unleashed in 1994 between the EZLN and the Mexican government, a boom began in both the practice of human rights defense and in intellectual production about human rights. This was due in part to the human rights abuses generated by the militarization and paramilitarization of many Mayan communities, and also to the fact that the Zapatistas themselves quickly created and mobilized human rights activist networks to defend themselves. Further, as the movement developed, it increasingly made indigenous rights a fundamental part of its discourse (Le Bot 1997; Leyva Solano 1998; Díaz-Polanco 1997; Ce Acatl 1996). In the context of war and low-intensity warfare the discourse of human rights appeared systematically in the reports of civilian observation commissions and in the denunciations of repression (against indigenous leaders and activists) and of the abuse of power by the military and paramilitaries, especially in the case of the Acteal Massacre in December of 1997.[13]

The similarities and differences between the Mexican and the Guatemalan states, and between Chiapas and Guatemala, are perhaps many more than we can discuss in this introduction. We have pointed briefly to some that we feel are of greatest significance. One more similarity emerges clearly from the contributions to this volume: the concept of human rights at the end of the twentieth century is intimately bound up with questions of indigenous rights and indigenous rights movements (see Speed and Reyes, Speed and Leyva Solano, Kovic, and Sieder this volume).[14]

But in spite of the similarities that we suggest make the comparative study of communities in Chiapas and Guatemala fruitful, the differences the reader will find in the essays of this book also make this comparative exercise interesting. The contributions to this volume point to a broad variety of practices and interpretations among the Mayan population, demonstrating that global-local-state interactions are very complex and diverse even within a geographically limited area. It is worth noting that this diversity is marked not only by a border between two nation-states but also by great variations extant within each state and even within particular Mayan linguistic subgroups. The Mayan experience is of course much more varied than the division between Guatemala and Chiapas. Within each state, different communities and regions have had unique historical processes, distinct interpretations of Mayan culture, and different engagements with human rights. For example, the meaning and uses of human rights may be different for the Tzotzil Mayans expelled from their home communities and living in the city of San Cristóbal (Kovic this volume), than for the Tzeltal Mayans of the Lacandon jungle who are part of an armed resistance movement (Speed and Reyes this volume), or for the Chol Mayans who ally themselves with paramilitary groups and the former state party (Speed and Leyva Solano this volume). Along the same lines, human rights can prove meaningful and useful in different ways for the Q'eqchi' Mayans in a process of social healing in Panzós (Sanford this volume) and for the K'iche' Mayans in Totonicapán (Ekern this volume).

At the dawn of the twenty-first century this diversity reflects a vast divergence from the notion of the homogeneous nation-states. It leads us to consider human and indigenous rights in the context of the current neoliberal states whose multicultural politics reinvent the states themselves and present new challenges not only to indigenous peoples but also to the nations as a whole (Bastos 2001; Sieder 2001; Díaz-Polanco 2006). In the following section, we turn to an analysis of these dynamics.

Human Rights and Neoliberal Globalization

In the post–Cold War march of neoliberal democracy throughout Latin America, authoritarian regimes that had for a number of decades favored policies of nationalism, economic protectionism, and the use of social services and agrarian reform as part of their governance practices gave way to governments that embraced electoral politics, opened markets and natural resources to foreign goods and capital, and eliminated social services and programs. The downsized neoliberal state, as it has emerged in the past two to three decades, reduces its social welfare undertakings and removes all restrictions on the economy designed to protect those citizens with fewer resources, a process epitomized by the so-called structural adjustment measures pushed by international financial institutions in many countries in Latin America. Responsibility for the mediation of social inequality is "privatized," passed from the state to industry and business (corporate social responsibility), to communities and individuals, and especially to professionalized advocacy groups in civil society such as NGOs (Álvarez et al. 1998; Bickham Mendez 2005; Berger 2006). Thus in neoliberalism, as the market is prioritized and the state divests itself of responsibility for social welfare, relations among social groups are increasingly defined by market forces and mediated by civil society itself (Guehénno 1995; Hardt 1998; Schild 1998; Gill 2000; Berger 2006).

Notably, democratization and neoliberalization were accompanied in many Latin American countries by the states' adoption of the discourse of human rights and, where populations were diverse, that of indigenous rights and multicultural politics. Constitutional reforms neoliberalizing economies and policies also recognized (for the first time, in many cases) the pluricultural composition of a number of states including Bolivia, Colombia, Ecuador, Guatemala, Brazil, and Mexico (Assies, van der Haar, and Hoekema 2000; Van Cott 2000; Sierra 2001). These reforms entailed a shift from previous assimilationist approaches to governing diversity to a new multiculturalist approach that entails the state recognition of distinct groups within society and some measure of self-regulation for them.

Of course, this was not a unilateral, state-driven process. Human rights and indigenous rights struggles had already been well under way in Latin America as populations struggled against repressive authoritarian regimes and sought to overcome centuries of systemic racism and oppression. Indigenous struggles had made significant progress in some countries and were exerting considerable pressure in others. However, with the globalization of neoliberal democracy and the concurrent decline of the national revolutionary model of resistance, human rights emerged as the basis of social movements throughout the hemisphere (Brysk 1994, 2002; Escobar and Alvarez 1992; Wilson 1997b; Jelin 1996). As the NGOization tied to neoliberal state downsizing combined with the new emphasis on legalism and rights struggles as the appropriate form of political participation (Brown and Halley 2002), human rights seemingly became the only discourse available in which to frame or enact resistance. The global spread of the human rights discourse has rapidly influenced the terms and forms in which individual and collective social actors articulate their struggles and their demands.

A number of questions are raised by this ostensibly predestined, evolutionary spread of human rights throughout the hemisphere and the effects of this process on local populations and their cultural understandings and political subjectivities. There are three interrelated debates that the authors of this volume address. One set of questions has been focused on human rights specifically as a Western concept and discourse, and asks how its fundamentally individualist and universalist tenets may diverge from or (at least potentially) converge with those of groups who are compelled to use the discourse in their various struggles. Another set of questions focuses on the reconfiguration of state power and on the relationship of states to their populations, particularly their indigenous populations, and on the role human rights play in this process. Yet another set of questions focuses on local conceptualizations and appropriations of human rights and on the multiple forms of contestation articulated through this discourse. We will explore each of these sets of questions in further depth in the sections below.

Anthropological interest in the relationship between human rights and non-Western peoples is not new (see Messer 1993, 1995; and Nagengast and Turner 1997 for useful reviews). In a long-running debate regarding universalism and the applicability of universal notions of any kind in diverse societies with distinct moral value systems, many anthropologists took a relativist stance, arguing that any practice can be understood only in the context of the cultural logics of the social groups to which it pertains (Donnelly 2003; Downing and Kushner 1988). As Sally Merry notes, for many anthropologists the universal application of the concept of human rights represented "an artifact of Western cultural traditions raised to the status of normativity" (1997: 28), an ethnocentric imposition of liberal cultural values on indigenous and non-Western societies (see An'Naim 1992; Bell 2000; Downing and Kushner 1988; Donnelly 1989; Pannikar 1992).

Richard Wilson's 1997 volume *Human Rights, Culture, and Context* made a much-needed call for anthropology to move beyond the universalist-relativist dualism. Wilson's suggestion that we focus on the local actors and broader networks of power is particularly important in the current context of globalization in which, from a relativist perspective, the assault on local cultures is intensified, constituting "cultural imperialism with a global reach" (Merry 1997). Focusing on the various engagements of local peoples with this globalized discourse, some suggest, allows us to comprehend the complexities of the lived processes and avoid absolutist dualisms (Cowan, Dembour, and Wilson 2001; Goodale forthcoming; Merry 2006).

Taking the insights developed in these studies as our point of departure, in this volume we focus on the engagement of a variety of actors with human rights in a particular local setting: the Maya region as we have defined it. Some might suspect that the concept's widespread appropriations by actors with divergent political projects make human rights little more than a vehicle for the globalization of old discourses (conservative, revolutionary, religious) couched in new, less overtly contentious language (see López García this volume). Yet as the combined contributions herein reveal, the reality is considerably more complicated. When the object of study becomes the varied spatial and discursive sites in which global discourses and local cultures meet, we find that the process of interaction is varied, complex, and frequently contradictory. Even when considering how indigenous communities engage with human rights (as distinct from the state, military, and other social actors) in both Guatemala and Chiapas, multiple and divergent understandings and uses of the discourse abound. For some groups, the Western concept of human rights is sufficiently foreign to render it incomprehensible or unworkable within a particular cultural worldview (Pitarch, Ekern this volume), and in some cases indigenous communities may find themselves compelled to utilize human rights discourse to advance their claims even when it is not particularly resonant with their own understandings of their situation (Ekern this volume). Still others find the discourse resonates with or validates their experience in some way, and they may actively mobilize it (Speed and Leyva Solano, Kovic, Stanford this volume), or they may find parts of the discourse useful and may engage with it in struggles over meaning, regardless of its level of compatibility or contradiction with their own worldview (Otzoy, López García this volume). Whatever the case, it is clear that human rights discourse has dramatically replaced other potential discourses of resistance for indigenous peoples (Gledhill 1997).

Nevertheless, it is not clear that the anticipated homogenization of cultures under the weight of advancing Western discourses has occurred. As people increasingly utilize the discourse, the social, epistemological, and political effects are multiple, and, importantly, not unidirectional. First, conventional (liberal, universal) propositions of human rights are actively involved in a dialogue with other ethical and political conceptions, effecting mutual permutations and continually reshaping each other. "This interactive reshaping takes place between differing perspectives within the Western liberal tradition, but also . . . between Western ideas of human rights and indigenous Mayan conceptions of personhood, society, and justice" (Pitarch and López 2001: 11). Further, even when the use of the discourse of human rights can be understood in a particular context as strategic, that appropriation, and the moral and conceptual engagement it implies, inevitably reshapes local understandings. That is, human rights are not only affecting political relations in the Mayan region but also the conceptualization and interpretations of the nonindigenous actors involved. In effect, there is an ongoing intercultural dialogue in which such concepts as human rights are continuously reinterpreted, as are local identities and political subjectivities.

That said, it is also clear that the dialogue of Mayan communities with other social actors takes place in the context of highly unequal power relations. It has become common among cultural theorists of the subject to associate globalization with the homogenizing effects of global capital (Jameson 1991, 1999; Giddens 1990), a perspective that takes into account the determinative force of change wrought by global markets and flows of capital, commodities, people, and information. From this point of view, the globalization of legal doctrines and norms such as human rights that accompany global capitalism forms part of a process that necessarily implies cultural change in ways that replace local norms and understandings. In other words, when Mayan conceptualizations come up against the globalizing force of capitalism's legal norms, the Mayan understanding is far more likely to be the one required to change.

These are not simply abstract processes in which the global effaces the local through sheer processual force; rather they are situated in actually existing and evolving relations of power and domination. Recent studies have considered how the state has used human rights, and indigenous rights in particular, as a means to circumscribe indigenous resistance, autonomy, and power, while indigenous communities use them to different ends in struggles for empowerment (Hale 2002; Postero 2001; Speed 2005). We can observe this process at work in the communities of Chiapas, where in cases in which local practices violate international and national human rights standards, Mayans are forced by the state, or petitioned or "trained" by NGOs, to rethink their norms (Speed and Collier 2000). It is thus important to recognize that the construction of culture takes place in a dialogic process, but one that remains weighted against local peoples in a variety of ways.

We hope that this volume will continue the process of moving anthropological thought on human rights in the direction of studying the different conceptualizations and appropriations, as well as the effects of the discourse of human rights in local populations, specifically those of indigenous peoples with distinct conceptual systems and practices. Thus, while we have sought to avoid confining ourselves to the now ubiquitous debate between universalists and cultural relativists, the book does make an intervention in this discussion.

Taken collectively, the essays in this volume demonstrate that, in the local contexts of distinct Mayan communities, the discourse and practice of human rights can be foreign to, distinct from, and incompatible with local concepts and social norms (the relativist argument) and yet can be appropriated, reshaped, and made relevant and useful for the social actors involved. That is, while we all (both academics and Mayans) recognize that universal human rights involve concepts largely external to Mayan communities and that their usage is determined by the global spread of the doctrine and its legal regimes,[15] it is not in all cases accurate to characterize the usage of human rights as simply a form of Western cultural imperialism. This is demonstrably not the case where Mayan communities are actively engaging with this discourse, negotiating and reformulating its meanings. The essay in this volume authored by Irma Otzoy, herself a Mayan intellectual, represents one such engagement, one in which Mayan women endeavor to bring Mayan culture into dialogue with Western feminist notions of women's rights. The various discussions of the process of cultural interaction throughout the book reaffirm that Mayan culture, far from being homogeneous or static, is in a continual process of change, one forged in dialogue with nonlocal discourses and social actors.

HUMAN RIGHTS AND THE NEOLIBERAL STATE

The simultaneous reframing of both state discourse and indigenous struggle in human rights terms also raises questions about how human rights discourse is working within specific processes of power, including neoliberal state power and the more deterritorialized if nonetheless tangibly felt power of capitalism in its neoliberal forms. Is this a felicitous confluence of state goals and Mayan aspirations that, after considerable negotiation, may bring about full recognition, rights, and "multicultural citizenship" (Kymlicka 1996) or "ethnic citizenship" (De la Peña 1995; Bastos 1997; Harvey 1998a; Villoro 2002; Zárate 2002; Leyva Solano 2005)? Or is the flourishing of the discourse of human rights part of a process in which relations of power between states and indigenous populations are being reconfigured in ways that facilitate new neoliberal forms of governance?

Some analysts have argued that the parallel spread of neoliberalism and of the discourse of human rights is due either to a response to increasing needs as the welfare state is left behind (Donnelly 2003) or to horizontally spreading resistance to the harsher consequences of neoliberalization (Bengoa 2000; Brysk 2000; Ignatieff 2003; Yasher 1999). These analysts view human rights from below as a process inherently contestatory to neoliberal globalization.

Others have been concerned with how these discourses function within the new forms of governance undertaken by neoliberalizing states (Gill 2000; Postero 2001, 2007; Gustafson 2002; Hale 2002, 2006b). These authors suggest that human and indigenous rights discourses are working within neoliberal Latin American states in several ways. First, as Rachel Sieder (2002) suggests, recognizing human rights and the rights of ethnic minorities or indigenous peoples was critical to establishing the authority of the democratic state. Some have viewed the recognition of rights principally as a concession on the part of political elites struggling to maintain legitimacy and authority even as they were increasingly unable to meet the material needs of their populations or to finance corporativist social pacting (Van Cott 2000; Collier 2000). Others have considered how rights and law serve to legitimate power, replacing the use of repression and force to maintain political power with the increasing deployment of political discourses and strategies of inclusiveness (Gill 2000). Still other analysts have focused on how such multicultural politics of recognition (in Taylor's 1999 sense) ultimately work to limit the force of collective indigenous demands and to divide indigenous people into those acceptable to the state and those whose demands are outside the range of the permissible (Gustafson 2002; Hale 2002, 2006b).

But human rights may also be working as more than a new justificatory discourse of power. The neoliberal mandate for reduced state intervention in social life requires the participation of all subjects in managing and regulating society, thus rendering inclusive policies and processes of subject formation the priorities of rule (see Rose 1999; Burchell 1996). Both individuals and collectivities are potential self-governing subjects, hence both individual human rights and collective indigenous rights articulate with the formation and legitimation of neoliberal forms of power. In fact, it has been argued that indigenous claims to autonomy can fit well within a neoliberal logic of self-management, as long as those claims can be contained within the legal framework of state recognition.

Nancy Postero has demonstrated how in Bolivia the "indigenous subjects of neoliberalism" (2001: 7) get constituted through the state's multicultural practices, which work to structure indigenous political participation in ways that imbue them with rationalities proper for adequate—and acquiescent—integration into economic markets. Postero shows how state policies and NGO trainings inculcate concepts of individuality and self-regulation. Thus neoliberal multiculturalism—in Charles Hale's (2002) sense—may cede rights to indigenous people, but with the effect of remaking them as subjects less likely to frontally challenge neoliberal economic and political policies.

Not only NGO programs engage in subject making. The law itself may provide a privileged space for the state to engage in neoliberal subject making because of its inherent delimiting, normalizing, and regulating power (Brown 1995, Gledhill 1997). Nivedita Menon argues that "modern forms of power do not simply oppress, they produce and regulate identity [and] law is an important technique by which this is achieved" (2004: 205). Concepts such as culture and identity are fluid and mutable, and once defined and codified in law, they become fixed and thus more easily limited and controlled. This is not a minor issue for Mayan peoples, who by no means have a unified identity and culture. How will they be defined in law? In what ways will the recognition of their rights as indigenous people potentially limit them and their aspirations in the future?

RIGHTS AND RESISTANCE IN MOVEMENTS AND NETWORKS

There is a third, and of course related, set of issues addressed in this volume concerning the engagement of Mayan people with human rights. While it is important to consider how power works through human rights in ways that may be regulatory, it is also vital to account for the ways in which human rights can serve to challenge structures of power and thus contribute to emancipatory processes (De Souza Santos 1998). To what extent is resistance based on legal rights claims or presented in rights language necessarily proscribed, and in what ways can local appropriations, reconfigurations, and redeployments work to further indigenous struggle?

As Hale has recently suggested, while rights may be part of the neoliberal project, previously they remained outside the realm of broad public consideration, and in the current political juncture all social actors can engage in the struggle to "shape their content and their reach" (2006b: 76). Some analysts are thus concerned with the ways that the globalization of human rights discourses offers opportunities for resistance to power both by putting rights questions on the table and by providing new possibilities for local social actors to reshape them in pursuit of their own goals.

For example, some anthropologists have considered how human rights are appropriated and deployed by indigenous people and other social actors in processes of collective memory and social healing in the wake of extreme violence (Amadiume and An-Na'im 2000; Sanford 2003; Sanford this volume; Theidon 2004; Cowan, Dembour, and Wilson 2001; Bastos, Hernández, and Méndez in press). Others have focused on how indigenous people and other local actors have appropriated the discourse of human rights and reshaped it based on local subjectivities—what Merry (2006) has referred to as the "vernacularization" of rights talk and others have analyzed as a new "cosmopolitanism" on the part of indigenous people (Clifford 2005; Goodale 2006b). In this volume, Christine Kovic demonstrates how human rights discourse takes on new significance in the hands of the poor, of the diocesan human rights center, and of faith-based grass-roots organizations when it is redeployed based on local experience and as a form of contestation to economic injustice. Shannon Speed and Alvaro Reyes (this volume) explore how indigenous Zapatistas are redeploying rights discourse based on local political subjectivities in ways that challenge the project of neoliberal state power. This is possible as Xochitl Leyva Solano (2001, 2006b) has pointed out, because the struggles against neoliberalism and capitalism have permitted the construction of moral grammars (Honneth 1996) that sustain transnational political agendas. Among the most relevant of such grammars shared within the neo-Zapatista networks Leyva Solano found those based on struggles for recognition and for human, indigenous, ethnic, or women's rights.

All these analyses suggest that while the globalized use of human rights discourse opened up by democratization and neoliberalization is inevitably constrained by power relations, indigenous people do demonstrate considerable agency in making use of the opportunities opened and the support provided, while engaging in the process of struggle to shape their content and reach. Precisely because human rights are globalized, demands for rights find support from a vast array of international sources. These range from institutional agencies such the World Bank, the Interamerican Development Bank (IDB), and the United Nations (UN), which support legal reforms of the state with the goals of promoting democracy and advancing market reform (see Sieder this volume), to European and American networks of solidarity and antineoliberal globalization and social justice activists (Le Bot 1997; Keck and Sikkink 1998; Reygadas 1998; Waterman 1998; Escobar 2000; Leyva Solano 2006b). While the first set of these demonstrates the intimate relationship of human rights to neoliberal capitalism, the financial and logistical support they provide to local groups may also be empowering and useful for rights movements at particular junctures. Further, the latter set of networks, from mainstream human rights organizations and faith-based solidarity groups to activists seeking more radical social change, can be mobilized in support of local goals in a myriad of ways.

The strengthening of civil society impelled by neoliberal state downsizing and the end of state mediations of social inequality (Jackson and Warren 2005) and the related emergence of transnational advocacy networks (Keck and Sikkink 1998) have undoubtedly opened new possibilities for social struggle.[16] As Margaret Keck and Kathryn Sikkink argue, "transnational networks multiply the channels of access [of domestic actors] to the international system, and help to transform the practice of national sovereignty" (1998: 1–2). Local social actors, including indigenous Mayans, are seizing the spaces and opportunities opened by democratization and human rights, mobilizing networks constructed around human rights advocacy, and appropriating the discourse of rights and reshaping it based on local concepts and subjectivities, remaking it as a potentially more challenging tool.

Structure of the Book

We have arranged the essays in three sections—global politics and nation-states, cultural contentions, and political engagements. These sections do not directly coincide with the three sets of theoretical questions laid out above. Those questions run through all of the works in the volume to differing degrees. Rather, the division of the essays into sections is based on our estimation of the emphasis and perspective of the authors in approaching these questions.

The first set of essays addresses how broad processes and philosophical models take shape in distinct nation-state contexts (Carmack, Sieder) and looks at the effects of these models on the indigenous population in the current global order (Sieder, Stavenhagen).

The essays in the second section focus on the disconnects and misunderstandings between liberal, Western human rights discourse and practice, and that of indigenous Mayans. These range from the inherent disjuncture between Western and Mayan concepts, and how the distinct notions are negotiated (Pitarch, Otzoy) or not (López García), to the incompatibility of the legal systems based on these divergent conceptualizations (Ekern), to the (externally imposed) misinterpretation of human rights violations as "vertical" (i.e., perpetrated by the state) when they are in fact "horizontal" (Stoll).

In the final set of essays, the authors are concerned with the ways in which human rights works as a discourse of empowerment or resistance. The articles explore how people in particular local contexts are appropriating, understanding, and putting into practice the discourse of human rights in ways that resonate with their own experiences (Speed and Leyva Solano, Kovic) and that facilitate their own goals, which vary from social reconstruction and healing (Sanford) to the creation of an indigenous autonomy that challenges neoliberal logics (Speed and Reyes).

We do not understand these themes as independent of one another, even in the case of the second and third sections, which might seem diametrically opposed. On the contrary, as the sum of the essays shows, all of these processes are complex, interrelated, sometimes contradictory, and sometimes complementary. The reader will find that the contributors' analyses correspond with each other in a variety of ways, but also that they frequently diverge. The fact that as a group these essays treat so many problems, and focus on human rights in so many ways, demonstrates the breadth of the implications that this theme has for the indigenous Mayans of Chiapas and Guatemala, and for indigenous peoples throughout the Americas. This diversity of analyses also reflects the fact that the authors (like the Mayas they write about) have differing engagements with human rights, as well as different positionalities from which they produce their knowledge (see Haraway 1988).

Two broad tendencies or currents exist among the contributors. A number of us have long been involved in human and indigenous rights activism in the region and elsewhere and thus draw on the strength of that critical engagement with the actors involved; others (whose engagements with their research subjects might have been equally intense, just not activist oriented) have approached the topic from a more strictly academic perspective, embracing the critical distance provided by an academic standpoint. The differences between these two tendencies are both epistemological and methodological. For example, it is notable that for the most part those interested in reflecting on the state and on rights struggles have had some kind of activist engagement (Hale 2001, 2004, 2006a; Naples 2003; Speed 2005; Leyva Solano 2006a; Sanford and Angel-Ajani, 2006; Leyva Solano, Burguete Cal y Mayor, and Speed in press). For these scholars the practices and discourses about peoples' rights, the Mayan organizations and movements, and their relationship with the issues of power, neoliberalism, and democracy are central and emerge from their activist engagement. The contribution to this volume by a female Maya academic intellectual could be cited as part of this current. Otzoy affirms approaching her work as a woman and as Maya and points out that her principal interlocutors are the Mayan communities, not the academics. Other contributors critique precisely such activism, thus, sometimes, logically distancing themselves from activist undertakings and, in general, from a focus on what is Maya and what is non-Maya (e.g., human rights). We believe this diversity of viewpoints makes for one of the volume's strengths, providing the reader with a variety of analyses from a range of perspectives.

The goal of this volume is to contribute to the anthropology of human rights by providing a sustained look at one particular region, the Maya region, and at the broader webs of power in which it is embedded. Notwithstanding this regional focus, the contributions are comparative, demonstrating that global-local-state interactions are quite complex and diverse even within a geographically limited space. We hope the volume will contribute to new understandings of the ways in which human rights are situated within structures and discourses of global and state power, but also, perhaps most important, of the agency with which local actors, Mayan peoples, are engaging with human rights in an ongoing process of resignification, contestation, and accommodation. Exploring these questions in the particular local context of the Maya region contributes to our understanding of broader questions of culture, power, and agency in globalization.

Notes

We thank Jutta Meier-Weidenbach for her assistance translating some sections of this introduction and Vivian Newdick for editorial assistance. We also thank Jennifer Bickham-Mendez, Kathleen Dill, and Angela Steusse for their comments on an earlier version. The final responsibility for the facts and ideas presented remains with the authors.

1. For Kirchhoff, Mesoamerica was part of the area of the superior agriculturalists of the American continent. To define it, Kirchhoff used linguistic, geographic, and ethnic criteria, openly criticizing the classifications applied in his era that identified "cultural areas" based above all on biological criteria and on those of geographic politics (Fábregas 2000). Immanuel Wallerstein affirms that area studies was probably the most notable academic innovation after 1945. It manifested the new imperial power of the United States, but at the same time prompted multidisciplinary studies of a region, which helped demonstrate the artificiality of the "clear institutional separations of knowledge in the social sciences" (2006: 40, 42).

2. Although, without using the concept "Maya region," diverse speakers of Mayan languages in Chiapas, Guatemala, and Quintana Roo are daily engaged in the process of constructing new sociocultural relations. Since the end of the armed conflicts in Guatemala and Chiapas, one sees Guatemalan Mayans cross the border to Chiapas and Quintana Roo to hold Mayan ceremonies and discuss Mayan cosmovision and spirituality. This is a form of living and constructing a transnational Maya space.

3. Mayistas are scholars who study the Mayans and who may come from anywhere in the world. See, for example, the 220 speakers from twelve countries participating in the First International Mayista Congress: they came from France, Spain, Germany, Denmark, Poland, Russia, Japan, Canada, the United States, Guatemala, Honduras, and Mexico (De la Garza 1992: 6).

4. Papers presented included Rodríguez y Rodríguez 1989; O'Dogherty 1989; Toledo 1989.

5. Papers included Ordóñez Cifuentes 1992–94; Alejos 1992–94; González-Ponciano 1992–94.

6. In Guatemala there are twenty-two ethnolinguistic groups of Mayan origin (PNUD 2005: 61, 63). According to the social demographic profile of 2004, there are fourteen indigenous languages registered in Chiapas, of which the Mayan languages Tzeltal, Tzotzil, and Chol are the most commonly spoken. Tojolobal and Mam are also Mayan languages spoken in the state. Non-Mayan indigenous languages include Zoque and Zapotec (INEGI 2002: 59). This marginalization is readily apparent to anyone who has visited indigenous communities and rural areas of Chiapas and Guatemala, particularly in the lack of basic services available to their residents. There are a variety of statistics available that measure this marginalization; we provide a few of them here to give a sense of the problem, though we are aware of their limitations. In 1998, 60 percent of the Guatemalan population was indigenous, but 90 percent of it lived in poverty and 76 percent in extreme poverty (Sieder and Witchell 2001: 63). In 2002, Guatemala only registered 41 percent of its population as indigenous (PNUD 2005: 79), but on average those municipalities with an indigenous majority were the ones with the lowest

index of human development (PNUD 2005: 114). By 2006, 56 percent of the population were still officially poor and 21 percent of that live in extreme poverty. See Comunidad Económica Europea, *Guatemala. Documento de estrategia 2002–2006*, ec.europa.eu/external_relations/guatemala/csp/02_06_es.pdf.

In Mexico in 2002, the indigenous population represented 7.3 percent of the population, while in Chiapas it is 26.8 percent (INEGI 2001: 69). The percentage rises to between 40 percent and 100 percent in some regions such as the highlands, the Northern Zone, and the Lacandon jungle, bringing it closer to the Guatemalan indigenous-nonindigenous ratio. In 2000, the National Council of Population and Housing (CONAPO) also identified those indigenous regions as having the highest level of marginalization in the state and in the country (qtd. in Gobierno del Estado de Chiapas 2003: 31).

Literacy rates are a limited referent, but they can give us a sense of the conditions of exclusion experienced by indigenous people in Chiapas y Guatemala. In 2002, the illiteracy rate among Guatemalan indigenous people was 47.7 percent, while it was 20 percent for nonindigenous people. The figure rises to 58.3 percent when one looks at indigenous women, and to 78 percent in some departments such as Chiquimula (PNUD 2005: 362). Chiapas also has a higher illiteracy rate than the national average. While the official average for the country was 10 percent in 2000, in Chiapas 23 percent of the population as a whole was illiterate, increasing to 29 percent for women. Levels reached as high as 60–70 percent of the adult population in some municipalities of the highlands (where the indigenous population is highest) (INEGI 2002: 74–76).

7. The interview was conducted during the V Congress of the Latin American Legal Anthropology Network (Red Latinoamerico de Antropología Jurídica, RELAJU), Oaxtepec Morelos, October 17, 2006.

8. The close economic ties between the Central American region and the Soconusco at the time lead to the Soconusco joining Guatemala at that moment (1823). This caused diplomatic quarrels leading to the Soconusco's independence until its reintegration into Chiapas and Mexico was achieved in 1842 (Pineda 1999; De Vos 1993).

9. But in spite of this, or maybe because of it, Chiapas remains a "hinge" entity pulled by both Central American and Mexican forces and processes depending on each particular historic situation. One example of this was the refugee crisis of the early 1980s, in which Chiapas's social and political dynamics were affected by the genocidal politics of its southern neighbor.

10. These numbers refer to the end of the 1990s and were taken from Sieder and Witchell 2001: 63. In Guatemala "the indigenous sectors represent almost half of the agricultural producers, but control only 24% of the cultivated land" (PNUD 2005: 132).

11. As José Alejos (1992–94: 451) points out, there is a "culturalist myth" affirming that the Guatemalan sociocultural problems are centered on the dichotomy be-

tween Indians and Ladinos, and this is used to explain the totality and complexity of the Guatemalan reality. But for Alejos, "these approaches carve a political substrate in stone and today, as in previous eras, serve as a modern ideological pillar of the prevailing system of domination." Thus, he adds, the causes of the conflicts, which lie in the system of economic exploitation and social inequalities, are hidden behind cultural differences.

12. For analyses of the postrevolutionary Mexican state, see Joseph and Nugent 1994.

13. Many sources might be cited here; we limit ourselves to the reports produced by the National Network of Civil Human Rights Organizations (Red Nacional de Organismos Civiles de Derechos Humanos 1998) and by the Secretariat of Judges for Democracy (Secretariado de Jueces para la Democracia 1997).

14. While we have emphasized here the strength of the human rights discourse in Chiapas and Guatemala, it does not mean that the discourse is absent entirely from other areas of the broader Maya region. In Yucatán the human rights discourse has become more present due in part to the creation of the National Human Rights Commissions (Comisión Nacional de Derechos Humanos, CNDH). There are also autonomous associations in Yucatán engaged in human and indigenous rights work. These are mostly narrowly focused groups that acquire local strength principally when they articulate with national and transnational movements for the defense of human, political, and indigenous rights. Prior to 2006, we found only one anthropologist writing academically about human rights in Yucatán (Krotz 2004a, 2004b), but the subject has been taken up by lawyers (Cantón Osalde 2001; Mendoza Freya 2003; Baeza Martínez 2005), members of the (governmental) Human Rights Commission of Yucatán (Comisión de Derechos Humanos del Estado de Yucatán, CODHEY), and by some associations of organized civil society (see the electronic bulletin *El Varejón*, www.indigna cion.org; Equipo Indignación 2001). In Yucatán, studies of legal pluralism and indigenous rights (Krotz 1997, 2001) are more numerous than those on human rights.

    In Campeche an incipient interest in human rights questions among social scientists has been focused on indigenous conciliation courts (Gutiérrez Rivero 2001; Collí Ek 2004; Gabbert 2006). In Quintana Roo, on the other hand, the study of human and indigenous rights is linked more closely to the analysis of customary law and the traditional Mayan judges (Reyes and Ek Cituk 2001; Buenrostro 2006; Estrada, Bello, and García 2006). This interest correlates directly with the legal situation created locally because of the constitutional and legal modifications of 1992, 2001, and 2003 (Krotz 2001). In Campeche, Yucatán, and Quintana Roo independent unionists working in the rope-making industry, in shoemaking, fishing, and university sectors have also taken on the defense of human rights since the 1980s. See www.geocities.com/rebeldecaribe/ and www.geocities.com/rebeldecaribe/CONTRAPODER.html., accessed October, 2006.

15. Several articles in this volume note the frequent Mayan perception of human

rights as being brought into the community by outsiders, whether it is the government, the UN, or NGOs, and their concern that this obstructs their own local autonomy (Ekern, Speed and Leyva Solano, Stoll).

16. Among the kinds of transnational networks that Margaret Keck and Kathryn Sikkink discuss are those of corporate and economic actors, as well as scientific and activist networks. The latter, which they call "transnational advocacy networks," provide the focus of their study. These are characterized as having "voluntary, reciprocal, and horizontal patterns of communications and exchange" (1998: 8). They are advocacy networks because "advocates plead the causes of others or defend a cause or proposition," in other words, "they are organized to promote causes, principled ideas, and norms, and they often involve individuals advocating policy changes that cannot be easily linked to a rationalist understanding of their 'interests'" (8–9).

GLOBAL POLITICS AND NATION-STATES $\quad$ 1

Cultural Rights and Human Rights
A Social Science Perspective

The Problem of Cultural Rights

The issue of cultural rights within the general debate about human rights forms part of a wider concern about the location of culture in international discourse.[1] The contributions of the United Nations (UN) have proven rather modest in this field. Article 15 of the International Covenant on Economic, Social and Cultural Rights, adopted by the UN General Assembly in 1966, mainly refers to the right of everyone to take part in cultural life, to enjoy the benefits of scientific progress and its applications, and to benefit from the protection of scientific, literary, or artistic works. Article 13 posits the right of everyone to education, which "shall be directed to the full development of the human personality and the sense of its dignity." While cultural rights are also referred to in numerous international instruments, as well as in several United Nations Educational, Scientific and Cultural Organization (UNESCO) conventions and recommendations,[2] the full implications of cultural rights as human rights remain to be explored. This essay aims to contribute to the debate from a social science perspective.

Cultural rights are closely related to other individual rights and fundamental freedoms such as the freedom of expression, the freedom of religion and belief, the freedom of association, and the right to education. Cultural rights have not been credited with much importance in theoretical texts on human rights and, as Asbjørn Eide has pointed out, are treated rather as a residual category. Yet states do have obligations to ensure the respect, protection, and fulfillment of each of these rights, and these obligations should be spelled out in the case of cultural rights and their various interpretations (Eide 1994: 233–38).

While some cultural rights can be dealt with exclusively within the framework of universal individual human rights, the relationship between culture and human rights is such that a broader approach is warranted. Lyndel Prott argues that cultural rights—particularly those pertaining to the preservation of cultural heritage, the cultural identity of a specific people, and cultural development—are sometimes considered "peoples' rights," and she calls for renewed efforts to frame such issues in international legal terms (1988: 92–106). In this essay I shall discuss some ideas concerning these issues.

If cultural rights are to be understood as any individual's right *to* culture, then ideally this term should have an unequivocal meaning. Yet even a cursory look at the way in which some international documents and legal instruments have dealt with the concept of culture shows a variety of usages. The right of a people to its own artistic, historical, and cultural wealth is stated in Article 14 of the Algiers Declaration on the Rights of Peoples, adopted by a nongovernmental meeting of prominent experts in 1976. It has no legal standing in international law, not having been sanctioned by an intergovernmental body, but as Ian Brownlie (1988) recognizes, it has had "a certain influence," particularly to the extent that its ideas were reflected in the African Charter on Human and Peoples' Rights, adopted by the Organization of African Unity in 1981.

UNESCO has asserted the right of every people to develop a culture and has proclaimed a "right to cultural identity,"[3] whereas the Algiers Declaration refers to the right to respect of cultural identity, and the right of a people not to have an alien culture imposed on it. The rights of persons belonging to ethnic, religious, or linguistic minorities to enjoy their own culture, to profess and practice their own religion, and to use their own language, in community with the other members of their group, are found in the International Covenant on Civil and Political Rights (Art. 27), and they were reaffirmed in the 1992 UN Declaration on the Rights of Persons Belonging to National or Ethnic, Religious and Linguistic Minorities, which also calls on states to take measures enabling persons belonging to minorities to develop their culture.[4]

The Genocide Convention, adopted in 1948, defines genocide, which it declares a crime under international law, as the commission of certain acts "with intent to destroy, in whole or in part, a national, ethnical, racial or religious group, as such" (Art. 2). Besides the actual killing of people, these acts include "causing serious bodily or mental harm to members of the group . . . forcibly transferring children of the group to another group, etc." Thomas Buergenthal rightly argues that by outlawing the destruction of national, ethnic, racial, and religious groups, the Genocide Convention formally recognizes the right of these groups to exist as groups, which surely must be considered the most fundamental of all cultural rights (1988: 49).

Underlying Conceptions of Culture

A careful reading of the above instruments will show that they refer indirectly to various distinct conceptions of culture that are not always clearly spelled out in the texts and that are in fact often used rather loosely in general discourse. A systematic treatment of cultural rights as human rights will require a somewhat more rigorous conceptualization of cultural terminology.

CULTURE AS CAPITAL

One common view identifies culture with the *accumulated material heritage of humankind* in its entirety, or of particular human groups, including monuments and artifacts. According to this position, the right to culture would entail individuals' equal right of access to this accumulated cultural capital. An extension of this view is the right to cultural development. Many governments and international organizations have established cultural development as a specific process of cultural change, which some people see as parallel or complementary to other forms of development, for example, economic, political, or social development.

The argument appears to go like this: if economic development means increasing goods and services, a rising gross national product (GNP), and a better distribution thereof among the population, then cultural development would mean "more culture" and better access to culture by more categories of people. Very often this is interpreted as a purely quantitative process: the publication of more books, the establishment of libraries, the wider circulation of newspapers and magazines, the building of museums, a higher number of TV sets, national budgets for cultural activities, and so on. The quantitative growth of cultural services is sometimes equated with the concept of cultural development, yet relatively little attention has been paid in official reports to the more qualitative dimensions of this process. What are the nature and the contents of such services? Can an increase in the number of TV channels really be equated with cultural development?

It is often assumed that there is consensus on the meaning of "cultural development," but it makes for a doubtful proposition. One could argue, for instance, that many of the general statements about the right to cultural development—implying more of the so-called cultural services—too often hide the fact of underlying cultural conflicts in our societies, cultural conflicts similar to social, political, and economic ones. These conflicts occur over the recognition and identity of culturally defined groups, or about the nature of "national" culture, or the aims of cultural policies. One widely accepted proposition proclaims the existence of a universal culture, one that only some people can enjoy, while others may not have access to it. It follows that a right to culture should entail a more equitable access to this universal culture.

This, however, is not the only possible approach, for the right to culture may also be interpreted as the right to a group's own culture, and not necessarily to some general or supposedly universal culture, because these two concepts are not necessarily coterminous. In fact, it has been pointed out repeatedly that so-called universal culture more often than not means the worldwide imposition of Western culture through the hegemonic practices of Western powers from the time of colonialism onward. To be sure, UNESCO's efforts at universalizing the cultural heritage of humankind are a step away from the Eurocentric tradition.

CULTURE AS CREATIVITY

A second widely held view does not necessarily regard culture as accumulated or existing cultural capital, but rather as the *process of artistic and scientific creation*. Accordingly, every society has certain individuals who create culture (or, alternatively, who interpret or perform cultural works). Within this perspective, the right to culture means the right of individuals to create their cultural oeuvres with no restrictions, and the right of all persons to enjoy free access to these creations (museums, concerts, theater, libraries, etc.). Cultural policies are therefore intended to further the position of the individual cultural creator in society (the artist, the writer, the performer), and this creator's right to free cultural expression has become one of the most cherished human rights in contemporary times. The cultural creator in fact symbolizes the freedoms of thought and expression, which have emerged as two of the motivating forces behind human rights struggles throughout history. Let us simply remember the international outcry that usually occurs when artists or writers are banned, exiled, or imprisoned (let alone executed) by authoritarian regimes (Aleksandr Solzhenitsyn, Kurdish writers in Turkey, or Salman Rushdie come to mind).

The view of culture as the result of the labor of cultural specialists has led to a widely held distinction between "high" and "low" culture. In Western countries, at least, cultural debates revolve around the relative weight and significance of elite culture and popular culture, the latter being defined as belonging to the sphere of the performing arts, usually channeled through the mass media and targeted at specific audiences by the cultural industries (e.g., pop music and pop stars, cult films, fashionable ways of dressing, youth culture promoted by highly paid and publicized promoters and performers). There is another view of popular culture that I will deal with below, but official policies directed toward the development of culture usually focus on supposedly elite culture. In this case, cultural rights are easily identified with the rights of the cultural creators, the cultural specialists.

CULTURE AS A TOTAL WAY OF LIFE

A third view of culture comes to us from the discipline of anthropology. It takes culture to mean the sum total of the material and spiritual activities and products of a given social group, which distinguishes it from other similar groups. Thus understood, culture is also seen as a coherent, self-contained system of values and symbols, and as a set of practices that a specific cultural group reproduces over time and that provides individuals with the required signposts and meanings for behavior and social relationships in everyday life.

The peoples of the world are the carriers of many thousands of distinct cultures. In some instances, all or most of a country's population share a common culture; in others, a state is made up of a variety of different cultures. There is no consensus about the actual number of existing cultures or about criteria for the definition of membership (who belongs, who is excluded), though this is a crucial issue, particularly in relation to the problem of cultural rights. Similarly, there is no hard and fast way to draw a line distinguishing one culture from another. This is neither possible nor indeed necessary for our understanding of cultural dynamics. Generally speaking, specialists estimate that in contrast to the world's more or less two hundred independent states, there are about ten thousand distinct ethnic groups or ethnies, based mainly on linguistic differences. Linguistic differences serve as one of the main criteria, but by no means the only one, for distinguishing one culture from another.[5]

Cultures are not static. On the contrary, every identifiable culture is historically rooted and changes over time. Indeed, cultural change and the constant dynamic recreation of cultures are universal phenomena. A culture may be said to have particular vitality if it is capable of preserving its identity even as it incorporates change, just as a specific human being will change over time but retains her or his distinct identity.

There is, however, a danger in this approach of treating culture as an object, a "thing" that exists separately of the social space in which various social actors interrelate. Anthropology reminds us that the ethnic (cultural) identity of any group depends not so much on the content of its culture as on the social boundaries that define the spaces of social relationships by which membership is attributed in one or the other ethnic group (see, e.g., Barth 1969; Thompson, Ellis, and Wildavsky 1990).

Following from this critique, recent scholarship treats culture as something that is constantly constructed, reconstructed, invented, and reinvented by ever-changing subjects; the emphasis here is on the way people perceive and speak about their culture, rather than on the culture itself (which by this criterium would have no objective existence outside of the individual's subjectivity). Customs and traditions are inherent elements of all observable cultures, yet traditions are constantly being invented and reinvented, and customs, by which people carry on their daily lives, regularly change to conform to varying historical circumstances, even as they strive to maintain social continuity. National cultures, which are very closely linked to state activity through governmental educational and cultural policies, are imagined collectively in historical processes, and nations are sometimes described as "imagined communities." So while cultures are given objective existence (people are born into a culture, social groups are identified by their cultures), they are also subjectively and variously constructed and fashioned by myriad individuals in continuing social interactions (Hobsbawm and Ranger 1983; Anderson 1983).

Why and how cultures persist, change, adapt, or disappear constitutes a special field of inquiry, and such questions are intimately related to economic, political, and territorial processes. At any given time, in any given area, there may be majority and minority, dominant and dominated, hegemonic and subordinate cultural groups. UNESCO's World Commission on Culture and Development writes: "A country need not contain only one culture. Many countries, perhaps most, are multi-cultural, multi-national, multi-ethnic and contain a multiplicity of languages, religions and ways of living. A multi-cultural country can reap great benefits from its pluralism, but also runs the risk of cultural conflicts" (UNESCO 1995: 25). The International Commission on Education for the Twenty-First Century argues that one of the problems of the future is "the multiplicity of languages, an expression of humanity's cultural diversity. There are an estimated 6,000 languages in the world, of which a dozen are spoken by over 100 million people" (UNESCO 1996: 40).

While so-called culture wars (ideological tensions and conflicts over cultural issues such as education, language, cultural policies, etc.) may occur in well-integrated societies without actually splitting them asunder (generally because other kinds of social, economic, and political institutions help keep the contenders together), in other cases cultural issues have become powerful mobilizing forces in political strife around the world.

Consider just one instance among many: The Serbo-Croatian conflict that triggered the breakup of Yugoslavia had much to do with long-standing rivalries between the national elites of the two republics over linguistic and religious issues. After decades of linguistic debates over the nature of "Serbo-Croatian" or "Croato-Serbian," in 1966 a large number of Croatian intellectuals published a declaration insisting that Croatian was a distinct language and should be officially treated as such. One author writes that "the attempt to divide the languages was labeled nationalistic and was suppressed through a strong political campaign" (Neçak-Lük 1995: 119). Other examples could be readily provided, but we should note that these are not exclusively cultural conflicts, but rather political ones over cultural issues. The way societies handle cultural differences among their populations may become highly politicized, and these problems are often resolved at the political level (Young 1976).

Are Cultural Rights Culture Specific?

If culture is understood in this wider, anthropological sense, rather than simply as accumulated cultural capital or the product of the talents and labor of a small number of cultural creators, it can be argued that cultural rights in their collective sense are culture specific, that is, that every cultural group has the right to maintain and develop its own specific culture, no matter how it is inserted or how it relates to other cultures in the wider context. This idea is now referred to as the right to cultural identity (Burgers 1990b; Stavenhagen 1990b: 251–58).

The approach raises a number of important issues regarding the right to culture. Basic to the Universal Declaration of Human Rights and the general instruments of human rights is the principle of nondiscrimination and equality. During the post–World War II debate on human rights, it was argued that if the principle of nondiscrimination were strictly adhered to, then everybody would have equal access to all the "goods" in the human rights basket, be they civil and political rights or economic, social, and cultural ones. Yet whether access alone really suffices to ensure these rights' enjoyment by everybody remains a major question in the discussion of cultural rights.

It may be argued that the enunciation of the principle of nondiscrimination is not sufficient within the framework and processes of present-day societies to provide all individuals with equal access to all human rights. Moreover, even if true nondiscrimination were a reality for everybody (which it is not), it would still not necessarily ensure the enjoyment of specific cultural rights. A case can be made for the need to develop procedures and mechanisms that allow the affirmation and enjoyment of specific cultural rights, because only such mechanisms can actually *guarantee* cultural rights.

A second question following from the one above is whether the concept of cultural rights can be adequately encompassed by a notion of universal individual rights, or whether they should be complemented by a different approach, that of collective or communitarian rights. There are persuasive reasons for the latter idea. The principles of nondiscrimination and equality, as set out in the Universal Declaration of Human Rights and the International Covenant on Civil and Political Rights basically relate to the rights of individuals. However, when we refer to cultural rights, as well as to a number of social and economic rights, a collective approach is often called for, since some of these rights can only be enjoyed by individuals in community with others, and such a community must have the possibility to preserve, protect, and develop its common culture. "Cultural freedom—states the Pérez de Cuellar report—is a collective freedom. It refers to the right of a group of people to follow or adopt a way of life of their choice" (UNESCO 1995: 25). Beneficiaries of these rights may be individuals, but their content evaporates without the preservation of the collective rights of groups. Cultural rights pertain to persons belonging to specific cultures and shaped by these cultures who engage in collective action, share common values, and can only be the bearers of these common values by joining with other members of their own group (Burgers 1990a: 63–74).

This line of reasoning necessarily poses the question what kind of collectivities might be the logical subjects of such rights. Who are the bearers of these rights? Who are the actors, in sociological terms, that can claim these rights and to whom they are applicable? This is a complicated issue because it leads directly into the discussion of the rights of minority groups —cultural groups or peoples—a concept that occasionally appears in international human rights instruments but that is rarely adequately defined.

Cultural Diversity and Universal Human Rights

When we speak of cultural rights we need to take into account the cultural values that individuals and groups share, values they often hold dear and that shape and define their collective identities. The right to culture implies respect for the cultural values of groups and individuals by others who may not share these values; it means the right to be different. How else are we to interpret the fundamental freedoms of thought, expression, opinion, and belief that are enshrined in the Universal Declaration of Human Rights? The fact that different cultures and civilizations do not necessarily share the same values must thus be accommodated. Perhaps humans hold many values in common, but cultures may differ regarding others as a result of, for example, different histories or social organization. These differences occur across state boundaries and civilizational fault lines, but also within countries when culturally differentiated peoples share a common state and its territory.[6]

But stressing the diversity of cultural values runs counter to the major thrust of human rights thinking in the world today, which sees the universality of human rights as the foundation of the international human rights edifice. Individual human rights must not only be universal in scope (that is, they must apply to all human beings) but the underlying values must also be universally shared. All human beings are equal; no matter what distinguishes them, they have the same rights. Yet when we speak of the respect for different values as essential to the concept of collective cultural rights, does that very distinction not imply a rejection of universality to recognize the specificities of different social groups (UN 1986)?

Whereas some scholars would deny the validity of this line of reasoning, arguing that cultural relativism jeopardizes the concept of human rights itself, the real world is clearly composed of a multiplicity of culturally distinct groups and peoples. Unless the debate on cultural rights acknowledges the particular issues relevant to each cultural group, we may only be talking about meaningless abstractions.[7]

This issue was recognized by the American Anthropological Association (AAA) as early as 1947, when the United Nations Commission on Human Rights was still discussing various drafts of the declaration. At the time, the executive board of the AAA submitted a statement to the commission, raising the question of how the proposed declaration could be made to apply to all human beings. The Universal Declaration of Human Rights should not, said the American anthropologists, be conceived only in terms of the values prevalent in Western Europe and America. The association argued, first, that individuals realize their personalities through their culture, hence the respect of individual differences entailed a respect for cultural differences.

Second, the respect of differences among cultures was validated by the scientific fact that no technique of qualitatively evaluating cultures had been discovered. Third, standards and values were relative to the culture from which they derived, so that any attempt to formulate postulates that grew out of the beliefs or moral codes of one culture must to that extent detract from the applicability of any Declaration of Human Rights to humankind as a whole. Finally, the AAA suggested that "only when a statement of the right of men to live in terms of their own traditions is incorporated into the proposed Declaration, then, can the next step of defining the rights and duties of human groups as regards each other be set upon the firm foundation of the present-day scientific knowledge of Man" (AAA 1947).[8]

Thus even as the declaration was drafted a half century ago, American anthropologists considered it to embody the values of only one culture, and they questioned the automatic applicability of these standards to other cultures. In more recent years, particularly as African and Asian states have joined the UN, many third world nations have also embraced this position, and it was highly visible at the World Human Rights Conference in Vienna in the summer of 1993.

The African Charter on Human and Peoples' Rights, for one, illustrates some of the difficulties intimated above. Article 17 takes from the Universal Declaration of Human Rights the stricture that "every individual may freely take part in the cultural life of his community," and adds that "the promotion and protection of morals and traditional values recognized by the community shall be the duty of the State." Surely morals and traditional values are culturally defined, and what "community" does this article refer to?

Chapter 2 of the charter refers not to rights but to duties. This offers an interesting counterpoint to the question of rights. Article 29 states, inter alia, that the individual shall have the duty "to preserve and strengthen positive African cultural values in his relations with other members of the society." If to preserve and strengthen positive African cultural values is spelled out as a duty, the existence of a countervailing right to African cultural values may be assumed. If it is every African's duty to strengthen and preserve these values, then every individual must have the right to enjoy them as well.

It should be noted that in its formulation, Article 29 distinguishes African values from non-African values. It also posits a certain unity or homogeneity of African values, since it makes no reference to possible internal diversity. And finally, if there are positive African values, then by implication there must also be negative African or non-African values, ones that need not be strengthened or preserved. What, however, are these positive African values, and how are they defined? If this appears like a tough intellectual challenge, it is surely even more difficult to apply the concept legally. Just raising this problem means opening up a Pandora's box of difficulties.

There is another dimension to the problem of cultural rights. We should be concerned not only about respect for variations of cultural values across international boundaries and among different regions, historical traditions, and political systems but also within countries. Most of the signatory states of various international human rights instruments are themselves mosaics of different cultures. Whether these are the cultures of ethnic groups, minorities, nationalities, or nations, in fact very few countries are culturally homogeneous. What does this diversity mean in terms of human rights and the right to cultural development? If we understand the right to cultural development not only as that for individuals to innovate and receive more cultural services but also as the right to one's own culture—the culture of the group into which one is born, in which one lives, and with which one identifies—that is, as the right to cultural identity, then we must again ask, how are the objectives of cultural policies defined? When we speak of more and better education, what will the content of this education be? When we speak of cultural development, which cultures will be developed, and by whom?

We must perforce return to the question of cultural definitions. Over the past half century, development was frequently identified as a process of nation building, an important aspect of which has been the development of a "national culture," particularly in the countries of the so-called third world, many of which achieved political independence during this time. Yet the conveniently ambiguous term of *national culture* leaves open the question of whose nation and what kind of nation is to be developed. Walker Connor has rightly suggested that the development of modern states has been more of a process of "nation-destroying" than one of "nation-building" as numerous nonstate peoples have in fact been destroyed or eliminated in the name of the modern nation-state (Connor 1972).

As the term has been used in recent history, nation building generally implies a melting pot of peoples, or else a process of national integration or of amalgamation. This means that the various ethnic and cultural groups who for one historical reason or another find themselves living within the defined borders of an internationally recognized state are expected to give up parts of their cultural identity to either adopt the values of the dominant or majority groups or else to mix and create something entirely new (this is generally assumed to have constituted the process of nation building in the United States). But usually the social groups who wield political power determine the model to which national culture is to adhere, in other words, they decide the form and contents of educational and cultural policies.[9]

Who are the people in power? On analysis, we may find that they often belong to one of the hegemonic cultural groups, who may be a majority or a dominant minority. And because they are the dominant group, they can define the national culture in terms of their own cultural identities. Hegemonic cultural groups who have the ability or power to define the national culture then expect all other groups to conform to this model, even if that means, in the long run, the destruction of other cultures.[10]

The relationship between a cultural hegemon and other culturally distinct groups (whether referred to as peoples, nations, or minorities of various types) is a complex issue that has serious implications for the definition and enjoyment of cultural rights. When a given ethnic group extends its cultural hegemony over weaker groups, a violation of cultural rights occurs. In extreme cases, this has been labeled "cultural genocide," but the Genocide Convention or other legal human rights documents do not actually refer to this notion.[11] More commonly, the process is referred to as "ethnocide," and it occurs all over the world (Stavenhagen 1990a: 85–92). Ethnocide, the willful destruction of a people's culture, is a far cry from actual genocide—the physical destruction of a people or a part thereof such as occurred in Bosnia and in Rwanda in the early and mid-1990s—but it is nonetheless a serious breach of international human rights standards.

The attempts by hegemonic ethnic groups in control of the state to homogenize national culture, and resistance to such policies by the subordinate groups, is becoming a subject of international concern, and the issue has been taken up by the relevant UN bodies such as the UN Subcommission on the Prevention of Discrimination and the Protection of Minorities. A growing number of states now recognize their multicultural heritage and some encourage the different groups on their territory to preserve and develop their separate cultures. Human rights discourse also refers to the right to be different. When we talk about cultural rights, we also mean the right of groups within a country to be able to maintain their own cultural identities, to be able to develop their own cultures, even (or especially) if these are distinct from the mainstream or dominant model of cultural development established by the so-called ethnocratic state.[12]

There have been bitter arguments between the universalists and the contextualists on these human rights issues, the former arguing that the Western liberal conception of human rights has universal validity, the latter maintaining that distinct cultures have different ways of dealing (or not) with human rights. In fact, the differences between the two extreme positions are not insurmountable. Most political theorists now recognize that even the most liberal and individualistic human rights policy, one that is neutral and impervious to any kind of cultural differences—one that is "difference blind," so to speak—must nevertheless take such differences into account as sociological and often political facts of life when building a solid human rights edifice. To the extent that cultural identities are structured through collective interaction among socially and culturally defined individuals, it is clear that the respect for the individual rights of members of minorities or disadvantaged and marginalized groups must go hand in hand with the rights of such groups to preserve and develop their own identities. One political theorist, referring to Canada, argues that the liberal politics of individual rights must be expanded to include the politics of difference and of recognition (Taylor 1994).

Human rights policies are not entirely neutral because they are the result of the values shared by the majority or dominant culture in any given society at any one time. The fact that they are dominant does not necessarily make them universal. If culture is recognized as continuous practice—rather than a set "thing"—then the evolution of human rights thinking in different cultural contexts should be seen as an ongoing, dialogic process rather than an either-or scenario.[13]

International Standards and Cultural Rights

The Universal Declaration of Human Rights does not mention minorities or any other human group except the family. When the Human Rights Commission drafted the declaration between 1946 and 1948, some states wanted to include specific provisions on cultural rights of minorities. However, the predominant view then was that this was not a general human rights issue, but relevant only to some specific multicultural societies, mainly in Europe. Due to the commission's inability to achieve consensus on this point, the declaration deals with everyone's right to participate in and contribute to the cultural life of the community in a very general way, a statement that lends itself to various interpretations.

Understandably, several states and many individuals were dissatisfied by the way in which the declaration dealt with cultural rights and the rights of minority peoples. But we do well to remember that at the same time that the declaration was adopted, the General Assembly passed another lesser-known resolution, in which it stated that "the United Nations cannot remain indifferent to the fate of minorities," adding that "it is difficult to adopt a uniform solution of this complex and delicate question, which has special aspects in each State in which it arises" (UN 1984: 116).

Article 27 of the International Covenant on Civil and Political Rights is one of the few concrete results of earlier discussions in the UN on the question of minorities. It says: "In those states in which ethnic, religious or linguistic minorities exist, persons belonging to such minorities shall not be denied the right, in community with the other members of their group, to enjoy their own culture, to profess and practice their own religion, or to use their own language." This is the only article in the international bill of human rights that specifically addresses the question of the cultural rights of minorities.

This text may be considered a step toward the recognition of the rights of cultural minorities, and perhaps even as a move beyond the abstract and universal consideration of individual human rights toward the idea of group rights. Nonetheless, some observers have commented that Article 27 falls far short of what is required in international instruments to ensure the protection of minorities and of their cultural rights. Numerous states refuse to recognize the legal or even the cultural existence of minorities within their borders. Article 27 makes for too weak a provision to protect and promote the cultural rights of minorities since, without state interference, the general historical tendency is toward the destruction of minority cultures—through the power structures in modern societies, the economic system, the impact of the mass media, as well as common educational policies. Unless the rights of cultural minorities are thus taken seriously and states and international organizations develop mechanisms to actively promote, protect, and strengthen minority cultures, the latter will be lost even without a willful intention to destroy them.

The UN Declaration on the Rights of Persons Belonging to National or Ethnic, Religious and Linguistic Minorities, adopted by the General Assembly in 1992, takes a more positive view. Article 1 proclaims that "States shall protect the existence and the national or ethnic, cultural, religious and linguistic identity of minorities within their respective territories, and shall encourage conditions for the promotion of that identity."[14] However, the declaration falls short of ensuring the collective rights of cultural minorities. Article 4 speaks about measures to be taken by states "to create favourable conditions to enable persons belonging to minorities to express their characteristics and to develop their culture, language, religion, traditions and customs," in short, to express their identity. Yet it adds this restrictive caveat: "Except where specific practices are in violation of national law and contrary to international standards."

As we have seen, national law may at times be restrictive of the cultural rights of minorities, so this provision in Article 4 raises the issue of the relation between national law and international human rights standards, including those of the declaration itself. Asbjørn Eide considers that

> the limitations set by national law, however, must not go beyond what is permissible under international human rights law. States cannot, by the use of national law, prohibit groups from developing their culture, unless the development is contrary to international standards. What is

involved, in particular, is to prevent that 'development of culture' is used to maintain traditions which constitute violations of human rights, such as discrimination of women, imposed marriages, the maintenance of caste systems or other forms of systemic discrimination, female circumcision, or other forms of violations of international standards. It underlines the point, which is essential in all issues of accommodation, that groups cannot demand to preserve those aspects of their culture and identity which are incompatible with universal norms. (1994: 100)

The danger here is that some outside body might wish to set itself up as a judge of other peoples' cultures, a situation that recent historical process flatly rejects and that obviously contradicts the right of peoples to self-determination. Regarding the possible conflict between group rights and individual rights from the standpoint of international human rights, one might suppose that individual human rights should have primacy whenever they are threatened by group rights (including cultural rights). No universal consensus exists about this problem, however. Jürgen Habermas argues cogently that "a correctly understood theory of rights requires a politics of recognition that protects the integrity of the individual in the life contexts in which his or her identity is formed" (1994: 113).

A case in point that has received widespread attention in recent years relates to the rights of indigenous peoples, defined as the descendants of those populations that inhabited a given territory before the arrival of a conquest or settler society, to which they were thereafter subordinated. In contrast to nations that achieve or regain their political sovereignty in later years (decolonization), indigenous peoples the world over, who have often suffered severe discrimination and marginalization and have frequently been denied full citizenship, demand not only equal rights with all other citizens but also the recognition of their own collective identities (including cultural identity, social organization, and territorial links) and an inclusion as equal partners in the wider society. Collective cultural rights are an important part of indigenous group claims. Some states have made progress in recognizing these rights (Bolivia, Canada, Australia, Norway); others (e.g., Chile, India, the United States), however, resist recognizing such rights and insist rather on the concept of the all-inclusive "civic" nation that rejects the legal and political recognition of subnational collective identities.

Convention 169 of the International Labor Organization (ILO) is one of the few international legal instruments that refers specifically to indigenous peoples. A draft Declaration of Indigenous Rights (including cultural rights) has been discussed in the UN Human Rights Commission since 1996, with still no practical results ten years later.[15] The Organization of American States (OAS) is considering a similar declaration for the Americas. While indigenous organizations wish their members to be called "peoples," many states reject this terminology because of its implications in international law. Indigenous peoples' rights are essentially cultural rights.

Cultural Rights and State Policies

How do states deal with these issues? In most countries in which minorities exist, state policies are designed to assimilate or integrate them into the prevailing model of the national culture. In some cases this might prove a shared objective. For example, in immigration states, where people come from various parts of the world, the immigrants may actually want to shed their traditions and become part of the new melting pot. However, even in societies that sustained the idea of the melting pot for many generations, this ideal has increasingly come under criticism. Too often, policies of national integration, of national cultural development, actually imply a policy of ethnocide, that is, the willful destruction of cultural groups.

There is increasing, though somewhat controversial, support for the view that minorities have a right to internal self-determination, which is less territorial than cultural; and to maintain and preserve their separate identities within the larger national society, sometimes within a framework of autonomy (Hannum 1992); Stavenhagen 1993; Tomuschat 1993). Governments tend to fear that if minority peoples hold the right to self-determination in the sense of a right to full political independence, existing states might break up through secession, irredentism, or the political independence of such groups. State interests thus presently supersede the human rights of peoples (Levy 2000). Some states, indeed, use the argument of cultural relativism to weaken, if not actually repress, human rights within their jurisdiction.[16]

Indigenous Peoples: A Case for Cultural Rights

The struggle for the rights of indigenous peoples illustrates well some of the issues discussed here. I shall refer briefly to the 40 odd million indigenous of the Americas, particularly in Latin America, where over four hundred distinct groups have been identified.[17] The UN defines indigenous peoples as follows: "Indigenous communities, peoples and nations are those which, having a historical continuity with pre-invasion and pre-colonial societies that developed on their territories, consider themselves distinct from other sectors of the societies now prevailing in those territories, or parts of them. They form at present non-dominant sectors of society and are determined to preserve, develop and transmit to future generations their ancestral territories, and their ethnic identity, as the basis of their continued existence as peoples, in accordance with their own cultural patterns, social institutions and legal systems."[18]

In the draft Declaration of the Rights of Indigenous Peoples, which was still under discussion in the UN Human Rights Commission as of 2006, cultural rights figure prominently, such as the right of indigenous peoples to be protected against cultural genocide and ethnocide; and "the right to the restitution of cultural, intellectual, religious and spiritual property taken without their free and informed consent or in violation of their laws, traditions and customs." The intellectual property rights of indigenous peoples include "sciences, technologies and cultural manifestations, including human and genetic resources, seeds, medicines, knowledge of the properties of fauna and flora, oral traditions, literature, designs and visual and performing arts," in sum, their "cultural heritage," which falls within the scope of what I have called collective cultural rights.[19]

Convention 169 of the ILO on indigenous and tribal peoples, which has been ratified by seventeen states since its adoption by the ILO General Conference in 1989, is the only international treaty specifically dealing with indigenous peoples. The convention stipulates that indigenous "peoples shall have the right to retain their own customs and institutions, where these are not incompatible with fundamental rights defined by the national legal system and with internationally recognised human rights."

Struggles for indigenous rights occur under the umbrella of these international documents, which provide a framework for more specific regional human rights instruments and for new legislation undertaken at the national level in a number of Latin American countries. For centuries, indigenous peoples were oppressed, exploited, and marginalized under a strict colonial regime in Latin America. During the independence period (since the early nineteenth century), the indigenous underclass (consisting mainly of poor subsistence peasants, migrant workers, and serflike rural laborers) found itself neglected and ignored by the ruling classes in their vision of building modern nation-states. Such states were thus built on the backs of

Indian labor, and even though Indians enjoyed formal equality as citizens in some countries, they lacked most of the attributes of full citizenship. During the twentieth century government policies attempted (with some success) to assimilate and incorporate Indian populations into the (non-Indian) mainstream. Still, Indian identities survived, persisted and, in some cases, even thrived. In Bolivia and Guatemala, Indian populations constitute a demographic majority. In other countries such as Ecuador, Mexico, and Peru, they make up significant minorities, especially in certain regions in which their demographic density is high. Indians are no longer only a rural population: economic changes and massive migrations have brought them increasingly into the large metropolitan areas, where indigenous identities are undergoing rapid transformation.

Under these circumstances it was only a matter of time before indigenous peoples began to organize themselves socially and politically to demand their basic rights, challenge established government policies, and claim adequate representation in the political process. The organizing process began in the 1960s and 1970s, and within two decades indigenous peoples emerged as new social and political actors in Latin America. Their claim to cultural rights has become an important mobilizing principle: the recognition of their identities, the public use of their languages, bilingual and multicultural education, access to mass media, the protection of their intellectual property and cultural heritage, control over their natural resources, respect for their traditional social and political organization, and the recognition of their customary legal systems within the wider framework of national law.

Among the more insistent claims of indigenous organizations in Latin America are the right of peoples to self-determination and the right to autonomy. Whereas international law accords the right to self-determination neither to indigenous peoples nor to minorities, indigenous organizations tend to insist on this right. These issues are the subject of political struggles in contemporary Latin America, and Indian intellectual and political actors play an increasingly important role in these controversies (Stavenhagen 1995).

Many Latin American states, most notably Colombia, Ecuador, Nicaragua, and Venezuela, have adopted new constitutions or constitutional amendments since the early 1980s that include references to indigenous cultural rights. Others have enacted modest or far-reaching legislation concerning their indigenous populations. In 1996, a strenuously negotiated peace agreement put an end to a thirty-year-old civil war in Guatemala in which the majority indigenous populations were either victims or active participants. The cultural rights of indigenous peoples constitute a crucial element of this peace agreement. In Mexico the indigenous peasants of Chiapas who rose up in arms against the national government in 1994 advanced claims for autonomy and cultural rights in the peace negotiations, although they finally broke off. Yet Mexico reformed its constitution in 2001 and recognized (limited) indigenous rights. In December 2005 an Aymara Indian leader was elected president of Bolivia by a substantial majority, and the new government has announced a constitutional assembly to "refound" the Bolivian nation. One or several collective cultural rights are being implemented in a variety of Latin American countries, particularly in the field of language and educational policies. Things prove more complex and difficult regarding territorial rights, control over natural resources, or intellectual property and customary law.

The Maya people of Mexico and Central America are directly involved in these struggles. Guatemala's peace process includes an Accord on the Identity and Rights of Indigenous Peoples, signed in 1995, that identifies specifically the Maya, Garífona, and Xinca who constitute a majority of the country's population. During the years of war, military repression, and violence, indigenous peoples' resistance took the form of organized cultural activities including the Academy of Maya Languages and similar organizations. The cultural rights of indigenous peoples have played a prominent role in the post–civil war environment. Due to a complex of political factors, the popular referendum on constitutional reform did not receive a majority vote in 1999, making the accord not constitutionally entrenched, but the debates over cultural rights form part of the demand for general human rights, and the Maya indigenous movement has been actively involved in the process (Warren 1998).

Toward Multicultural Citizenship

As Latin American nations struggle to redefine their relations with indigenous peoples and thus themselves, the idea of cultural or multicultural citizenship has become a useful concept. By this I mean the recognition of indigenous people qua peoples with their own legal status and the right to self-determination; indigenous communities as subjects of public law with autonomic rights, indigenous languages as national languages, the demarcation of their own protected territories, the right to the management of their resources and their development projects, respect for their internal norms of local government and their customary legal systems, cultural and religious freedom within the community, as well as political participation and representation at the regional and national levels. It is not only a question of ensuring individual and collective rights within the existing state structures but also of redefining the very notion of state and nation. Cultural citizenship as far as indigenous peoples are concerned should have two essential points of reference: the unity of the democratic state and the respect for individual human rights within the autonomic collectivities and units that may be established. Neither pure individualistic liberalism nor the corporativist structure of a centralist state (such as exists in Latin America) satisfy the requirements of multicultural citizenship: this can only be achieved through democratic practice, dialogue, tolerance, and mutual respect.

It is within the framework of some of the issues set out above that the argument for the development of cultural or multicultural citizenship has emerged as a constructive approach to the cultural rights of groups within the modern nation-state. The anthropologist Renato Rosaldo and his colleagues, for example, argue for the need for cultural citizenship among the Hispanic populations in the United States, meaning thereby the reclaiming and reconstruction of the social and geographic spaces of Latino communities. "Cultural citizenship," Rosaldo writes, "operates in an uneven field of structural inequalities where the dominant claims of universal citizenship assume a propertied white male subject and usually blind themselves to their exclusions and marginalizations of people who differ in gender, race, sexuality, and age. Cultural citizenship attends not only to dominant exclusions and marginalizations, but also to subordinate aspirations for and definitions of enfranchisement" (1997: 37).[20] Furthermore, cultural citizenship means empowerment, "a process of constructing, establishing and asserting human, social and cultural rights." It is to be thought of as "a broad range of activities of everyday life through which Latinos and other groups claim space in society and eventually claim rights. . . . [it] allows for the potential of opposition, of restructuring and reordering society" (Flores and Benmayor 1997: 14–15). In a similar vein, the Peruvian historian Rodrigo Montoya (1996) suggests that "ethnic citizenship" be recognized for indigenous peoples who wish to use their own language and reproduce their own culture within the wider society.

From the perspective of political theory, Will Kymlicka argues for a form of differential citizenship in multicultural societies such as Canada, where different identities should be accorded recognition not to fragment a fragile nation but, on the contrary, to integrate and strengthen it. "Shared values," he suggests, "are not sufficient for social unity. . . . The missing ingredient seems to be the idea of a *shared identity* . . . [that] derives from commonality of history, language and maybe religion. But these are precisely the things which are not shared in a multination state." Kymlicka calls on liberal states to "insure that there is equality *between* groups and freedom and equality *within* groups" (1995: 188–94). Similarly, the philosopher Charles Taylor holds that "liberalism can't and shouldn't claim complete cultural neutrality." He proposes a politics of "mutual recognition" in multicultural societies (1994: 62–73). Also within the liberal perspective, Jeff Spinner (1994) pleads for a new form of "pluralist integration" of culturally distinct groups in the United States.

The cultural rights of distinct ethnic groups in existing states can thus be considered under the framework of ethnonationalist struggles or from within the approach of liberal citizenship. Whether group claims for cultural rights fall into one or the other of these camps depends on particular circumstances, and they are not necessarily mutually exclusive. Pluralism is but one of a number of policies that might satisfy claims to cultural distinctiveness. Multicultural citizenship constitutes another frame that promises the greater empowerment of and participation by disadvantaged collectivities, even as nation-states are challenged to reconsider their traditional and often legally enshrined perceptions of themselves.[21]

Notes

This is a revised version of an earlier text published in Halina Nieç, ed., *Cultural Rights and Wrongs* (Paris: UNESCO Publishing, 1998); and in "Cultural Rights and Universal Human Rights," in Eide 1995.

1. Homi Bhabha (1994: 2) argues that "the representation of difference must not be hastily read as the reflection of *pre-given* ethnic or cultural traits set in the fixed tablet of tradition. The social articulation of difference, from the minority perspective, is a complex, on-going negotiation that seeks to authorize cultural hybridities that emerge in moments of historical transformation" (emphasis added).

2. See the Declaration of the Principles of International Cultural Co-operation,

proclaimed by the General Conference of UNESCO on November 4, 1966 (UNESCO Web site, portal.unesco.org, accessed December 7, 2007).

3. The UNESCO Declaration on Cultural Policies states, inter alia, that "1. Every culture represents a unique and irreplaceable body of values since each people's traditions and forms of expression are its most effective means of demonstrating its presence in the world. 2. The assertion of cultural identity therefore contributes to the liberation of peoples. Conversely, any form of domination constitutes a denial or an impairment of that identity" (UNESCO 1982).

4. General Assembly resolution 47/135 of December 18, 1992.

5. The World Commission on Culture and Development speaks of ten thousand distinct societies living in roughly two hundred states (UNESCO 1995).

6. On civilizational fault lines, see Huntington (1997).

7. For a critique of relativism in human rights and of collective and peoples' rights from an individualist and universalist perspective, see Donnelly (1989: 109–24); and the same author's "Third Generation Rights" in Brölmann et al. 1993.

8. Note the pre–gender conscious wording of the text.

9. For the idea that the constitution of a social identity is an act of power, see Laclau 1990.

10. The World Commission on Culture and Development has this to say about the problem: "More is at stake here than attitudes. It is also a question of power. Cultural domination or hegemony is often based on the exclusion of subordinate groups. The distinction between 'us' and 'them' and the significance attached to such distinctions is socially determined and the distinctions are frequently drawn on pseudo-scientific lines so that one group can exercise power over another and justify to itself the exercise of that power" (UNESCO 1995: 25).

11. At the time of the UN debates leading to the adoption of the Genocide Convention, some states wanted to include cultural genocide as an international crime. See Ermarcora 1984: 312–18.

12. On issues of cultural identity and identification see Hall and du Gay 1996.

13. "This is precisely why a more dynamic approach to the understanding of human rights is needed which stresses the interplay and mutual determination of 'internal' and 'external' factors and relationships, and recognizes the central role played by human action and consciousness" (Preis 1996: 313).

14. General Assembly resolution 47/135 of December 18, 1992.

15. The UN Declaration of Indigenous Rights was finally adopted in June 2006.

16. This argument is made by Adamantia Pollis in comparing the human rights records in Africa and Asia, where emphasis on "cultural distinctiveness" has been strong (Pollis 1996).

17. Estimates of indigenous peoples the world over vary from 100 to 200 million, mainly concentrated in southern Asia (where they are known as "tribal" populations). They are also found in Africa, Europe, and the Pacific, as well as in the Americas.

18. United Nations, E/CN.4/Sub.2/1986/7/Add.4.

19. For a conceptual analysis of indigenous rights, see Stavenhagen 1996.

20. William Flores and Rina Benmayor add: "For Latinos, community is essential to survival, not only in terms of neighborhood or geographic locale, but also in terms of collective identity . . . Latinos have organized by barrio or on a city-wide basis for cultural identity, group survival, and political representation (1997: 16–17).

21. These concerns have been taken up, among many others, by UNESCO (2000).

Perspectives on the Politics of Human Rights in Guatemala

My anthropological studies of the Mayan peoples in Guatemala (Carmack 1973, 1979a, 1979b, 1988, 1995; Carmack and Mondloch 1983) have been focused on political issues, largely within a neo-Weberian theoretical framework. The key concepts that I employ revolve around the concepts of power and authority, their interaction, and their impact on sociocultural institutions. Methodologically, I attempt to integrate ethnohistory with ethnography, microhistory with macrohistory, and controlled comparison with general comparison. These same theoretical and methodological approaches provide the framework for the study to follow on human rights in Guatemala, although for reasons of brevity specific references to these approaches have been largely excluded.

In previous writings I have attempted to apply a genre of historical anthropology to general historical periods of Mayan history in Guatemala, which in a previous book (Carmack 1995) I refer to as the prehispanic, colonial, early republican, and modern periods. Research on each period, of course, poses difficult methodological problems such as appropriate kinds of comparison, access to relevant data, the critical analysis of primary and secondary sources, and so on. A particularly acute problem raised by research on recent Mayan history is that of advocacy, of attempting to be both a good social scientist and an active participant in the serious political struggles in Guatemala. Nowhere is this problem more evident than in the case of human rights in Guatemala.

In *Harvest of Violence* (Carmack 1988), other colleagues and I shared personal insights into the violation of human rights in different Mayan communities of Guatemala during the decades of the 1970s and 1980s. Our goal was mainly to inform U.S. citizens, and especially their political representatives, of these violations and to advocate for a modification of U.S. foreign policies and relations with that country. In a sequel to the *Harvest* volume being prepared by a group of anthropological scholars (Little and Smith n.d.), our main goal is to understand sociocultural developments in Guatemala—including those involving human rights—since the end of the civil war. In the present essay, I draw on information and ideas appearing in both of these volumes.

My primary concern in the present essay lies with the political dimensions of human rights advocacy, on the one hand, and with opposition to that advocacy, on the other. I confine my study to macrohistorical developments at the national level despite the obvious relevance that, for example, microhistorical studies of human rights at the Mayan community level would have in a fuller discussion of the topic.

I will start with a general review of the political contexts within which the concept of human rights was created historically, followed by a brief discussion of the relationship among human rights, cultural relativism, and political ideology; finally, I will examine the specific case of human rights advocacy and violation in Guatemala during the final decades of the twentieth century in terms of the issues raised in the preceding accounts.

Historical Overview of Human Rights Advocacy

Jack Donnelly (1989) defines human rights as "the equal and inalienable rights (in the strong sense of entitlements that ground particularly powerful claims against the state) that each person has simply as a human being . . . a particular social practice that aims to realize a distinctive substantive conception of human dignity" (66–67).

Although the idea of human dignity is held widely by most peoples, the "distinctive substantive conception of human dignity" known as human rights is unique to the Western liberal tradition. This holds for the complete list of human rights found in the Universal Declaration of Human Rights including, without distinction, civil, political, economic, and social rights. Liberalism recognizes the individual as prior to the community and the state, and it advocates protecting each person's human rights against the state. This liberal conception emerged in late medieval and early modern

Europe, and it was closely associated with the rise of capitalism, the separation of individuals from primordial groups and of the economy from politics: "The recognition of separate individuals possessing special worth and dignity precisely as individuals, [is] the basis for human rights" (Donnelly 1989: 70). While these rights were primarily promoted by the bourgeoisie, it became necessary for political reasons to make them universal. As liberalism spread, these rights increasingly became the norm around the world, and even though they have never been completely realized or applied equally to all social sectors, the ideal was created and implementation begun.

According to Ronald Glassman (1989), classical liberalism, an outgrowth of the Enlightenment, dealt with political and economic rights, but not with the issue of social inequality; this was directly related with the liberals' concern to free up the economy for industrial capitalism and to provide the right to vote and voice. One reaction against this early form of liberalism was Marxian socialism, but another reaction was modern liberalism, representing an attempt to retain the capitalist market but eliminate its destabilizing inequalities.

Classical liberalism arose during the transition in Europe from feudalism to capitalism and was "the credo of the trade-capitalist commercial classes of city and countryside" (Glassman 1989: 164). These classes—gentry, yeoman, merchant, artisan—created the institutions needed to free up the capitalist economy, institutions such as the limited state, political and economic freedom, law and order. Classical liberalism's main flaw, it is often noted, was that its form of democracy generated "wealth differentials too great to sustain the class balance necessary for the stability of the democratic polity" (Glassman 1989: 165).

Ronald Glassman sees the conservatives of today as intellectual heirs of classical liberalism, heirs who are largely reacting against the excesses of the socialist response to liberalism. The conservative critics have been most intelligently represented in the past by such figures as Alexis de Tocqueville and Max Weber, and in the present by Friedrich von Hayek and a host of neoliberal advocates. Contemporary liberalism as espoused in the United States and in Europe is an alternative response to classical liberalism and advocates the need to provide greater social equality, thus preventing the injustices, instability, and revolutions that accompanied the classical liberal-democratic agenda. Influential scholarly exponents of this modern liberalism would include such figures as John Maynard Keynes (1935) and John

Rawls (1961). The contemporary liberals, taking into account neoconservative arguments about the loss of freedom that accompanies state interference with the economy, advocate a democratic type government, limits on state control, free markets, and the acceptance of some economic inequality. The important revision of classical liberalism consists of accepting inequalities only to the extent that those at the top use their wealth and power to benefit those at the bottom: "A system in which the talents of the better endowed are recognized and rewarded, but only if their superior talents are put to the use of all and to the benefit of the least advantaged" (Glassman 1989: 50).

Anthony Giddens (1981) finds limitations in all three of these political interpretations of human rights and of the role of the modern state. He argues that the state is far from being primarily a specialized organ of moral integration as modern liberals would have it, or an instrument of the dominant economic class as the Marxists or socialists claim, or the bearer of irreconcilable values as the conservatives argue. Nor is the state to be understood as only the most obvious source of power, while a pervasive ubiquitous power embedded in the discourses of modern institutions dominates social life, as some Foucauldian thinkers seem to argue.

Giddens (1981: 212) reminds us: "The recognition of a 'public sphere' in which a range of freedoms and rights are in principle universalized . . . rests historically upon a political inheritance that . . . seems unique to the West." Nevertheless, these freedoms and rights in the West "had to be fought for in virtually all of the now 'liberal democratic' societies, often through bloody encounters" (222). Furthermore, it is often overlooked that these achieved rights were not only the result of class conflict but also "were in most Western countries substantially influenced by the imminent threat or actuality of military conflict: that is to say, by the two world wars" (228). The process was not one of liberal democratic states creating basic rights, but one of these states being created, at least in part, in the struggle over such rights.

The historical record seems to suggest, then, that the modern democratic state has never functioned primarily as a moral or neutral entity granting rights to its citizens. Rather, these rights have had to be exacted from the state through struggle and negotiation. The specific historical background of the Western states and their unique geopolitical struggles constitute other important factors in the acquisition of such rights. It would seem to follow that if the process of achieving human rights has been difficult in the dominant countries of the modern world, how much more so must it be for dependent countries like Guatemala where political, economic, and ethical ideals have been imposed from the outside and local bourgeois and proletarian classes have remained weak and poorly defined.

The purpose in reciting this history is to provide a clear and realistic understanding of the kinds of processes involved in protecting human rights in a given setting. It is a profoundly political as well as moral undertaking. History teaches us that it involves the promotion of a political agenda whose origins can be traced to a particular cultural tradition (Western European), type of state (democratic), philosophy (liberalism), class conflict (aristocratic/bourgeois/proletarian), and geopolitical arena (the states system of the modern world). However supportive of the goals of human rights movements we may be, and impatient for concrete results, we must expect that all the factors mentioned above will be brought to bear in some complex fashion in the unfolding struggle for human rights in Guatemala and elsewhere.

Cultural Relativism, Political Ideology, and Human Rights

The political basis of human rights, whether derived from liberalism or some other cultural tradition, raises serious questions for anthropologists and others around the world who have adopted the concept of cultural relativism. The anthropologist Elvin Hatch (1983; see also Scupin 1995) suggests that we need to differentiate between (1) "cultural relativity," trying to understand cultures on their own terms rather than according to some outside standard; and (2) "ethical relativism," granting equal moral recognition to the values and norms of the diverse cultures of the world. Ethical relativism itself requires the assumption of a particular moral position and has been difficult to accept for most Westerners, anthropologists included, who oppose widespread cultural practices such as vengeance homicide, racial discrimination, and the subordination of women. Hatch suggests that we distinguish between understanding cultural differences and approving of them, and attempt to establish universal humanitarian rights and standards recognized by all peoples. This will be difficult to carry out in practice, of course, especially for non-Westerners who have long experienced the unrelenting drive of Western nations to impose their beliefs and ethics on others.

Liberal scholars working within diverse disciplines are often more optimistic than Hatch about the possibility of achieving universal consent on human rights and other liberal goals. While recognizing that non-Western societies may not have "invented" the idea of individualistic human rights—although most of them strongly advocated human dignity through social participation—they claim that almost all of these societies have been radically transformed as a result of contact with the liberal societies of the West and that this has made agreement on universal rights more feasible. A concrete manifestation of this accommodation is the nearly universal acceptance by the diverse nation-states of the world (but not necessarily by all the social groups within these states) of the Universal Declaration of Human Rights (1948) and the International Covenant on Civil and Political Rights (1976).

Liberal scholars have further argued that the goal of human rights as historically created in the West was precisely to deal with social conditions in which the "traditional" societies were breaking down, resulting in isolated individuals who were in need of protection and support: "Modern markets ... created a whole new range of threats to human dignity and thus were one of the principal sources of the need and demand for human rights. And at roughly the same time, the modern state, both as an autonomous social actor and as an instrument of the newly ascendant bourgeoisie, was creating new institutions and practices that enabled it to invade the lives and threaten the dignity of a rapidly increasing number of people in new and increasingly ominous ways" (Donnelly 1989: 64). Human rights may have been originally a liberal initiative to solve particular social problems, but given the current domination of the world by liberal regimes, they are now widely thought to be not only the most appropriate but also the best political device for protecting the many peoples of the world against the liberal (especially neoliberal) regimes themselves.

For many scholars any regime other than the liberal democratic type fails the human rights test: the conservative regimes fail, for which the United States is often cited as an example, because in their emphasis on liberty and property over social rights they necessarily violate social human rights; traditional regimes, exemplified by nativist groups, fail because they base rights on group status rather than on inalienable individual rights; communitarian regimes, especially communist states, fail because they place rights of the state above rights of the individual; and authoritarian regimes, as certain past Latin American so-called development dictatorships, fail because favored social segments rather than individuals receive protected rights. One conclusion often drawn from this kind of thinking is that the social democratic welfare regime championed by the Scandinavian countries constitutes the only type of political system that can be counted on to fully guarantee human rights (Donnelly 1989: 87).

It further follows from this liberal perspective on human rights that the greatest threat to civil and human rights in the world today comes from the aforementioned regimes which would deny or not fully implement the universal human rights agenda. According to Larry Diamond (1994), constraints must be imposed on these flawed regimes, and "only the international community can impose these constraints, and only the credible threat or application of military force can make them effective." This international version of the liberal agenda would therefore include the creation of a "global system of law and order" that would be enforced by "international institutions" (3). Intervention of some kind—we are told that the use of force will not always be possible—would be appropriate for regimes failing to protect basic human rights. Diamond, in fact, advocates a standing army for the United Nations (UN) with at least one hundred thousand troops to enforce the international order (now in 2008 the number of troops would seemingly have to be considerably higher). Where national sovereignty conflicts with the internationally prescribed system of rights, the international order must prevail. Thus, according to this international perspective, the advocacy of human rights has a broad and profound political aim. As argued by Diamond (5): "The active promotion of democracy and human rights must be a major pillar of our strategy for building a new world order . . . [and it is] no less important than the pursuit of collective security."

The implications for cultural relativism and liberal ideology are transparent: human rights are part of both a cultural program and a political ideology—specifically Western culture and the agenda of welfare-state liberalism—an agenda profoundly wedded to ideas about individual rights over social rights, universal culture over specific cultures, and norms over competitive powers. The liberal ideology for the achievement of human rights is historically associated with Western capitalism and welfare democracy, and it seeks the replacement of conservative, authoritarian, traditional, and communitarian regimes. Beyond that, certain variants of modern liberalism advocate the creation of a new international order, backed by an enhanced central authority that would curtail the sovereignty presently exercised by individual nation-states. Given this list of political implications, it is not surprising that human rights advocates face opposition from several political directions.

Not everyone, of course, would agree that this is the only cultural direction or political agenda involved in the struggles for human rights, and certainly many would strongly disagree with its specific ideological claims. I for my part, despite human rights' laudable aims, see the discourse as an agenda, at least as expressed by some, that can be dangerously idealistic, even ethnocentric, and therefore only a partial answer to the problems of terror, violence, exploitation, and the violation of human rights in the modern world. We must tread cautiously here, given the charged atmosphere of world politics. Furthermore, the liberal ideology just described for protecting human rights is often the only effective countervailing source of opposition to the most cruel and vile repressive forces operating in specific social settings. Yet it is useful to understand that the argument for human rights always has a political dimension and that sometimes the political interests of those who push for human rights are not as universal or lofty as claimed. Furthermore, some account should be taken of political ideologies beyond the liberal one. For example, the conservatives surely have a point when they argue that legitimizing human rights without also transforming social conditions rife with unresolved differences of power and respect can only result in temporary, sometimes fictional, solutions to problems. Power is an inevitable and probably necessary factor in society (Murphy 1971), and a just and fair disposition of it cannot be achieved through ideological and legal means alone. Radical ideologies, of course, are also relevant to the issue of human rights advocacy and violation, and they deserve more attention than they are receiving at this present juncture of world history.

Politics and Human Rights in Recent Guatemalan History

The above comments on human rights and their political implications seem particularly relevant to the case of Guatemala, where Latin American–style authoritarian regimes ("reactionary despotisms") reigned supreme for over one hundred years (Baloyra 1983) and remain a continuing threat to recent more democratically oriented governments. From the classical liberal regime of Justo Rufino Barrios of 1873 to the despotic military regimes of the

1970s and the 1980s—with the exception of the brief interlude of Juan José Arévalo-Arbenz—the Guatemalan state ruthlessly violated the basic human rights of its underclasses. Internal bourgeois and proletarian groups certainly existed in Guatemala during this long period, and they struggled to establish democratic institutions and social welfare programs (Dunkerley 1988, 1994). However, despite some successes—again mostly during the 1944–54 period—these groups were far too weak to challenge the power of the old political, military, and business elites.

The human rights failures of the Guatemalan regimes should not be seen as isolated or solely national ones, for they were closely linked to Guatemala's dependent or peripheral position within the world economic and political system. As Lars Schoultz (1981) pointed out in an important book, core countries like the United States paid scant attention to the Guatemalan regime's denial of basic rights to its people and applied much of the political and economic pressure that made this denial seem necessary. In fact, Schoultz claims that U.S. government and private interests have harassed "progressive Latin American political movements whose policies are designed to meet basic needs" (379). Nowhere was this more evident than in the events of 1954, when the United States and other world-system forces were decisive in thwarting the struggle for basic human rights by lower- and middle-class Guatemalans (Handy 1994).

The election of civilian presidents in the 1980s, 1990s, and in the early twenty-first century brought renewed attempts within Guatemala to establish a liberal democratic political system that would guarantee the human rights of all its people. This development has been accompanied by changes in the world system. On the one hand, Guatemala has been drawn more tightly into the modern world system on neoliberal terms, a process that is said to sacrifice not only social welfare programs but also human rights on the altar of the world market (Abell 1999; Robinson 1996; Hale 2002). On the other hand, the previously mentioned "revised" liberal agenda to create an international order that includes the protection of human rights has also made considerable progress. While Guatemala remains peripheral to the dominant powers of the world, and continues to be pressured to provide wealth and political support to the core countries at the expense of the rights of its people, for the first time in Guatemalan history the external pressures on the government now include the mandate to improve its human rights record and promote meaningful social welfare reforms (Booth

2000). It became obvious to all during this period that Guatemala was an "international pariah" in human rights, and this materially affected such profoundly political matters as the peace talks with the guerrillas, convincing refugees to return home, access to foreign aid and loans, and the recognition of the Mayan Indians as legitimate "multicultural" entities within the nation-state (Hale 2002: 487–99).

During the 1970s and 1980s, the open advocacy of human rights in Guatemala proved a dangerous undertaking. As the civil war was winding down in the early 1990s, for example, Tom Barry (1992) reported that human rights advocates in Guatemala were still being accused of engaging in "an international 'conspiracy' promoted by the guerrillas" (37, 38). The human rights ombudsman, Ramiro de León Carpio, was described as "an isolated figure," at least until he was suddenly projected into the presidency in 1993 (with the downfall of President Jorge Serrano Elías, who had attempted to abolish the sitting congress). Susanne Jonas (2000) recounts how De León Carpio, despite occupying the presidency, was unable to make much human rights headway because of open opposition from entrenched powers such as the military and business sectors. Subsequently, however, the UN established a human rights mission in Guatemala (Misión de Naciones Unidad para Guatemala, MINUGUA), replete with a four-hundred-person advocacy team. Between 1994 and 1996, the mission monitored all human rights activities in the country, and despite both passive and active opposition of all kinds from the government itself and from other reactionary sectors, it was able to lay the groundwork for institutionalizing effective human rights in the country. Under this kind of intense international pressure, human rights progress was made in Guatemala, highlighted by the signing of the peace accords in 1996 that ended the thirty-four-year civil war.

Nevertheless, in April of 1998, two days after the Catholic Church had issued a report on human rights violations from the war period, the author of the report, Monseñor Juan Gerardi, was cruelly assassinated (his head was crushed with a brick). This was a clear signal that the advocacy of human rights would continue to be a politically charged and highly dangerous activity in Guatemala. Another setback during this time period was the intense bickering over the proposed constitutional reforms needed to legalize the peace accords. Central to the reforms were human rights issues such as protecting human rights institutions within the country, eliminating clandestine security units, respecting the rights of indigenous peoples, reducing the power of the army, and improving the economic conditions of the poor (Jonas 2000: chap. 3). The two most important conservative parties in congress, the National Progress Party (Partido de Avanzada Nacional, PAN) and the Guatemalan Republican Front (Frente Republicano Guatemalteco, FRG), were opposed to the reforms, although the reform package was finally approved in October of 1998 (in large measure because the FRG members abstained from the vote).

These same parties failed to support in a consistent way the reforms in the national referendum that followed. These reforms were defeated in May of 1999, with only 19 percent of the registered voters participating. As pointed out by Jonas (2000: 189–218), the Mayas were the main supporters of the referendum, while Guatemala City and other Ladino areas constituted the decisive opposition. This sequence of human rights setbacks provided the backdrop for the presidential election in December of 1999, in which the FRG candidate emerged victorious. The party "of human rights violators and peace resisters" was firmly in control of the state, and the record on human rights by the subsequent conservative Grand National Alliance (Gran Alianza Nacional, GANA) regime, from 2004 to the present, has been only a moderate improvement.

In retrospect, the recognition of the political dimensions of the human rights movement in Guatemala helps us understand the movement as, at least in part, a response to the vicious civil war of the late 1970s and 1980s, and as an attempt to counter the gross repression of the general population by the ruling military regimes. The victims of this repression correctly understood the political nature of these violations and their source primarily in the political-military institutions of the state. It should be noted that there has been much less understanding on the part of the Guatemalan population of the external sources of support for these violations, direct or indirect, from the United States and other world powers (Booth 1998).

The main opposition to repression in Guatemala has taken two forms in recent decades: (1) the revolutionary insurgents, even though they had some problems of repression of their own; and (2) the human rights advocates, organized around diverse institutionalized formats—the National Commission for Human Rights, the Mutual Support Group (Grupo de Apoyo Mutuo, GAM), the human rights ombudsman, MINUGUA, and many other national and regional human rights groups, as well as international human rights organizations such as the United Nations Human Rights Commission, Amnesty International, America's Watch, and so on. The civil war insurgents took the direct approach to eradicating repression by countering physical power with physical power, although the protection of human rights always formed part of their political ideology. The human rights advocates took the indirect approach, attempting to counter power with authority by legitimizing human rights as a moral force backed by international laws and institutions. Almost all observers agree that without such international backing the peace accords and the institutionalization of human rights groups in Guatemala would not have been possible.

In important ways these two social movements and their ideological perspectives are reactions to the old political struggle between conservatives and liberals over what the modern world is like and how societies ought to be governed within it. On one side is the conservative claim by the generals, the right-wing political parties, and some political moderates in Guatemala that society operates, and should operate, on the basis of competing powers, balancing each other out to some extent but in the end tipping the outcome toward the strongest. On the other side is the claim by human rights groups and centrist democratic parties that society is, and should be, a system of law and order that summarizes the best thinking of the people, who therefore yield to it; this is the liberal, humanitarian challenge to the conservative position. From the conservative perspective, progress and stability are achieved through the clash of power and its associated competing values, while from the liberal perspective they are achieved through subjection to agreed-on norms and values. Lest we consider this to be largely a third world conflict, Robert Kagan (2003) has effectively argued that a very similar ideological split defines the important differences between the United States and most of Europe on the issues of human rights and the war in Iraq.

The conflict between these two political ideologies in Guatemala was not generally phrased in terms of human rights until recently, although the same basic issues have always been debated under different terms. As already noted, the conceptualization of political struggle over human rights is closely associated with the increasingly connected nature of the world's societies and the domination of that world system by liberal-democratic core states (see Wallerstein 2002). Other scholars argue that even conservative (or neoliberal) leaders of the core states have had to employ the politics of human rights and multiculturalism, however begrudgingly (Forsythe 1989; Hale 2002). To the extent that governments in countries like Guatemala openly continue to oppose human rights, this is a clear indication of just how weak liberal democracy is there and of how deleterious conservatism can be when carried to extremes.

In this regard, the claim made by Carol Smith (1990) in her summary of recent Guatemalan history up to 1988 is of particular interest. She notes that toward the end of the civil war period the Guatemalan military regime began to adopt a modest development agenda for the Mayan Indians and to institute programs that included some economic and political rights for them. She sees this as largely political propaganda, because the regime remained profoundly authoritarian and a gross violator of the human rights of Indians and other sectors of the population. This type of military-dominated government with a human face would seem to be the kind of regime that Donnelly and other liberal scholars argue on historical grounds has never effectively protected human rights and is unlikely to do so in the future.

But Smith (1990: 173–74) further argues that there was emerging in Guatemala, even though incipiently, "a historically new form of resistance that is being generated throughout the Third-World . . . made up of anti-state political groups that stress democracy, local autonomy, multiculturalism, and individual human rights." It is noteworthy in light of our previous discussion that while these groups share important features with the liberal agenda (i.e., support for democratic institutions and human rights), they also share features with the so-called communitarian agenda, specifically in their support for the so-called third generation of human rights, including the 1996 UN Resolution and International Labor Organization (ILO) Covenant 169 to support the group rights of indigenous peoples (Cojtí Cuxil 1996). We have been told by liberal scholars that group rights, the communitarian agenda, cannot in the long run guarantee human rights, but in the context of Guatemala these new groups and their communitarian ideals should not be discounted. In countries like Guatemala with large indigenous populations, the native groups have the potential of generating considerable power along with moral suasion (Warren 1998) in opposing the conservative, and if necessary even the liberal, forces that now dominate the discourse and practice of human rights.

In recent updates of Smith's argument about the importance of civil society for the future of Guatemala, Jonas (2000) rejects the view that internal reactionary and external neoliberal forces make the defeat of peace, human rights, and the "revolution" inevitable. We must consider "agency as well as structure" (224), she says, and the main actors will come from such civil sectors as marginalized classes seeking true citizenship for the first time, Mayas struggling for indigenous rights, and the political forces from the left countering the resistance from the moderate right. But the international community will be necessary too, occasionally intervening to support the internal pro-peace forces.

In a similar vein, Charles Hale (2002) notes that neoliberalism has taken a position in Guatemala and elsewhere that accommodates multiculturalism "while retaining the prerogative to discern between cultural rights consistent with the ideal of liberal, democratic pluralism, and cultural rights inimical to that ideal" (491). The goal of states such as the Guatemalan one is to reconstitute the Mayan communities "in its own image" rather than to destroy them. Although the Mayas have much to gain by occupying the "spaces opened by neoliberal multiculturalism," their fundamental cultural and human rights will be achieved through adopting a more radical "politics of Mayan collective empowerment" (523).

In the quest for human rights in Guatemala, scholars have perhaps exaggerated the significance of leftist and international forces, while underemphasizing the potential importance of internal more moderate and conservative forces. Jonas and other scholars, however, are certainly right on target in concluding that all future progress in the struggle for human rights in Guatemala will be "subject . . . to the ups and downs of the 'normal' political arena, rather than the certainties of a controlled negotiating environment" (2000: 239). History teaches us that power will be needed along with authority to finally institutionalize the full spectrum of human rights in Guatemala.

Conclusion

I have outlined some of the important political issues associated with human rights advocacy in general world history and in the specific case of Guatemala. Almost everything remains to be filled in, including a clarification of human rights violations and advocacy in Guatemala for the several historical periods mentioned at the beginning of this essay. The decline of the communitarian regimes in Eurasia and the rise to further prominence of the liberal-democratic states within the modern world system correlate with the current emphasis on human rights around the world and the likely continuation of this emphasis in the near future.

Anthropologists and other scholars will want to continue participating as advocates of human rights, especially in cases such as Guatemala where the violation of basic rights has been so blatant and tragic for the Mayas and other ethnic groups that they have studied. The discussion above should not be taken as an argument against such advocacy, but rather as a reminder that the issue of human rights has political as well as moral dimensions. Surely the forces struggling for human rights—including Mayan communitarian rights—in Guatemala can benefit from the support of outsiders, especially from sympathetic students of their cultures. But the victims of human rights abuses need this support to be effective. Understanding the underlying political ideologies and realities behind both the advocacy and the violation of human rights will in the long run help ensure that support for the Mayas and the other peoples of Guatemala whose basic rights have been systematically violated for centuries will not be seen as interference but as strategic collaboration.

Legal Globalization and Human Rights
Constructing the Rule of Law in Postconflict Guatemala?

L egal globalization is a complex phenomenon that involves the trans-
nationalization of certain legal institutions, frameworks, and ideas (Dezalay and Garth 2002a, 2002b; Merry 1988, 1997, 2001; Santos 1998; Trubek et
al. 1994; Wilson 1997a, 2000). It is not new and indeed has historically
constituted a central pillar of imperial systems—one only needs think of the
spread of Roman law or English common law across large parts of the world
to understand the power and enduring nature of legal transplants. However,
during the second half of the twentieth century, and particularly during its
last two decades, the pace and impact of global legal exchange accelerated
rapidly. Increasingly, it makes less and less sense for the legal systems of
individual nation-states to be examined as bounded national entities, as
they are inevitably and increasingly affected and shaped by external and
transnational phenomena. This is linked principally to economic globalization, as trade integration and new forms of capitalist production and con-
sumption generate changes in legal regulations across large areas of the
world.[1] However, other forms of legal globalization also have a profound
impact on states and on relations between states and their citizens. One of
these is the spread of human rights doctrine.

In one sense human rights can be understood as the international legal
framework of treaties and conventions that codify the inherent rights of
human beings and the obligations of states toward them. Since the Universal Declaration of Human Rights (1948) and the International Covenants on

Civil and Political, and Economic, Social and Cultural (1966) rights, the trend has been toward the increasing codification of the rights of specific groups—and the corresponding obligations of states toward them—within the human rights framework. So, for example, the rights of indigenous peoples have been codified in the 1989 International Labor Organization Convention 169 and the 2007 UN Convention on the Rights of Indigenous People. The rights of women have been laid down in a universal standard for the global community in the UN Convention for the Elimination of All Forms of Discrimination against Women (CEDAW) of 1979. The rights of children were codified within the UN Convention on the Rights of the Child (CRC), approved by the UN General Assembly in 1989 and subsequently ratified by most states in the international system. However, acknowledging the formal expansion of human rights norms at the international level tells us little about what this means in specific local contexts. Anthropologists have placed particular emphasis on the processes by which human rights are elaborated, understood, interpreted, and contested through human interaction in particular contexts. They make the important point that while the legal doctrine of human rights is based on their universalism, there is in fact no universal or standard understanding of what they actually mean in practice (Wilson 1997b, 2000; Speed and Collier 2000; Merry 2003; Sieder and Witchell 2001). While many may celebrate their expansion and supposed global reach, human rights evidently remain highly contested terrain.

Social movements have long used the idea of human rights to oppose and resist state violence and oppression "from below" or "from outside" (Keck and Sikkink 1998; Sikkink 2005).[2] However, since the end of the Cold War human rights has also become one of the central concepts in the legal reorganization and reform of the state in the wake of armed conflict or authoritarian regimes. In this sense it constitutes a fundamental component of the globalization of certain politico-legal norms, values, institutions, and models "from above." A range of international organizations and powerful states in the international system now promote the spread of liberal legal norms (such as the inalienable rights of the individual) and institutions in the name of strengthening democracy, promoting the market, nation building, and securing peace and security within the international system. The promotion of these top-down efforts increasingly occurs within the rubric of "rule of law construction" or "rule of law strengthening," which in turn implies extensive international efforts to support the reform of judicial systems in developing, transitional, or fragile states. As Yves Dezaley and Bryant Garth observe, there is now a burgeoning global industry dedicated to the import and export of the rule of law (Dezaley and Garth 2002a; Domingo and Sieder 2001; Carothers 1999). The promotion of human rights is just one dimension of this.[3]

In this essay I focus on postconflict Guatemala and consider what prevailing global trends in rule of law construction might mean for human rights and access to justice, especially for the most vulnerable and excluded sectors of society. How do internationally supported justice reform initiatives affect relations between the state and society? And what role do different local and international understandings of human rights and the rule of law play within such processes?

The rule of law and the protection of fundamental human rights have been conspicuously and disastrously absent in Guatemala. During thirty-six years of armed conflict over two hundred thousand people were killed (some 2 percent of the population in 1980), the great majority of them civilians murdered by the military and by paramilitary forces. Over fifty thousand of these were disappeared—more than in any other country in Latin America in the twentieth century. Since the negotiated peace settlement of 1996, international agencies, including the United Nations (UN), have focused their efforts on attempts to strengthen the domestic justice system, respect for human rights, and respect for the rule of law. The idea of protecting human rights was at the heart of postwar attempts to reform the justice sector. However, international trends in rule of law construction have combined with local factors to produce unanticipated and paradoxical effects on human rights in practice. I suggest this is partly because the rule of law means very different things to different domestic and international constituencies. It is also a consequence of certain historical trends in state formation and current patterns of state (re)organization and state-society relations, which are leading toward what I term a situation of "illegal pluralism."

In the following section I reflect on the historical relationship between law and state formation in Guatemala. I then go on to detail the nature of the postwar reforms of the justice sector and different and competing discourses on human rights and the rule of law. Finally, I consider some of the implications of justice-system reform within the current context for the prospects of securing human rights in contemporary Guatemala.

Law in Guatemala

A number of features have historically characterized the Guatemalan state and its society, all of which have profound implications for current attempts to reform the country's justice system. First, racism and discrimination against the majority indigenous population are endemic, together with acute and persistent levels of socioeconomic inequality. Second, the military has tended to dominate the political and legal institutions of the state and has deployed extremely high levels of violence against the civilian population to secure order and elite rule. Third, the purchase of state legality is weak—the majority of the population mistrusts the official justice system, viewing it as inefficient, corrupt, and operating to the benefit of the powerful. Consequently there is a high degree of legal pluralism—the overlapping coexistence of different legal and regulatory orders (Santos 1995)—and an enduring distance between popular mechanisms for conflict resolution and the state judiciary.[4]

During the colonial period semiautonomous and subordinate legal spaces existed for the majority indigenous population who, as in the rest of the Spanish Americas, were subject to the laws of the República de Indios. These provided for the segregation and limited protection of indigenous people at the same time as they guaranteed their continued exploitation. A dual legal system operated, with nonindigenous governed by the laws of the República de Españoles. Legal interactions and mediation among the crown, *peninsulares,* criollo elites, and the indigenous populace were central to the reproduction of colonial society. Traditions of engaging with the law were as deeply rooted as the existence of separate legal spheres for Indians and non-Indians. In the early republican period attempts to raise taxes and to introduce liberal reforms and legal institutions, such as trial by jury and a new penal code, contributed to a conservative-led indigenous revolt in 1837 that initiated three decades of conservative rule. The conservatives restored the Leyes de los Indios, and a paternalistic attitude of the state toward the indigenous population prevailed.

After the victory of the liberals in 1871, the dual legal system was abolished in the name of universal citizenship, and state laws were used to aggressively promote the production of coffee for agroexport. Yet citizenship was far from universal: forced labor arrangements were intensified and the consolidation of a professional army allowed for their more rigorous policing by an increasingly centralized state. Although communal land titles were not subject to the kind of wholesale assault that occurred elsewhere in the isthmus during the 1880s and 1890s, state law actively promoted the privatization of so-called *tierras baldías* in favor of new coffee elites. However, while the legal order in Guatemala became highly centralized and militarized under liberal rule, subordinate semiautonomous legal spheres for local conflict resolution continued to exist within indigenous communities. It declared an ideology of assimilation, but in practice oligarchic liberalism in Guatemala continued to segregate the population along ethnic and class lines (Taracena Arriola 2002). During the early twentieth century new vagrancy laws were introduced to ensure a supply of unfree labor for coffee production and road construction, and the role of the military became ever more central in underpinning the economic order. Under the dictatorship of General Jorge Ubico (1931–44) the state's coercive apparatus and administrative purview was extended throughout the country.

The ten-year reformist experiment in social democracy known as the Guatemalan Spring (1944–54) was cut short by a U.S.-supported military coup in 1954. The subsequent rollback of the 1952 agrarian reform involved both the legal restitution of expropriated lands and high levels of extrajudicial violence against peasant organizers and political activists. As in the past, the law ascribed to an ideology of universalism (equality before the law), but operated almost exclusively for the benefit of the rich and powerful and coexisted with extreme levels of extrajudicial violence exercised by agents of the state. During the following decades the military consolidated its control over government, which was increasingly organized according to a national security, counterinsurgency logic. Following the emergence of a significant guerrilla movement in the 1960s, levels of state violence rose steadily, culminating in the genocidal campaigns against the indigenous rural populations carried out in the early 1980s under the military regimes of Generals Lucas García and Ríos Montt (Ball, Kobrak, and Spirer 1999; REMHI 1998).

Throughout the armed conflict the judiciary was entirely subordinated to the military, and most disputes were resolved by extrajudicial mechanisms with resort to extreme levels of violence.[5] According to the Commission for Historical Clarification (CEH), the UN-backed investigation into human rights violations that occurred during the armed conflict, the singular failure of the judicial system to act as a check on the de facto exercise of power and the systematic abuse of human rights by the state made for a significant factor actively facilitating the violence. The armed forces' control over the government also further accentuated the authoritarian character of the law and its arbitrary application. Civilian elites tended to rely on the military to mediate disputes, further weakening the purchase and relevance of the judiciary.

Following the transition to elected civilian government in 1985, demands for a more effective rule of law increased. This was due to a number of factors. On one hand, organized civil society groups increasingly resorted to international human rights law as a form of leverage to frame their demands for fundamental protections, rights guarantees, and social justice. On the other, as the international community became increasingly involved in efforts to bring an end to the armed conflict, they focused attention on how to strengthen weak state institutions such as the judiciary to ensure a sustainable peace. Lastly, rising levels of crime and insecurity meant that securing law and order had become a major electoral concern by the mid-1990s.

Human Rights, the Rule of Law, and the Peace Accords

At the end of the armed conflict the judicial system remained under-resourced, inefficient, inaccessible—particularly to indigenous people, women, children, and the poor—plagued by corruption, lacking independence from other branches of state, staffed by poorly trained, mediocre, and undermotivated professionals, and subject to the de facto power of elite groups. Opinion polls taken in the late 1990s indicated extremely low levels of citizen confidence in the judiciary.[6] Unsurprisingly, most Guatemalans continued to perceive the law as something that benefited the rich and powerful, not as a resource to protect their fundamental human rights.

"Human rights" lay at the heart of the postwar project to strengthen the rule of law. The 1996 peace settlement advocated the democratic modernization of the justice system, particularly of the criminal justice system, through institutional reform. The peace agreement that dealt most comprehensively with the reform of the justice sector was the Agreement for the Strengthening of Civilian Power and the Function of the Army in a Democratic Society, signed in September 1996, but in total five of the thirteen accords made express reference to the justice sector. The different reforms advocated aimed to encourage the peaceful resolution of conflicts via the courts and reduce resort to extrajudicial and arbitrary, violent means. They also aimed to ensure respect for human rights and due process guarantees within the judicial process. Additionally, the settlement emphasized the importance of securing greater accountability of state officials and institutions before the law, and also of improving access to justice for the majority of the population. Such changes implied little less than a root-and-branch transformation of the prevailing legal culture and practice. Rather than simply a means to punish or to protect privilege, the courts, it was hoped, would come to be seen as an instrument for all citizens to secure accountability and restitution.

Reform of the criminal justice system was based on what was referred to as a *garantista* model, one in which guarantees for the fundamental human rights of the accused were made central to legal procedures. Considerable advances were made in this respect throughout the 1990s. Like other countries in Latin America, Guatemala reformed its Penal Procedures Code (Código Procesal Penal, or CPP). A new law came into force in 1994, and a series of further amendments were approved by the congress in 1996, introducing a framework for criminal justice based on ensuring human rights guarantees for detainees. This emphasized the rights of the accused to due legal process, particularly the presumption of innocence, habeas corpus guarantees, and the right to legal defense.[7] Past practices such as the admissibility of confessions as the sole basis for convictions (which encouraged coercion and torture to extract confessions and secure convictions) were abolished. Other important measures included the separation of investigative and adjudicative functions—previously judges had investigated crimes and issued sentences, making them in effect both prosecutors and judges and raising potential conflicts of interest. Criminal investigations and prosecutions were delegated to a separate institution, the Public Ministry, in the expectation that judges' independence would be strengthened.

The peace accords mandated a doubling of budget allocations to the justice sector between 1995 and 2000 and a massive extension of its institutional coverage throughout the country. Prior to the end of the conflict only two-thirds of the country's municipalities had an office of justice of the peace, or *juzgado de paz*, but by the end of the 1990s every municipal center had a local court. In 1997 the multisector Justice Strengthening Commission was set up according to the terms of the September 1996 Agreement for the Strengthening of Civilian Power and subsequently undertook a unique process of consultation on the reform of the justice system with different civic and professional groups throughout the country. The commission's comprehensive and wide-ranging recommendations, published in April 1998, included a series of measures to increase judicial independence and reduce corruption, professionalize the judiciary, guarantee basic rights, increase access to justice, and make it more multicultural (Comisión de Fortalecimiento de la Justicia 1998). Many of these recommendations were subsequently incorporated into the judiciary's five-year Plan for Modernization (Plan de Modernización del Organismo Judicial), approved in mid-1997 and supported by the World Bank, the Inter-American Development Bank (IDB), the United Nations Development Programme (UNDP), the U.S. Agency for International Development (USAID), the UN Verification Mission in Guatemala (Misión de Naciones Unidad para Guatemala, MINUGUA), and the governments of Sweden, Japan, Switzerland, and Canada, among others.

The peace settlement's focus on human rights meant that during the years immediately after the signing of the accords strengthening the rule of law was on everyone's agenda. However, the rule of law meant significantly different things to different sectors. For the panoply of international agencies supporting the implementation of the peace accords and the reform of the Guatemalan state, the rule of law came to be seen as a panacea for many things. It was championed as a central part of democracy promotion and strengthening, for example by USAID. The World Bank claimed it was fundamental to strengthening national economic performance. The UNDP, MINUGUA, and a host of bilateral donors advocated it as an essential component of postconflict reconstruction and of sustainable and equitable development. Unsurprisingly, the aims of these different external agencies did not always coincide, and considerable competition and duplication occurred in practice.

For Guatemalan human rights activists, such as the widows association Coordinadora Nacional de Viudas de Guatemala (National Committee of Guatemalan Widows, CONAVIGUA) or the families of the detained-disappeared the Grupo de Apoyo Mutuo (Mutual Support Group, GAM), the rule of law meant an end to impunity and the trial and punishment of those individuals responsible for gross violations of human rights during the armed conflict. This implied putting military officers on trial, making them accountable for their crimes, and also providing material and symbolic restitution for the victims of those abuses. Such demands were supported by the peace settlement, which had included a mandate for a UN-led investigation into past violations, or a so-called truth commission. The results of this commission, made public in 1999, found the Guatemalan state guilty of gross human rights violations including genocide and recommended the judicial prosecutions of those responsible (CEH 1999).[8] A variety of different national NGOs and civil society organizations continued to press for justice in human rights cases in the wake of the peace settlement, campaigning for an end to military impunity. These groups provided evidence and witness testimony for a number of paradigmatic cases pursued before the domestic courts. When these efforts were frustrated or blocked, victims' groups and NGOs took the cases to the Inter-American Court of Human Rights (IACHR) and, following the example set by the Augusto Pinochet case, attempted to pursue criminal proceedings in the courts of other countries, for example in Spain and in Belgium (Sieder 2001).

However, for many ordinary citizens—who were not part of the vocal but relatively small sector that constituted organized civil society—the rule of law increasingly meant tough policies on law and order to provide greater security. While violations of civil and political rights by the state declined relative to the 1980s and early 1990s, new forms of insecurity became generalized toward the end of the decade. Armed robbery, car theft, kidnapping,[9] child abduction for illegal adoption, drug trafficking, homicides and rape, gang-related violence, and money laundering became commonplace (Vela, Sequén-Mónchez and Solares 2001). Official figures are notoriously unreliable, but one study estimated that the total number of reported crimes increased by 50 percent between 1996 and 1998 (Call 2000: 9). Rising levels of crime undermined citizen confidence in the legal system, as this, in turn, proved unable to tackle the public security problem. The new Penal Procedures Code appeared to have particularly contradictory effects: in the face of the postwar crime wave, the rights protection afforded to detainees by the *garantista* model became the subject of acute public criticism, with calls for more hard-line measures and revisions to the code increasingly gaining ground. Paradoxically many citizens blamed human rights for crime and impunity; they were widely viewed as something that gave too much protection to suspected criminals, many of whom were routinely released after arrest due to lack of evidence. Tough law-and-order policies became increasingly popular. In 1995 the government of Alvaro Arzú extended the death penalty to anyone convicted of kidnapping. Subsequently the Guatemalan Republican Front (Frente Republicano Guatemalteco, FRG), led by former military dictator Ríos Montt—whose regime was accused by the UN's Historical Clarification Commission of perpetrating acts of genocide against the indigenous population in 1982 and 1983—was elected to office in 1999 on a law-and-order platform. In May 2000 the congress rescinded the law allowing the president to grant pardons in capital cases, bringing Guatemala into violation of both the American Convention on Human Rights and the International Covenant on International and Civil Rights (HRW 2001: 4). In addition, citizens increasingly took justice into their own hands, as the incidence of lynchings and death squad–style killings of suspected criminals increased after 1996 (MINUGUA 2002; Godoy 2002; Gutiérrez and Kobrak 2001). In short, the legacy of armed conflict and authoritarian government, combined with increased insecurity in the wake of the war, had contradictory impacts on popular expectations about human rights. Although the UN agencies in particular placed great emphasis on educating citizens about their human rights as an essential part of postconflict reconstruction, this alone unsurprisingly could not ensure greater respect for fundamental human rights in practice.

Multiculturalizing Justice

In addition to strengthening respect for human rights and due process guarantees, the attempt to multiculturalize Guatemalan justice constituted another central aspect of postconflict reforms to the justice system. The peace settlement identified the historic exclusion of Guatemala's majority indigenous population as one of the causes of the conflict. It therefore advocated a series of measures aimed at making state institutions reflect the cultural diversity of the country and at reducing discrimination. Such initiatives partly reflected the tendency in international human rights thinking toward recognizing the collective rights of indigenous peoples as human rights.[10] They also echoed regional trends in state reform. Since the mid-1980s a number of Latin American countries had initiated constitutional and secondary reforms to reconstitute themselves as pluricultural and multiethnic nations (Van Cott 2000a; Assies et al. 1999; Sieder 2002). The partial nature of this recognition of indigenous rights continues to be hotly contested by indigenous groups across the region. Nonetheless, a variety of community-based forms of justice were recognized to some degree as part of the wave of multicultural reforms. In part this was a response to long-standing indigenous demands for greater autonomy. But such legal decentering was also at the heart of the legal reconstitution of the neoliberal state in the 1990s across much of Latin America.

The peace accords underlined the need to ensure access to justice for Guatemala's majority indigenous population: some 50 to 60 percent of the overall population of 12 million, comprising twenty-two different ethno-linguistic groups and including the most impoverished sectors of the populace. Multiculturalizing the justice system involved a number of measures to improve indigenous access to state justice and to promote nonjudicial forms of dispute settlement. Initiatives included increasing the free legal defense for those accused of crimes, particularly the numbers of indigenous or bilingual defense counsel lawyers and legal interpreters. It also involved encouraging the use of community-based mechanisms for dispute resolution and other forms of alternative dispute resolution (ADR) in order to resolve conflicts outside the courts. The Accord on the Identity and Rights of Indigenous Peoples, signed in 1995, committed the Guatemalan government to constitutionally recognize indigenous peoples' right to use their traditional forms of justice (customary law).[11] However, according to the terms of the peace settlement the constitutional reforms had to be ratified in a popular referendum, and in the event these were defeated in a vote held in May 1999. This meant that the autonomy of indigenous community authorities to apply their own resolutions or forms of law was not officially recognized. Their decisions and adjudications could therefore be challenged by those who viewed them as illegitimate or illegal.

Nonetheless, different forms of community-based conflict resolution were increasingly promoted within indigenous areas of the country as part of overall efforts to reform the justice system. In line with the peace agreements, and with the recommendations of the 1998 Justice Strengthening Commission, international agencies and bilateral donors supported the increased use of ADR mechanisms and a greater recognition of indigenous customary law, supposedly as complements to the formal justice system. However, the promotion of community justice was seen primarily as a means of improving access to justice and of dejudicializing certain kinds of conflicts, rather than as a means to guarantee indigenous peoples collective rights to legal autonomy. In effect, such initiatives aimed to remove minor legal claims from the courts, thereby freeing up the latter and increasing the efficiency of the judicial process. They were also intended to increase access to justice by providing more culturally appropriate and affordable forms of justice and conflict resolution for the majority of Guatemalans.

The promotion of ADR is a key feature of legal globalization and transnationalized forms of rule of law construction (Salas 2001). Not all ADR concerns the poor—indeed a major area of ADR expansion is that of arbitration in commercial law, promoted in particular by the World Bank. However, many international agencies and donors support ADR under the broader remit of furthering greater access to justice for underprivileged groups. In theory, informal dispute-resolution processes are more accessible in terms of the language they employ. Procedures are often lauded as simpler, cheaper, more flexible, and faster than those deployed in the courts and as involving a greater degree of participation by the parties to a conflict, who are encouraged to reach consensual settlements. Such alternative remedies were also strengthened in the penal procedures codes introduced throughout Latin America in the 1980s and 1990s.[12] In Guatemala USAID was one of the main external development agencies supporting the strengthening of community-based dispute settlement in the wake of the peace settlement. In 1998 the agency initiated a program that resulted in the establishment of various community mediation centers in predominantly indigenous rural areas, featuring local mediators trained by USAID in dispute settlement techniques who served on an *ad honorem* basis (Hendrix and Ferrigno 2003). Other international agencies also supported the promotion of ADR and of dejudicialization as part of overall efforts to increase judicial efficiency and access to justice for marginalized sectors. For example, a major loan approved by the IDB in 1998 aimed at strengthening judicial institutions and improving access to justice in deprived rural communities included plans to finance eight justice administration centers (CAJS). These were promoted as a low-cost means to decentralize and integrate justice-sector services, and they included ADR as a key component (Beibersheimer 2001: 119–20; Hendrix 2000: 861).

Civil society organizations and local communities differed in their responses to these ADR initiatives. Some welcomed them as a means of extending access to justice, pointing to their accessibility and low cost. However, many indigenous rights organizations rejected them as external impositions. They argued that such innovations effectively undermined indigenous authorities and indigenous law by imposing external techniques of mediation and training local mediators—instead of recognizing the authority of indigenous community leaders. These activists worked to strengthen *el derecho maya,* or Mayan law, by promoting various alternative forms of community-based forms of conflict resolution through their network of local paralegals, and by working to strengthen community authorities in their exercise of Mayan law.[13] In addition, indigenous rights organizations continued to lobby for an amendment of the constitution to formally guarantee indigenous peoples' legal autonomy (as specified in ILO Convention 169, ratified by Guatemala in 1997), even though the prospects for such a reform appeared increasingly remote. It seemed that at times prevailing trends in justice-sector reform to strengthen human rights and the rule of law were at odds with indigenous activists' perceptions of their rights, which were premised on demands for greater autonomy from the state.

The promotion of different models of community-based justice should be understood within the overall context of transnational trends in rule of law construction and current internationally promoted preferences for the decentralization of the state. In effect, the promotion of different kinds of ADR represents a process of legal decentralization. While in some cases this has increased the autonomy of indigenous communities, such a decentering of state law also effectively reduces the direct responsibilities of the state for legal redress in certain spheres, in effect privatizing law by devolving responsibility for dispute resolution to local communities. What are the implications for human rights of the ways in which the state is being legally reconstituted within the broader context of legal globalization? And in the case of a state like Guatemala, which remains highly dependent on foreign loans and development aid, how do current trends in international development assistance interact with historical traditions of legality and illegality?

Legal Decentralization: Toward Illegal Pluralism?

Initiatives to decentralize the legal system in Guatemala aimed at making justice more accessible and multicultural were implemented within a highly problematic legal context. A number of significant improvements were made after 1996, in particular the extension of the network of courts throughout the country. Yet the justice system overall continued to be highly ineffective and injurious to fundamental human rights. This was partly a consequence of institutional shortcomings and weaknesses, some of which were slowly addressed by the reforms advanced by the Justice Strengthening Commission. Other more intractable factors, however, included the lack of will among political and business elites and justice-sector employees to support fundamental reforms and secure effective legal accountability, as well as the increasing colonization of the Guatemalan state by organized crime.

Judges, lawyers, and public prosecutors continue to be highly vulnerable to internal and external intimidation, interference, and corruption. Powers to promote, discipline, or dismiss judges and public prosecutors are concentrated in the Supreme Court. In a study carried out in 2001, some 25 percent of judges interviewed and 87 percent of public prosecutors acknowledged that they had been the target of pressure either from their superiors or from interested parties to alter the course of investigations and cases (*Central America Report*, August 17, 2001). Low salaries and poor training also foment corruption. Disciplinary procedures remain inadequate, and officials charged with malfeasance rarely face criminal prosecution. In addition to bribery, justice officials also face intimidation. Constant harassment and threats mean that many are scared to testify, investigate, or judge impartially. Private insurance companies in Guatemala consider judges and magistrates to be such a high risk that they cannot obtain life insurance, and in 2001 the Supreme Court declared it lacked the funds to pay for an insurance scheme for its employees.

The public prosecutor's office, or Public Ministry (MP), undoubtedly remains one of the weakest links in the judicial process. In 1999 one study for USAID found that in Guatemala City alone, of approximately ninety thousand criminal complaints filed in a year, success in prosecution in statistical terms approached zero (Hendrix 2000: 837). In the face of the manifest failure to deliver results and of the personal danger often involved in making a legal representation, most victims of crime do not file complaints with the MP, and those that do tend to drop them after a short time. The continued influence of military intelligence and elite groups over judicial institutions means that powerful individuals and groups who break the law continue to enjoy impunity. These forces work to prevent thorough criminal investigations and bring pressure to bear in trials to protect the guilty. This is the case when military officers are implicated in human rights violations, but also in instances of drug trafficking, embezzlement, and other crimes. Human rights activists have signaled the existence of an extensive clandestine network operating throughout state institutions in the justice sector and in the public security forces that works to systematically obstruct the course of justice. This network, often referred to as "parallel powers" (*los poderes paralelos*), originated in military intelligence structures and is led by members of the armed forces and supported by members of the Policia Nacional Civil (PNC), the MP, and the courts. Its multiple activities include: carrying out parallel investigations;[14] the manipulation of crime scenes; mislaying, altering, or inventing evidence and testimonies; hiding crucial information; bribing police, prosecutors, and judges; finding so-called fall guys to take the rap (usually a lower-ranking military officer); and, when necessary, threatening or murdering witnesses and officials. This network has entrenched interests in criminal gangs: a number of high-profile cases indicated the ways in which it uses common criminals to gather information and threaten and attack its targets (Goldman 2002). After years of campaigning by human rights activists, in March 2003 an independent investigative commission into clandestine, parallel groups in Guatemala was set up under the auspices of the Organization of American States (OAS) and the UN. The commission was charged with investigating organizations tied to narco-trafficking, arms trafficking, and human rights violations and was given the right to subpoena police and judicial archives. However, political obstruction involving a series of objections to the commission's proposed mandate on constitutional grounds meant that by the beginning of 2006 it still had not been set up.

Much of the impetus for reforming the justice system in Guatemala comes from international agencies or embattled human rights organizations and civil society groups. In contrast to other countries in Latin America, the Guatemalan domestic private sector has not been a major player promoting justice reform efforts. Neither have the main political parties prioritized justice reform as part of their programs. In other words, justice reform has constituted part of the conditionality for donor funds to support the peace process, yet the demand from local political elites and citizens for concerted reform has remained weak. In addition, the judiciary itself has displayed considerable resistance to change. Despite institutional improvements and some notable advances, judicial training remains poor, selection and appointment by merit is still not general practice, and the tendency to make appointments on the basis of clientelism or nepotism persists. Neither periodic purges of incompetent or corrupt personnel nor improved training and institutional reform have proved sufficient to secure meaningful advancements in judicial performance and credibility. Some observers have criticized the emphasis justice reform programs placed on institutions, pointing out that it was justice operators themselves who proved to be some of the main obstacles to successful, nationally owned processes of reform (Pásara 2002).

By December 2004 the peace process effectively came to an end when MINUGUA closed its doors for good. The popular lack of faith in the justice system combined with certain "donor fatigue" in the face of poor results suggested that the postconflict window of opportunity to reform the legal system was closing. Citizen mistrust of the justice system and the resort to extrajudicial and violent means of conflict resolution has deep historical roots in Guatemala. Overhauling the justice system and changing popular attitudes in such a short space of time was always going to be a Herculean task. Nonetheless, the failure to deliver more effective justice through the courts since the end of the armed conflict, combined with continued disregard for the law on the part of local elites and rising crime, dangerously eroded confidence in state institutions. A survey conducted by the Research and Social Sciences Association (Asociación de Investigación y Estudios Sociales, ASIES) in 2000 concluded that only 6 percent of the population felt their basic rights were fully protected by the legal system (PNUD 2001b: 112). The credibility of the judiciary was greatly undermined by popular perceptions of widespread corruption and the ability of politicians to avoid accountability by securing favorable rulings through the courts. Such perceptions, in turn, further encouraged preferences for unofficial, punitive, and authoritarian mechanisms to provide security and resolve conflicts.

A widespread sense of insecurity continues to characterize daily life for Guatemalans, and in many senses this has worsened during the first years of the twenty-first century. Surveys conducted in seventeen Latin American countries revealed that Guatemala had by far the highest rate (55 percent) of those polled declaring that a member of their family had been a victim of crime at some time during the previous year (IDB 2001: 14–15). The government's failure to implement coordinated policies to improve public security and the inability of the courts to effectively sanction criminals led people to turn to a range of private solutions. These include a growth in vigilante activities, the use of private security firms, and an increase in private gun ownership. In addition, there has been a steady rise in extrajudicial executions including lynchings and widespread so-called social cleansing—particularly death squad–style murders of young men allegedly linked to the criminal gangs or *maras* that now control most of the capital's impoverished neighborhoods. In June 2001 the Association of Private Security Firms reported that some eighty-five private security firms were legally registered, comprising some forty-five thousand agents (*Prensa Libre*, June 17, 2001); in 1999 MINUGUA estimated that some two hundred private security firms were in operation throughout the country. This means that for every serving police officer in Guatemala there are now three private security guards, many of whom lack adequate training or regulation and who have sometimes been involved in acts of violence themselves.[15] In addition, the fact that their services are only available to those who can pay for them makes access to security even more unequal, reinforcing existing socio-economic inequalities. Those who can afford such private services are less and less willing to contribute economically toward improving state security services. The rate of reported homicides has continued to rise. One comparative study estimated that the annual rate of violent deaths in Guatemala reached seventy-seven per one hundred thousand inhabitants in 1998, second only in the region to El Salvador (eighty-two per one hundred thousand) and compared to approximately ten per one hundred thousand for the United States (Call 2000: 9).[16] Only 10 percent of all homicide cases are sent to trial, and very few of these result in convictions (HRW 2001).[17] All social classes use extrajudicial execution as a means of conflict resolution. Yet collective mob executions of suspected criminals by indigenous communities dominated the headlines in the late 1990s. According to MIN-UGUA's figures, the average rate of lynchings and attempted lynchings was roughly two per week. Between December 1996 and December 2001 some 421 lynchings and attempted lynchings occurred, involving 817 victims and leaving 215 people dead (MINUGUA 2002). Commonly cited reasons for lynchings include the breakdown of community structures and cohesion resulting from the armed conflict, lack of confidence in state institutions, and the population's lack of understanding of existing due process guarantees. (Popular expectations of justice seem to demand the immediate incarceration of the accused or their public sanction and repentance, whereas recourse to the courts often involves the release of the accused for lack of evidence or on bail.)[18]

The rapid privatization of justice and security is not exclusive to Guatemala, nor are its most spectacular and violent manifestations such as lynchings and death squad killings of suspected delinquents (Caldeira 2000; Vilas 2001). Across much of Latin America the weakness of the rule of law and the rise in crime during the 1990s made such responses a regional trend. However, the combination of the increasing privatization of conflict resolution and security provision with the decentering of state law that has featured in internationally promoted judicial-reform initiatives raises serious questions about the state's ability to protect the basic human rights of its citizens in the future. It could be argued that through strategies of legal decentralization the neoliberal state sheds its central responsibility for guaranteeing and enforcing the pact of common citizenship. Through such strategies certain social spaces and actors are effectively abandoned as the state renounces its traditional coercive and protective functions. This allows other actors to assume these functions: for example, indigenous communities engaged in local conflict-resolution procedures, private security firms engaged in protecting the private property of the wealthy, or international law firms offering commercial arbitration services to business sectors. The effects of such privatization, fragmentation, and decentralization of the law are multiple and contradictory: on the one hand, they allow greater space for local autonomies and may in this way contribute to more effective and accessible forms of regulation and dispute resolution. On the other, however, the restructuring of the legal functions of the state often serves to aggravate existing inequalities and social exclusion. The rich and privileged are better able to secure greater protection for themselves; the poor are vulnerable to the predatory actions of powerful individuals and groups within officially sanctioned semiautonomous spheres. Such trends reflect the more general features and effects of the neoliberal state: the privatization of state functions, increased inequality, and a reduced institutional capacity to intervene in society to address those inequalities. The state in Latin America has never, in practice, been able to create and secure unified legal orders. However, the privatization of law that is occurring as a consequence of neoliberal reordering poses new and complex challenges to those seeking greater access to justice, respect for fundamental human rights, and more democratic forms of citizenship. Certain internationally supported efforts to strengthen the rule of law may, paradoxically, be contributing to a more fragmented and weaker legal order in the future. The combined effect in a context such as that encountered in Guatemala, where a historically rights-abusive justice system has been colonized by military intelligence and organized crime, may be to consolidate a kind of illegal pluralism—the overlapping of different legal and regulatory orders—where the line dividing the legal from the illegal becomes increasingly difficult to discern.

Conclusions

In the late twentieth century states were rightly condemned for abusing human rights. Yet today as human rights violations are increasingly carried out by a multiplicity of actors, our focus needs to be on what kind of institutions and practices and what kind of state can guarantee human rights for the most vulnerable sectors of society. In this essay I have emphasized the ways in which the law is reconstituted within a global context and have argued that an analysis of processes of legal globalization and particularly of internationally promoted models of justice reform is vital for understanding postconflict processes of legal change. Negotiated settlements to armed conflicts offer important opportunities to reshape state institutions and to challenge existing practices and attitudes. However, such possibilities are constrained by long-run processes of state formation and by the ways in which law has historically been configured, exercised, engaged with, and understood by different groups in society. The Guatemalan case illustrates that the international promotion of judicial reform and an increased awareness of human rights do not necessarily translate into effective respect for the human and constitutional rights of all citizens. In certain contexts claims for the rule of law can mean advocating highly authoritarian measures. Social pressure from below for due process and the rule of law is weak in Guatemala—what is demanded instead is rapid and invariably highly punitive forms of justice. Despite increased public concern with the law, the judiciary's legitimacy is low and perhaps even declining. Moves to tackle discrimination and increase sensitivity to cultural differences within the justice system are undoubtedly a positive feature of the peace process. Yet strengthening ADR and a recognition of greater legal autonomy for indigenous peoples in the name of multiculturalizing the state cannot be separated from the question of how to build a strong and legitimate state that provides effective protections for all citizens, particularly those who are most disadvantaged and marginalized. The decentralization of law has advantages and disadvantages—it brings law closer to everyday lived experience, but in the context of a weak state colonized by criminal groups, it can also open greater spaces for abuses by powerful actors and further marginalize the poor. In contrast to the rational spread of law so widely presupposed by classic paradigms of state modernization, what we may in fact be seeing in Guatemala, and many other parts of the world, is the consolidation of illegal pluralism as part and parcel of the neoliberal restructuring of the state.

Notes

I greatly benefited from the opportunity to discuss the ideas developed in this chapter at the Institute of Latin American Studies London, the 2003 Congress of the Latin

American Studies Association in Dallas and the University of Bergen in Norway. I am particularly indebted to Maxine Molyneux and Carlos Flores for their comments and encouragement and gratefully acknowledge the financial support of the British Academy for fieldwork in Guatemala. Some of the material included in this chapter appeared in "Renegotiating 'law and order': judicial reform and citizen responses in post-war Guatemala," *Democratization,* Volume 10, No. 4 (December 2003) pp. 137–160.

1. Many analyses of legal globalization have focused on the spread of transnationalized forms of law making such as the private law of business sectors (*lex mercatoria*), which appear to operate almost independently of nation-states. See Teubner 1996; Appelbaum, Felstiner, and Gessner 2001.

2. Margaret Keck and Kathryn Sikkink's celebrated "boomerang effect" occurs when local actors not only attempt to secure respect for human rights by bringing pressure on their respective governments from below but also engage in transnational networks to bring pressure to bear on governments from outside (1998).

3. As Thomas Carothers (2001) points out, governments, multilateral agencies, and bilateral donors have different aims and motivations for supporting rule of law construction and judicial reform; some may seek to improve human rights, some to guarantee greater security for private investment, others to tackle transnational crime. Unsurprisingly, their agendas often conflict.

4. Contemporary research on legal pluralism focuses on the imbrication of different legal orders in a given field, territory, or space and is particularly concerned with the ways in which the legal ideas and processes of subordinate groups are constrained and shaped by dominant legal frameworks. Legal pluralism is understood not as a plurality of separate and bounded cultural systems, but rather as a plurality of continually evolving and interconnected processes enmeshed in wider power relations. For discussions of legal pluralism, see Merry 1988, 1992, 1997; Moore 1986; Griffiths 1986; Starr and Collier 1989; Fuller 1994; Santos 1987, 1995; Benda-Beckmann 1997.

5. A thorough analysis of the legal apparatus of the counterinsurgency state is set out in Alberto Binder et al., "Informe sobre la participación del sistema judicial en la violación de los derechos fundamentales durante el enfrentamiento armado," a draft document prepared for the UN Comisión de Esclarecimiento Histórico, on file with the author.

6. A poll commissioned by the Supreme Court in 1997 revealed that 88 percent of those surveyed considered the justice system to be inadequate; four out of five admitted they had little or no confidence in the system. See Pásara 2002.

7. A state legal defense office, the Instituto de Defensa Penal Público, was set up to provide legal counsel to criminal detainees who could not afford a lawyer. While the institution remained hopelessly underfunded and could not hope to meet the scale of demand, the fact that it was created was nevertheless important.

8. An amnesty law was passed in December 1996 as part of the peace negotiations.

However, this law specifically exempted amnesty for crimes against humanity (genocide, torture, and forced disappearance).

9. One UNDP study indicated that in 1997 the rate of kidnappings in Guatemala was similar to that in Colombia: approximately seventeen per one hundred thousand inhabitants per year. See PNUD 2001a: 45.

10. These were explicitly recognized by the 1989 International Labor Organization's (ILO) Convention 169 on the rights of indigenous and tribal peoples, currently the only international instrument on indigenous rights that is binding on signatory states. The tendency to frame indigenous rights as human rights is also evident in the UN and Organization of American States draft declarations on indigenous rights, both of which may eventually become binding international and regional instruments.

11. Indigenous peoples' right to their customary law, including their authorities, norms, and procedures was recognized within international human rights law in the form of ILO Convention 169. This was ratified by Guatemala in November 1995.

12. In September 1997 the Guatemalan congress approved a series of amendments to the 1994 Penal Procedures Code, which aimed to promote the greater use of conciliation and mediation.

13. In 1999 one Mayan rights organization, the Defensoría Maya, published a study, financed by USAID's Justice Programme, in an attempt to systematize and promote its work (Defensoría Maya 1999). Indigenous rights organizations have continued to call for the constitutional recognition of indigenous peoples' right to customary law at the same time as they promoted its use in practice.

14. The existence of investigative structures parallel to the official judicial process came to light when families of kidnap victims, frustrated with the inability of the police and the criminal justice system to secure their release, turned to military intelligence, revealing a network run out of the presidency that coordinated operations between the MP and the Presidential General Staff. See *Prensa Libre,* August 13, 2000.

15. In June 2001, the PNC had 18,314 operatives (UN 2001).

16. The overall homicide rate (which includes intentional and unintentional killings) for Latin America in the 1990s was thirty per one hundred thousand, making the region the most violent in the world. Call 2000: 9.

17. The text cited was the Report of the UN Special Rapporteur on the Independence of Judges and Lawyers, Param Cumaraswamy, March 2000.

18. During the armed conflict authoritarian and violent means such as torture and summary execution were used to resolve disputes, and whole communities were obliged to bear witness to and participate in atrocities. In addition, an entire generation of Mayan men were militarized through the civil patrol structure and schooled in the immediate, violent, and summary resolution of conflicts, a function that was effectively delegated to them by the armed forces. Many instigators

of lynchings have been identified as former paramilitary heads, who are now community leaders, and in some instances reports indicate that attacks were premeditated rather than spontaneous. The municipalities in which lynchings have occurred most frequently also rank among the poorest and the most disadvantaged in the country, where the impact of robberies characterized as minor by the state legal system, is keenly felt (MINUGUA 2002).

CULTURAL CONTENTIONS 2

The Labyrinth of Translation
A Tzeltal Version of the Universal Declaration of Human Rights

The Universal Declaration of Human Rights is, as its title indicates, a text with universal aspirations. Nevertheless, for people everywhere to fully understand the declaration's meaning, it has to be translated into their languages. Thus how the document is translated is crucial. Words and expressions are not neutral means of communication; they ascribe specific cultural meanings to the things to which they refer. In the case of translation between European languages—which share a history of political and moral ideas derived from Christianity and the Enlightenment—the difference is hardly perceptible, even in cases in which the translator goes to great lengths to be as faithful as possible to the original. In contrast, between more distant languages and cultures, the linguistic translation implies an intercultural translation. Cultural references have to be altered and adapted, and faithfulness to the original becomes impossible if one wants to maintain the true sense of a text. Therefore, if the principles of human rights are deeply linked to modern occidental culture, how does a non-Western culture translate these concepts into its own vocabulary and categories of thought? In this chapter, I look at certain aspects of and difficulties related to the translation of the Universal Declaration of Human Rights from Spanish into Tzeltal,[1] a Maya language spoken in the state of Chiapas, in the southeast of Mexico, by around four hundred thousand indigenous peoples.[2]

The translation of the declaration into Tzeltal (Gobierno del Estado de

Chiapas 1997) was done in 1996 by Miguel Gómez Gómez and Juan Santiz Cruz (as his assistant), indigenous persons from the municipality of Cancuc. It was published as a small, twenty-eight-page pamphlet with a parallel text in Spanish by the Center for Indigenous Languages, Art, and Literature (where Gómez was then working). The center was a Chiapas state government institution in the city of San Cristóbal de Las Casas involved in the translation of laws, statutes, rules, agreements, and the like into indigenous languages. This sudden concern with disseminating among the indigenous population knowledge about its rights derived from the Zapatista uprising of 1994 and from the San Andrés peace accords. But in contrast to what usually happens with government or legal texts translated into indigenous languages, the translators in this case were genuinely concerned that the resulting text could be understood by its readers (or listeners). As we shall see, the translation adopts the rhetoric and content of Tzeltal discourse, with the intention of turning it into a meaningful text for its potential readership. It is this effort that makes it an exceptional and particularly valuable text.

During the summer of 2000, I was able to work with Gómez—whom I had known for some time—in San Cristóbal de Las Casas to try and understand his translation and the difficulties he had encountered.[3] We dealt directly with the Tzeltal text—without consulting the original version in Spanish—attempting to clarify issues of form and content while at the same time discussing the more general ethnographic elements relating to "rights." This allowed me to translate the text back into Spanish: the work therefore meant translating a Tzeltal text originally translated from the Spanish into Spanish again. Later in this essay I will present and comment on this second translation. In a certain sense, this task can be seen as the opposite of what anthropologists generally do: if we usually "translate" indigenous culture into European culture, in this case, the Tzeltals have translated European culture into indigenous culture. This change of direction should reveal as much about indigenous (and European) culture as the translation generally done by anthropologists.

A Note Concerning the Dissemination of the Concept of Human Rights in Chiapas

Before moving on to look at the text itself, a few words should be said about the context. Indigenous peoples' exposure to the doctrine of human rights is a relatively new phenomenon in Chiapas. The first attempts at propagation were made at the end of the 1970s, but a more genuine effort did not begin until the end of the 1980s, and it did not become widespread until the 1990s. Those responsible have been nongovernmental organizations, along with the Catholic Church and some evangelical churches. (The Centro de Derechos Humanos Fray Bartolomé de Las Casas [Fray Bartolomé de Las Casas Human Rights Center, CDHFBC] which forms part of the diocese of San Cristóbal de Las Casas, was established in 1989 and is probably the most important institution in Chiapas dedicated to the promotion and defense of human rights.) Government human rights institutions appeared later in Chiapas. Information regarding human and legal rights was first made available as part of workshops held by nongovernmental organizations in which religious or revolutionary education, or both (the teaching of history and contemporary social analysis with a proselytizing objective), came to dominate. However, by the 1990s priorities were reversed and these organizations' educational curricula came to highlight human rights.

The importance attached to human rights also depended on the organization in question. In practice, the organization interpreted and provided information on human rights in line with its political and religious orientations. This meant not only that some aspects were emphasized over others but also that in many cases human rights served as a generic label under which politically motivated programs were promoted. In the case of Chiapas, the invocation of human rights frequently acquires a factional quality and is associated with more immediate political tactics. One has the impression that "human rights are not for everyone," but rather for groups considered morally superior and therefore deserving of such rights (Pitarch 2004b). This may happen everywhere, but in the indigenous regions of Chiapas, perhaps because of the novelty of this kind of politics, it is particularly evident.

As a result, the indigenous population is exposed to many different, and quite distinct, versions of "human rights." What is more, before actually reaching a larger segment of the indigenous population, concepts of human rights have to pass through a series of filters that progressively modify them. If we take the case of the diocese of San Cristóbal, which probably has the best network for the dissemination of rights (and where, in analogy with the so-called theology of enculturation, activists talk of "the enculturation of human rights"), the input comes from the activists who prepare the indigenous catechists. The catechists then instruct grassroots indigenous promoters (who make up the human rights defense committees in communities with Catholic majorities) entrusted with informing a majority of the population, which tends to be only the men. In this context, it is likely that they emphasize such things as the existence of individual rights to be able to better defend themselves in dealings with Mexican institutions. But talk of "women's rights," for example, rarely occurs in this environment, and if the women of the community do have any knowledge of these rights, it likely came from other organizations with projects dedicated to sexual and reproductive health. On the other hand, given that human rights activists seldom speak indigenous languages, it is difficult to know what a particular indigenous population—whose members often have a limited knowledge of Spanish—might understand by human rights. Notions of human rights thus go through a labyrinthine process of interpretation, translation, and adaptation that often renders the original ideas unrecognizable.

In contrast, the text we are now going to look at implies a direct translation from Spanish into Tzeltal, without this chain of intermediaries. As it is a written text and not an oral one—and thus one more difficult to disseminate among the indigenous population—it offers a rather exceptional example of the translation of human rights in Chiapas. It is, in some senses, a learned version of the process of translation. However, for the reader it has the great advantage of revealing—through a contrastive process—cultural extremes. If we really are witnessing the beginnings of a long conversation between Western concepts of human rights and indigenous ones concerning personhood and society, Gómez and Santiz's translation of the Universal Declaration offers an ideal means to approach the issue.

Law and Rights: Two Key Words in the Translation

The Universal Declaration of Human Rights uses two principal terms—*law* and *rights*—whose translation into Tzeltal is both difficult and compromising. In general, indigenous translators usually choose to keep these words in Spanish in their translations.[4] But in the text under discussion here, Gómez and Santiz decided to translate them into Tzeltal, and it is worth examining the terms used because they reveal the ways in which the Tzeltals might interpret the declaration.

The term *law* is consistently translated by *mantalil,* and the declaration is translated as *mantalil jun,* or "book of law." *Mantal* (*mantalil* without the generalizing suffix -*il*) is what one says to somebody about what they should or should not do; in other words, *mantal* is advice. Nevertheless, sometimes it is understood as something akin to "order," "dictate," or "rule." In fact, in his Tzotzil Dictionary[5] Robert Laughlin (1975) translates *mantal* as "advice, order, epidemic." In the declaration, the word *article* (article 1, 2, etc.) is translated as *mantal* (first *mantal*, second *mantal*, etc.). *Mantal* likely comes from the Spanish *mandar* (to order, command, or send for). If this is the case, it must have passed into Tzeltal relatively early on as today the Tzeltals do not recognize it as a word of foreign origin.

In the context of the Universal Declaration of Human Rights, the translation of "law" as *mantalil* has wider implications. *Mantalil* is essentially the advice and rules given to children and adolescents to ensure socially appropriate behavior. Although the themes that the term *mantalil* covers are very broad, it deals in particular with questions of posture, gesture, and social etiquette, especially with regard to showing respect to relatives and neighbors. To quote Gómez: "So when you are a parent, you give *mantal* to your children, part of *mantal* is giving a sacred word, good words, good words so that your children understand. . . . What we're looking for is that a child who is behaving badly begins to think, to think good things, do it this way, behave yourself, don't do bad things, so you're making him think." Children should follow the *ch'ul be mantal,* the "sacred path of advice."

In short, *mantalil* is an ethic for life. It is an ethic developed in and with relation to the body, not the soul (here the multiple indigenous souls are not relevant).[6] The process of creating the body is effectively continuous and only at an advanced age—older than forty perhaps, when a man or woman is a grandparent—is a person considered to have acquired sufficient maturity to be considered a "correct" body. Nonetheless, this development is as much physical as it is moral: each aspect is a necessary condition for the other. From a Tzeltal perspective, this ethic (*mantalil*) intervenes decisively in the formation of a person, though not spiritually (as we imagine in the West) but corporally. *Mantal* is thus not only used and understood as an ethical discourse; over a lifetime one actually acquires *mantal* as if it were something substantive, so that a person can accumulate a lot or little *mantal.*

This ontogenetic development begins at birth and stops with death, or rather, it ends a little before death, with the deterioration of mental faculties, when the body's optimal maturity is considered surpassed. The Tzeltal term denoting an older person, *k'otem* (from the verb *k'ot*, "to arrive"), means "finished," "complete," or, "with a fully formed body." The eth-nonym that the Tzeltals use to describe themselves, *batz'il winik* (true men, genuine men), should be interpreted in this way, that is, as beings that have turned into authentic human beings because their bodies behave as morally correct bodies. Gómez explains it thus: "Because you are not born with *mantal*, at the moment of birth, a creature doesn't have *mantal*, until you begin to walk, begin to focus, that is when the creature receives the love of its father, the love of its mother, at that moment, then it begins to feel affection, it is born, a year passes, it begins to feel the love of its sibling, when it is a little bigger it begins to feel the love of the people, there it begins to acquire its way of living, its way of thinking, its way of doing things, because a child cannot simply stand up, it cannot live by itself, it has to be controlled through *mantal*." In this way, the fetus inside the mother's womb does not receive *mantal*. Neither do the dead, because "I don't believe that [the *ch'ulel* of the dead[7]] receive *mantal*; many speak of life in their prayers, they talk of *ch'ulel*, our spirit, therefore that would be another person that is going to be disciplined, as it is not all of us, because they say that here you have everything, in contrast, the spirit doesn't." As far as I understand, Gómez reasons that the soul *ch'ulel* cannot have *mantalil* because it lacks a body ("here you have everything, in contrast, the spirit doesn't") and, as we have seen, the body is the necessary condition for the moral development of a person.[8]

If the generic term *mantalil* constitutes an ethic, it also represents an aesthetic. For the Tzeltals, this constitutes an essential dimension of the term. Not only are words of *mantalil* inherently beautiful and emotionally stirring but they also reveal the beauty of the world, as well as its goodness. For example, a friend from Cancuc traveled to a hamlet in the lowlands and there met some elderly people who were sitting listening to a particularly beautiful birdsong. Given its exceptional beauty, the song made them reflect on the world. My friend referred to this birdsong specifically as *mantal*, in other words, as a sort of ethical advice that the birds offered to those able to pause and listen. This episode also reveals that *mantalil*, or ethics, is not produced solely in relations among human beings but also includes the relationship between human beings and the world. This is an issue that Gómez had me take note of in relation to the Universal Declaration of Human Rights. He considers Tzeltal ethics more universal than that of the

United Nations (UN) because the latter does not include the nonhuman world: "*mantalil* for me is also very big, *mantal* is the good that exists in the world, how one should relate to the people, how one should respect one's neighbors and everything else that surrounds us, the trees, what the birds say, all that, everything is joined to us and forms part of our blood. I believe that when we are talking of the universal we have to also consider the right of (or respect towards) everything that exists in the world, how one relates to the world, because we rule in all the space that we have, with the *aja-wetikes* [mountains], although we don't see it." Thus important is not only the relationship between human beings and the world but also that human beings are themselves part of the fabric of the world.

Let us now look at the second key concept, that of rights. In the declaration, the term *rights*—describing both the sphere within which it is determined what should and should not be done and the possibility of demanding something ("to have rights")—is consistently translated by the expression *ich'el ta muk,* which means "respect." (The expression is made up of the transitive verb *ich,*' meaning to receive, obtain, or take something; *ich'el ta muk* can be literally translated as "receiving something greatly, with force.") Therefore, to have rights is translated as commanding respect, to be respected, and human rights are translated as "respect for human beings." From these meanings one can deduce that in Tzeltal the notion of rights is interpreted within the logic of reciprocity and complementarity. In fact, the verb *ich'* also means "to get married to someone," in the sense that one receives a husband or a wife.[9]

Here the authors of the original declaration and the Tzeltal translators clearly start from different premises. If for the former all human beings are equal, for the latter human beings are not only distinct from one another, but also powerfully unequal, arranged in asymmetric hierarchies. Precisely this makes reciprocity and complementarity necessary. For example, there is no exact equivalent in Tzeltal for the word *fraternal,* used in the original declaration in the sense of affection between equals:[10] siblings are older or younger siblings, never equal; a hierarchy shapes their relationship. In the same way, husband and wife are unequal, and this is what makes them need each other. This asymmetry also explains why not all human beings possess the same respect or, in this context, the same rights. Respect is not something given but something acquired as one goes about fulfilling one's obligations.[11] Only when a person carries out his or her social responsibilities will he or she be worthy of respect or rights. From this it follows that respect and rights are progressively acquired throughout life. In reality, children hardly have rights at all, given that they benefit from their parents without giving anything in return. They are not inserted into a scheme of reciprocal obligations or, to be more precise, they build up a debt that they will have to repay later on.

For instance, for the Tzeltals, this perspective renders almost incomprehensible an article such as 16.2 in the Universal Declaration of Human Rights, which reads, "Marriage shall be entered into only with the free and full consent of the intending spouses." This is considered unjust: given that the young woman has been benefiting from the care and attention of her parents throughout her childhood without offering anything in exchange, the parents should receive something when handing their daughter over for marriage. Moreover, an intimate relationship exists between achieving the condition of being a human and being worthy of respect. For this reason Gómez observes that "the creature that is inside the belly of their mother does not have rights, it is the rights of the mother, because if the creature is inside the mother it has never heard that there exist laws. While it has yet to be born, it is not a person. For this reason, it is very important when it begins to tread the ground [*stek' lum k'inal*], that is when I believe it begins to be a person, because it is then part of society, it is protected by its father and mother, and they begin to respect it a little."

Human Rights as *Mantalil*

The Universal Declaration of Human Rights has been translated into Tzeltal following the verbal genre of *mantalil*. This is something that emerges as much from the content of the translation as from its style.

The Tzeltal text, despite being a written document, has the flow and characteristic links of spoken language. It is difficult to know whether the translators were imagining a finished product to be read in private or a text that would be read in public, such as on the radio or among small groups in indigenous communities. (Perhaps this difference does not really exist, as the few indigenous people that do read Tzeltal tend to do so as if it were still an essentially oral language, which, in effect, it is.) In any case, the mode of expression is clearly oral, and the way it is written assists in its being read aloud (e.g., in the use of the enclitic *-e*, which indicates where to end a sentence and make a pause). Even so, it does not completely avoid the decontextualization implicit in written texts. In the normal context of Tzeltal oral expression, priority is given to dialogue, and in this case the audience—even if comprising small children—would show its attentiveness through forms of approval or by asking questions that clarify certain aspects of what has been said.

It is significant that the Tzeltals of Cancuc to whom I read aloud fragments of the text recognized without much difficulty that it dealt with advice about how to live appropriately, that is, they understood it as a kind of *mantalil*. While it was difficult to identify exactly what they recognized as *mantalil*, it is certain that these were details of style not content because they often did not understand the meaning of what was stated in each article in the declaration. (Something similar also happens, of course, when a Spanish or English speaker reads a fragment of the Universal Declaration of Human Rights and can immediately recognize it as a legal document without knowing exactly the particular text in question.) The people I consulted insisted that words of *mantalil*, if sufficiently eloquent and solemn, "attract the heart." "A single word is enough to seduce an audience," one person said with regard to *mantalil*, whose rhetoric makes liberal use of emotive tropes, such as that of elderly folk listening to birdsong. This provokes an emotional response that the Tzeltals associate with *ch'ul*—however difficult it might be to define—the domain of the sacred. The fact is that the spoken form of the declaration's translation is sufficiently eloquent and solemn; although it is written, it manages to be recognized by its listeners as a *mantalil* text, thus provoking an inclination to listen to something important "to live correctly." The content of the Tzeltal translation, however, presents other problems. Some parts of the text have been translated rather literally, making it difficult for Tzeltals to understand their meaning. This seems to occur above all in two types of circumstances: First, when the Spanish becomes more technical, for example, when using the language of international politics ("shall strive by teaching and education to promote respect for these rights and freedoms and by progressive measures, national and international, to secure their universal and effective recognition and observance, both among the peoples of Member States themselves and among the peoples of territories under their jurisdiction"), or simply when the translators do not understand the sense of the Spanish text, which sometimes happens.[12] And second, when the subject spoken about does not have a near equivalent in local experience ("Technical and professional education shall be made generally available and higher education shall be equally accessible to all on the basis of merit").

In contrast, other parts of the declaration have abandoned such faithfulness to the original and have been translated adapting fairly well to the type of Tzeltal language used in *mantalil*. For example, the first paragraph of the preamble to the declaration states:

"Whereas recognition of the inherent dignity and of the equal and inalienable rights of all members of the human family is the foundation of freedom, justice and peace in the world." In Tzeltal, this sections reads, "In order to enjoy well-being and health here in the world in which we live, it is of great importance that we do not hinder nor harm the respect owed to every group of human beings' desire for happiness." This adaptation generally occurs with the more generic declarations—or one might say, those with a moral character—most probably because they allow for a more flexible interpretation. But however much the translation has adapted itself to Tzeltal common sense, the declaration's articles still have not really turned into an indigenous *mantal*. The content of the text maintains a strange character, and at times the declarations clash with traditional points of view. After all, the translators were not able to completely ignore the original Spanish. Rather, they interpreted the declaration's *sense* as if it dealt with Tzeltal ethics.

The clearest example of this is that the translators have written the Tzeltal text by following an ontogenetic pattern, in much the same way as a *mantalil*. They did not deliberately alter the declaration; rather, they took as a given that the logic of the UN essentially resembled the Tzeltal logic of the *mantalil*: they read the text as if it were akin to a indigenous moral discourse. Consequently, the first articles of the declaration must begin with the respect that persons are due from their birth and infancy, and as the articles progress, so does the age of the person. In the words of Gómez: "Because I feel that this human rights law functions from one's birth, until you gradually become a good citizen, until you're old, it follows the growth of a person from birth until . . . well, here it doesn't say until death, but we can imagine that it is until death, as then you are not a person, but something else, that doesn't have rights anymore. Do you believe that on dying, rights don't matter anymore?" According to Gómez, the first article ("All human beings are born free and equal") deals with those just born; the second article ("Everyone is entitled to all the rights and freedoms set forth in this Declaration") deals with children and the domestic context within which people should be respected. For this reason, the articles relating to marriage and higher education are found further on in the text. In fact, the translation contains overinterpretations that strengthen this logic of personal growth; in article 3, for example, the English states, "Everyone has the right to life, liberty and security of person." It is translated by "All human beings should be respected during their life on earth, helped to mature in their words, as well as cared for during their growth." Whereas the English version leaves age indeterminate, the translation refers clearly to a child—given that we are still dealing with article 3—and therefore freedom is interpreted as the maturing of the word and security is interpreted as the care necessary for growth.

Translations

For reasons of space, instead of the whole text of the Universal Declaration of Human Rights, only its preamble and articles 1 through 6, 15, 16, and 18 are presented here. From a Tzeltal point of view, the initial words, however rhetorical they might be, are the most important, and in fact Gómez accords greater value to the preamble than to the articles themselves. For this reason I have chosen to maintain the preamble complete. Of the declaration's twenty-nine articles, the nine I have chosen are the least technical and therefore perhaps those that give the translators the most leeway.

In what follows I present the original English text of the declaration, followed first by its translation into Tzeltal and then my translation from Tzeltal back into English. The latter is the most literal translation possible because what interests me here is not so much flow or meaning, but that the differences and similarities between the original and the Tzeltal translation become as visible as possible.

THE UNIVERSAL DECLARATION OF HUMAN RIGHTS

YAK'EL TA NA'EL TA STOJOL SPAMAL BALUMILAL TE YICH'EL TA MUK' KIRSANUETIK

SO THAT IT IS KNOWN ON THE WHOLE SURFACE OF THE EARTH THE RESPECT FOR HUMAN BEINGS

Observations: The translation uses the term *spamal balumilal,* "the surface of the earth," although more literally it means "the flat surface of the earth," the flat area found on top of the nine horizontal levels that make up the earth. It is a more restricted space than that suggested by the English term *universal.* This is the space that living human beings inhabit, and implicitly excluded from this dimension are the souls of the dead, whether they be found in the center of the earth or in heaven. On the other hand, the expression does indicate that the text should be recognized along the length and breadth of this space, which encompasses all human beings.

Human being is translated here and throughout the text as *kirsano* (pl. *kirsanuetik*). The word is one borrowed from the Spanish *cristiano* (Christian). It is likely that the Tzeltals recognize the term as Spanish in origin because in Tzeltal words have the accent on the final syllable, while *kirsano,* like all other borrowed terms, has the accent on the penultimate syllable. According to Gómez, he and his collaborator tried to avoid the term *winik* (man), much more common in other translations, because it does not include women, at least not explicitly. This choice is not explained only by some sort of political correctness: the text needs to *emphasize* that the declaration includes women as well as men. Furthermore, the choice of *kirsano* provides some extra benefits. Among the Tzeltals of Cancuc, *kirsano* is usually used to distinguish human bodies of skin and bone from other types of beings such as spirits, the dead, souls, lords of the mountain, and monsters. If someone comes across a being of some sort during the night, they wonder whether it is a *kirsano* or not, if it is a human body or not. These other beings have some human qualities, but their bodies are not really their own. Conversely, the category of *kirsano* includes human beings that are not indigenous, such as Europeans or the "cannibals" in the Lacandón Forest, despite their great cultural distance.

Adopted and proclaimed by the General Assembly of the United Nations in its resolution 217 A (III) of 10 December 1948.

Ch'uunbil sok pukbil sk'oplal ta Muk'ul Chajpajibal ta Spamal Balumilal ta yajtelul juklajuneb xbuluchwinik A (III) chiknaj ta sk'aalel lajuneb yu'un lisiembre ta ya'wilal 1948.

Accepted this word in the great deliberation of all the peoples, and disseminated over the whole surface of the earth in folio number two hundred and seventeen, which was proclaimed on the tenth of December of the year 1948.

(First paragraph): Whereas recognition of the inherent dignity and of the equal and inalienable rights of all members of the human family is the foundation of freedom, justice and peace in the world;

Te yich'el ta wenta te lekil utsilal sok sbuts' k'inal li' ta lu balumilale, ja' tulan sk'oplal te manchuk ya yich' k'axumtayel ta ich'el ta muk' te sk'anojel yo'tanik ta spisil juju chajp te kirsanuetike.

To enjoy well-being and health here in the world in which we live, it is of great importance that we do not hinder nor harm the respect owed to every group of human beings' desire for happiness.

Observations: The European words *freedom, justice,* and *peace* have been replaced in the Tzeltal translation by two expressions that are culturally closer: *lekil utsilal* and *sbuts k'inal.* The first, which I translate as "well-being," means "a lot of goodness" and is understood as being a contented person, protected, out of danger, without enemies, who lives well and can go where he or she pleases in harmony with the rest of the world, the human as well as the natural and nonhuman ones. The expression *sbuts k'inal,* which I translate as "health," means that a person is physically healthy ("they have an appetite," "they have the strength to work") and furthermore that they are not scared, worried, ashamed, or depressed. In Tzeltal, the language of health and illness is the principal means through which the quality of social and political relations, both collective and personal, is expressed. It is not an exaggeration to say that the Universal Declaration of Human Rights is proposed, in its Tzeltal version, as a means of improving the health of human beings.

To achieve this well-being and health, the respect that one should show for the desire for happiness should not be hindered in any way (in the sense that nobody should "cross" [*k'axumtayel*] the path of another person). The expression *sk'anojel yo'tanik,* which I translate as "happiness," means "what our hearts desire," or "the way of being" of a person or community. It is not a rational or reflexive desire (which would correspond to the head), but a desire that comes spontaneously from the heart and originates in the past.

With reference to a community, it comes close to the notion of tradition or customs. According to Gómez, in Chamula (a traditionalist municipality where Mexican legal rights are frequently subordinated to indigenous custom), "they conserve their customs and their traditions because they most likely want it that way, even when it is ugly, but it is an issue for them, they are content with their way of being." This contentedness with their way of being is precisely *sk'anojel yo'tanik*. In other words, "the equal and inalienable rights of all members of the human family" have become, in the Tzeltal version, the respect for a way of being, the traditional practices of a particular group of people that live in a community. The "human family" has become "every different group" of human beings, who probably have their own hearts' desires. "Group" is the translation of *chajp*, which can be applied to a group of relatives or to a lineage, for example, but it does not communicate the idea that its members should treat each other "fraternally," as the declaration insists at various points. As we have seen, the relationship between siblings is deeply hierarchical. Tzeltal Catholics call each other *kerman,* borrowed from the Spanish word *hermano* (brother or sibling), in an attempt to establish a more egalitarian relationship, although it does not work entirely.

(Second paragraph): Whereas disregard and contempt for human rights have resulted in barbarous acts which have outraged the conscience of mankind, and the advent of a world in which human beings shall enjoy freedom of speech and belief and freedom from fear and want has been proclaimed as the highest aspiration of the common people;

Ta skaj te ma ba tsakbil ta wenta sok te ma ba ich'bil ta muk' te kirsanuetike, bayel binti chujkul ko'em ta pasel ta swenta yu'un ayuk bit'il ya xyanej te snopibale; sok a'aybil stojol sk'oplal te binti ut'il ya sk'an yo'tan ya xchajpan sbaik, bit'il ya sk'an xkuxinik ta lum balumilal. Manchuk ayukik ta xiwtesel sok ta wokolajel, yakuk ya'aybeyik slekil yutsilal te binti ut'il ya sk'an xchajpan sbaik ta swenta xch'uunel te yo'tanike.

Due to the fact that it (the law) is not recognised nor human beings respected, much hardship has occurred. In order to think well and so that there exists the change that our hearts desire, there is a good, upstanding word with which to organize ourselves and according to which we can live life on earth: may there be no fright nor suffering; may we enjoy well-being; and may we be able to organize ourselves according to the thoughts of our hearts.

Observations: Again the ideas of freedom (of words and beliefs) have been substituted here by the idea of the heart's desire; *xch'uunel yo'tanik* is "the heart's thought," to believe with one's heart, to believe emotionally. It is the equivalent of believing in something good, and from an indigenous perspective, once one believes in something good, it becomes less likely that one will experience frights or suffering. Its opposite—"fear" in the English version—has been translated into Tzeltal as *xiwtesel*, which I translate as "fright." The concept is equivalent to those of scare or fright as used in the ethnographic literature on Mesoamerica: something gives a person a fright (e.g., something that suddenly appears in the night, or a fall) and as a consequence the person falls ill. In Tzeltal, in a situation of *xiwtesel*, it is likely that the soul *ch'ulel* abandons the body. Therefore it is not a question of vague fears, nor a state of more generalized dread; neither is it necessarily a fear of something specific, but a fear of being given a fright. *Xiwtesel* is the consequence of this fear. The "good, upstanding word," or the Universal Declaration of Human Rights, should help avoid this type of fear, which is basically the fear of falling ill. But there is something else: on "thinking well," that is, on believing the words of the declaration, it becomes less likely that "bad things" occur. This idea resembles one suggested by Benjamin Lee Whorf's (1956) writings on the Hopi, for whom positive wishes and a general benevolence help produce desired outcomes. For a thought to be effective, it should be consciously and intensely experienced, as well as well defined, firm, and loaded with intentions. I understand that the Tzeltal expression *xch'uunel yo'tanik*, to believe something strongly in the heart, has this same sense of placing thoughts and good intentions at the service of any undertaking's future success.

(Third paragraph): Whereas it is essential, if man is not to be compelled to have recourse, as a last resort, to rebellion against tyranny and oppression, that human rights should be protected by the rule of law;

Tulan sk'oplal te yakuk yich'ik kanantayel ta lek yu'un mantalil te yich'el ta muk' binti ay ta swentaik spasel te kirsanuetike, swenta ma ta k'opuk ya sle ich'el ta muk' te kirsanuetike, yu'un me jich ma'yukik ta tsalel sok uts'inel yu'un te mach'a ya spasik mantale.

It is of great importance that all people are cared for by the good law (*mantalil*) of respect, so that there are no conflicts owing to a lack of respect for people, and likewise, so that there exists no deceit nor mistreatment, they make the law (*mantal*).

Observations: According to Gómez, the law (*mantalil*) protects: "As you would protect a child, giving him the goodness of your heart, telling him to respect other men, so that the child doesn't do bad things . . . the law looks after you so that they don't mistreat you, so that they don't frighten you or make you suffer, well protected by the *mantalil,* what people want to do." Here rebellion is translated as *k'opuk,* meaning "conflict" or "dispute," above all a verbal dispute (*k'op* is word as well as dispute [Gossen 1974]). It should be noted that the translators are not putting themselves in place of the authors of the text; it is they (whoever they may be) that "make the law"; the translator is simply the bearer of the word.

(Fourth paragraph): Whereas it is essential to promote the development of friendly relations between nations;

Ja' nix jich tulan sk'oplal te junuk nax ya yich' sabik ta muk'; sok smuk'ubtesel spasel ya'tel te juju sejp muk'ul k'ejel lumetike.

Furthermore, it is of great importance that there exist mutual respect, and that the task (of the law) extend itself to each and every one of the great peoples.

(Fifth paragraph): Whereas the peoples of the United Nations have in the Charter reaffirmed their faith in fundamental human rights, in the dignity and worth of the human person and in the equal rights of men and women and have determined to promote social progress and better standards of life in larger freedom;

Ta yich'el ta wenta te Muk'ul Chajpajibal ta Spamal Balumilale, xchajpanobeyik sk'oplal ta swenta yich'el ya muk' slekil yutsil yo'tanik sok yantik binti tulan sk'oplal ta stojolik ta spisil winik antsetik; sok lok'em sk'oplal yu'unik ta swenta spasel ya'telul ta slekubtesel bit'il ya xkuxinik ta lek.

To receive the great deliberation for the whole world, the groups have agreed (this) so that the well-being of the heart is respected and other things of summary importance for life and to which all men and women are entitled; and this word is made public to improve the goodness of life.

Observations: This paragraph is a good example of how very abstract and general concepts (that have universal pretensions) in the original Spanish text tend to be redirected in the Tzeltal translation toward more concrete and local interpretations. Hence "faith in fundamental human rights" becomes "that the well-being of the heart is respected," and the "dignity and worth of the human person" becomes "other things of importance for life." "Social progress" and the raising of standards of life "in larger freedom" become in Tzeltal "to improve the goodness of life."

(Sixth paragraph): Whereas Member States have pledged themselves to achieve, in co-operation with the United Nations, the promotion of universal respect for and observance of human rights and fundamental freedoms; and

Ja' nix jich te juju sejp Estadoetike, yak'oj sk'op ya'yejik te junax ya yak' sbaik sok Muk'ul Chajpajibal ta Spamal Balumilal ta swenta stulantesel sk'oplal yich'el ta muk' sok spasel ya'telul ta lekil utsilal ta stojolik te kirsanuetike; sok

Furthermore, every state has given their word to respect the agreement of the great deliberation of the whole world, so that the word of respect is strengthened and so that we work to improve the well-being to which people are entitled; and

(Seventh paragraph): Whereas a common understanding of these rights and freedoms is of the greatest importance for the full realization of this pledge,

Ta skaj te yu'un pajal jich snopojibal te yakuk xk'otok ta pasel te ich'el ta muk'e, ja' tulan sk'oplal ta swenta xch'uunel spasel ya'telul te binti chajpanbile

So that this work in favor of respect can enter in equal measure the understanding (of all), it is of great importance that each and every group work in favor of this agreement.

(Final paragraph): The General Assembly proclaims this Universal Declaration of Human Rights as a common standard of achievement for all peoples and all nations, to the end that every individual and every organ of society, keeping this Declaration constantly in mind, shall strive by teaching and education to promote respect for these rights and freedoms and by progressive measures, national and international, to secure their universal and effective recognition and observance, both among the peoples of Member States themselves and among the peoples of territories under their jurisdiction.

Te Muk'ul Komon Tsoblej ayich' ta muk' te mantal ta Spamal balumilal yich'el ta muk' ta spamal k'inal te kirsanuetike, melel yu'un jich pajal tabil ta nopel ta juju sejp lumetik, ja yu'un te juju tul te yajwal lume, snail chajpajibaletik sok snaul te sp'ijubtesele ya sk'an ya yak'ik ta a'yel sok snopel bit'il ya yich' pasel ya'telul ta yich'el ta muk' sk'anojel yo'tanik sok ayuk ta stojolik te binti ya sk'an yo'tan ya sapasik te kirsanuetik, yakuk muk'buk ta pasel ta juju sejp k'ejel lumetik ta swenta te pajaluk ya xk'ot ta tuuntesel ta selekil yutsilal te binti chajpanbile, sok ta juju chajp tut lumetik te banti wentaibilik ta jujun Estadoetik jich' bit'il yajwal banti ayik juju chajp slum sk'inalike.

The Grand Assembly gives this law (*mantal*) of the whole world in favor of the respect for all people on the earth, because it has been genuinely agreed on by all peoples in an equal manner. For this reason, every person in every place, every organization, every house of study should become aware of (the law) and teach it so that respect is achieved for the desire for the way of being and thinking, and that each and every one of the great peoples and every one of the other smaller peoples, and the respect and goodness contained in this agreement, reaches everyone in equal manner, all peoples subject to all states, as well as every portion of peoples in other places in the world.

ARTICLE 1

All human beings are born free and equal in dignity and rights. They are endowed with reason and conscience and should act towards one another in a spirit of brotherhood.

Spisil kirsanuetik k'alal ya xtojkik ayikix yich'el ta muk' ay ta slekil yutsilal sok pajal ay snopibal sjol yotanik te ja' jich ya sk'an ya xjech ich'bey sabik ta muk.'

All human beings from the moment they are born have the respect and well-being of the world, and have the same understanding of the heart's thoughts, and desire great mutual respect.

Observations: The Tzeltal version of this article does not deal with adults, but with human beings that have just been born or are very young. According to Gómez, the text is explained thus: "From birth a person has respect, and their behavior will be in accordance with what their father and mother teach them, when they are a little older, the child knows how he is going to behave or conduct himself, as he has learnt it from his father, from his mother . . . from the moment the creature arrives it should be respected and it should have good things, the best things, in learning, behavior and the experiences of its father." The expression "have the same understanding of the heart's thoughts" (*pajal ay snopibal sjol yotanik*) is explained in the following way: "Although it is a creature, it is born with understanding, and comes with its thought, how it should behave. It [i.e., the text] is talking about thought, intelligence: from the heart to the head, the heart is moving (beating) at the moment the creature is born, that means that it is thinking, that's why we talk about the heart's thoughts, it's when the whole body is moving. When it is in the womb, we don't know if the creature is thinking because its mother is feeding it, it is the mother's thoughts, its father's blood, but when the creature is born, its heart begins to move, it's independent." In other words, before being born, the fetus is not really a human being. It feeds from its mother's blood and its father's blood (sperm), but above all its heart is not beating and therefore it does not have a conscience independent of its mother.

Among the Tzeltals, a person has two consciences, or two "thoughts": those of the heart and those of the head. The conscience of the head only exists potentially and grows along with the development of the person, but that of the heart is totally formed at birth. Newborns deserve respect (or, they already have rights) because they have their own conscience. This is what the translation of the declaration states, but the majority of Tzeltals would almost certainly qualify this statement by explaining that a newly born child should be respected, but not in the same way as an adult, whose conscience (of the head) has developed appropriately. In other words, a child is not worthy of the same respect (it does not, and cannot, have the same rights) as an adult.

Everyone is entitled to all the rights and freedoms set forth in this Declaration, without distinction of any kind, such as race, color, sex, language, religion, political or other opinion, national or social origin, property, birth or other status.

Spisil kirsnuetik ay me ta stojol spisil binti ya sk'an yo'tanik spasel jich bit'il chajpanbil sk'oplal li' ta mantalil jun, ma'yuk me mach'a ay ta tsael bit'il ay stalelik, bi yilel sbak'etaltil me winik o ants, sk'op ya'yejik, xch'uunel yo'tanik, binti u'til xchajpanoj sabik, ja' nix jich banti wejtem tojemik, bit'il swentainij sbaik ta stak'inik o ay yantik binti u'til kuxinemik.

All human beings deserve to do what their hearts desire, inasmuch as it is in accordance with the word of the book of law (*mantalil jun*). Nobody can be separated from their way of being (their character, their tradition), for what their body looks like, for being a man or a woman, for their conversations, their hearts' beliefs, for the group to which they belong, or where they were born, or for their living conditions, or if they have money, or if they have a different way of life.

Observations: According to Gómez, while the previous article referred to a small child, this one refers to a person who is a little older, perhaps an adolescent, which is why it mentions the ways in which human beings organize themselves. Religion here is translated as "their hearts' beliefs," in the sense of the emotional thoughts mentioned above, but directed at thinking good things. On the other hand, Gómez insists on translating "economic situation" in the original Spanish with *bit'il swentainij sbaik,* which means "living conditions," because in his opinion money itself is not as important as the availability of other resources (land, health, etc.) in indigenous communities. Nevertheless, to respect the original, *ta stak'inik* ("if they have money") has been added. "What it means is that we depend on life, it gives the idea that we are dependent, on how we get on with our neighbors, with the rest, how we depend on our maize, our beans, if you have food, you don't depend on money anymore, if you behave yourself, if your behavior is good, you get on with people . . . the people in the communities don't go along with the idea of money: 'I have my food, my maize, my beans.'"

Everyone has the right to life, liberty and security of person.

Spisil kirsanuetik ich'bil ta muk' xkuxinel ta lum k'inal, kolemuk ta ch'iel k'opojel sok ayuk me kanantayel ta stojolik.

All human beings should be respected during their life on earth, helped to mature in their word, as well as looked after while growing up.

Observations: This article continues to refer to the respect due (or rights of) a child or adolescent. The rights to life, liberty, and security are interpreted as obligations, fundamentally family ones, related to children. Here the maturing of their word is equivalent to a growth in thought and conscience, which is related to the head. In other words, they should be educated. Education is that which allows children to relate to each other in a socially appropriate manner. Although the Spanish text does not mention the process of growing up, the expression *kanantayel ta stojolik* specifically means to help or look after a child, throughout its growth, so that it does not suffer any physical harm.

ARTICLE 4

No one shall be held in slavery or servitude; slavery and the slave trade shall be prohibited in all their forms.

Ma'yuk me mach'a ay ta mosoinel sok ta abatinel ta jich nax, makbil me sk'oplal sok oy smulilal ta pasel.

Nobody can be subjected anymore to a situation of tied labor or as a porter; this is prohibited and to do it is a crime.

Observations: Here the translators have substituted the terms *slavery* and *servitude* with "tied labor" and "porter." They could have translated these terms in a more abstract fashion, but they decided to use two more specific local terms that have a strong emotive charge in indigenous social memory. I translate *mosoinel* as "tied labor," a term that derives from the Spanish *mozo* (unskilled laborer), a word used to describe *peones*, or agricultural laborers, on the estates, ranches, and commercial plantations of Chiapas, where indigenous people found themselves obliged to work because of a lack of available agricultural land. For the Tzeltals of Cancuc, this is a somewhat remote period in their history (occurring in the first few decades of the twentieth century, before President Lázaro Cárdenas implemented a policy of agrarian reform), but it is vividly recalled in oral tradition: the exhausting work, pitiful wages, the mistreatment and abuse, the estate shop, and the condition of servitude caused by debt are all remembered. However, for other Tzeltal and Tzotzil Indians, this state of *mosoinel* lasted until the 1960s, or even into the 1970s (Toledo Tello 2002, Bobrow-Strain 2007).

The term *abatinel,* which I translate as "porter," has also left a deep mark on indigenous oral tradition. The people of Cancuc remember the time in which they were forced to carry *a mecapal* (a way of carrying a load on the back with a supporting band across the forehead) batches of salt, pig lard, maize, or even rich Ladino people from Ocosingo or Salto de Agua to San Cristóbal de Las Casas. Such stories do not leave out how Ladino women traveling on seats mounted on the backs of indigenous people did not climb down to urinate, thus soiling the porters. In some ways, the category of *mosoinel* includes that of *abatinel.* The difference is that the former stayed in one place, the estate, whereas the latter generally lived in his or her village, but was ordered to carry loads (*abatinel* is a servant, but in the sense of an errand boy) and therefore moved from one place to another. However, it is possible that here these two terms are used as a semantic pair to give a more formal feel to the text, much as they would in oral performance.

As far as I know, the words *mosoinel* and *abatinel* are only used in relation to servitude under the *kaxlanetik* (Ladino or mestizos) but they are not used among indigenous peoples themselves (although sometimes the work conditions are not much better). Therefore, the abstracted slavery and servitude mentioned in the original text has become strongly ethnicized in the translation: "The *kaxlanetik,* or mestizos, cannot subject us to slavery or servitude."

ARTICLE 5

No one shall be subjected to torture or to cruel, inhuman or degrading treatment or punishment.

Ma'yuk me mach'a ya yich' k'aesel swokol ta uts'inel sok k'alal ya yich' chukel yu'un smul, ma'yuk me mach'a ya yich' kuyel ta chanbalam, ta jich ma jichuk.

No person can be made to suffer (physical) mistreatment, even though they may be in prison for a crime; no person can be treated as an animal, this cannot be.

Observations: Given that the declaration is interpreted in a precise way, as specific dictates, the translators felt obliged to specifically introduce the fact that it is not permitted to treat people badly in prison, given that it is common practice in the prisons of Chiapas and that until recently many indigenous people considered it normal.

ARTICLE 6

Everyone has the right to recognition everywhere as a person before the law.

Spisil kirsanuetik ay me yich'el ta muk', ma wentauk banti ay, sok ay yich'el ta muk' binti u'til ya sle chajpanel.

All human beings must be respected, wherever they may be, and they must be respected so that they are able to defend themselves.

ARTICLE 15.1

Everyone has the right to a nationality.

Spisil kirsanuetik banti wejtem tojkemik ay me ta swentaik ta ich'el ta muk' te yu'un ja' slumalik.

All human beings should be respected in the village where they were born and grew up, and to which they belong.

ARTICLE 15.2

No one shall be arbitrarily deprived of his nationality nor denied the right to change his nationality.

Ma'yuk me mach'a joil nax ya yich' jelontesbel banti slumal wejtem tojkem te me ma jichuk snopibal yu'une, te me ma jichuk sk'an yo'tane.

No person can be forced to live in a different village to the one where they were born without their consent (of the head), or if they do not wish it (in their heart).

Men and women of full age, without any limitation due to race, nationality or religion, have the right to marry and to found a family. They are entitled to equal rights as to marriage, during marriage and at its dissolution.

K'alal ya sta ya'wilalik te winik antsetike, ma me stak' ta makbeyel yo'tanik bit'il ya yik sabik, ayinuk yal xnich'anik, ma wentauk me pajal stalelik, xkuxinemik o xch'uunel yo'tanik, sok te bit'il ya xkuxinike pajal me ak'a ya'aybeyik slekil yustsilal binti ay ta ewentaik spasel k'alal ya yik sabike sok te me ay patil yijkitay sbaike.

When men and women reach their age, their desire to join together and have children cannot be obstructed. It does not matter if they do not have the same way of being, customs or beliefs of the heart; and during their life together they must receive life's bounties in equal measure because they now live in new circumstances, and also it cannot be obstructed if they want to stop being together.

Observations: This is one of the articles of the declaration that most contradicts Tzeltal common sense. That the couple may have different ways of life or beliefs does not present any problems, but the idea that young women may decide for themselves whom to marry (as implied in article 16.2) does. The issue is relatively simple: young women have lived fourteen or fifteen years in their parents' house, being fed and clothed, and otherwise taken care of, but they have hardly worked in exchange. The idea that they can get married and go and live in their new parents-in-laws' house (just when they reach working age) without offering anything in exchange thus verges on the absurd from a Tzeltal perspective.

The statement that the man and woman "are entitled to equal rights as to marriage, during marriage and at its dissolution" is practically impossible to translate into Tzeltal because there does not exist a concept of property in common, that is, of the two individuals in a marriage sharing property equally. In Tzeltal and Tzotzil communities, with patrilineal patterns of social organization, women inherit neither land nor goods; in fact, they hardly own anything at all (with the exception of their back-strap loom); not even their children are really theirs. Even in the communities in which women are able to receive land or other goods in theory, in practice it remains a rare occurrence. Therefore the translators did not exactly know how to translate into Tzeltal the idea that the married couple has the same rights if the marriage dissolves. In fact, the Tzeltal version does not really acknowledge this point, and it seems that the translators have not assigned it much importance.

Marriage shall be entered into only with the free and full consent of the intending spouses.

J'a nax me te me yu'un jich sjol yo'tan stukelik te pajal ya staik ta nopel ta jtulutule, ya me stak' yich' sbaik.

Only if the thoughts of both persons' hearts (the man and the woman) so wish, can they join together.

ARTICLE 16.3

The family is the natural and fundamental group unit of society and is entitled to protection by society and the State.

Te bit'il ya xnujp'ejike ja' me lom tulan sk'oplal ta kuxinel, ya me sk'an ya yich' ich'el ta muk' sok ayik me ta kanantayel yu'un te Estadoe sok spisil te kirsanuetike.

When they are together (man and woman), this is a commitment of the greatest importance for life; and they are worthy of the greatest respect and care on the part of the state and all other people.

ARTICLE 18

Everyone has the right to freedom of thought, conscience and religion; this right includes freedom to change his religion or belief, and freedom, either alone or in community with others and in public or private, to manifest his religion or belief in teaching, practice, worship and observance.

Spisil kirsanuetik stak' snop binti sk'an yo'tan, ta sk'oponel jch'ul tatik, ja' nix jich xaal stukel me ya staik ta nopel te me ya sk'an yak'ik ta ilel, bit'il ya spasbeyik ya'telul ta jtulutul o ta komon manchuk me jamal chikan ta ilel o stukel ya swol sbaik ta spasel te ya'telule.

All people may think what the heart desires to talk to our holy father; furthermore, if they want, they may change the way they think and take on a different belief, and what they do may be seen, and their work (ceremonies) may be carried out individually or collectively, and these activities can be carried out in public view or by gathering together in a small group.

Observations: The translators interpret the article as a text that relates to freedom of worship. This idea is not unfamiliar to the Tzeltals and Tzotzils, among whom there exist a whole host of churches and religious tendencies, and among whom the change from one religious affiliation to another is incessant. Yet these churches are generally intolerant of one another, and particularly of those who "have no religion," that is, those who practice shamanic rituals. Such practices are acknowledged by the translators with their reference to those who gather together "in a small group."

It is interesting, on the other hand, how change in religious affiliation is expressed. One can "think what the heart desires," in other words, the head can accept the religious belief that the heart desires, but one can also change such thoughts and take on a different belief, which is not necessarily what the heart desires. It appears rather to be a change of belief that owes itself to a reflexive attitude "given by sight" (*yak'ik ta ilel*) that depends on the thoughts of the head.

Epilogue

I trust that the fragments presented above have managed to convey the tenor of the Tzeltal translation. I would now like, by way of conclusion, to return to certain aspects that have been dealt with above.

The text of the Universal Declaration of Human Rights in Tzeltal represents a genuine effort to shift the European text into indigenous idiom. Precisely for this reason, it constitutes an exceptional case in the context of the dissemination and interpretation of human rights among the indigenous people of Chiapas. For one, as mentioned earlier, the propagation of knowledge about human rights is subject to the bias of the organizations and institutions responsible for this task. But more importantly, it is unusual for indigenous people, generally speaking, to be interested in turning human rights into something culturally accessible and coherent. The human rights discourse is identified and classified as a foreign language, and it is precisely this external character that makes it a valuable tool: it is language used to facilitate indigenous society's self-representation in the modern world. If indigenous people (organizations and activists) invoke human rights principles, it is because, on the one hand, they provide a common formal language and a relative advantage in the communities' dealings with the Mexican state and its institutions and because, on the other hand, they stir the sympathy and assistance of Mexican and international organizations and activists. In contrast, the principles of human rights do not seem to play any role in the social relations *among* indigenous peoples themselves, when they are not being mediated by state institutions (or churches or NGOs), especially when they have a local character: community, neighbors, relatives.

In reality, the discovery of the existence of rights does not mean that indigenous people show an interest in the specific content of legal texts. As the human rights activist Adela Bonilla explained to me about his work with indigenous peoples: "They know they have rights, but they are not familiar with them."[13] This "having rights," whatever they might be, appears to be essential. In this context, rights work almost magically.

Essentially, there are two distinct logics also operating in distinct spheres. The Tzeltal concept of personhood differs significantly from that embodied in Western practice and texts, especially in legal texts. As we have seen, in the local indigenous case, the moral and judicial life turns on reciprocity and social obligations. If a woman is mistreated by her husband and she reports him to the town council, the authorities will want to know if she adequately fulfills her domestic functions; if not, the mistreatment appears justified. The existence of inalienable rights, or a "respect" that exists independently of whether or not it is deserved through adequate social behavior or etiquette, responds to a very different logic from the conventional Tzeltal one.

The Universal Declaration of Human Rights is based on the assumption of the existence of transcendental moral principles. In this perspective, moral principles are by nature independent on the context and circumstances in which relations among persons take place. By contrast, indigenous traditional morality is attuned to the specificity and contingency of human relationships. Se and Karatsu's (2004: 275) analysis of the Japanese, who "tend to regard morality as keeping good terms with others or fulfilling social roles smoothly," applies as well to the Tzeltal. Being moral entails acting properly in a given social situation. In this "situational view of morality" (Se and Karatsu 2004: 274–277), instead of abstract moral principles such as liberty, justice, or equality—which are practically impossible to translate into Tzeltal—what is assumed is the relational and situational nature of the self.

Until now the ideologies of human rights and social reciprocity have been kept distinct and unrelated. Moreover, the moral order clearly sides with the logic of reciprocity, obligations, and acquired respect. Regardless of how much some book might speak about women's rights, the majority of women would accept that wives who do not fulfill their obligations deserve a punishment. However, this could change in the near future if women (to continue with this example) have different options available to them and are able to appeal to the Mexican courts, traditional community justice, or some other judicial system. This change is already occurring in the cities and in nearby communities, and among indigenous members of some churches. With increasing frequency, indigenous people hear about inherent rights: the rights of all "Christians" (indigenous and nonindigenous people), the rights of women, the rights of children, and so on, acquired simply by being "Christian," woman, or child. This new normative pluralism undoubtedly diversifies, complicates, and enormously enriches the panorama of indigenous life in Chiapas.

Nevertheless, we cannot simply take for granted that the traditional ethic of rights as acquired respect is disappearing with the appearance of alternative normative systems. As demonstrated by how indigenous people participate in new religious practices ("conversions") or use the Mexican public health care system and other new medical practices, the logic by which they make their choices frequently remains essentially traditional (Pitarch 2003). In spite of new experiences and pressures that accompany the modernization process, my impression is that it is still too soon to hold that the indigenous people of Chiapas have formulated a clear notion of the person as an entertainer of rights. To use the terms of Marcel Mauss (1971), the traditional concept of *moi* (self) does not seem to be losing ground, at least not yet, to the concept of *personne* (person) in its sense as a bearer of duties and rights by virtue of being a citizen or simply a human being. Furthermore, there is no reason to suppose, as Mauss did, that this is an inevitable progression (Carrithers 1985).

Regarding the translation discussed in this chapter, I have shown how it implies an effort to make compatible two distinct logics by domesticating the unknown and making it familiar. In the Tzeltal version of the Universal Declaration of Human Rights, the doctrine of human rights reappears as a text that is to a significant degree conceptually indigenous. If the translators had tried to present an untransformed declaration reflecting its original form (although I doubt they would have been able to do so) such a document would have had little meaning for the Tzeltal. Important dimensions of the principles that give life to the idea of human rights are lost in translation. As is often said, misrepresentation is translation's bedfellow, at least in a meaningful translation. For example, the more abstract and universal claims of the declaration become something more concrete and local; the terminology of the Tzeltal version expresses more immediate indigenous social and historical experience. Much as was the case with the translation of Christian doctrine in the first decades of the evangelization of the Nahuas (Burkhart 1989: 12), for the doctrine of human rights to become meaningful in local terms, it should be made to agree with indigenous ways of naming things and of convincing. Despite the fact that it is a written text, the framework within which the translators set out their ideas is essentially oral. In contrast to the declaration in Spanish (or English), the indigenous version is directed at specific persons virtually present in the text as an audience. The translators, or their Tzeltal listeners, are not familiar, for example, with the abstract notion of slavery, but they know the specific condition of being a *mozo* in the commercial agriculture of Chiapas, or the work conditions of a porter of goods or people. In its ambition to be truly universal by being available in other languages, the declaration becomes intensely local.

This does not mean, however, that the resulting text is free from ambiguities or contradictions. The translation works well in many sections, but not in others. The reasons for this have nothing to do with the quality of the translation (although at times the translators do not adequately understand the meaning of the Spanish text and in certain sections the translation becomes incomprehensible). Rather, the explanation lies with the difficulty of the task itself. In many cases, the translation distorts and adapts European concepts so as to make them compatible with Tzeltal logic. In other cases the translation becomes so literal as to make it impossible to understand. In addition, at times the translators combine European contents and indigenous rhetorical devices that are mutually incompatible. Undoubtedly, to Tzeltal ears certain sections must seem unconvincing or simply strange. Translation between culturally different languages is unavoidably beset by these types of contradictions.

In any case, the result of the translation is a Tzeltal text in which the Universal Declaration of Human Rights is transformed into something new and distinct. It neither represents a true conventional indigenous discourse nor is it a faithful rendering of the logic in the original European text. In short, the text has become a zone of engagement, a boundary line at which indigenous and modern European cultures meet to interact. The translation assumes a Tzeltal cultural form, but this form is itself modified during the translation process. Despite the radical differences that separate these respective ethics, in this case they interact, exchange ideas, and adapt themselves. In a word, they are in dialogue; a dialogue transforms them.

Notes

Thanks to Miguel Gómez Gómez, Martha Moreno, Adela Bonilla, Alma and Meño, and Tim Trench.

1. This text was originally written in Spanish and thus dealt with the Spanish version of the Universal Declaration of Human Rights, which formed the basis of the Tzeltal translation.

2. The majority of Tzeltals are campesinos that work small plots of maize, beans, and other crops such as coffee for export. The men sometimes leave the community on a seasonal basis to obtain wage labor. Nevertheless, indigenous peoples are increasingly leaving their small villages in the mountains and establishing themselves in cities—San Cristóbal de Las Casas, Tuxtla Gutiérrez, Comitán, Ocosingo —working in the service sector. A section of the Tzeltal population is thus becoming urbanized, and consequently the cities in Chiapas are rapidly becoming "Indianized." For a magnificent study of the transformations of indigenous society in the region in recent decades, see Rus 1995.

3. All quotations of Miguel Gómez Gómez are taken from interviews with the author, July–August 2000, San Cristóbal de Las Casas.

4. In a different Tzeltal translation of the Universal Declaration of Human Rights (Amnistía Internacional 1998: 29–35) that is more literal and concise, rights become in Tzeltal *jrerechotik,* "our rights"; "law" is translated as *sts'ibayik te leyetik,* "written laws"; "the Declaration" is simply *jun,* "book."

5. Tzotzil is a Maya language closely related to Tzeltal.

6. I comment here on certain points I have dealt with in greater detail elsewhere (Pitarch 1996, 2004a).

7. A person's soul is called *ch'ulel,* that on the death of the body travels to a place inside the earth where it lives with other *ch'ulel.*

8. In the light of debates occurring in Mexico and Guatemala regarding indigenous or Maya customary rights, it is noteworthy that the translators interpret the law (*mantalil*) as ethics. (In fact, this happens with any legal text, even with those that

have a more statutory character.) It is not a question of a series of substantive customary norms, but that of a general ethics of behavior, which is furthermore intimately connected to the domestic or family environment. From indigenous people's own perspective, the attempt to place on the same level indigenous or Maya so-called customary rights with more positive rights might be considered logically unviable.

9. In the sixteenth-century Tzeltal vocabulary described by Friar Domingo de Ara (1986: 308), *ych* (*ich'*) is translated as "to take, receive a woman, to have." *Ychahc* is the son of a sister, and *ychab ychab xcopogh* is "to talk a lot." It also means "to get married" in Mariana Slocum and Florencia Gerdel's Tzeltal dictionary (1981).

10. But of course this implies that we are all children of the same father, a notion that does not entirely work in Tzeltal.

11. As a result of religious preaching, some Catholics or evangelicals state that "respect" is granted by God to all humans in equal measure. My impression is that beyond the rhetoric and in everyday practice this idea does not really work.

12. The language of the modern nation-state is incomprehensible for the majority of Tzeltals, but, with a few exceptions, I do not believe that in the future it will entail great difficulties of translation and understanding.

13. Author interview with Bonilla, August 16, 2000, San Cristóbal de Las Casas.

Are Human Rights Destroying the Natural Balance of All Things?
The Difficult Encounter between International Law
and Community Law in Mayan Guatemala

In a paper presented at a seminar about the dilemmas of democratization in Guatemala, the Mayan leader Benjamín Son singled out "impunity, violence, and a lack of balance between human rights and obligations" as the most important social problems of postwar Guatemala (Son 2000). Son is the founder and longtime director of one of the biggest NGOs in the country, an organization that moreover works in accordance with a manifest indigenous agenda. Because he also has a reputation for being one of the most insightful indigenous leaders of Guatemala, I asked him, on another opportunity, to elaborate, and he answered:

The focus of the human rights discourse is off the mark. In the communities, the focus is on the community as such. The correct approach is to talk about rights and obligations simultaneously. The problem is not the lack of rights, but that the obligations are not respected. Let us take an example. A family cuts down trees in the communal forest. This is prohibited. Therefore the family has to be sanctioned. However, the family in question turn to MINUGUA [Misión de Naciones Unidad para Guatemala, the UN peace mission to Guatemala whose mandate includes human rights monitoring] to denounce the community's decision. The international observers conclude that the case belongs to the courts. The judge decides to fine the family. The fine goes to the state. The family continues to cut down trees. MINUGUA only talks about the rights of the family. There is no mention of their obligations. In this manner the damage is not repaired.

This way of looking at offenses and crimes as ruptures of an order or a balance that call for mending the injury to restore an equilibrium or harmony forms part of a set of normative traditions in Guatemala that until recently were known as customary law. Today it is known as Mayan law.

To explore the above assertions, this article discusses the encounter between a local and oral legal tradition in Guatemala and the international system of human rights. It does so, first, by reviewing two books about Mayan law in light of what I learned during fieldwork in Son's hometown, and second, by analyzing two specific conflicts that took place there during the late 1990s and that locals commonly regard as evocative of this encounter. The municipality in question is Totonicapán, a fairly large town in the western highlands that constitute the heartland of Mayan Guatemala: of Totonicapán's approximately 110,000 inhabitants, around 90 pecent are Maya. The two studies discussed (Esquit Choy and Ochoa García 1995; IDIES 1999) contain analyses of authority, power, and law in Mayan communities. My fieldwork in Totonicapán (during 2000, with frequent visits both earlier and later) focused on a similar theme: the formation of leadership and community in Mayan Guatemala (Ekern 2006).

The encounter between customary law and human rights can be examined from different angles. Theories from, for example, legal anthropology, comparative law, human rights studies, and development studies may all be relevant. Here, I have been inspired by anthropological approaches that study customary law or custom as a variation of the legal systems of modern state-based societies, and furthermore by a proposition that claims that human rights "serve to articulate political claims which make sense in a particular social context" (Dembour 1996: 33), or to be specific, that make sense in societies in which the state plays a dominant role in defining and expressing the political and social orders. Human rights talk is talking with reference to the state.

The expansion of the state is also usually what provides the context for the study of customary law. For one, this is so because the modern nation-state constitutes the frame of reference for most researchers and thus provides a "natural" contrast to the society under study, just as the latter society effortlessly serves as "the other" in a modern-traditional dichotomy. Second, if studies in this field used to carry an evolutionary frame of reference —and regarded custom as a precursor to law—today "development" and "modernity" typically frame investigations, and thus research either searchs for ways to ease the transformation from traditional to modern or sets out to scrutinize the foundations of modernity itself. Within an evolutionary perspective, customary law was thought to be subject to the fallacies of oral memory, and for that reason many anthropologists found a worthy case in demonstrating how stateless societies, too, might exhibit sophisticated systems for creating and applying the rule of law. In discussing modernity and the workings of state-grounded political orders, the situation is often the opposite: anthropologists show how apparently fixed and stable bureaucratic institutions based on written rules are constrained by conflicting interpretations and constant negotiation. Contemporary investigations of state penetration in traditional societies focus on the different elements that constitute notions of personhood (or self) and agency in so far as the norms defining correct social behavior are always grounded in specific conceptions about possible and right ways to live together as humans and to construct political institutions. Whether the corresponding laws are transmitted orally or through written texts will, of course, make a difference. Yet in both cases the process we see as "legal" will be based on tacit assumptions about human agency and a set of ideas about how to sanction transgressions of the order (see e.g., Harris 1996).

If the difference between customary law and the law imposed by a state principally resides in the political organization of the societies in question, the exploration of the contrasts between human rights and customary law will also prove useful for examining the characteristics and impact of human rights. A human rights focus enables systematic comparisons of state power and authority because, in international law, states become subjects and must submit to the scrutiny of other states, international organizations, and nongovernmental organizations (NGOs) that ostensibly seek to protect the welfare of the citizens. Human rights transform state power into something contingent by positing an international order. Additionally, the constitutive charter or founding myth of human rights is to be found neither in tradition nor religion (as is frequently the case with customary law), nor in any idea about the origin of a particular nation; instead it focuses on the human being as such—the inherent value of each and every individual under the state. Even as it criticizes the state, human rights talk encourages individualization and state penetration at the cost of traditional polities such as clans and indigenous communities.

It should come as no surprise, then, that many Mayas find the work of human rights activists—governmental or nongovernmental—to actually reproduce and even to further state power in their communities and therefore conclude that, at least locally, human rights are out of place. The cases to be discussed below demonstrate how, to comply with international law, Guatemalan law enforcement officials are led to violate local law. It appears that compliance with human rights contributes to a situation of impunity because the community cannot carry out its own justice. The view of human rights as a kind of alien law is enhanced when seen against the backdrop of an indigenous political philosophy that puts more weight on the survival of the community than on the caprices of the individual. In this way encounters between Mayan customary law and state and international law in the rural areas of Guatemala become "total social events." International recommendations about human rights implementation are transformed into something much more significant than simple suggestions for using the legal system of the state to prevent people from taking justice in their own hands.

The present article begins by presenting some of the basic principles of Mayan law, with an emphasis on what could be termed its legal philosophy and its administration of justice. Then I trace some of the conflicts that arise as Mayan society copes with the efforts of the Republic of Guatemala to institutionalize its legal order. Finally, a discussion of two specific cases will serve to elucidate the diverse meanings that the message of human rights may take on in Guatemala. The conclusion is that promoting human rights in Guatemala involves more than building a multicultural and human rights–compliant state; it also implies bridging different philosophical traditions.

The Holy, the Equilibrium, and the Community

At first sight, Son's assertion that "the correct thing is to speak simultaneously about rights and obligations" appears to be a purely normative remark. Yet it is also a descriptive statement because the local language, K'iche' (the most widely spoken of the Mayan languages, with 1 to 2 million speakers), has no word for expressing the concept of right as something claimable in the abstract. Consequently, if one wishes to avoid the Spanish term *derecho*—the use of Spanish is the common solution among human rights activists—one has to rephrase the sentence and say something like "what one receives when obligations are fulfilled," for instance, the right to inherit that a son receives when he complies with the duties to his father.

Similarly, if Son's suggestion is taken to mean that the problems of Guatemala are caused by too many people demanding this or that without offering anything in return to society, it becomes a trivial allusion to government shortcomings widely accepted all over the modern world. However, a more detailed examination of the words he chooses when, for instance, he compares crime to damage and observes that punishment ought to function as compensation suggests a conceptual framework based on customary law in which connotations follow pathways different from those prevailing in a Western legal tradition. Thus in K'iche', the term *makaj* alludes to punishment as well as to sin, and it easily denotes whatever is deficient or broken. The important thing is to reestablish the original state of equilibrium and harmony in all relations, because if it is not repaired everyone will suffer from the resulting lack of order.

In their book *Respect for the Word* (*El respeto a la palabra*), the historian Edgar Esquit Choy and the anthropologist Carlos Ochoa García examine what has been called the Mayan legal order (1995). Both authors have Mayan languages as mother tongues (Kaqchikel and K'iche', respectively) and they use their intimate knowledge of the spoken word to construct what they believe is the inner logic of a Mayan normative tradition. This tradition is generally well known because it has been explored since the 1950s through a long series of anthropological investigations of Mayan social life all over Guatemala. The new element in the writing of Esquit and Ochoa is its political ambition in comparing Mayan customary law with the national law of Guatemala and arguing that even if the former so far has been subordinated to the latter, it is now time to establish an equal relationship (1995: 59). In this endeavor Esquit and Ochoa may count on broad support from the international community and from human rights circles all over the world.

Esquit and Ochoa begin by claiming that customary law, as it might be observed in daily conflict resolution or discussed with local Mayan leaders, is a coherent system transmitted orally from one generation to the next through socialization in the family and by ensuring that all families take turns in serving in a local hierarchy of civic and religious public office that, together with the group of merited elders who have successfully completed their duties, make up the local Mayan political authority. Through the existence of a cycle of fiestas (community festivals), or a sacred calendar, all the positions and functions in the hierarchy are integrated, and Esquit and Ochoa dedicate the second half of the book to an empirical analysis of this cycle in four selected municipalities. However, even as this study convincingly demonstrates long and continuing traditions—including ritual practices that date back at least two thousand years—few anthropologists will support Esquit when he writes that this is possible because of the inherent logic of the tradition. On the other hand, as an argument in favor of equal rights in a state founded on written doctrine, the claim does have considerable merit.

Subsequently, the authors examine this inner logic and conclude that it has three characteristics: For one, all norms reference the sacred (*tyox*) aspect or part of any phenomenon. Within the Mayan tradition there exists a kind of archetype for any social role, behavior, or life trajectory that is tied to morality and respect for the sacred. The lives of the ancestors offer prescriptions, or blueprints, subject to divine sanction for how to do what has to be done. In this way, everything and everyone has its own path or life's way. One has to respect and obey "the grandfathers and the grandmothers" as well as the rules of tradition, because "it is in the past that the norms that govern contemporary life are formed and stabilized" (38). The elders, who make up the highest local authority, are known as *k'amal b'e*, "those who know the way." Second, the world is a balanced and harmonious whole. Any action should respect this fact and also be balanced in itself to keep up the order. Third, human society forms part of this divine order and is consequently superior to the individual and to any particular family. Everyone should show respect for, obey, and follow the ways that best secure and perpetuate the community. There is little room for those who defy these principles.

Transgressions of the order are thus conceived of as sins and crimes because they threaten the whole community. Contraventions cause *makaj*—sin, fault, embarrassment. *Makaj* also indicates the need for purification or cleansing. Hence the Maya who prays asks everyone—not only God—to forgive and also to forget the sin. There is no original sin, but the imbalances created may cross categorical boundaries between domains that citizens of modern nation-states likely consider separate, for instance regarding personal responsibility. It might be necessary to consult a religious specialist (*ajq'ij*) to find out whether an illness, for example, has been caused by divine punishment or provoked by humans with evil intentions (i.e., by witchcraft).

Mayan Law in Practice

In the late 1990s, the Rafael Landívar University in Guatemala carried out a research program to identify Mayan judicial practices with the precision needed to incorporate, as much as possible, such custom into the country's legal order (IDIES 1999). This integration is called for by the peace accords, an ongoing legal reform, and the International Labor Organization (ILO) Convention 169 about the rights of indigenous peoples that Guatemala ratified in 1996. These initiatives are also good examples of promoting human rights in Guatemala and therefore enjoy substantial foreign funding. As long as current legislation remains in force, however, Mayan law is in fact extralegal or even illegal, even though in practice, Mayan law and Guatemalan law have been cohabiting since 1524. Today, the former is principally applied to solving family conflicts, disputes involving natural resources, and cases of misdemeanor such as theft and public disorder. Type and motive of the crime notwithstanding, the procedure always relies on mediation and aims to restore balance and reconfirm community consensus. Only if the negotiation fails, or when the damage is serious—for instance, murder—are the cases brought before the nearest *kaxla'n* (alien) judge.[1]

All cases are thus first brought before the local Mayan authorities. The quantity and the function of their duties (known as *patan*, meaning "sacred work" or "service," or *k'axk'ol*, "pain"), as well as their areas of competence may vary considerably from one community to the next. Yet all share a number of traits such as belonging to a hierarchical order or team of duty-holders and having a one-year term. At the top of the hierarchy there is a group of elders (Spanish, *principales*; K'iche', *ajawab'*) who have previously performed inferior services and now function as the heads of the system. However, in Totonicapán and in many other places, the power of the elders has been circumscribed since the 1970s as popular voting at community assemblies has become standard procedure for choosing all duty-holders. In general, all married men (as well as their wives because the duty really demands a sacrifice from the entire household, with long hours of unpaid work and less ordinary income) have to serve periodically. Thus the Mayan local authority makes for an efficient social glue that in addition to attending to a variety of community services plays an important role in conserving the community and its customs. It thus ethnifies the area in so far as this order is exclusive to the municipality's Mayan population.

Over the past thirty years the system has changed significantly due to the continuing pressure from the surrounding Hispanic society (and indeed from all the forces of modernization and globalization). Economic diversification means that not all men continue to work in accordance with the growth cycle of maize. Religious change has meant that not everyone now still belongs to the same congregation. This has brought about the downfall of the religious branch of the hierarchies (the *cofradías*) almost everywhere, and it has curtailed the powers of the so-called indigenous mayoralties (*alcaldías indígenas*) through which the Guatemalan state appropriated the hierarchies and indirectly ruled its Mayan population. Importantly, many of the religious hierarchies have their origin in state demands; thus, in the 1930s, the principals in Totonicapán started to name vice mayors (*alcaldes auxiliares*) to do liaison work with the municipal mayor and, for instance, report births and deaths to the authorities. Today the office of the vice mayor is the highest one, and his authority often eclipses that of the elders. Moreover, the Guatemalan state legally recognizes the figure of the vice mayor: successive Municipality Acts (from 1946, 1957, and 1988) assert that the municipal mayor appoints the vice mayor. Yet in Mayan areas at least the mayor has always respected the local community's decision, and in line with Mayan campaigning and the peace accords, a new law from 2002 has paved the way for the municipal recognition of indigenous forms of self-rule. Some places also have an indigenous mayor (*alcalde indígena*) who is the leader of all the vice mayors and who may work alongside the elected mayor. This office, however, has been extralegal since 1944.[2]

Somewhat apart from the self-rule tradition stands the figure of the Mayan priest (*ajq'ij*), an office exercised by a person with special gifts. Elder priests generally act as principals too. According to the material the Institute of Economic and Social Research (Instituto de Investigaciones Ecónomicas y Sociales, IDIES) collected in three municipalities in the province of El Quiché, people seek the advice of the priests in cases of conflict between spouses or between parents and children, but in other cases they seek out the vice mayoralty. In Totonicapán, where Mayan priests are few, the vice mayors also attend to family conflicts. In both cases the person consulted will listen to and speak with the contending parties and attempt to mediate. In cases of theft the vice mayor will hear witnesses, if there are any, to confirm or refute the accusation. If there are doubts one may consult a priest or a principal who will eventually make an appeal to divine the forces at work by way of a Mayan ceremony. The goal is always to reconcile the opposing parties and to repair the damage.

The most common misdemeanors in Mayan parts of Guatemala are theft and verbal aggression. The latter category has to be understood in the context of a strong emphasis on respect and harmonious relations characteristic of Mayan society, as well as with regard to the predominance of oral communication. Typical family conflicts involve the failings of spouses to comply with their obligations, for instance, when a man drinks too much and neglects his work. Only when such cases become very serious and consistent do people see the *kaxla'n* judge. This is also the instance that may authorize a divorce. However, at the tribunal, the parties face a kind of law that differs markedly from Mayan law as it underlines the importance of written testimony and pays scant attention to mediation. Taking a case to court thus not only ups the ante but also changes the nature of the conflict.[3] From a Mayan point of view, rules requiring evidence to be in conformity with the law and the need for written and legally confirmed declarations in effect take the case out of its context. Moreover, Guatemalan courts seek to identify one culprit and a single chain of events; they do not seek to make amends for an injury. Few judges and lawyers, moreover, speak any Mayan language, and because it is costly to hire a lawyer and a scribe, the vast majority of Mayas feel heavily discriminated against in their encounters with the country's legal system (IDIES 1999).

For all these reasons the contending parties generally accept the decision of the vice mayor (and of the elders). For the thief, for example, locally administered customary law also offers an opportunity to purge him- or herself of accumulated shame. But if the perpetrators do not accept the decision of the principals, they are forcibly brought to the tribunal. In some places there are "preventive" prisons for this purpose, though not all local Mayan self-rule institutions possess the necessary authority to incarcerate. In the aftermath of the civil war—which also meant an overall debilitation of the national legal system and the militarization of many communities— spontaneous justice in the form of lynching has spread all over the country, particularly in the Mayan areas, where, since 1995, around thirty alleged thieves and rapists have been beaten, whipped, and burnt to death by the mobs of a Mayan society that lacks a consolidated authority.

The Difficult Encounter

The report from the Rafael Landívar University about the K'iche'an juridical system also suggests that the percentage of cases resolved through the application of Mayan law might be similar to that brought before the legal system of the state, and furthermore that the distinction between misdemeanor and crime in the latter system corresponds to that between restoration and ostracism as forms of sanction in the former. In this regard, lynching may be an expression of the contemporary impossibility of ostracism, or it might be that the old system of local authority is no longer respected.

For problems involving land rights and marriage the situation is more complex. Both societies accept the concept of private property, but Mayan law curbs this right by the communal ownership of forest and noncultivated lands, as well as by norms preventing sale of land to people outside the community. In some places, municipal archives contain property registers, and the principals supervise all land transfers. However, neither of these two institutions are legally recognized in Guatemala. A court case involving land has to base its proceedings on certified copies from the national (state-run) property register (Registro Nacional de la Propiedad). In the predominantly Mayan provinces of the country this register rarely includes more than 30 percent of cultivated land,[4] but nowadays an increasing number of Mayan peasants are registering their lands to secure it, although this operation is costly, involves field inspection, and requires the recognition of all neighbors. The dramatic population growth over the past fifty years has resulted in a considerable division of family inheritance into increasingly smaller slices. Moreover, the areas of forest and marginal lands between the communities have been much reduced. These developments have caused a steady rise in the number of unresolved boundary conflicts that dominate local political agendas and obstruct economic improvement.

Guatemalan authorities also do not accept the traditional Mayan wedding. This consists of a ceremony that takes place in the house of the parents of the groom under the supervision of a Mayan priest, who then later takes on the role as the couple's adviser during their marriage. The requirements of carrying out either a Catholic (Christian) or a civil ceremony, and of registering the marriage in the civil register, amount to a further weakening of the authority of local leadership. Here as in land cases we see how the application of Hispanic justice penetrates Mayan society and transforms it, and much more directly so in the case of civil law than of criminal law. In Mayan tradition, religion, law, politics, education, and public administration all interlock to unite in one single entity, one single moral community in a very immediate sense. Any interference of the specialized national institutions of the Guatemalan state in these areas will thus give rise to considerable conflicts. One might therefore ask whether it is genuinely possible to incorporate Mayan law into a modern legal system.

Esquit and Ochoa identify the school system, the church, NGOs, the state, the tribunals, and political parties—as well as other institutions whose structure breaks the inner logic of Mayan society—as particularly responsible for forcing the encounter between the two societies and thus pushing the Mayan one toward what they call "Westernization" (1995: 56). The tribunals undermine the powers of the priests, the school replaces the parents and particularly the elders in their all-important roles in community socialization, the political parties and state (and municipal) administration displace the hierarchies and the vice mayoralties in their quest for the common good, and the NGOs chip at the responsibilities of local and central authorities for maintaining communal harmony. The two authors lament these trends and conclude that "the whole population should assume an attitude of creativity, tolerance, and respect when facing the cultural diversity of Guatemala" (59).

The Ambiguous Role of Human Rights

In view of their dramatic description of the clash between the Mayan and the Hispanic societies, Esquit and Ochoa's plea to show tolerance may appear meek. Yet both clearly seek to put both legal traditions on an equal footing so as to prepare the terrain for a new and reformulated encounter between Mayas and Ladinos in a multicultural society, that is, one encompassing two distinct traditions. The human rights–based argument about equal treatment underpinning the peace accords follows a similar logic, but as we have seen, it is not only a question of rendering equal two traditions previously ranked asymmetrically but rather one of internal reform—in both traditions.

As was the case with her sister republics in Central and South America, Guatemala was founded, as a state, by invoking the ideals of the European Enlightenment. Furthermore, like Europe, Latin America has played an active role in developing human rights law and, through the UN and the Organization of American States, continues to do so. Human rights do not express alien ideas, so it is no coincidence that belligerent parties on both the right and the left of the national political spectrum took the human rights discourse as the starting point for peace negotiations and accepted the UN as an arbiter. Moreover, this union of nation-states emphasized its presence by establishing a mission charged with supervising the human rights situation (MINUGUA). Furthermore, the peace accords, along with the ILO Convention 169, bestow on the international community a decisive role in the transformation of Guatemalan society: typically donors justify aid to Guatemala by conceptualizing the effort as building peace through improving the human rights situation.

In this manner, human rights arrived in Mayan communities in the form of white four-wheel-drive Toyotas with blue UN flags up front and staffed with educated youth from Europe and North and South America. Initially, this group struggled to comprehend the powers of the elders, for theirs is an eminently oral authority. In 1997, two years into their mandate, a high-ranking MINUGUA official confessed to me that bringing rural people together to inform them about the peace process and about human rights had proven very difficult at the beginning. Help came from a Mayan notable's warning that principals could not simply be summoned; only the principals can give the necessary permission to summon a communal assembly. Once MINUGUA learned to cooperate with local authorities, the situation improved.[5]

The anecdote about the sovereign authority of the elders reveals that it does not suffice to preach reform only to the state. The frequent news dispatches from Guatemala during the first half of the 1990s telling of violent clashes between human rights activists and patrollers further suggest the need to understand the inner workings of the Mayan community.[6] In a national context, the main dividing line appears to run between groups of conservatives and activists from the so-called popular (i.e., left-wing) organizations. In a local context, however, the most important dividing lines are closely connected to the two issues discussed above: community autonomy and the place of alien law in the exercise of local authority. Human rights talk easily undermines the local order.

Human Rights and the Community

The anecdote told by Benjamín Son about the family who continued to fell trees even after they had been fined by the *kaxla'n* state is not exceptional and in fact alludes to a long-standing conflict about the exploitation of the communal forest located in the community of Chuipachec just above the town. By collecting and comparing narratives from two groups of residents and from the various state agencies that were involved—the Human Rights Ombudsman (Procuraduría de Derechos Humanos, PDH), the prosecuting authority (Ministerio Público), the National Forestry Agency (Instituto Nacional de Bosques, INAB), as well as an association of water committees, organized as an NGO and calling itself Ulew Che' Ja' (UCJ, or Earth Tree Water)[7]—and taking into consideration the agreement with which the conflict was solved on June 3, 1998, it is possible to piece together the following story.

Chuipachec, the uppermost hamlet of the urban canton of Palín, is situated at the rim of the great communal forest that begins just above Totonicapán town.[8] For the families that live there (approximately forty in 2000) the extraction of timber and firewood has always been of great economic importance. Rapid deforestation over the past few decades has resulted in growing anxiety about the water supply to the town, and with increasing consciousness about the need to conserve the forest, there were acute worries about a group of residents who used chainsaws and pickups to actually increase logging. Their opponents, organized in the local water committee, contacted the central leadership of the UCJ to pressure the loggers. At the communal assemblies, they managed to condemn the first group and prohibit excessive logging. However, the perpetrators did not respect this decision, and as a consequence the assembly decided to cut their water supplies. At this point, it should be mentioned that the two groups in question also correspond quite closely to two extended families (i.e., clans) with a long history of antagonism. In reply to the water blockage, the group of loggers went to the tribunal, that is, the Office of the Prosecutor, after first having complained to MINUGUA and the Human Rights Ombudsman. Initially, the rest of the community had not wanted to take the extreme measure of blocking the water supply, but it appears some pressure to do so came from the UCJ leadership, which wanted to set an example of resolute action.

The prosecuting authority determined that there were two separate offenses but little evidence. An arbitration ensued, resulting in an agreement —verified by UCJ, INAB, and the Swiss development program Helvetas Pro-Bosque—stipulating that the water supply immediately be reopened to the loggers, who for their part had to promise to reforest the affected area. In case of a further violation, the water would immediately be cut again.

Two years later it seemed that the loggers had emerged victorious. Every Thursday they climbed up the hills to make amends under the supervision of an employee of a government project protecting the water sources in the area. I joined the group one Thursday and was told that they were innocent because "[this issue] involves interests—we do not know what kind—of the other group." However, when "the tribunal changed the sanction," they decided to accept the penalty because "authority belongs to God," because of fear of being cut off from "the holy liquid" once more, and also, I learned, because compliance also meant the accumulation of a considerable amount of moral capital. They had even become active members of the UCJ. On the other side of the conflict, the group that had spearheaded the confrontation appeared to be regretful as they observed how their adversaries "think they have more rights because they reforest more."

Perhaps the most revealing detail of this story, however, may be how it became, in the words of one of the leaders of the groups, "a typical case of how human rights favor the guilty," and curiously, how two years later everyone assumes that MINUGUA gave support to those sanctioned by the community, even though no one remembers exactly how or whether MINUGUA was involved at all. Nor did anyone remember this incident at the MINUGUA office when I visited there in 2000, but employees did confirm that the case would have constituted a violation of the right to due process and thus probably did merit mediation. Tellingly, the K'iche' language employs a single word to refer to all outside authorities, q'atb'al tzij, which literally means "instructor of law," but that above all alludes to alien authorities, among whom MINUGUA now also ranks.

Perhaps the most famous story told in Totonicapán to illustrate how human rights "protect the delinquent" and "collide with our law" is that of the imprisonment of two youngsters in the community hall of the canton of Chuanoj during the first week of July 1997. The following week, in the presence of a judge, the police broke the door to the assembly hall and seized the two boys and a shoulder bag that belonged to one of the members of the vice mayoralty and contained the seal of the canton, several archival records, and other effects of the vice mayoralty, presumably as evidence. After much correspondence with the Court of First Instance in Criminal Matters of Totonicapán to have the bag returned, in November the community decided to block the Pan-American Highway that runs through the canton of Chuanoj. An impressive array of institutions such as MINUGUA, the Catholic Church, the provincial governor, and the Human Rights Ombudsman tried to mediate, and for the second time, the case reached the front pages of Guatemala's newspapers. Finally, and with a hundred policemen surrounding the community, a MINUGUA representative returned the shoulder bag.

Chuanoj, with its six hundred families, is renowned for being the best organized of all the forty-eight cantons of the municipality of Totonicapán. It boasts a vice mayoralty of fifteen persons that includes the representatives of various development committees in addition to the traditional functionaries and is headed by a popularly elected vice mayor. The authorities of Chuanoj have kept an archive of their proceedings since the 1950s, although the institution has changed a lot since then and the principals today have to content themselves with finding "just another chair" at the general assembly. Generally speaking, contemporary vice mayors are young men with a formal education, and their leadership experiences stem from running development projects.

From the archives of the community the following narrative may be reconstructed: On July 2, acting on information from two residents, the vice mayor ordered the capture of two boys for stealing a bull calf. During interrogation, the two "completely admitted to being the perpetrators," though they did not admit being guilty of a series of thefts and assaults that the community had suffered in the preceding three years. The document concludes that "they were kept in detainment until morning to present them to the community." The following day the two boys were presented to the majority of the residents who had been called upon "to validate the theft of a bull calf." The group decided to throw the families of the "robbing individuals" out of the meeting, and then, considering that "this is not the first time they rob," the Chuanoj general assembly decided that the culprits should "pay for the injuries and the damage a sum corresponding to 5,000 quetzales (USD 700) . . . and be expelled from the community, and if not, be detained." Furthermore, the assembly decided that "if anything [happens to anyone in] the Corporation of Authorities . . . the thieves will be held responsible and also their families." Minutes 10–97 of Chuanoj were signed by four hundred residents. Later that day relatives of the two boys called the tribunals in Totonicapán town, and the judge decided to intervene.

Immediately after the youngsters' removal by the police, the community wrote an open letter to the people of Guatemala, stating that "the Community of Chuanoj declares: its disagreement with the violent and intimidating actions of the security forces . . . that drastically penetrated the community in the presence of various communication media . . . and the judge in office." The document then explains the events and details the decision of the community: "The residents stood up and took the decision to judge [the perpetrators] before the community, complying with the [Peace] Accord of Identity and Rights of Indigenous Peoples and particularly the [ILO] Convention 169, through which the indigenous communities are given the powers to take their own decisions in accordance with their own cultural practices [*vivencias culturales*]. What is regrettable is the behavior of the juridical authorities . . . either they ignore or they do not comply with these accords, [thus] always protecting the individuals that conduct themselves at the margin of the law."

It should be mentioned that no leader in Chuanoj denies that the youngsters were maltreated and submitted to violent interrogation. One informant even explained that "we made them go down on their knees on sharp rocks" because they had read somewhere that this had been an ancient Mayan practice. Not without reason did the judge who ordered the capture (and hence, release) of the boys conclude that it had been a case of illegal detention, of clandestine captivity, torture, and abuse of minors because the thieves were fifteen and twenty-three years old.

On October 1, the vice mayor dispatched a letter to the judge asking for the return of the shoulder bag, and on November 3, he sent another letter with the signatures of all the members of the town and a reference to the minutes 23–97 of the community that "demands the immediate return of the objects that are community property, explains [that] our authorities have sent five delegations without receiving any answer . . . [and consequently] the community will only wait 48 hours to have its rights and the patrimony of the community resolved." Still without answer, four days later the community wrote another letter of warning repeating the demand and backed up with four hundred signatures (or thumbprints): "From that moment [of 'the abusive plundering of the woolen bag by the hands of the armed authorities'], the community of Chuanoj has become conscious of the flawed application of the law" and how "the peace signatures only have benefited common delinquency and not the equality of rights." Finally it is announced that "we are ready to keep the protest going until we have in our hands the stolen goods."

Apart from the formalism and a narrative style that with instructive clarity reflect the importance of law in public affairs in Guatemala, what attracts attention is the forceful behavior of the community as such, as well as its belief in the necessity of asserting its sovereignty. When asked why Chuanoj was so well organized, all local leaders pointed out that "it is our way of being." They are proud of the belligerence demonstrated against "the authorities [of Guatemala]" on this and other occasions. As regards human rights, they add that "Chuanoj doesn't want to relate to them because those who stand to gain are the thieves. We don't burn people. We just apply the norm of Chuanoj." Nevertheless, the same leaders do not hesitate to invoke international law, for instance, ILO Convention 169, to back up their position.

Promoting Human Rights in Mayan Guatemala

The conflict between the authorities of Chuanoj and the republic of Guatemala over who has the power to sanction juvenile delinquents obviously reflects an effort by the Mayan community to maintain the boundary that separates it from the external world. This is necessary because, for one, this world is *kaxla'n* or alien, and second, because the actions that the *kaxla'n* world takes in cases of disorder simply do not work. Once again Chuanoj residents were able to watch how *kaxla'n* justice was slow and soft and how criminals were set free the day after they were handed over to the police. In a sum, state law is "good for nothing" (*no trae ningún beneficio*), or as a young leader from Chuipachec put it: "Unfortunately, human rights were written in another country." In addition to defending Mayan community autonomy, such allegations echo Mayan communitarian logic with its emphasis on reestablishing respect and restoring damage, directly and visibly, instead of focusing on an individual in conflict with society. In this way the cases of Chuipachec and Chuanoj confirm the claims about a separate Mayan tradition put forward in the two studies I discussed earlier. Furthermore, the vigor with which the authorities of Chuanoj defended the town's norms strongly indicates that the act of defending autonomy is itself as important as the issue being defended. In light of such cases and focusing on how competing leaders achieve moral authority in communities like Chuanoj, I argue that the latter conclusion indeed is fundamental: if a distinct tradition is to survive, it needs an autonomous space in which to reformulate itself. The "inner logic" of which Esquit Choy and Ochoa García speak resides not in a particular practice, but in defending a room for it.

Like their colleagues in Chuanoj, the present generation of Mayan leaders in Totonicapán generally recognizes that human rights have a bad name. At the same time they realize, however, that Guatemala's submission to international human rights instruments has brought many benefits to their people. For instance, Pedro Ixchíu, who served as president of the Board of the Mayors of the Forty-Eight Cantons (and thus as indigenous mayor) in 2000, commented that "thanks to human rights we may feel as equals. However, there are clashes. Take, for instance, communal work. In the community, [only] those who work are entitled to voice an opinion." It is in this respect that Benjamín Son goes further when he calls to mind that community law contains a concept of community obligation that ought to be included in human rights.

These Mayan leaders are quick to point out that the action taken by Chuanoj residents do not serve as a good example of Mayan law. For one, in Chuanoj there exists a profound imbalance because of the absence of elders in the vice mayoralty. In a modern political idiom, this would mean to suggest that the town has a lack of checks and balances in its political structure. If on that fateful evening the young vice mayor of Chuanoj had had access to a council of elders, who in addition to giving advice could also have calmed down the agitated populace, the story would have likely taken a less violent course. In a setting in which age still commands much respect, the absence of elders, or guides, in effect constitutes a power vacuum and a lack of examples to follow, and this easily opens the door for shortsighted solutions.

Furthermore, both defenders and critics of the action taken in Chuanoj point to the fact that the war left a legacy of authoritarian and corrupt practices in many vice mayoralties as the office of the military commissioner—typically filled by an elder (who also was appointed by the army) to do liaison with the military—grew unduly in importance. In conjunction with growing pressure from the forces of modernization, the end product is a rapid weakening of the legitimacy of the Mayan institution of self-rule. The violent outcome of conflicts in many Mayan communities appears to reflect a general crisis of Mayan authority.

Meanwhile, in the national context, human rights have become frequently cited across the entire political spectrum. This development has become possible for two reasons. First, human rights discourse is a political discourse in so far as it "represents the language of not-yet-realised—and ever-to-be-identified—political claims at the same time as they are phrased in terms of eternal truth" (Dembour 1996: 20). Second, it is a political discourse which rings particularly true in the world of modern nation-states. For, as Dembour also maintains, these truths are not totally universal, but rather belong to political settings in which the state plays a predominant role. In Mayan communities human rights appear inappropriate because as a discourse they do not have the same political resonance: in Mayan society working for the survival of the community is more important than fighting for the freedoms of individuals. To rephrase Dembour again: Human rights can be validated generally only in societies that possess the political institutions that implicitly form the foundation of these same human rights.

The focus of human rights, and therefore also of the work of MINUGUA, is the relationship between individuals and the state. The local community disappears from view because human rights activists are averse to making the community responsible for any abuse, and in any case the human rights observers are in Guatemala to supervise a state with nasty antecedents. Within the Mayan community, however, people only acquire rights through gaining the respect of the ancients and through participating in communal work. Therefore the defenders of the community do not comprehend the inviolability of the person. They conclude that MINUGUA and human rights behave just like any other *q'atb'al tzij*. Consequently we have a situation in which conflicting parties might position themselves in accordance with their conceptions of personhood, even if this posture is at odds with their political goals. For example when, out of sympathy with Mayan victims, European human rights activists support individual Mayas who have been expelled from their communities and in the process find themselves aligned with the state they originally intended to oppose.

For Mayan society, which still primarily exists in the form of hundreds of small communities, the challenge is double: on the one hand, there is the desire to build a community that can overcome the strong parochialism of its legal system; on the other, there is a wish to reconcile the communal balance with individual rights. This endeavor leaves ample room for profound discussions between human rights activists and Mayan leaders, and if the latter should include novel principles in their communal workings, the former should attempt to bring the ideas of community balance and harmony to the nation.

Notes

I thank Benjamín Son, Pedro Ixchíu, Efraín Tzaquitzal, Pedro Hernández, the vice mayoralty of Chuanoj, Pedro Ajpop, Candelaria Gutiérrez, Benito Canastuj, MINU-GUA's office in Quetzaltenango, the Ministerio Público, the Human Rights Ombudsman in Totonicapán, and three anonymous readers. The original Spanish version of the article was written in 2000 (during fieldwork in Guatemala). The present version closely follows the original text but includes some observations made at later dates.

1. In Guatemala, the dominant Spanish-speaking population is generally known as Ladinos. In K'iche' the term for Ladino is *mu's; Kaxla'n* means "foreign" or "alien." State institutions are typically referred to as *kaxla'n* or *Spanish*, even if they are generally staffed with Ladinos.

2. My fieldwork in Totonicapán focused on changes in Mayan self-rule over the past three decades and the concomitant changes in notions of community and leadership. Briefly told, by making development a community issue, accepting project administration as a meritorious activity, and gradually substituting residence and community service for kinship as criteria for community citizenship, the rule of the principals has been replaced by a kind of community democracy (Ekern 2006).

3. The Criminal Procedures Act from 1994 does allow for oral proceedings, but this new law has met with much passive resistance from judges and lawyers. By 2003, a commission named by the Supreme Court had prepared a new unified procedures act that allowed oral evidence also in other fields of law. It will take many years before the principles of orality and immediacy will be standard in Guatemalan law. (Information collected during a review of the Norwegian support to the judicial system in Guatemala in 2003.)

4. Information given at the property register in Guatemala City in 1995.

5. Personal information from Birgit Gerstenberg.

6. "Patrollers" refers to former members of the local militias (Patrullas de Autodefensa Civil, PAC) that the army set up in 1982 to combat the guerrillas. Presumably also ex-patrollers were manipulated by the army to intimidate and discredit political activists.

7. Ulew Che' Ja' is both a Mayan organization and an NGO because it was founded by

traditional leaders as an association of water committees. Later it registered legally to comply with the rules of development cooperation.

8. The municipality of Totonicapán consists of forty-eight communities known as cantons (*cantones*). Generally, the canton is also the unit that a local Mayan political authority represents. Originally being a union of intermarrying clans, large cantons may fission along clan boundaries. Chuipachec is on the verge of leaving Canton Palín.

"Here It's Different"
The Ch'orti' and Human Rights Training

On September 28, 2000, the popular Guatemalan news program *Notisiete* reported on a strike by city bus attendants due to commence the following day as the workers faced the persistent threat of redundancies as part of a "modernization" plan for transport services. A reporter interviewed one representative of the attendants who, showing uncertainty and common sense at the same time, stated, "They would be satisfied in receiving human rights training, like the drivers." In fact, many drivers, as well as many other professionals, have received human rights training to such an extent that it appears as something necessary to carry out a whole host of professions. Mockingly, one "trained" bus driver told me: "Even the shoeshiners will have to be given human rights training." Behind this sarcasm one can point to a desire that gives rise to, with varying intensity and to different degrees, governmental and nongovernmental organizations; the desire to extend, through training, the universal discourse of human rights to all corners of the country and to all its peoples. This training is justified as necessary for the attainment of a truly democratic and modern Guatemala that would put an end to the secular state of corruption, the disregard for people's dignity, and to irrational and violent atavisms, of which the most widely known stigma today is lynching.

On the same day as it covered the impending strike, the press reported on the latest lynching incident in Guatemala in Pueblo Nuevo, Ixcán, Quiché: Manuel Andrés Ramírez was lynched accused of having stolen a horse that he sold in the neighboring village, Cuarto Pueblo. More than twenty-four hours elapsed between the capture of the alleged thief and his lynching, allowing the arrival of the National Civil Police, a justice of the peace, representatives of the Misión de Naciones Unidad para Guatemala (UN Verification Mission in Guatemala, MINUGUA), and representatives from the attorney general's Office of Human Rights. It did not matter that more than one day had passed to calm tensions, nor were the human rights representatives' pleas to respect the suspect's right to life of any use. In fact, the villagers' attitude did not even change when faced with the coercive threat of the police. According to the newspaper *Al Día*,[1]

> members of the community and others from Mayalán, Xalbal, and Victoria 20 de Enero, carried out a type of public trial. [This was] when a man got hold of the accused, who had been tied to a newsstand, and threw him into the crowd who, with punches, stones, and sticks, beat him to death. . . . Human rights organizations yesterday denounced the actions that are being carried out in the interior of the country, and demanded thorough investigations by the police authorities to detain and bring those responsible to justice. They likewise declared their concern that these acts may be on the increase in the interior of the country and for this reason explained that campaigns to educate and create awareness will be carried out with the intention of curbing these acts.

Faced with the uncertainty and confusion that the unstoppable wave of lynchings (about five hundred between 1996 and 2005) is causing—even greater when one considers that it began just as peace accords were signed in Guatemala—the only thing national social and political organizations can agree on appears to be the need for general human rights training. Conversely, there is no agreement on the causes of the violence. Some see in it the application of a form of Mayan justice.[2] Mayan organizations, on the other hand, believe that the application of Mayan justice would avoid these lynchings, which to them result from the climate of violence that Guatemala has experienced for at least four decades and in the more or less underground activities of paramilitary groups. Another line of explanation considers the lynchings a "popular" response to the slowness and inefficiency of the official justice system. Some analysts also see the ultimate responsibility lying with the state, which has failed to properly deal with the problem of common crime. They also believe that it is significant that the lynching phenomenon's beginning coincided chronologically with the execution of two peasants who were given the death penalty for the rape and murder of a young girl, an execution that was broadcast by all media and turned into a spectacle, seemingly as an invitation to violence. In reality, it proves very difficult to find a cause that comprehensively explains the lynchings. Many are triggered by robberies or other attacks on life or property, though not all of them are. Nor is it possible to view them within simple cause-and-effect parameters. For example, in Pueblo Nuevo, Ixcán, on July 8, 1998, two women were accused by some fellow villagers of having killed a young man through acts of witchcraft. The assistant mayor and the executive committee of the local cooperative, which had served judicial and executive functions in the community, called a meeting to deal with the issue. The meeting was transformed into a type of indictment trial in which the family of the deceased accused the women, who denied any responsibility. A doctor from Médicos del Mundo working in the community also spoke, claiming that the young man had died of AIDS. The angry villagers did not accept this explanation and started to beat the two women, spraying one of them with gasoline. The lynching was not carried out thanks to the intervention of other villagers and because the justice of the peace of Cantabal, who attended the assembly meeting, approved the inclusion in the affidavit of a copy of the statement in which the community accused the two women of witchcraft. Subsequently a case for murder proceeded to the public ministry of Cobán, in which the two accused women appeared in court as presumed perpetrators of the crime.

Another example from June 29, 1998, in Almolonga, Quetzaltenango, makes clear the impossibility of general explanations for lynchings. When a truck that was to take the carnival queens of the government school Pablo Gazona Nápole away would not start up and the children could not attend the event as a result, enraged parents attacked two teachers, beating them and then spraying them with gasoline.

The confusion as to the violence's causes is experienced at all political and social levels. In a recent interview, the president of the republic asserted the difficulties of systematizing the causes, since one was not only dealing with acts of "popular justice":

"The most serious part of this is that the lynchings that were said to be caused by common crime are now said to be due also to religious problems, to political problems, and to economic problems. They have just told me, I hope that it is not true, that in the lynching,[3] when I went to talk with the people, [they told me that] one of the dead, one of the people lynched, who were father and son, were competitors in the transport business of the one who instigated the lynching."[4]

In situations like this, one easily ends up with knee-jerk reactions in search of a solution, considering exemplary punishments. MINUGUA reiterates at every opportunity the need for judicial prosecution and for the punishment of the instigators, while the Catholic Church has considered the possibility of refusing communion in the communities in which lynchings take place.[5] Even governmental organizations such as the Guatemalan Institute of Tourism (INGUAT) aim to set an example by taking communities in which lynchings have occurred off tourist routes. The town of Todos Santos Cuchumatán, where a Japanese tourist and the tour bus driver were lynched, has been "seriously warned" (*La Hora,* Novermber 28, 2000).

In this way authorities hope citizens will pass from mob rule to civil society, from atavism to modernity. The Modernization Unit of the Judicial Organization, on request from the Modernization Unit of the Justice Sector, has designed a pilot study in collaboration with MINUGUA and the Department of Education (Program of Civic Values) that aims to carry out human rights workshops to prevent lynchings in those areas in which they have been most frequent. Notebooks and worksheets have been created and directed at school principals, teachers, and school advisors "who will turn into multipliers."[6] The Department of Education (MINEDUC) has also prepared two educational manuals that will reach 300,000 secondary and 1,500,000 primary school students. Moreover, dramas on radio and television in K'iche', Q'eqchi, and Spanish have been broadcast to make people aware of the seriousness of lynchings. Evaluations of these workshops highlight the effectiveness of the multiplier effect created by directing the campaign mainly at leaders and educators and assert the need to extend the courses to other areas.

To modernize and to eliminate all types of atavism there does not seem to be any way other than human rights training.[7] In this view, the state has the task of updating the design of an institutional framework for the protection and respect of universal human rights through the creation of different types of "modernization brigades," the establishment of training networks, and the signing of all international agreements that deal with this topic.[8] The Guatemalan state therefore integrates human rights training into the wider framework of the country's modernization; for this reason the training usually has a more technical than moral character. Once the institutional scaffolding has been created, citizens, the state hopes, will respond by getting some sort of training themselves.

There were other principles for the Indians' development. Most prominent during the past century were those to "improve the bread," "ladinize," or "have a revolution" (see González-Ponciano 1998; and Cojtí Cuxil 1989, 1994). All are precepts that come from outside the indigenous communities and that deal with the benefits of homogenizing, whether one is talking about blood, culture, or ideology. Many of these attempts at assimilation have failed, often leading to a claim of Indians' "intractability."

This article aims to assess to what degree the new principle of universal human rights training—at times imposed without any understanding of the cultural molds into which it is applied—reproduces past errors and, in presenting itself as beyond critique, prevents any possibility of dialogue and is therefore doomed to failure. The suggestions that I put forward here are based on research that I have been conducting for some years with Mayas-Ch'orti' and Ladinos from western Guatemala and on specific conversations on the subject carried out in Tunucó Abajo during the summer of 2000.

Modernization and the Ch'orti' Panorama Following the Project and Training

Everyone who stresses the need for human rights training has an image in mind of a country "trained" to enter into modernity. In this perfect image one glimpses a bus in which drivers and attendants are aware of the dignity of the people they are transporting, and in which they do not forget to give passengers their change but have forgotten to give the *mordida* (kickback) to the police. One glimpses a country in which the police arrive following a traffic accident and one would not have to blush at affidavits in which officers claim that someone "committed suicide by cutting himself down with a machete" (Zapeta 1999: 120–21) or that a policeman killed a child in the street "in self-defense." A country in which citizens and the administration are not tied up in inextricable bureaucratic webs; a country, in short, in which, following the detainment of a criminal, democratic justice works quickly and effectively. A country's transformation has to be the government's mission, and in this way the National Progress Party (Partido de Avanzada Nacional, PAN) administration has systematically stated its modernization project: "The mission of the new Executive Organization is to facilitate in a coordinated and harmonious fashion the existence of certain conditions that guarantee life, liberty, justice, security, peace and the integral development of a person. All of this with a devotion to the principles of the primacy of the person, equality before the law, solidarity, efficiency, effectiveness, integrity, transparency, customer service, decentralization and citizen participation in the search for the common good."[9]

The fulfillment of the mission depends, among other things, on well-organized training processes. Essentially, if training is seen as a fetish, one can perhaps expect magical results. It does seem miraculous that the Modernization Office of the executive body and the public administration have succeeded in reducing the administrative steps necessary for collecting road tax from 211 to 15. More miraculous still is that the administrative procedure for the collection of value-added tax has been reduced from 1,223 steps to 45. These achievements not only affect administrative bureaucracy; Álvaro Arzú's government also claims to have achieved a good level of modernizing success in rural areas. Some of the achievements are related in the following words of the peasant Don Paco, disseminated by the secretary of planning and programming:

> At first they came to fix the school, which was so dilapidated that it was falling down. They added two classrooms and employed two new teachers. The following year they gave the kids some nice, free books. Later they organized the mothers, they trained them, and now they take turns so that the children can have their breakfast every day. I decided to send all my children to the school, and they even gave my daughter a grant to study. We are happy.
>
> We had to name two community health supervisors who now vaccinate the kids, monitor the expectant mothers, and if anyone gets ill they notify the doctor so that he comes. The midwife Chona is trained and registered, and no kid has died since then. The good thing is that Chilo, my sister's son, because he's bright, they put him in charge of the community first aid kit where we now buy cheaper medicines. It's great because before, we got ill, we even died, and nobody did anything for us.
>
> Nineteen years ago we formed a committee to ask for electricity. Oh God! How many times I traveled to the capital—and nothing. We had lost all hope, until at the end of last year in the end they did it for us. . . . Now we no longer have to use candles at night. . . . How the children used to get

burnt! Now we even have radio, and in the community hall between all of us we bought a television. (Secretaria General de Planificación 14)

This account, with the addition of the novel component of human rights, could be considered paradigmatic of how rural modernization hopes to be achieved. By means of governmental and nongovernmental development projects, dressed in fetishistic terminology (sustainable development, diversified production, a gender component, human rights, etc.), the miracle, through sufficient training, will come about.

If this modernizing miracle is possible, why is the implementation of an ideology making peasants aware of the need to know, value, and respect universal human rights not? One problem in this intellectual equation is thinking that there are no substantial differences between designing an administrative or an otherwise technical change and creating an ideological one, and that one can use similar mechanisms to reduce bureaucratic steps, introduce better heaters, and train people in human rights. But evidently there are many very notable differences. Another problem lies in the unquestioned status of the human rights discourse, which is extended indiscriminately to indigenous peasants and Ladinos, to industrial builders and bus conductors, and to officers in the new National Civil Police. Yet local assessments of the discourse by Mayas-Ch'orti' peasants make clear that it is neither considered in its entirety nor universally understood. When I read the list of human rights to the people I spoke to in Tunucó Abajo, they showed disagreement, sometimes saying, "here it's not the same" or "here it's different," either because they believed that to be the case or because, I think, they did not understand exactly the content of my words.

There are some preconceived notions about the desired transformation. The implementers of the rights discourse know the starting point and establish a suitable goal, with no questions asked. To achieve this goal (and fulfill their mission), they set in motion the most efficient machinery available. Modernization is achieved with typically vertical schemes in which reconsideration, negotiation, and dialogue are prevented.[10] The targets of modernization only appear interested in being trained.

Human rights training follows a treelike scheme similar to the ones used in rural areas of Guatemala when teaching the use of "appropriate technology" or proper health care. This involves the creation of an institutionally coordinated framework and the teaching of trainers who will in turn train others ("multipliers") in every corner of the country, especially in rural areas where the technology is the most "inappropriate," where health and "environmental sanitation" are the most precarious or, in the case that concerns us here, where ignorance about human rights is most evident. It is obvious that this vertical design, from top to bottom, impedes dialogue and makes change impossible since the end branches of the tree have few opportunities to become involved.

Three terms can be used to describe those who can foster change: trainers, facilitators, and multipliers. In other words, we are dealing with people who transmit what they have learned and who hope that the chain of learning will continue in a similar fashion. The training scheme followed is based on classical approaches to formal education directed at children, where trainers are teachers who teach pupils who do not have ideas regarding the topics being taught. It also resembles military hierarchical schemes, with the executive levels at the top and levels of blind and automatic obedience below. That is to say, the trainer, somewhat illogically, is expected to be the most uncritical and automatic in his or her conduct.

It is possible to evaluate the impact of some modernization and training processes that have been in operation for longer than human rights training and for which results are clearer. I will look at these to challenge the authoritative and interventionist models that, by being considered unquestionably good, make debate virtually impossible; these are projects that are persistently repeated, persistently fail, and rarely reflect on the principles that underwrite them.

The apostles of eugenics, for example, would be surprised to see how tens of thousands of Ch'orti' are still surrounded by hundreds of thousands of Ladinos. Defenders of the theory of ladinization would also be surprised to see how the Ch'orti' communities shatter all of their theoretical ideas.[11] The principles of modernization have changed, but, one after another, they have failed, at least partially. In recent decades the emphasis has been placed neither on biology nor on culture but on the economy and on health, and always in an authoritative way: modernization will arrive when the appropriate technology, the appropriate health model, and the appropriate environmental sanitation are in place.

It is not difficult to hear the Ch'orti' peasants sometimes themselves blessing the modernization schemes, repeating arguments similar to those of Don Paco, the idealized peasant of the Planning and Programming Secretariat of the Presidency (Secretaría de Planificación y Programación de la

Presidencía, SEGEPLAN) propaganda. "Now that we're getting over it, it's lovely to see the community with latrines," said Don Valentín in 1992 when, as a result of a cholera epidemic, more than fifty latrines were built in Tunucó Abajo. He received training in "environmental sanitation" and was one of the promoters in the community installation work. Today it is the chickens that are grateful for that work since many of the latrines have been converted into chicken coops. Some say that it would have been different if the latrines had been not Turkish but "seated" like those of Jocotán. "Those would have caught on," says Don Valentín now; perhaps that is true, and perhaps this type of latrine will soon be installed, though those latrines might end up being used as fish tanks. The solar heaters distributed through another project by the Bethania Clinic today serve as rabbit hutches.

On occasion the projects do come together, at times automatically and at others with specific adjustments that leave the promoters and trainers without arguments to explain why some projects "stick" and others do not. While the introduction of sewing machines failed with the Lantiquín, the project proved a success in the Q'eqchi community of San Lucas. According to Didier Boremanse, the Indians performed *wa'tesink* rites on the machines to feed their spirits, serving as a "symbolic mechanism to integrate the sewing machines, or say objects (and techniques) into the local culture that traditionally did not form part of that culture" (1998: 240).

One is often led to believe that the culturally foreign object ends up being accepted via a decoy or a culturally emotive trick.[12] The attitude typified by this type of trick is widely used to disseminate something or to train people.[13] It is construed as a white lie necessary for the Indians' own good, but my impression is that interactions based on forms of deceit or condescension never lead to lasting changes.

Many promoters, when evaluating their project's impact on completion, end up thinking, without necessarily saying so, "these intractable Indians!" They cannot understand why the indigenous population does not adopt something good, or does not adopt it well, especially since they carried out a needs assessment beforehand and installed the project themselves. But often there is no ongoing and honest dialogue, only, as mentioned above, one based on tricks. Those who wanted to introduce a nixtamal machine into Ch'orti' communities first asked: "Do you want your wives not to have to spend so many hours milling?" Evidently the answer was yes, but it turned out that the dough made with the machine was not sufficiency kneaded, one of the basic prerequisites of making a good tortilla and a reason to celebrate the social value of women. If the dialogues continue to be handled in this way ("Do you want heaters that do not use wood?"), there will not only be a dialogue of the deaf but also considerable uncertainty.

Maya-Ch'orti' Cultural Molds and Human Rights Panoramas Prior to Training

For the peasants of the region, human rights have not yet arrived, although they have heard about them on the radio and are awaiting their arrival. Yet organizations such as the Fund for Social Investment (FIS), World Vision, the International Fund for Agricultural Development (IFAD), and the Peace Corps have already arrived, and with them roof tiles, community halls, and sewing machines, though still no human rights as of yet. Don Simeón, a peasant from the village El Tablón, told me,

> At the moment I don't know anything about human rights because I don't even know what they are. I don't know what type of people have meetings, I don't know if they have meetings, because I have never had a conversation with them. I have wanted to find out something about them, but I don't know how they behave, if they go to the villages or they don't, or if they only go to the towns . . . I don't know. From what I've heard on the radio, human rights is something that we all have to have; as Guatemalan citizens, we have the right to work honorably and not to be isolated, or that if some are valued more and others less, we would all have to be valued equally by our rights . . . but I don't know . . . here those people have not arrived yet.

This moving image of human rights, imagined as a foreign entity that arrives headed by spokespeople setting themselves up in offices, is common in Guatemala. As David Stoll affirmed for the town of Nebaj, human rights arrive when the Human Rights Bureau establishes an office in the town (1999a: 348). Or, as Stener Ekern states in this volume, "human rights conquer the Mayan communities in the form of four-wheel-drive Toyotas." In this approach everything is conditional; human rights here begin with institutionalization followed by training. Don Simeón would see little difference between the arrival of human rights and that of steamrollers to build the new road to Florido.[14]

In the giddy race to spread awareness and disseminate ideas about universal human rights, manuals and pamphlets are designed to prepare trainers who will spread the word further. One of the manuals used in Guatemala is Hugo Ávila's *Education Manual in Human Rights* (n.d.). The booklet is aimed at trainers new in the field and its content is divided into background information and practical suggestions for activities. It has not been formally published but MINUGUA distributes it electronically or through photocopies. According to the author's introduction,

> The information activities are aimed at helping participants know and understand what human rights consist of in general, the rights of indigenous villages, children's rights, women's rights, the rights to a healthy environment, the rights of people living in special conditions and the rights of people living with HIV/AIDS. This material has been selected because it comprises the main themes in human rights about which we Guatemalans must acquire knowledge and on which we must reflect to achieve a harmonious coexistence. The suggested activities are aimed at helping participants study in depth the knowledge acquired during the information activities or that they reflect on specific situations. The trainer must always bear in mind that human rights education has as its principal objective that each member of society understands what his or her rights and his or her obligations are and that they exercise them within a framework of respect, free from discrimination. It requires therefore that the people to whom training is directed develop an analytical attitude, constructive criticism, and commitment in relation to the different aspects of life in their community. That is to say, that they be citizens capable of proposing and generating change for a life worthier for all. It is intended therefore that these people are generators of human rights knowledge in each one of its environments.

In this manual's approach, as in other human rights analyses done in Guatemala, the fundamental principle of equality stands out: if this idea has not already been interiorized, the training should be responsible for fostering its acceptance. However, the appeal to human rights, even more than universal principles, is linked to context. When I spoke to Don Simeón about indigenous rights and the possibility of reporting discrimination, he said, "It is possible to directly report the Ladinos who don't want to give us a break." Though said half in jest, this suggestion accords with the type of reports presented to MINUGUA. According to one official from this organization, more than two-thirds of reports they receive about human rights violations are not dealt with, and not only because they do not fall within the mandate assigned to MINUGUA but because they are not human rights violations at all. On this matter, he referred to some common themes: people who reported their neighbors because the latter's animals had invaded their land; reports of neighbors who had allegedly thrown stones on the roofs of their houses or had insulted them. There was even a mother who reported her son because he got drunk a lot and did not work in the cornfield. According to Stoll, after the "arrival" of human rights in Nebaj, the Ixils complained about the violation of their human rights as much when ambulance drivers arrived late to pick up a patient as when a teacher disciplined a child (1999a: 349).

On the other hand, it proves difficult to interiorize discourses about equality without first taking into account preexisting discourses about foretold destinies or envy: "Our grandparents told us that we should never be envious nor desire what a brother or another human being or neighbor has because what he has is his mission, if he is a scientist, his mission was to be a scientist, if he is a farmer, his mission was to be a farmer, and so on. We should never be envious because what we are is our mission from the moment we are born. Each one of us carries our vocation with us. (Lima-Soto 1995: 76). Accounts like the former, which comes from Comalapa, are common among indigenous Mayas, and they also exist among the Ch'orti'. As Mancho from Tuticopote told Brent Metz, "God gives us a spirit that determines our weaknesses and our strengths." Pedro Súchite from Pelillo put it more explicitly: "God establishes the destiny of everyone, some are destined to work with machetes, others to travel, others to work in commerce . . . even in God's destiny, the language that each person will speak is assigned" (Metz 1995: 197–98). What has been written about predetermined destiny ("mission" or "vocation") can be summarized with the classic argument of Luigi Tranfo about the Otomies, according to which, despite the efforts of humans to control their world and to avoid destruction and illness, there exists an imponderable link to the sacred calendar and to the *tono*, which determines destiny according to the willingness of the gods (1975: 197).

It is true that these discourses exist and they are often said to account for the fatalistic and resigned character of indigenous people. Yet although it seems contradictory, this discourse at present coexists with another, according to which desire, curiosity, and effort can affect the natural course of events.[15] In fact few groups are as unfaithful to fixed ideas or attitudes as the Maya, and few are as willing to listen to new notions or novel versions of already extant knowledge.[16] Trainers and promoters therefore have at their disposal two ways of justifying the need for explicit or implicit imposition: either as a weapon against a paralyzing fatalism, or as a necessary strategy against the impossibility of reaching agreement since Indians "are not serious," "they cannot be trusted," or because "it is not possible to talk to them because they do not have an opinion." In the case of human rights training models, such phrases are repeated time and time again.

I will now focus on evaluative comments made by the Ch'orti' in reference to three of the topics Ávila's manual deals with, namely, human rights in general (particularly the respect for human life), the rights of childhood, and women's rights. The commentaries were collected by the author during the summer of 2000 in Tunucó Abajo. They come from the conversations that arose out of the suggested practical activities in the manual.

For human rights in general the activity suggested consists of the participants identifying human rights and reflecting on their importance. The facilitator requests that each of the participants select one human right from a list that will have been prepared earlier. Each participant represents one human right and will explain to his or her colleagues what this right consists of (and may prepare a poster with the name of the right). Afterward, each one of the participants expresses his or her opinion on which of the rights is the most important. At the end of the activity the votes cast for each right is counted. Normally in these activities, respect for human life is the right that proves to be the most important. Those who voted for it are asked to explain their choice, and those who voted for other rights will be asked to explain their reasons. Later, the facilitator will point out that, in fact, respect for human life is the most important because without it, the other rights have no meaning. However, it is important to emphasize to the participants that all rights are important because even with the respect for human life, without freedom, security, work, education, health, and the like, life is not worthy. It is also necessary to impress on the participants the significant role the state plays as the main body committed to these rights, and that all Guatemalans have the right to demand the state's compliance with the protection of human rights.

It seems obvious that the trainers will understand that respect for human life is the most important and that no other crime is more serious than one in which a life is taken. However, this is not so obvious for the Ch'orti', nor does it seem obvious for others such as Mayas Ixil, K'iche', Mam, and Poqomchi'. These communities "consider as seriously harmful acts the following: murder; manslaughter ('to give death to another person'); rape ('of a child by an adult'); kidnapping ('stealing children'); physical violence toward parents; serious wounds ('to cut a person down with a machete'); adultery; the theft of animals, 'especially work animals such as oxen or horses'; incest ('sleeping with your sister'); and usurpation ('taking land'). The K'iche' community would add to this list slander; the Mam and Poqomchi' communities, lack of respect toward authority; and the Poqomchi', the robbery of agricultural products with the intention of selling them, and not fulfilling a promise" (Universidad Rafael Landívar 1998: 47). The list of universal rights prepared beforehand by the trainers thus clashes with another list similarly prepared beforehand; for the trainers, the majority of the "seriously harmful acts" mentioned above do not appear as attacks on human rights. Training might therefore easily not meet expectations because, evidently, it does not occur on a blank slate.

One particular case helps illustrate how, for the Ch'orti', respect for human life acquires different meanings depending on the situation and how not all persons have the same right to life and not all lives have the same value. I remember how some years ago in Tunucó Abajo, the brother-in-law of my host, Doña Gregoria, arrived at her house. Two months had passed since he had killed another peasant with a machete; during this period he had roamed and hid in the mountains. Since his house and his cornfield had been burned, and because revenge was likely, his wife and six children had taken refuge in a disused farmhouse close to Doña Gregoria's house. She lamented the sad life that awaited them and referred to her nieces and nephews as "these poor little Joes." In reality, the children were not "Joes" in a strict sense because it is a term used for orphans. But their designation as "Joes" made clear that sooner or later the father would fall victim to revenge, or at the very least would have to remain in hiding or so far away that it would amount to the same thing as if the children had no father at all. Some material signs also made them resemble real "Joes": all were in rags, seminaked, dirty, undernourished, and gave the general impression of having been abandoned. After her brother's brief visit Doña Gregoria told me: "He is going to die." She spoke in the same tone we might use when referring to someone with a terminal illness. Exactly two months later the sons of the man whom he had murdered killed Doña Gregoria's brother with machetes.

Tunucó Abajo is a community that has one of the highest records of machete killings; in the past five years at least fourteen deaths have occurred. During the summer of 2000, I asked whether those who had committed these machete crimes had a right to have their lives protected, and why. I was told that their lives were no longer worth living, and heard many reasons justifying this: they generally could not go back to cultivating their fields and even in the best-case scenario, a long time would have to pass before they would be able to do so again. They would not be able to extend or consolidate any social relationship, not even with their family. "Nobody will want to be his compadre; if he is not married no woman will want to marry him, and if he is married, he will not be able to be with either his wife or his children. It's not good for him to walk to the village, nor on a path . . . perhaps they spend their time eating grass . . . they have to live like animals." In other words, respect for human life can clash with the question of whether some lives are really worth living. This becomes evident when acts of revenge are carried out: the murderer, wanting to stop living like an animal, starts becoming more conspicuous again, perhaps visiting his family more regularly or even daring to be seen along well-used paths. In the end he turns into an easy target and is killed. In some ways one could almost talk of suicide.

On the other hand, it is believed that killers will undoubtedly go to hell. When they die their loss does not provoke the same feelings as does the loss of other people. In fact, a murderer is not given the farewell "of a man," but is buried without a wake and with his feet pointing to the east rather than the west, as would be the custom. Moreover, the spot at which the murder took place is transformed into a dangerous and forbidden place for people in weakened states such as children, the sick, and the old because they might be *achucuyados* (bewitched) by the dead.

Probably in the past, systems of material restitution were in place that prevented murders and may have even prevented these machete killings. Other Mayan communities show similar patterns. When material restitution does not occur, probably due to changes in the line of authority or the imposition of legal norms from another community, revenge appears as a means of balancing out the negative.

Restitution not only helps avoid conflicts but also leads to the foundation and strengthening of alliances. If someone does not comply with the right to restitution, the community in return may not see the need to respect that person's physical rights. For example, if the costs that parents incur with a daughter are not restituted (with initiations, presents and "donations," or a dowry) by the young man who "steals" her, the young woman's life immediately loses value. In fact, her life is debased in such a way that violence possibly directed at her may be viewed differently than violence directed at a girl formally united with a young man (via some form of payment). In the latter situation, the girl's parents and even the community would intervene if the young man mistreated her. Doña Margarita García from Tunucó Abajo explains it as follows:

> They can secretly go out if she is happy with the boy, but if it goes on in secret, if he is hitting her, it's as she wishes, because she doesn't want to be alone. . . . It would be different if they had received the dowry . . . but since it was her decision to pick the boy, if they are hitting her, they hit her . . . it's now nobody's responsibility . . . it's like a hen that goes out looking for a cockerel . . . who is responsible for that? Another thing is if the father received the dowry, if they are hitting the girl he has to go and see . . . if it's true that the boy [is hitting her], if they are fucking with her, he is going to say: don't hit the girl, you did not find her on the street, you came to look for her at home. . . . [If there has been a dowry] there is always a solution, and for those who do it in secret there is never a solution.

For the Ch'orti' a clear-cut discourse on universal and equal rights to life will thus not prove very effective if parallel discourses on rights to restitution, for example, are not dealt with simultaneously.

On another occasion we talked about the rights of childhood in Tunucó Abajo. The suggested activity in Ávila's manual aims to make the participants aware of certain beliefs that society has about children and that it is possible to discuss children's rights. To do this, the facilitator will present on the blackboard the following myths and beliefs concerning children: (1) Children are human beings without rights whose only duty is to respect their parents; (2) parents have the right to discipline their children by hitting them and using strong and humiliating language; (3) indigenous children must learn Spanish at school to improve themselves; (4) children must have the same religion as their parents; (5) children on the street are inferior to other children; (6) indigenous children are used to poverty and therefore remain unaffected by not having drinking water, electricity, education, or any free time; (7) sexual relations between adults and children are normal and thus deserve no special attention; and (8) adults should always decide on behalf of children because children do not have experience, do not understand much, and easily make mistakes. Afterward the workshop participants generally say that these beliefs represent mistaken ideas that their society has about children.

The facilitator then proceeds to ask each participant his or her thoughts concerning the beliefs on the board. The aim is to generate group discussion about children's rights. The facilitator will point out that such beliefs often obscure children's problems and thus lead to a violation of their rights as a consequence. At the end of the workshop, the facilitator will present counterarguments to the commonly held beliefs:

(1) Children are human beings who have all rights established by the Convention on the Rights of the Child and the Childhood and Youth Code. They also have obligations, among them, to respect their parents.
(2) Parents have the right to discipline their children, but not by physical or verbal mistreatment. Mistreatment only produces physical or psychological problems in children.
(3) Indigenous children have the right to have their mother tongue respected and that education be provided in this language. Indigenous children have the right to express themselves in their own language.
(4) Children can have the religion they choose.
(5) All children, whether they are on the street or not, are equal, and all have the same rights and obligations.
(6) All children have the right to an adequate standard of living with drinking water, electricity, education, and health services. Poverty presents an obstacle for the proper development of a child. If we believe that indigenous children are used to poverty, we will never be able to do anything to better their living conditions.
(7) The sexual abuse of children constitutes a serious human rights violation and is not justified under any circumstances.
(8) A child's opinion should always be taken into account in decisions that affect him or her.

The intercultural dialogue with respect to children's rights seems easier than the one discussed before. Indigenous populations clearly understand both the list of "incorrect myths" and the corrected one, although they will not completely agree with either one. For example, the ideas expressed in myths 6 and 7 do not reconcile with Ch'orti' ideology in any way, but neither do items 2 and 4 of the corrected list. The corrected list aims to make them understand that children are just like adults, but here the Ch'orti' are in total agreement: "Here it's different; children are not people in the same way as adults." Moreover, it is precisely the duty of parents to raise children to become adults, and this is achieved "bit by bit . . . setting them examples, teaching them how one should talk to people, give them their little machete and teach them how to work, or if it's a little girl how to make tortillas." Raising a child to be an adult can involve "lashing them hard" if one is dealing with a "wild" or "rude" child: "If parents aren't interested in scolding or lashing their boy, or even their girl, suddenly they'll end up with a spoiled *ixchoco* "child"; this is the responsibility that we have as parents. The lash is suitable only for some *ixchocos*." The Ch'orti' believe that a child grows into adulthood from the progressive accumulation of heat: children are born "cold" and "tender," their stomachs are "tender" and "watery," and their veins are equally tender in such a way that although a child is born with "his or her spirit, his or her pulse," it is weak and born into the world almost "empty of understanding." Little by little children accumulate heat, so that "the little tender one goes on maturing like a little piece of fruit," his or her stomach gets "more solid," and his or her understanding develops. Between the ages of fifteen and twenty the process of heat accumulation concludes. In this belief system the behavior of a child "with a strong character"—a child that is angry, rude, or without respect—proves incomprehensible and contemptible: it is considered abnormal to accumulate so much heat at such an early age, and it is also pernicious because it means the child is turning away from the correct course of his or her upbringing. A suitable formative process will make the child have "good blood" (meaning he or she will be affable, humble, polite, respectful, and the like). However, incorrect upbringing will result in "bad blood" (a stubborn, sensitive, or easily angered personality). Therefore severely lashing and scolding the child will result in "reducing the blood pressure," "softening it," and returning it to its normal "pressure." A child who is made to cry, who loses "strength," "pressure," and "heat" in his or her blood through tears, is made to see the benefits of directing his or her life along the path of humility and respect. Faced with a child turning away from the correct path, a parent has no other choice but to make him or her cry. If trainers offer other forms of punishment that can produce tears and stabilize the child, a reasonable intercultural dialogue is possible. But if trainers insist that hitting and verbal abuse always produce physical and psychological damage in children, dialogue becomes more difficult.[17] If punishment and scolding are understood therapeutically, the right to not suffer physical harm clashes with the right to health. With impeccable logic, Don Paulino, now a helper in the Tunucó Abajo health post, suggested, "Is it not true that injections hurt?"

The Tunequeño people are also in complete agreement concerning their children's free choice of religion: there is no way for them to do it.

> Perhaps they are not tender? If their bodies are tender to carry a load of wood, their spirit is also tender to decide on what belief is best for them. Is it possible for an *ixchoquito* to decide whether he wants to be a Catholic or an Evangelical? This would be the end of time. It's the father and the mother who must make him see what is best and what is not best for him. One must set examples for children: if there is a celebration of the Word over there you go with the little one; if it's a wake they are at the wake from when they are very tender. This is how understanding is awakened. And when they grow up they can change, but only then are they responsible.

In fact, the responsibility is also something that results from the accumulation of heat. The example of the load is useful for understanding the meaning of responsibility: someone who has accumulated enough strength will be able to carry the weight of heavy loads, as well as be able to carry the burden of making a decision. Until this happens, parents help with their physical strength and with their responsibility for their young ones. Likewise, the opinions of children are regarded as insignificant because they are irresponsible, and the expression of children's opinions can variously give rise to laughter or annoyance.

Part 4 of the manual refers to women's rights: "The objective is that the participants reflect on certain beliefs of Guatemalan society regarding women and that they discuss the topic." The facilitator presents on the board the following myths and beliefs concerning women: (1) Women are human beings with less rights than men; (2) women do not have the intellectual capacity to hold public office; (3) married or engaged women cannot go out and form friendships without the consent of their husbands; (4) married or engaged women can only work if their husbands authorize it; (5) women should not be given credit because they are unreliable in their commitments and do not have the means of payment; (6) it is not necessary for women to study because one day they will get married and have their husbands to support them; (7) women should not use birth control because their natural role is to have all the children that God gives them.

The manual continues: "These myths or beliefs are mistaken ideas that society has about women." The facilitator proceeds by giving each of the participants the opportunity to participate individually or in previously formed groups and ask them what they think of the myths or beliefs and what arguments could be used against them. Again, the objective is to generate a group discussion about women's rights. The ultimate "counter-list" will look like this:

(1) Women have the same rights and obligations as men and differences should not be made between them. To do so constitutes a human rights violation.

(2) Men and women both have the same aptitude for holding public office. The law does not establish differences between them.

(3) Married or engaged women, although they have certain obligations that come from matrimony, are free to go anywhere and form whatever friendships they choose.

(4) Women can freely decide whether to work or not and are able to choose the type of work they want to do.

(5) Women have the right to receive credit. In rural areas of Guatemala it has been proven that women who have received credit complied strictly with their obligations to repay it.

(6) Even though a woman may get married, she has the right to education and to select technical or university studies.

(7) Women have the right to use family planning methods whenever they deem necessary.

The facilitator will likely close the discussion by suggesting that, among other things, the myths expressed in the first list often render women's problems invisible, making rights violations possible.

For the Ch'orti' the lists contain sometimes contradictory or unrelated notions. In the discussion I had after reading the manual, I asked if men and women were complementary. The question has to do with one of the principles on which Mayan spirituality is based.[18] Although my interlocutors agreed that men and women complemented each other in work, the discourse of complementarity that has come from the Altiplano remains somewhat foreign to the Ch'orti': men and women are neither equal nor complementary; they are separate, different, and each one has a mission from birth to which other obligations and rights are added through more or less explicit contracts.

The most important and most explicit of these contracts between a man and a woman is established by marriage. This contract basically admonishes the man to bring home maize and the woman to have the tortillas ready so that they can be eaten at home or in the field. The fulfillment of this contract involves the men spending a great deal of time in the field, with the women, in turn, spending a lot of time at home. A woman who is selfless with her time fits the model of socially congruous and esteemed behavior. In this way, husbands, friends, and in-laws are won over, relations with neighbors and friends are strengthened, and the fear of solitude is mitigated. A woman considered good for nothing, who does not spend enough time at home to make sufficient or good tortillas, turns into someone who loses value, not only within the family circle but also in the community, which sees her as someone likely to cause conflicts because a good-for-nothing woman is also a gossiping woman.[19] The time a woman spends at home establishes a boundary differentiating diligence, a value socially attributed to good wives, from "ruin," an attribute seen as particularly negative. In this way, women who are "good for nothing," "ruinous," and "too delicate for hard work" are distinguished from those who "know how to do diligent work" and who are "patient." The latter are "soft," humble, and receptive to advice from mother-in-laws, allowing therefore the consolidation of the most difficult, though basic, social relations: that of mother-in-law/daughter-in-law and that of wife/husband. On the other hand, the "delicate" woman, careless, caring more about "going for walks" and "chatting" than about attending to the kitchen, will soon create conflicts with her mother-in-law and will generally end up splitting the family union. The time dedicated to cooking, the base of the couple's relationship, unites the fundamental social units, while carelessness results in food losing its value, being transformed into one of the main reasons for family crises. Although I will not discuss it here, a similar discourse exists that deals with men who fail to fulfill their side of the contract.

The manual talks of a woman's right to go out as much as she chooses.

However, for the Ch'orti' the binding force of commitment (of the contract) is so strong that it clashes with this right. While it is not forbidden for a woman to carry out other tasks, go to the village, or take charge of a cooperative, everything is subordinate to the need to make tortillas. If one tries to impose the right in opposition to this commitment, conflicts will arise. A constructive dialogue, on the other hand, might be initiated by considering the issue of time management because everyone recognizes that natural limitations exist that arise not from impositions but from the fact that "time cannot be extended." Doña Felipa recognized that "only Doña Gola and Doña Gregoria are able to go to Mass, to make a flying visit to the Feminine Promotion [an organization of the Jocotán parish] . . . [because] Doña Gola is on her own, she doesn't have to attend to any man, and Doña Gregoria's children are grown up." Leadership is founded on men, but in my understanding this does not involve a prejudice against women, but a question of effectiveness: men interact with more people, and this helps fulfill the requirements expected of a good leader such as oratorical skills (and if they exist in both Ch'orti' and Spanish, even better). However, the commitment that men have to women involves spending a certain amount of time in the field, which in reality means that leadership is restricted to a few men who, as well as having more "spark," have more help or know how to organize their time better. One leader of the village El Rodeíto told Claudia Dary, "Ten years ago we started to form a committee to improve the village, and they made me secretary because I was one of the few who could speak Castilian [Spanish] well, and I knew how to read a little. Later, we formed a school committee and I was made president. Now I am president of the road committee, I am also vice president of the agricultural committee and president of the church committee. Now they want to name me president of the central committee, because the organization wants there to be a central committee. I said that I couldn't accept because with so many posts I no longer have time to attend to my field" (1998: 237).

Although the wives of men with religious responsibilities have always held leadership posts (see Girard 1949: 292–93), and midwives and healers have always enjoyed a position of respect, only recently have some women started to be leaders in community projects owing to new ways of managing time. Except for some minority opinions that allude to the dangers of sexual relations with other men, these novel roles for women have not caused much gender resentment. Deep down there was never any opposition to women going to the village, selling their handcrafts, or taking charge of shepherding calves. Furthermore, it is considered normal that the money they earn through their activities is exclusively theirs.

In conclusion one might say that struggles for meaning in human rights training will mainly occur because neither the trainers nor those being trained arrive as blank slates, but instead work from "prepared lists" of various kinds. If this fact is ignored and models are imposed from above yet again, another phrase will need to be coined: "These intractable trainers." And if we replaced the term *trainers* with others such as *colonizers, evangelists, apostles of eugenics* or *of ladinization, revolutionaries, neoliberal modernizers, apostles of universal human rights,* or *Mayan neospiritualists,* a new history of the centuries past could be written, a history of ignorance, failure, and above all, of deafness. Another history is possible if "motivating agreements" (Watanabe 1990: 136) are established in a true dialogue, or what Richard Wilson calls "active syncretism" (1999: 137). As Don Paulino said, "[If] we find the words to reach another companion, we will succeed in finding the way."

In other words, the possible alternative to so many centuries of imposition could be a dialogue between the local versions of rights and duties and Western human rights perspectives. If both versions confront each other in an egalitarian way, the agreements will prove not only more valid but also more effective.

Notes

1. *Al Día*, September 28, 2000.
2. Those who claim this—somewhat contentiously—justify it by indicating that all lynchings have taken place in the west of the country and none in the east, which is for the most part Ladino.
3. This refers to a lynching in Chichicastenango.
4. Interview with López Portillo, Radio Nederland, October 10, 2000.
5. Catholic Church sources in Guatemala have confirmed the possibility of suspending Eucharistic rites in places where villagers have carried out lynchings. The assistant bishop of Guatemala, Monsignor Mario Ríos Montt, claims that "we don't like adopting this attitude, but there are things that we cannot change in any other way. . . . Crimes of this type cannot continue in the face of indifference in the local community, and it is the responsibility of the Church to react to the events" (*Noticias,* May 31, 1999). He indicated that the church considered those participating in lynchings as criminals and that—once there was evidence—measures would be taken in parishes where the first lynchings were reported.

6. http://www.asies.org.gt/carta38–2001.htm.

7. Every new lynching ignites condemnation of the villagers ("savages," "cavemen") and a reiteration of the need for training. Faced with the recent lynching of the justice of the peace of Senahú, Hugo Martínez Pérez, the magistrate of the Supreme Court of Justice, Amanda Ramírez, affirmed that "orientation of these villages will be carried out with the objective of making them aware" (*Siglo* xxi, March 15, 2001).

8. Such as the setting up of different agencies in charge of responding to accusations of human rights violations and the signing of international agreements such as the International Labor Organization's (ilo) Convention 169 on Indigenous and Tribal Peoples.

9. pan leaflet, distributed in the town of Jocotán, Guatemala, 1999.

10. It is clear that the organizers know the added value of words, and their presentations usually contain certain new words, for example, *horizontality, decentralization,* and the like. See, for example, the program principles of the current government's new secretary of planning and programming: "The focus of economic planning in previous decades was based on ideologies and doctrines that made its practical application dependent on a vertical, centralized, aid-assisted, and non-participative scheme, evident in a model that carried out the process as a simple exercise to demonstrate good intentions for the future of the country. From the signing of the Peace Agreements, the segeplan adopts and promotes the pluralistic, participative, democratic, and decentralized nature of planning, a characteristic that is fundamental for the construction of a firm and lasting peace, one economically and socially sustainable. This context made clear the need to transform the focus of planning, with the aim of adapting it to the requirements of the changing environment, increasing its efficiency and effectiveness to give a suitable response to the problems of the country and facilitate its incorporation into the processes of modernization and globalization" ("Informe de gestión del gobienro, secretaría general de planificación," government dossier, 2000). However, the magic of the words does not change the realities, and the system appears to be working in much the same manner.

11. In Pacrén, for example, a community close to the mestizo village of Jocotán, the Ch'orti' language is retained, and many of the women still use traditional dress. Yet economically the community is far removed from the agricultural subsistence model: its members are traders, and many buy and sell in places far from their home. Some, with a formalist economic mentality, say of their neighbors of the village Tunucó Abajo, four kilometers up the mountain, that they are primitives who continue "paying" the land and participating in economic wastefulness to receive the souls of the dead. However, those of Tunucó Abajo have practically lost the language, although many women retain the dress. In Pelillo Negro, one of the most remote villages of Jocotán, Ch'orti' is spoken, but the women do not use traditional dress, the community boasts a fair number of Evangelicals, and for many years it has not carried out "payments to the land."

12. Along similar lines, many congratulate themselves on the ease with which sorghum was introduced to the region some decades ago. The trick was in the name. It was accepted, promoters say, because it was introduced with a name full of emotive meaning, "gravel." Another name might have made acceptance harder.

13. In the case of training, they resort to using expressive incidents instantly recognized to attract attention. The training methodology employed by the trainers at times resembles the strategies that street vendors of remedies use: their words aim to quickly produce a laugh or amazement so that people come closer and buy.

14. The history of the Mayan communities is often constructed starting from the things that arrived from outside and in the end get lost and fade away. One woman from Santa María Cauqué (Sacatepéquez) summarized the history of her community throughout the past decades: "First came religion, the factories came, the earthquake came, the agriculture of broccoli and peas came, and then the government came, trying to get rid of the Chinese" (Goldín 1998: 59).

15. My suggestion is that the Ch'orti' are even in the process of changing the lifestyle in heaven (López García 2001).

16. This idea, which I have discussed fully elsewhere (López García 1998), would contrast with the more idealized positions within Mayanism that stress faithfulness to the past as a fundamental mark of being Maya. For example, Otilia Lux de Cotí has written: "Grandparents and parents teach harmony and not to compete, to talk before taking action, to cooperate and not be ambitious, to respect and not take advantage, to listen and not interrupt, to be discrete and cautious and not foolish and imprudent, that is, to be loyal allowing the union with nature, with God and with people. The Maya has remained faithful to himself throughout his millennial life in Mesoamerica" (1995: 107)

17. With other Mayan groups, a dialogue on alternatives to lashing would prove much more productive. I have already said that the lashing intends to reduce the "pressure" and "strength" of the blood. As I have pointed out elsewhere (López García 1995), not only tears but also other bodily humors can be considered by the Ch'orti' as distinct types of blood. For example, among the Tzotziles of San Pedro Chenalhó, irate children must be "cooled" by quickly passing them over chili smoke, lit in such a way that the child will salivate and expulse his or her rage (Guiteras Holmes 1986: 104). Charles Wagley refers to something similar in Santiago Chimaltenango: irate children are calmed down by making them swallow tobacco, which renders them violently sick (1957: 140). Salivating, in the same way as vomiting or crying, involves the loss of "strength" in the blood.

18. In this process of the "reconstruction of the traditional," the cultural construction rests on the subordination of women. Therefore, following from the idea of complementarity, women find themselves without the means for change since such change is regarded not only as antitraditional but also as linked to Western cultural imperialism (Sieder 1998: 329).

19. See the analysis of Susan Tax with regard to Zinacantán (1980).

IRMA OTZOY 7

TRANSLATED BY CHRISTOPHER LUTZ,
ELISABETH S. NICHOLSON,
AND SHANNON SPEED

Indigenous Law and Gender Dialogues

> Three virtues are expected of intellectuals based on what we know
> how to do: presenting contrasting and reasoned information, provid-
> ing solidarity based in a critical understanding of intercultural con-
> flicts, and engaging in doubt.
>
> NESTOR GARCÍA CANCLINI, "ATAQUE A LAS TORRES GEMELAS: EL FIN DEL
> TÓTEM PROTECTOR"

Prologue

Before entering into the substance of this chapter, I want to let readers
know what they will and will not find here. First, this text was written
principally for a local audience in Guatemala. It was after this writing that I
received the invitation of the editors to include it in the present volume. It
would be easier to understand the text if readers were not only familiar with
the ethnographic literature on Guatemala but could also set aside for a
moment recognized academic protocol. While the average academic might
find some points trivial, for an indigenous audience they represent a kind of
cultural self-critique that we rarely engage in. Given that this text contains
certain references that are of an academic nature framed in language not
frequently used by a wider public, but also ones better understood by
indigenous interlocutors concerning their situations, I am attempting to
offer an argument intelligible to both audiences. Unfortunately, I do not
have an analytical model that perfectly fits my intellectual contribution.
Rather, I speak from the position of a native intellectual who is sensitive to

the political processes of a third world country and who seeks to contribute to the analysis of the sociocultural problematics surrounding the practice of rights in indigenous communities.[1]

Leaping from the Past to the Present

Guatemala has had a bloody and complex history from the sixteenth century and Spanish colonization to the civil war of the twentieth century. Indigenous peoples have suffered the harshest effects of these historical processes, yet they always maintained fierce cultural resistance. Today sharp contrasts between indigenous and nonindigenous groups remain. Statistically this translates into indigenous people comprising the social group with the highest levels of poverty, illiteracy, and suffering the negative effects of discrimination and political exclusion (Office of the High Commissioner for Human Rights 2003).

Following thirty years of civil war and the signing of the peace accords between the Revolutionary National Unity of Guatemala (Unidad Revolucionaria Nacional Guatemalteca, URNG) and the government in December 1996, Guatemala now has made a commitment to social reconstruction and thus to creating a new type of society: one more just for all of its citizens, especially those that have been historically excluded—women and indigenous peoples. The struggles of women and of indigenous peoples thus have special relevance and should not be conceived of as mutually exclusive in the achievement of their objectives. Rather, the two groups should see each other as potential collaborators, with the potential for genuine learning offered in the process of that collaboration.

What Do Women Celebrate in a Multicultural Country?

The Guatemala City celebration of International Women's Day on March 8, 2002, was a major event for many feminist activists. The morning's march was led by rural indigenous women, and the evening's musical event was organized and attended by Ladino and mestizo women.[2] On that day a young indigenous woman asked me the reason for this fiesta so widely publicized on the radio and in the press. When I told her it was International Women's Day, she replied, "But this only has to do with Ladino women, right?"

The newspapers were quite casual about the importance of the day. One only mentioned that the day had passed "without pain and without glory" and reported on the party held by the wife of a government functionary who with her friends had "invaded" his office and appropriated some of his expensive liquor ("Invasión femenina," *El Periódico*, March 17, 2002). Frankly, I am not as concerned about whether this day is celebrated or not as I am with the various meanings and interpretations it has in the public perception. From my perspective, more than a celebration of diversity, these forms of commemorating Women's Day reflect three distinct but inter-related dynamics: the generalized indifference of Guatemalan society to the significance of this day; the superficial way in which upper-class women claim as their own the achievements and struggles around women's rights; and the ethnic division even in the realm of women's activism. The lat-ter point concerns me the most, especially since, after the signing of the peace accords in 1996, Guatemalan society in general is supposedly com-mitted to a more inclusive and just sociocultural reordering. Precisely the almost imperceptible split in activism between indigenous and nonindige-nous women raised questions for me and ultimately motivated me to con-tribute some ideas to the relatively new and still inadequate discussions in the areas of gender, multiculturalism, and interculturality.

Progress has been made in recognizing the rights of Guatemalan women in certain social spaces (*Foro Nacional de la Mujer* 2002). However, intra- and intergender and interethnic obstacles remain to be overcome, and many distinct perspectives must still be *dis*covered. We live in a socially con-structed world in which women must struggle on social, political, religious, and intellectual levels—both nationally and locally—to achieve lives and bodies free of violence, to find voices, and to gain access to participation and decision making in sociopolitical matters. Beyond this, there is something more tangible, more worrisome because it is easy to forget in the name of "the cause": the internal diversity and inequity within feminist struggles. Although this type of ethnic conflict is not new, it has yet to be dealt with directly by both activists and academics.[3] Manuela Camus has referred the problem as a "desencuentro profundo" (deep disconnect) (2002: 2). In an environment of distrust, nonindigenous women still hold racist ideas and naturalize cultural differences, ignoring historical and everyday aspects of indigenous women's experience. Or, as one of the conclusions of the Inter-national Indigenous Women's Forum openly indicated: "There has not been a full appropriation by the feminist movement of the indigenous perspec-tive, but from our organizations we have retaken some crucial points from the feminist paradigm that are necessary for the advancement of our rights as indigenous women" (FEMI 2005). It is perhaps not the differences and the inequalities themselves, but the absence of any effective management of them at ethnic, social, and cultural levels, that is responsible for the *desencuentro,* the disconnect between the participants in the Guatemalan feminist movement. We yearn for the day when women can celebrate their human rights, both universal and local, in settings offering spaces both for divergent and for parallel causes. In the struggle to attain those rights, we find that indigenous women have rights both as *women* and as *indigenous* women. In the latter case we must be our own advocates without, in the process, rejecting the solidarity and sensibility of progressive nonindigenous people. Here I want to analyze two little-discussed levels of struggle that are at once congruent and incongruent with the lived experiences of indigenous women today. They are the socially and culturally intertwined struggles for the exercise of collective rights and for the enjoyment of individual rights.

In Guatemala, as in other Latin American countries, indigenous people have occupied a subordinate political position within the nation-state. Their persistent historic struggle for survival and recognition received a brief respite with the signing of the peace accords in 1996. One of those accords, the Accord on the Identity and Rights of Indigenous People (AIDPI), focuses on concrete areas of indigenous rights. Other accords including the Accord on the Strengthening of Civil Power and the Function of the Army in a Democratic Society make reference to the need for judicial reform and for the expansion of the scope of the justice system to encompass indigenous law or indigenous customary law.

Other international instruments also support the recognition of indigenous rights and law and the practice of customary rule, including the International Labor Organization's (ILO) Convention 169 on Indigenous and Tribal Peoples. This convention was ratified by the Guatemalan congress on March 5, 1996. But up to now there have been few concrete results from these documents because little has been done by the government to systematize, coordinate, or monitor a legal plan of action for indigenous law. Despite the 1985 Guatemalan constitution, which recognizes indigenous customs and forms of organization, and despite the government's ratification of Convention 169, the administration of justice in Guatemala has seen no significant change for indigenous people, and whatever the state has done has been contradictory and ambiguous (Yrigoyen Fajardo 1999).

Much of this lack of progress derives from a fear of dividing the country into different peoples or nations. Ironically, as a nation-state Guatemala has been constructed as a divided country in which indigenous people are politically excluded; this division correlates with what Carlos Fuentes calls the "legal country" and the "real country" (1985), and this is precisely the impediment to the integration of the nation-state (see Smith 1990).

Peace Commitments and Indigenous Women

The Office for the Defense of Indigenous Women (Defensoría de la Mujer Indígena, DEMI) was created in July 1999, to comply with the Peace Accords agreement to disseminate and promote the Convention on the Elimination of All Forms of Discrimination against Women and other international agreements signed by the Guatemalan government. At first DEMI had an office in Guatemala City and regional offices in Santa Cruz del Quiché and Cobán, Alta Verapaz.[4] Among other things, DEMI was charged with promoting and developing lawsuits or legal actions and planning programs within and among institutions to prevent, defend against, and eradicate all forms of violence and discrimination against indigenous women. It also provides legal and social assistance to indigenous women who are the victims of violence, mistreatment, discrimination, sexual harassment, or other violations of their rights. The office has provided assistance to its clients in the areas of labor problems, land conflicts, and other issues that fall under the purview of civil law or of the penal code, but mostly it has worked to resolve domestic violence cases. This has been especially true in DEMI's regional offices.[5] Using mediation based on local Maya practices to resolve conflicts has resulted in many successful outcomes for the parties involved, particularly those concerning paternity and alimony payments. Indigenous mediation has expedited the legal process and provided culturally sanctioned solutions. And mediation in the local indigenous Mayan language ensures that both parties, but women in particular, understand and can consent to the outcome.

A true recognition of indigenous customary law requires a systematic study and a variety of joint actions involving both the state and indigenous people, but even the practice of indigenous law in and of itself requires critical analysis by the indigenous participants. There are a number of possible conflicts between collective and individual indigenous rights that demand our attention, as does the very juridical validity of the coexistence of indigenous law and the legal code of the state. Much of the indigenous struggle thus far has been focused on the recognition of customary law before state legal institutions, but little attention has been paid to how indigenous law provides justice for indigenous women and men as individuals beyond the collective interests of their communities. Although some researchers have noted that the meaning of customary law with regard to nature and the divinities resides in the collective sense of the people rather than in the individual (see Dary 1997), Edgar Esquit, a Kaqchikel Maya historian, argues that indigenous people are more concerned with the effective functioning of the social order than with the possession of "rights" (qtd. in Dary 1997: 252). Indigenous law consists in large measure of regulations, forms of proper behavior, and rules with differing implications for female and male subjects. It is worth mentioning that indigenous authorities, in particular the *alcaldías comunitarias* (community authorities), as organizations that constitute part of indigenous customary law, are more often made up of men than of women.[6] Often it is said that "customary law is validated by consensus and by practice" (qtd. in Mayén 1995) among indigenous people. But if women's agreement is largely taken for granted, the consensus more resembles the social contract than a true acquiescence of all people in a community.[7] Thus a careful study is needed to focus on possible models to regulate and coordinate state or national law with indigenous law (here seen as the collective law of an indigenous people) and to examine both the achievements and the limitations of indigenous law with regard to individual rights in terms of gender. Unfortunately, some indigenous customary practices overlook the rights of indigenous women, and women themselves sometimes seem resigned to this. This dynamic is demonstrated in the two following cases, which used customary law practices of mediation as an alternative method for conflict resolution.

CASE ONE: SEÑORA CBG

Señora CBG is a woman who lived with a younger man.[8] Their seven-year relationship produced three children. The man later fell in love with a younger woman. To resolve his difficulties, the man brought together the grandparents, parents, and godparents from both sides to comply with the custom of delivering or "returning" the first woman to her family. The man, his wife Señora CBG, and their families went to the DEMI office believing that they needed to publicly legitimate the process. For its part, DEMI, seeing that the man firmly expressed his desire to leave the woman, could only insist, using all available legal pressure, that he pay a food allowance for the three young children. Although the whole process was defined by the man's intentions only, legally the separation was considered voluntary. As an aside, a note in the case states that Señora CBG was "emotionally and economically affected," barely touching on the devastating psychological and economic effects that the decision made by her spouse had on her future. With three children to care for, she had little time, opportunity, or resources to process the trauma, and the possibility of finding a new partner willing to share the burden of raising her children was practically nonexistent.

CASE TWO: SEÑORA JR

Señora JR lived with a man with whom she had a son.[9] When Señora JR's spouse decided to go to work in the United States, she continued to live in the house with her in-laws. Among the jobs the latter assigned to her was that of shepherding the family's livestock. While engaged in that work one day, Señora JR was raped by a man, got pregnant, and gave birth to a daughter. Her in-laws forced her to put the baby up for adoption. When her spouse returned from the United States, he legally recognized his paternity of the son they had together, but then threw his wife out of the house, accusing her of unfaithfulness. In addition, he legally removed the son from Señora JR's custody. Community authorities, and even her own mother, supported the man in his actions. Señora JR's report laconically records the type of aggression she suffered as a "violation of values and human principles." If I described the first case as "devastating" for the indigenous woman affected, this word cannot begin to describe the suffering and profound disgrace provoked in Señora JR by the loss of all that mattered to her as a woman, mother, wife, daughter, and daughter-in-law.

In both cases, the DEMI turned to the use of community customary law, leading to the violation of the women's individual rights. As a discontented DEMI representative put it: "The man has the last word." In the first case, while the man was legally obligated to a minimum childcare payment (but not alimony for Señora CBG, who is illiterate and would have difficulty supporting herself), the "return" of Señora CBG to her family can in no way be understood as an honest or responsible act for not "leaving her in the street." Rather, it should be understood as an abuse of her dignity as a person, treating the situation as if it were a matter of returning an object no longer needed and failing to take into account her own needs and desires. In the second case, Señora JR was indeed left in the street without even the moral support of her own mother. As a married indigenous woman she had no right to make decisions about her conjugal life, her own body, or her children. Even the rape she suffered was defined by her husband as an act of infidelity. The decisions he made were thus considered just by all concerned, making them appear logical and unquestionable even in the victim's eyes. Perhaps due to situations like these Claudia Dary (1997) reports that some Maya women see in certain customary law practices a continuation of oppression. In the two cases described here, the interests, wishes, and supposed honor of the men prevailed over the indigenous women's needs, feelings, voice, and dignity.[10] It is in this sense that the DEMI's *First Report on the Rights and Status of Indigenous Women in Guatemala* (DEMI 2003) should be understood when it states: "Even though the Maya worldview presents the concepts of harmony and complementarity between men and women, there are indigenous women who are victims of some type of violation of their rights in the bosoms of their families."

This concept of gender complementarity in Maya thought is currently being debated by and among women's rights activists in Guatemala, as well as by women researchers in the field of gender studies. The activists' positions range from seeing it as a key principle for demanding legal action and reducing inequities between indigenous men and women to a frank questioning of the idea because it finds a rhetorical grounding in Maya worldview, engendering a selective blindness to prevailing gender inequity that disadvantages women. A number of recent studies document this gender inequity at several levels (see, e.g., Palencia Prado 1999; Chirix García 2003). While indigenous men and women need to combine their efforts to survive in a world that oppresses them socially, culturally, economically, and politically, their efforts often complement each other in unequal proportions for the good of the family, community, or couple, and this inequality often comes at the expense of women's rights.

The Significance of the History of the Ancient Maya in the Struggles of Mayas Today

Although there are now indigenous people who talk about the problem of gender inequality in indigenous families, the mere concept of gender continues to be a problem for some indigenous leaders who view it with disdain and hostility. This adverse position originates from a conceptual and political problematic in the minds of those who think that gender struggle divides men and women, putting at risk the historic struggle that indigenous peoples have maintained against the state and dominant groups. In reality, however, concepts and issues of gender are often inadequately understood because they are linked to ideas, attitudes, and cultural forms pertaining to nonindigenous women.

But notions of gender and gender relations are neither new or unilineal in the history of the ancient Maya peoples. The construction of gender and the assignment of sexual and social roles have undergone many changes from pre-Columbian times in Mesoamerica, when gender was considerably more complex than we could possibly know today. Rosemary Joyce (2000) studied gender and power relations from the formative to the classic and postclassic Maya civilizations, and she notes that there was nothing "natural" about the social roles and status assigned to gender; they were, as they are today, constructs reflecting the power and belief systems of the times. Joyce finds that the power wielded by certain Maya women was not directly related to their gender, but rather derived from other social markers such as their age, caste, or occupation. Noble women in the classic period were recognized more for their status as mothers and only rarely as wives. She finds that the sexuality of men and women was equally represented during the formative period, but that men's sexuality was more emphasized during the classic period, while that of noble women was downplayed. During the classic period, the state demanded tribute in the form of weavings from plebian families, and it was the women who supplied these goods, suggesting women's economic value and political input. In the postclassic era, women dominated household affairs but had little influence or participation in the public arena.

Joyce sees in these Mesoamerican daily practices a logic of complementarity and interdependence rather than a hierarchical relationship between gendered social actors. Yet Susan Kellogg (2005), another scholar who has comparatively studied prehispanic and contemporary gender relations among indigenous people in Latin America, argues that this Maya complementarity in the classic period, although important, also regarded women's roles as secondary, active, and circumscribed at the same time. The notion of complementarity in the past is of much significance in the present as it has been frequently raised by indigenous women, whether or not linked to gender questions. If this principle suggests historical equity in the social relations of men and women, in current cultural practice complementarity is unequally weighted against women.

The history and legacy of the ancient Maya have much relevance in the political and cultural struggles of contemporary Mayas. Yet it is possible that we have greater fear of cultural transformations than our foremothers and forefathers due to historical trauma suffered intermittently. Culture constituted a powerful vehicle for change and dynamism among the ancient Maya, and had varied forms and expressions. In this sense, Joyce notes that artistic representations (e.g., illustrations) of dress and background constitute sites of discourse about identities and convey information about social processes including resistance and the transformation of ideologies of gender. Along the same lines, Kellogg notes that clothing rather than sexually differentiated bodies were the vehicle of gender representation for the classic Maya.

DEMI's *First Report on the Rights and Status of Indigenous Women in Guatemala* contains the ten "Specific Rights of Indigenous Women" ("Derechos Específicos de las Mujeres Indígenas"). These articles grew out of workshops and consultations with indigenous women's groups and organizations in different areas of the country. Of interest here, particularly with regard to the cases described earlier, is number 5, the right to modify customs and traditions that affect the dignity of indigenous women, which states:[11] "Considering that cultures are not static, but that they are constantly changing, there exist, nevertheless, situations that have endured, such as discrimination from birth for being a woman. These practices or customs which impair the development of women exist in all areas—the family, politics, education, and community" (DEMI 2003: 12). In light of this specific right, indigenous women today are clearly addressing those community leaders and authorities who dismiss the principle of the complementary equilibrium of gender rights inherited from the ancestral Maya worldview.[12] If a complementary equilibrium had been pursued, both the husband and the community authorities would not have objectified Señora CBG, but would have respected her voice and her dignity. They would not have taken away Señora JR's individual rights, especially her maternal rights. Injustice should not seek refuge in tradition. Indigenous women, in their demands for specific rights, say: "We have thought over the things we need to better our living conditions, and we are in a position to modify our points of view and those of others" (DEMI 2003: 12). Ultimately, indigenous women are asking that the universal right to equality with dignity and rights, in full concordance with the principles of the Maya worldview, be observed.

Others have discussed the importance of recognizing customary law in the application of justice in a country that is multilingual, multicultural, and multiethnic (e.g., Alarcón Osorio n.d.). Often the demand is that the legal recognition of customary law be granted without creating ambiguity or contradiction with state law, and that customary law be conceived as a system of law and not just of local habit (Yrigoyen Fajardo 1999). The current validity of indigenous law in indigenous communities has been demonstrated.[13] In the absence of government services in rural areas, indigenous law has functioned as the only alternative form of justice in many communities. Sometimes, even though a governmental judicial system exists in a community, it remains linguistically and culturally foreign to indigenous people, and women in particular prefer not to use it given their experience of mistreatment and racist discrimination at the hands of public servants who tend to be nonindigenous (DEMI 2003). In general, indigenous law offers alternatives to the bureaucratic and costly state judicial system. Further, the state can share in these advantages, not by freeing itself from legal responsibilities, but rather by partaking of a more efficient and democratic parallel system of justice.

Occasionally Maya cultural values in general have been praised (see Salazar Tetzaguic and Telón Sajcabún 1998), as has the nobility of customary law. Attributed to indigenous law are a series of principles and procedures developed that stress methodological flexibility, preventative intervention, and community participation throughout the process of a case.[14] Yet despite such benefits, it is necessary to examine the system critically so that the ideals of equity in the Maya worldview and in Maya communal justice become beneficial to *both* women and men. Even though Maya indigenous law contains elements of Mayan spirituality, consciousness, and ethics, it is not static but has changed and continues to change in accordance with historical circumstances and the sociocultural needs of the people (Yrigoyen Fajardo 1999).

Just as the solutions to national problems should not exclude certain parts of a society, the collective community practices of indigenous law should not exclude the individual rights of indigenous women. Only then will we be sure that our struggle against the discrimination and exclusion committed by state institutions does not conceal an element of subaltern oppression.

Indigenous law is not backward, and it does not exist in isolation. On the one hand, indigenous law is, can, and ought to be continually enriched, both politically and culturally. As Raquel Yrigoyen Fajardo (1999) states, it is possible to have multiple layers of justice in which the global and the local stand not in irreconcilable opposition, but through which intercultural oversight and the juridical pluralism of nations is permitted. The universal and intercultural aspects of the exercise of human rights do not automatically suppress the virtues and cultural identities of indigenous peoples. Thus, in an intercultural exercise, these cultures can open themselves to elements of justice that are shared without losing the cultural history of their origins. Although they are not present in current practice, indigenous peoples possess ancestral principles of potentially greater justice between men and women, which is why indigenous women's struggle for their rights does not have to succumb to universal cultural patterns. If we have come to understand that human rights are a creation of the Western world bound to a liberal democratic political model (Heinz Pohl n.d.), we must also see that non-Western peoples have values and cultural models that can contribute to Western cultures.

Diversity and Shared Struggles

While certain political and cultural values are identified with specific (and distinct) peoples, all of them have the potential to create intercultural spaces that are of mutual benefit. But no true intercultural dialogue can emerge if the cultural values or interests of one culture are imposed on another as an absolute model. In multicultural contexts, intercultural practice is as important as the safeguarding of the diversity of the individual projects it encompasses. In her critical linkage of modern theories of politics, culture, and feminism, Wendy Brown (1995) offers us insights on those values and political identities that appear liberating but that in reality harm us. In deconstructing basic notions of subjectivity, liberty, and equality, Brown leads us to examine them in their Western, liberal, and democratic political context, all of which have little to do with pluralistic justice. Brown questions subjectivity and the immersed "I" as a specific creation of modernity and liberalism. Women's experiences, she says, are constructs, historically and culturally varied, and infinitely interpreted. She suggests that rather than one standard policy of what is "good" for women, we need a political conversation about a complex and diverse "us," as well as more spaces for a cacophony of voices and opinions.

Our struggles for greater social justice for all demand that we not lose sight of the fact that these struggles are changing and complex, and that this change and complexity interpolates us sociopolitically. What is difficult about considering diversity is that it encompasses various culturally diverse axes that locate the person and the collective. At times an indigenous woman's cause locates her differently than her male counterparts or than nonindigenous women, but at times she is located close to nonindigenous women, while at others again, she is close to indigenous men. In other words, while the complex "I" of indigenous women struggling for our rights carries differential angles to the cultural values of nonindigenous women,[15] a complex "us" is relevant in collective efforts such as in feminist struggles or in the struggles of indigenous peoples.

Final Reflections

Through a brief examination of indigenous law I have tried to outline some aspects of gender inequality in indigenous practice and to note problematic elements in the feminist activism of indigenous and nonindigenous women by considering what an exercise of multi- or pluriculturality would mean. In both instances, intra- and intercultural disconnects are generated that merit intra- and intercultural dialogues so that we do not miss the opportunity to create a better path for our justice struggles.

In this debate, nothing will have great meaning unless we gain the attention of and provoke a cultural rethinking from the principal actors: indigenous women, indigenous men, and nonindigenous activists working for greater justice. We each have more to see and do. The history of the ancient Mayas has demonstrated that they had the ability to create and recreate their values and cultural forms. They experienced changes in gender roles and power while preserving a base of interdependence and nonhierarchy between men and women. In a similar way, the customary law of contemporary Mayas has been maintained dynamically, demonstrating that it is in a process of constant development and can be applied to aspects of local and of global justice. Indigenous peoples have maintained their culture dynamically, which is why contemporary Maya men and women have no reason to fear the struggle for women's rights. It is possible we are trying to maintain a more dogmatic cosmovision and a more static culture than our ancestors. It is not enough to defend culture based on difference if doing so does not offer a greater enjoyment of equality for both men and women.

If women's struggles are heterogeneous, a parallelism of causes will not stop their advancement. The needs and interests of indigenous women, or their struggles, do not have to be identical to those of nonindigenous women. It is these struggles and interests in conjunction at points of political convergence and a genuine cultural understanding between diverse women that will make advancements in social movements possible. A divided activism may be a flashing light pointing to an internal problem that requires attention. The polyphonic and heterogeneous nature of the movements means that one cannot assume the course of things or the role of each actor in the process. A review of what we have been able to do up until now may provide good lessons for moving ahead: Why, then, while indigenous women continue to problematize these issues, do indigenous men not problematize everyday authority, and women and men of diverse self-identifications not consider reproblematizing our common causes?

Notes

I have chosen to use Indigenous Law and not Customary Law because I agree with Yrigoyen Fajardo (1999) who states that the term *consuetudinario* (customary) connotes an implicit meaning of everlasting immutability, and because customary law can be applied and put into practice by non-indigenous people. For example, here is customary law in the Civil Code in which "custom," determines that daughters take the surname of the father first, followed by that of the mother.

1. I use *native* in the sense of self-definition and not as a colonial imposition as discussed by Trinh 1989. Generally when using *intellectual* I utilize the exclusive plural, but I utilize the inclusive plural when I know that I share specific contexts with indigenous women more generally.

2. Although "mestizo" is not an official ethnic identification in Guatemala (Adams and Bastos 2003: 398), a number of Guatemalan men and women with differing motivations and ideologies are now beginning to identify themselves as such both in and outside the capital city (see Hale 2003, 2005).

3. Other indigenous women have also pointed out the lack of cultural sensitivity in Mexico, regarding it as "the cultural breech between mestizo women and indigenous women" (qtd. in Hernández Castillo 2002a).

4. Recently the DEMI has opened up several more regional offices.

5. The mistreatment and abuse of indigenous women by their husbands has recently

been brought to public attention by DEMI's Huehuetenango office. See "Abogan por la mujer," *Prensa Libre,* July 17, 2006.

6. Until 2004 the Alcaldía Indígena de Sololá was presided over by a woman, and this was a first in the country. Recently, in the *departamento* of Quiché, of a total of seventy-two *alcaldes comunitarios,* three were indigenous women. "Asumen setenta y dos alcaldes auxiliares; tres mujeres," *Prensa Libre,* January 9, 2006.

7. See the critical reconstruction of social contract theories from Jean-Jacques Rousseau (2003) to Carol Pateman (1989) by Wendy Brown (1995). According to these theories of the social contract, consent ostensibly exists from civil society, workers, and women, with regard to the actions of the state, bosses, and men. Ostensible consent contributes to the legitimization of unequal relations of power and subordination.

8. The case is taken from Boleta Socioeconómica, case no. 52, September 7, 2001, Quiché region.

9. The case is taken from Boleta Socioeconómica, case no. 68, November 13, 2001, Quiché region.

10. It is important to indicate that this violation of rights is not in any way exclusive to customary law. It was 2001 before the penal code was changed so that both men and women could be charged with adultery. Prior to that date, only women could commit adultery. National law places predominance on men's honor, and the Guatemalan congress has been unwilling to prepare or debate legislation on sexual harassment.

11. In a similar manner, Mexican indigenous women have seen the need to rethink community customs, saying: "The customs we have should not harm anybody" (Hernández Castillo 2002b).

12. In opposition to the right to modify customs and traditions, there stands the "Specific Right to Recover Customs and Traditions That Strengthen Our Identity." This right is not applicable only to indigenous women, of course, and the principle of complementary equilibrium also does not apply exclusively to gender, but rather to many aspects of life, the most important of which is the environment. The consideration of this right and its relationship to the environment is not under discussion here.

13. This may only be a passing phenomenon, but considerable confusion has arisen when various lynchings were erroneously associated with communal indigenous law.

14. See, for example, the Saqb'ichil-Copmagua project "Investigaciones en derecho consuetudinario y poder local" (Saqb'ichil-Copmagua 2000; or Defensoría Maya 1999).

15. It has even been suggested that the notions of liberty held by Western women differ morally, culturally, and politically from the bourgeois male version of the same notion.

Human Rights, Land Conflict, and Memory of the
Violence in the Ixil Country of Northern Quiché

Some years ago, when the idea of peace accords seemed like an impossible dream, I was the object of undeserved respect for doing fieldwork where soldiers and civil patrollers still occasionally clashed with guerrillas. The Ixil country of northern Quiché Department was presumed sufficiently dangerous that the U.S. Peace Corps forbade its volunteers from visiting. Ironically, Peace Corps volunteers encountered far more danger around their headquarters in Guatemala City—from common crime. When I brought my family to Ixil country in 1988, I presumed that even though the army-guerrilla stalemate promised to drag into the next century, violence against civilians was dwindling. True, the army was still attacking refugees who refused to come down from the mountains. Anyone who defied the army in the area under its control was subject to swift intimidation or worse. But many Ixils were quick to assure visitors that the situation was now *tranquilo* compared with the living hell of 1980–82.

The same army that had wreaked havoc six years before felt obliged to honor certain guarantees to a population disinterested in further hostilities. This is why, long before the formal declaration of peace at the end of 1996, a counterinsurgency zone could feel safer than a crime-ridden capital. This also helps explain why, in the Ixil area, the most widely felt result of the peace process was an outbreak of highway robbery. Mass holdups are common in Guatemala, but they were unknown in northern Quiché until a few months before the peace signing, when masked highwaymen, gangs armed with anything from cheap pistols to AK-47s, began stopping buses and robbing passengers. With the army confined to its bases, its civil patrols disbanding, and the guerrillas demobilizing, the former monopolizers of armed force had stepped aside. The criminally inclined knew there was no one to stop them. And so the most widespread source of anxiety was not whether the two sides would comply with the peace agreement: it was women's fear of being raped by bandits.

This essay will address some of the paradoxes of demilitarization, democratization, and our customary way of talking about these issues in terms of human rights. Because the peace process is usually analyzed on the national level, I will be very local in my focus, concentrating on the three *municipios* in northern Quiché Department known as Ixil country. As is customary on these occasions, I will dwell on problems rather than accomplishments, even though much has been accomplished. By taking a detailed look at the peace process in one area, I will suggest how a popular way of interpreting Guatemala can make it harder to perceive certain issues. If I keep returning to limitations of the human rights perspective, this is not to denigrate it. Guatemala is one of a number of countries in which human rights pressure has led to significant changes in official behavior, if not in all the behavior engaged in by officials during unofficial moments. Yet if we think of human rights as a beacon that spotlights certain issues, the very intensity of the beam can leave other issues in shadow. So how can the human rights perspective put us in the dark?

Human rights is the latest of a series of master narratives or discourses—such as Christianity, development, and revolution—that have descended on Latin America with mixed results. As a master narrative—one that comes to dominate perceptions and subordinate or exclude other possible story lines—human rights is supposed to reflect the broadest interests of an entire country, just like Christianity, development, and revolution did. Such assumptions should always be suspect. For example, it is now proverbial that especially in its final decade, the army-guerrilla conflict was not very meaningful to most Guatemalans. As the civil war dwindled into a feud between two institutions, other conflicts rose to the surface. It would not be surprising if a human rights discourse that came into existence to combat state terror, and that was still required to fight impunity, was not as helpful in elucidating other issues coming to our attention.

By the usual definition, only an agent of the state can violate human rights. Protecting human rights therefore means constraining state power, in the sense of putting up moral, social, and judicial barriers against its improper deployment. But what if many Guatemalans do not perceive state power as the most serious threat they face? What about the many Guatemalans who apparently feel more threatened by criminals? It is easy to find situations in which Guatemalans are more concerned about their need for security than about what they perceive as the more abstract—or even foreign—concept of human rights.

Elsewhere in this collection, Stener Ekern, Julián López García, and Pedro Pitarch analyze the gap between how Mayas tend to understand rights and how lawyers and internationalists do. Mayas tend to condition rights on the fulfillment of obligations that are anything but equal for different categories of people. That can quickly produce harsh reactions to persons—more often than not, fellow *indígenas*—who they perceive as violators of community and order. The hundreds of mob lynchings of suspected criminals illustrate the problem. The demand for security can also translate into support for right-wing politicians—for example, many Mayas voted for Efrain Ríos Montt, the former army dictator whose Guatemalan Republican Front (FRG) won the 1999 election. A man responsible for gross violations of human rights is, even to some of the peasants who suffered from his army's offensives, a defender of law and order.[1]

Mayan peasants not only want a state strong enough to repress common criminals. They also want a state strong enough to deal with the land conflicts they face, which are often with each other. The peasant delegations taking trip after trip to Guatemala City to make the rounds of government offices are not just humbling themselves before state power. They also want the state to intervene in local disputes, effectively and on their own side, which often means intervening against other peasants. To illustrate the point, I will look at land conflicts between peasants, not because this is the most important issue facing the peace process, but because it is an issue that does not fit comfortably with human rights perspectives. Such has become increasingly evident in the Ixil country of northern Quiché Department, as human rights become the rationale for foreign activists to intervene in local disputes. Peasant rivalry over land makes it very unlikely that truth commissions will be able to recover and disseminate a single historical memory of the violence, that is, one with which most peasants agree.

International Aid and Reconstruction

The valleys and mountains of the *municipios* of Nebaj, Cotzal, and Chajul are populated by Ixil Mayas, most of whom combine subsistence maize farming with a trade or seasonal wage labor. There are also some K'iche' Mayas, some Ladinos, and a stream of foreign aid volunteers. In the late 1970s and early 1980s, this rather poor, conservative district hosted the guerrilla revival of the period. The three *municipios* became known as the Ixil Triangle, a stronghold of the Guerrilla Army of the Poor (EGP). Thousands of noncombatants were killed by the army. Thousands more died of starvation and illness as they hid from army offensives. Hundreds more were killed by the EGP to keep its wavering followers in line. In the process of regaining the upper hand, the army burned down all the villages outside the town centers, then put refugees into closely watched model villages and forced all the men under its control to join antiguerrilla civil patrols. By the late 1980s the army was guarding a surviving population of around seventy thousand, with another five or six thousand in the EGP-administered Communities of Population in Resistance, the CPRs of the Sierra, perched on the northeastern rim of Ixil country just before it drops to the Ixcán lowlands.

Since publishing *Between Two Armies in the Ixil Towns of Guatemala* in 1993, I have been involved in a debate over whether the insurgency grew out of the needs of the Ixils themselves or was imposed on them by the political-military decisions of the two sides. Many observers have accepted the guerrilla movement's explanation of itself as a broadly based response to worsening oppression that left Mayan peasants no choice but to take up arms. My position, based on interviews with survivors, is that armed struggle was not an inevitable outgrowth of Ixil experience with local exploiters and the state. Instead, I argue, the mere arrival of guerrilla organizers brought down ferocious reprisals from the security forces, which then radicalized a significant number of Ixils into joining the rebels.[2]

Even if the insurgency's local roots were deeper it is safe to say that after the early 1980s, most Ixils decided that this was not their war, in the sense that they had little to gain and everything to lose. The result was a local vocation for peace making that began years before the army and the guerrillas agreed to negotiate. In the EGP-administered CPRs, as well as in army-controlled settlements, Ixils started their own peace process by turning their backs on both sides. Thousands of men forced to serve in the army's civil patrols figured out how to subvert them from within through tactics of passive resistance. The guerrillas had their own problems with noncompliance and defection in the CPRs. Through lack of enthusiasm for their duties, whether conceived by the Guatemalan army through its civil patrols or by the EGP through its parallel vision of organized, fighting villages, Ixils communicated to both sides that this should be a conflict between military forces, not a fratricide. Their disengagement from the guerrillas and from the army turned the war into a ritual affair for each side to keep up its pretension to represent the national interest.

Let me now sketch what has been accomplished in terms of restoring the economy and the civil government. Of the problems facing Ixil country, a lack of financial support is not one. Ixils were an early target for international donations, not just because they had suffered heavily but also because the army decided to make them a showcase for its pacification programs. The EGP's local strength contributed to the army's decision, as did a fascination with the Ixils as a bastion of Mayan culture. Judging by the number of books, magazines, and documentaries that sported their image, Ixil women in their spectacular red skirts were the cover girls for a war not of their making. Before the violence, the nongovernmental sector consisted chiefly of the Catholic Church. Now there are also some twenty evangelical denominations, plus major programs by the United Nations (UN), the European Union (EU), the U.S. Agency for International Development, and an attending swarm of nongovernmental organizations.

In the towns, every block seems to boast a different *institución* dedicated to the common good. One *proyecto* follows another with the predictability of skyrockets going off at a fiesta. As to be expected from an aid bonanza, the steady succession of projects has boosted the most entrepreneurial Ixils, an upwardly mobile class of businesspeople, schoolteachers, and other professionals. Two- and three-story houses are going up on all sides, lines of pickup trucks bounce through the streets, and hundreds of youth have entered secondary school. The old index of poverty, seasonal migration to the coast, is in decline, but it is being replaced by costlier and riskier odysseys to the United States. The commercial ventures with which Ixils are trying to replace plantation labor, such as producing artisan goods for tourists, have a desperate air. The majority of Ixils are still trapped in below-subsistence maize agriculture, from which they perceive the only deliverance to be undocumented wage labor far to the north.

Still, certain favorable developments should outlast the aid bubble. First, a fiscal reform in the national constitution sends 10 percent of the national budget to municipal governments, which makes them less dependent on the ruling party for public works. Second, Ladino finca owners have been selling their holdings, which usually end up being parceled out to Ixil farmers. Third, a broader slice of the peasant population is producing coffee, which is the area's most reliable cash crop. Peasants are also restoring livestock lost in the war and experimenting with new crops and techniques.

Demilitarization and Insecurity

Given the amount of killing in Ixil country, it would be reasonable to expect that its inhabitants were still squirming under the military boot, at least until they were liberated by human rights activists and the 1996 peace agreement. What actually happened is more complicated. A decade before the official arrival of peace, the army was withdrawing from the management of the town halls because Ixil disillusion with the guerrillas was so evident. Out in the villages, though men were pressured to stay in the civil patrols until the peace agreement, elders quietly reasserted their authority. Since Guatemala's return to civilian government in 1985, elections in the three Ixil towns have been technically fair, control of town halls has shifted regularly from party to party, and opponents are not afraid to hold rallies that can turn into sieges of the municipal building. On such occasions, the local interpretation of democracy suddenly turns Athenian, with hundreds and even thousands of people assembling in front of the town hall to demand explanations from the balcony.

To give credit where credit is seldom given, I know of at least two occasions in which the army has rescued the losing side in plaza confrontations. In 1989, the garrison in Cotzal saved striking schoolteachers from angry civil patrollers (i.e., parents) summoned by the town's mayor. In 1996, the army stopped a mob from battering down the door of the Nebaj town hall to seize a youth accused of shooting a child. Since then, riot squads from the national police have come to Chajul more than once to protect the town's mayor from crowds accusing him of giving away their land to the new Visis-Cabá Biosphere Reserve. Elsewhere in Guatemala, the recent wave of lynchings has been attributed to manipulation by the army or behavior learned during the violence. But the lynch mob or *turba* is nothing new in Guatemalan social history, even if this particular manifestation of it is. The possibility of facing mobs was on the mind of Ladinos settling in Mayan areas in the nineteenth century. Perhaps mobs became more rare as the state consolidated authority. But it is also possible that foreign observers have downplayed the phenomenon, which is hardly unique to the Mayas, because it is not compatible with our idealization of Mayan culture.

Because the army-guerrilla conflict is increasingly explained in ethnic terms, as an inevitable consequence of the ethnic divide in Guatemalan society, I should mention what I have called "ethnic detente" in Ixil country —a surprising level of solidarity between *indígenas* and Ladinos that the war strengthened rather than weakened. Other areas could be different but, in Ixil country, members of both groups tend to avoid explaining current conflicts in ethnic terms; are often willing to criticize members of their own ethnic group for misbehavior toward members of the other; and frequently vote for members of the other ethnic group. The guerrillas can take some of the credit for indigenous/Ladino solidarity because they killed or chased away the most abusive Ladinos. The army can take even more of the credit because it made nearly everyone despise it. Another sign of solidarity is that despite many horrible memories and unresolved conflicts, Ixils and their neighbors have not been very interested in pursuing blood vendettas. There are probably more homicides than before the war, often between youth in rival gangs. But there are not nearly as many homicides as there could be in a population that dropped as much as 15 percent due to massacres and hunger. In keeping with their pioneer role in peacemaking, Ixils and their Ladino neighbors have developed a broad consensus against more political killing.

At the time of the peace accords, Ixils still dreaded the G-2, the army intelligence and death squad wing that took hundreds of lives in the early 1980s. Even in Nebaj, the capital of political confidence in the Ixil area, I heard stories about the G-2 delegating local youth to watch neighbors and warn them against joining the left's organizations. The army also developed its own spin on human rights for villagers tempted to drop out of the civil patrols. Just before the UN established a branch of its MINUGUA (United Nations Verification Mission in Guatemala) observer mission in Nebaj, the army sent civic action teams into the villages with the message: "You know, you're not really obliged to talk to MINUGUA. They're here for a matter of months, but we are here to stay." Threats such as these are why so many Ixils were grateful for the arrival of human rights monitoring networks. The first to open in Ixil country was the government's Procurator for Human Rights (PDH), followed by the Interdiocesene Project for the Recuperation of Historical Memory (REMHI), and then MINUGUA.

Only after the procurator's arrival in 1992 did the left's popular organizations surface in the towns and villages under army control. Having kept a low profile, the few Ixils belonging to these organizations were now reinforced by organizers sent out from the capital and by delegates sent in from the guerrilla-controlled CPRS. Even under the protection of human rights monitors, there was a notable contrast between the cautious approach of Ixils who had spent a decade under army control and the confrontationalism of visitors from the CPRS and the urban left. For example, when visiting cadres from the National Committee of Widows of Guatemala (CONAVIGUA) built up a roster of Nebaj women by distributing fertilizer and then led them into an antiarmy demonstration organized by the CPRS, many of the Nebaj widows quit.

For most Ixils under army control, responsible behavior did not include chanting slogans such as "army assassins, get out of here!" For Ixils who had experienced fifteen years of military occupation, that sounded like the same game that the EGP encouraged them to play in the late 1970s—with disastrous results. What army-occupied Ixils found more appealing was to invoke the national constitution in a diplomatic manner. First individual men, then entire communities, informed the human rights procurator that they wanted to drop out of the army's civil patrols. He would arrange a meeting with army officers who, because of all the national and international pressures being brought to bear, were obliged to acknowledge the constitutional right to resign.

Under the 1996 peace agreement, the army closed all but three or four of its bases in Ixil country and suddenly dropped out of sight, to the point that it was conspicuously absent from local peace ceremonies. As for the guerrillas, their demobilization in March 1997 was greeted with quiet awe rather than celebration. When the EGP commander Ricardo Ramírez visited his fighters at their final encampment in Ixil country, they had tough questions for him. Some of them were about immediate issues such as financial compensation. Others were much broader, such as "Why did we spend so many years in the mountains for so few concessions at the end?"

When I reached Nebaj six months after the peace agreement, in June 1997, the most widespread cause of anxiety was the aforementioned outbreak of highway robbery. However, Ixils were also worried about a new armed group that, unlike the gangs of bandits, did not rob travelers. Instead, it regaled them with political slogans. Dressed in olive green, its members were more numerous and better armed than the highwaymen, and they identified themselves as the Guerrilla Forces '97. They accused the mayor of Chajul of stealing land and said they were going to kill him.

The Land Issue

Die-hards who refuse to lay down their weapons are an inevitable complication in any peace process. But before getting back to the Guerrilla Forces '97, if indeed they were that, we should look at the most difficult issue facing the peace process in Ixil country, which has to do with land, although not quite as this tends to be understood by outsiders. When scholars and activists present Guatemala to an international audience, we usually stress the inequality of land tenure, the famous contrast between latifundia and minifundia, wealthy plantation owners and land-starved peasants. This is indeed a structural contradiction in Guatemalan society, and there is no shortage of confrontations between peasants and finca owners. Even in Ixil country, whose agricultural potential is so limited that most of it rests in smallholdings, the sizeable Finca San Francisco and Finca La Perla have long histories of conflict with peasants. Neighboring smallholders would benefit from parceling out the two estates. But even if this becomes possible, it will do little to alleviate land scarcity. One reason is that there is not enough finca land to divide among a rapidly growing population. Another is that the fincas are already occupied by resident laborers who, because they have worked the land for several generations, regard it as their own.

Let me now present three land disputes in the *municipio* of Chajul. All areas in question are located in the mountain valleys that descend toward the Ixcán and are warm enough to grow coffee, making them unusually attractive to both smallholders and *finqueros*.

FINCA LA PERLA VERSUS THE VILLAGES OF SOTZIL AND ILOM

The first conflict is over the Finca La Perla. It was the EGP's execution of La Perla's owner, Luis Arenas, in 1975 that set off the first wave of army repression in northern Quiché. From that point onward, political killing heightened tension between two classes of peasants in and around the plantation. One consists of Ixils in nearby villages that, in the early 1900s, were cheated out of the land on which La Perla sits. Here, especially in the land-starved villages of Sotzil and Ilom, the death of Arenas may well have been as applauded as the EGP claimed. Although many Sotzil and Ilom villagers used to work for La Perla part-time and to rent land from it, they are not to be confused with a second class of peasants—the finca's full-time *colonos*, or workers who live on the estate. For this mixed population of Ixils, Kanjobals, and Ladinos, the assassination of their *patrón* meant the end of a reliable wage. Seven years after the guerrillas killed Arenas, the La Perla *colonos* who the EGP thought it was liberating not only joined the army's civil patrol; they also helped the army commit a chain of massacres with a cumulative toll of at least three hundred dead.

Since then, through many vicissitudes, La Perla's resident workers have clung to the finca for survival. They expect to be the beneficiaries if international donors ever pay the exorbitant price demanded by the Arenas family. Meanwhile, the surrounding Ixil villages still regard the land as their own. In the case of Sotzil, it took advantage of demilitarization to join the National Indigenous and Campesino Coalition (CONIC). In retaliation, the finca stopped renting land to the villagers. On November 23, 1996, Sotzil chose the day the La Perla civil patrol was demobilizing to reclaim its ancestral lands. No sooner had the La Perla civil patrollers handed over their weapons than word arrived that the Sotzils were coming through the fence. The civil patrollers grabbed back their weapons and went out to defend the finca's boundary, killing one claimant and wounding several others.

In theory La Perla is a property that could be divided. But because peasants continue to have large families, they are reluctant to give up any claim, however much conflict it promises. There is a demographic issue here, which I wish we could subsume under the issue of political economy, as in "have a land reform, and with more equality in the distribution of resources, peasants will have fewer children." Unfortunately, the implications cannot be wished away like that. As the population continues to grow, what now seems the most obvious agrarian issue, the existence of estates, will become only a manifestation of the underlying scarcity of land.

The peasants at odds with each other around La Perla raise another uncomfortable issue. To mobilize international opinion, the Guatemalan left and its supporters have not only dwelt on the dramatic contrast between the plantation sector and peasant smallholders. They also want us to believe that the state is a central actor in land disputes. Actually, this is a necessary condition for fitting land conflicts into a human rights framework, since a human rights violation is, by definition, an act of commission or omission by an agent of the state. But what if the state is only an occasional enforcer (as when it intervened against the assassins of Enrique Arenas, a national political figure) and usually is only an ineffective mediator? Magnifying the state's role, as Richard Wilson (1997b) has pointed out, "verticalizes" conflicts between local actors into national and even international ones. This helps foreign groups justify intervention, but it also diverts attention from the local dimension.

THE K'ICHE' OF LOS CIMIENTOS VERSUS THE IXILS OF CHAJUL AND COTZAL

To illustrate how verticalizing a conflict obscures the local forces in contention, let us turn to a second dispute in the lower, coffee-growing valleys of Chajul, this one at a place called Los Cimientos. In the early 1990s, K'iche' Mayas from Los Cimientos told human rights organizations that they had been displaced by the war and that the army was preventing them from returning to their land. It was true that they had been displaced by the war. But it was not the army that was preventing them from going home. Blocking the way were the Ixils of Chajul, with whom the K'iche' have been feuding over Los Cimientos since the early 1900s. According to the Ixils, the K'iche' used national land-titling legislation to seize municipal land without their permission, just like plantation owners did. But the Ixil version of events, based on an indigenous ideology of ownership, was slow in reaching the international human rights community. This is why international volunteers, under the impression that they were protecting the K'iche' from the army, helped the K'iche' seize land being cultivated by Ixils.

Legal counsel for the K'iche'—Frank LaRue's Center for Legal Action and Human Rights (CALDH)—argued the case all the way to the Interamerican Court of Human Rights. The lawsuit was against the Guatemalan government, for failing to enforce the land rights of the K'iche' and compensate their wartime losses. Yet the state was not a principal actor at Los Cimientos in the way that the human rights perspective encouraged activists to assume. As soon as the case attracted international attention, the army stepped aside, so that foreign accompaniers could face their actual antagonists—Ixils from Chajul and Cotzal. However many court decisions the K'iche' won—because their title was indeed valid under national law—back at Los Cimientos they were still surrounded by hostile Ixils. The Ixil siege could be lifted only by national police enforcing an eviction order—a tactic the K'iche' tried before the war without success. This was the implication of using human rights activism to enforce a land title against indigenous peasants. In 2001, after seven years during which the two groups tore out each other's crops and every conceivable national and international agency tried to negotiate a compromise, Ixils armed with guns and machetes expelled the K'iche'. They spent more than a year as refugees before accepting a U.S. Agency for International Development (USAID)–financed finca on the Pacific Coast.

THE CPRS OF THE SIERRA VERSUS THE IXILS OF CHAJUL

For another example of how human rights discourse can be used to explain away peasant competition over land, let us return to the CPRs of the Sierra—the last of the displaced peasants who stayed with the guerrillas in the mountains rather than surrendering to the army. Their final refuge was in the forest clearings of northern Chajul, opened up by Ixils from Chajul before the war. So as refugees often must, the CPRs squatted on other people's land. Until 1991 they were under attack by the army, which viewed them as guerrillas. Then an army helicopter pilot attacked a CPR settlement while the UN representative Christian Tomuschat was watching. Human rights pressure forced the army to end its offensives, acknowledge the CPRs as noncombatants, and relax its blockade against them.

Because CPR members could now venture out to trade, the Ixils of Chajul felt that they should be able to travel in the reverse direction and reclaim their land. This the CPRs would not allow. Thanks to the international support they were getting, including a full-time complement of international accompaniers to discourage the army from resuming its attacks, the CPRs were emboldened to claim the land as their own. As had the K'iche' of Los Cimientos, the CPRs and their foreign supporters tried to blame the hostility of the Chajules on the Chajul civil patrol. The army connections could be used to turn the dispute into a human rights issue, yet the Chajules were defending land that was their own by national law as well as by local custom (for more details on this and the Los Cimientos dispute, see Stoll 1995, 1997).

After lengthy negotiations, punctuated by threats and brawls, the Quiché bishop Julio Cabrera persuaded the CPRs to accept a timetable for leaving.

In 1998 the majority of CPR households either returned to their home *municipios* or moved elsewhere collectively. One relocation to the nearby Zona Reina of Uspantán went well, but another to the Pacific Coast led to much hardship. The threats did not end immediately. Not long after the last EGP combatants left the local demobilization camp and returned to civilian life, the mayor of Chajul was ambushed by the aforementioned Guerrilla Forces '97. Judging from communiqués found at the scene, this heretofore unknown group was upset with the mayor because of his success in pressuring CPR leaders into giving up their land claim.

I should now emphasize what some readers do not need to be told—that the Guerrilla Forces '97 could be a charade to frighten Ixils away from the left. Assassinating even a hostile Ixil mayor has long been out of character for the EGP. A new insurgency would not serve the interests of a post-guerrilla movement trying to make its way in electoral politics, nor those of the CPR leadership. But staging a guerrilla resurgence might suit army officers who wished to remilitarize northern Quiché. Whether the Guerrilla Forces '97 consisted of army destabilization specialists, or CPR dissidents rebelling against the EGP's political agenda, or conceivably both, the tensions it is preying on are real. Nor are they just a product of the war or of the unjust distribution of land. Even total demolition of the local finca sector might not do much to alleviate peasant competition for land.

The kinds of land disputes described above—between finca dependents and surrounding villagers, and between successive cohorts of displaced peasants—have also cropped up elsewhere. In the early 1990s, as internationally sponsored refugees returned from Mexico and collided with civil patrollers, human rights activists blamed the army. Presumably it was the army, or renegade civil patrol leaders, who were sowing strife among peasants. But the conflicts run deeper than that, as demonstrated when bitter differences over land, dating to before the violence, welled up within the left's popular organizations in the Ixcán region and tore them apart. "One of the primary dynamics," a human rights observer noted of the land clashes in the Ixcán popular movement, "is the presence of two or more memories of what happened in the 1980s to those who stayed, those who returned, and those who stayed in Mexico. This mixed with historic feuds between families and the highly politicized atmosphere in the Ixcán, has made this conflict very complex and potentially explosive" (National Coordinating Office on Refugees and Displaced of Guatemala 1995).[3]

Land Conflict and Historical Memory

Let us now step back from land feuds to look at the implications for how peasants remember the violence and how the various truth commissions hope to uncover, then propagate, a socially useful historical memory. Once the commissions have collected, compared, and condensed the many memories of the violence, the resulting truth is supposed to identify perpetrators, end the army's de facto immunity from judicial accountability, and consolidate democratic institutions. If so, what complexities will this agenda face in the realm of peasant testimony?

The basic dichotomy in a human rights interpretation, between the state as violator and citizens as victims, is easy to find in decades of state terror in Guatemala. Amply documented by the Guatemalan opposition and its international supporters, the dichotomy has joined a series of other oppositions—between dictatorship and society, Ladinos and *indígenas,* finca owners and peasants, the army and guerrillas—that are widely agreed to define the country. Still, such dichotomies have their limits in explaining the problems and priorities of indigenous peasants. This becomes evident when peasants perceive their enemies to be each other rather than the class and ethnic antagonists that activists and scholars would prefer them to perceive. The same can be said for the wish to depict indigenous peasants as being in perennial opposition to the state. As Paul Kobrak (1997) has pointed out in his dissertation on the violence in Aguacatán, Huehuetenango, resistance to the state goes only so far in explaining peasants who have a long history of using the state against other peasants.

The quasijudicial nature of human rights discourse holds out the hope that a more or less objective version of events can be established. There should be an identifiable set of victims and an identifiable set of victimizers. In Guatemala, all the activists involved in truth campaigns wish to establish clear lines of responsibility to the army high command. There is no shortage of killing for which the army was directly responsible, because it was committed en masse by uniformed agents. Our knowledge about such events continues to grow, and hundreds of mass burials will keep exhumation teams busy for years. Since most of the mass killings point to the army, there will be no shortage of evidence fitting the human rights paradigm of citizens versus the state.

But what about all the killing that was internecine, between or within peasant communities, much of it small scale and out of view, but still remembered by survivors and victimizers? All parties concede that the violence could become very complicated, with people on either side (or neither) using the war to settle old scores and to disguise what they were doing. Thus it can become difficult to distinguish agents of the state (or a parastate like the guerrillas) from civil society—which is necessary to distinguish between a human rights violation and a common crime (Wilson 1996). Moreover, while there may be a single regime of denial (the state's) targeted by truth commissions, and perhaps a counterhegemonic regime of denial (the guerrilla movement's), there are also many local regimes of denial, maintained by killers who were using larger causes to pursue their own interests.

Inconveniently for truth commissions, blame is a many-headed beast. Blame is the parochial, self-interested version of a commission's more detached idea of responsibility. Who one blames for a disaster tends to be one's personal rivals: it is a moral judgment coexisting with a factual narrative (Ignatieff 1999). What is generally agreed in Ixil country is that the war was imposed by the two sides, on people who, while they may have cheered the guerrillas in village rallies, had no idea what was in store. What is less agreed is who is to blame locally. Thus most peasants I have interviewed blame the army for the majority of the killing and the guerrillas for some of it, in factual narratives attributing responsibility to institutional actors. But some peasants also blame neighbors, not just for particular deaths but for errors of judgment, such as cooperating with the guerrillas or giving names to the army, that brought on tragedies that might otherwise have been avoided. These are moral judgments that tend to diverge along preexisting fault lines in peasant society and that will be difficult for truth commissions to reconcile in all their multifarious contradictions.

Exhuming massacre victims is therefore likely to disinter differing assessments of blame. The first mass exhumation in Ixil country, in 1997 by REMHI, was of the victims of the June 1982 EGP massacre at Chacalté, Chajul. Since most large-scale killing was committed by the army, scheduling Chacalté for the first exhumation might seem unfair to the less homicidal guerrillas. But all the previous exhumations around the country had been of army massacres. This made the Chacalté dig a reminder that the EGP was also capable of mass murder (of something like a hundred people in this unusual case). Choosing Chacalté was also astute because fear of the army has retarded Ixil interest in exhumations. Digging up victims of the guerrillas showed that, contrary to what army officers claimed, the exhumations were not another maneuver by *los subversivos.*

But who was really to blame for Chacalté? If survivors overcame their fear, they could name current residents of neighboring villages who, while serving in the EGP's Local Guerrilla Forces (FGLS, the rarely mentioned model for the army's civil patrols), helped commit the massacre. If the ex-FGLS are forced to defend themselves, they will probably point out that, caught between army and guerrilla demands, their Chacalté adversaries had organized a civil patrol that was repressing guerrillas for the army. Hence, these victimizers will be able to argue, they could defend themselves only by attacking Chacalté. In cases like this, establishing who is to be regarded as a victim and who is to be regarded as a perpetrator is a function of how narrowly or widely one chooses to interview.

Lurking around the edges of church-, state-, and NGO-endorsed historical memory will be many contradictory attributions. Aside from determining exactly who was responsible for committing a massacre, a factual issue often resolvable, peasants will often have more than one memory of who was to blame. Victims in the eyes of their families and human rights groups may be accused, rightly as well as wrongly, of earlier offenses by the people who killed them. When survivors engage in reciprocal blame, pointing fingers at each other, it becomes harder to beatify one set as the victims and reject another as victimizers. The victim-victimizer distinction can still be made in particular episodes of aggression. But since most of the population is Mayan and poor, and since both sides used local people for killing, there is no shortage of cases in which victims in one time and place became victimizers in another, with rationales for committing a wrong being adduced from having been wronged on previous occasions that will often stretch to long before the arrival of guerrillas and soldiers.

The human rights movement still has many tasks before it in Guatemala. But like any discourse, human rights can be deployed too broadly, blinding us to complexities that need to be taken into account. The purpose of human rights agitation is to protect individuals from state abuses. But peasants may be more interested in a strong state that defends their interests, whether in punishing criminals or in constraining personal enemies from their own social class. Under the aegis of supporting peasants against human rights violations, human rights groups can take partisan positions in disputes in which outsiders should see themselves as mediators rather than advocates.

Notes

An earlier version of this essay appeared in the collection *Guatemala After the Peace Accords,* edited by Rachel Sieder and published by the Institute of Latin American Studies at the University of London in 1998.

1. The FRG administration's blatant corruption and incompetence cost Ríos Montt much of his popularity. Yet human rights organizations found themselves at loggerheads with hundreds of thousands of ex–civil patrollers demanding financial compensation for the years they were conscripted into the army's counter-insurgency campaigns. Once the FRG promised to pay the patrollers, human rights groups realized that it could buy the next presidential election in November 2003. Ultimately the FRG lost the election, by a large margin, but in the heavily indigenous Quiché, Huehuetenango, and Baja Verapaz departments it won the majority of municipal governments, including all three in Ixil country. Since then, a number of FRG mayors have defected to President Oscar Berger's ruling coalition, which may spell the end of Riosmonttismo as an electoral force. The lynchings, which tend to occur in Mayan areas, illustrate a basic difference between human rights guarantees for individuals and the collective obligations that indigenous villages enforce on their members. "In practice," observes Paul Kobrak (1997: 237), "the human rights community . . . concerns itself almost solely with the individual human rights guaranteed by the constitution—the village character of Mayan Indian life is seldom officially recognized." Ironically, with state institutions in disrepair, it is now the human rights community that is spearheading the application of liberal guarantees to indigenous communities.

2. The usual assumption about rural guerrilla movements is that they grow out of local conflicts, that is, they originate with basic problems facing peasants. If not, why would peasants sacrifice themselves in an uprising? Certainly there is a history of oppression in the Ixil area, perpetrated by Ladino labor contractors and finca owners. But in the 1960s and 1970s Ixils were making slow but steady progress in regaining control of town halls and moving into economic niches dominated by Ladinos. Elsewhere throughout the western highlands, *indígenas* were also displacing Ladinos from local power structures (Smith 1984). Far from seeing guerrilla warfare as a necessary stage in Mayan empowerment, I second Yvon Le Bot's (1997) argument that guerrilla organizing interrupted the process of empowerment by motivating the security forces to suppress a wide range of organizations that might be infiltrated by enemies of the state. When guerrilla organizers appeared, they did appeal to certain Ixils, but it is quite a leap to assume that early recruits represented the bulk of the Ixil population. So how did the EGP develop the Ixil support that it unquestionably had by the early 1980s? The

most important reason is how the security forces responded to EGP organizers. By accepting the EGP's claims to represent the people, and by kidnapping and murdering large numbers of suspects, the army convinced many Ixils that they had no choice but to support the insurgents. Yet the EGP was unable to protect most of its new Ixil supporters. When the army proceeded to massacre entire villages, it showed survivors that the guerrillas could not keep them safe. When the army forced survivors to join its antiguerrilla civil patrols, it showed Ixils they could survive by collaborating with the stronger side. For different interpretations of the violence in Ixil country, see the memoir by Yolanda Colom (1998) and the CPR study by Andrés Cabanas (1999).

3. For other descriptions of these conflicts, see Finn Stepputat (1999) on refugee returns to Nentón, Huehuetenango, as an apparatus of modernization coming into conflict with more traditional forms of peasant organization. Pilar Yoldi's (1996) portrait of Juan Coc, one of the leaders of the Xamán, Alta Verapaz, return, describes the successful resolution of a conflict between returnees from Mexico and finca squatters, in which the latter were incorporated into the new community. A more effective state could at least manage land conflicts, which is why in Nebaj local leaders and international organizations have persuaded the government to set up a new district court. Accompanying the new *juzgado de primera instancia* is a public prosecutor; a public defender; a contingent of national police; and a legal aid office run by law students from San Carlos University. Initially the docket consisted almost entirely of land quarrels. One of the first judges was said to have become so frustrated that he nearly quit, because the litigants rarely had the documentation he needed to reach a decision. Instead, he had to jawbone the parties into splitting the tract in dispute. As of 2006, complaints about corruption have become frequent. Yet mediation services run by popular organizations have helped some Ixil disputants avoid the costs of litigation.

POLITICAL ENGAGEMENTS 3

Global Discourses on the Local Terrain
Human Rights in Chiapas

In recent decades, accelerated processes of globalization have given rise to so-called global discourses, or sets of ideas and assumptions that enjoy broad currency throughout the world. "Human rights" has undoubtedly become one of the most widespread of such discourses, accepted in theory by virtually all governments, recognized as valid by most peoples, and deployed regularly by a wide variety of social actors including indigenous people seeking to redefine their relationship to the state. Because human rights are generally understood as "natural" and legitimate, the concept's different meanings and significations often go unquestioned, leaving un-addressed critical questions about the multiple and complex ways that the globalized discourse of human rights is being used and understood in different social contexts by the specific social or political actors involved.

In this article, we explore these complexities on the local terrain in Chiapas, Mexico, by examining the ways in which various local actors and groups understand and put into practice the discourse of human rights. Chiapas is in many ways a privileged place to observe interconnected global, national, and local dynamics. Long characterized by racial and ethnic polarization and a high degree of regionalization that gave rise to quite distinct local histories and identities (Viquerira and Rus 2002), the state of Chiapas is notable for its social, cultural, and political complexity. The Zapatista uprising that began in 1994 generated new levels of interaction among groups, as well as new levels of tension. While prior to the uprising there had undoubtedly been a great deal of interaction among local groups, as well as between local and nonlocal groups, the subsequent political mobilization, militarization,[1] and the influx of activists from outside the region generated an intensified interaction among indigenous communities and organizations, local elites, agents and agencies of the state, and national and transnational activists. All of these individuals and groups became political actors in the Chiapas conflict (Leyva Solano 2003a; Rus, Hernández Castillo, and Mattiace 2003), and in this context they have related to and engaged with discourse of human rights (Speed 2007; Stephen 1999).

In the context of exploring how human rights are working in Chiapas, we will address long-standing anthropological debates about globalization, human rights, and cultural imperialism. Anthropological discussions about human rights have been heavily overshadowed by the discipline's cultural relativist leanings. Many anthropologists have rejected the universality of human rights, arguing instead that they can be understood only in the context of a society's internal cultural logics, a position made explicit in the American Anthropological Association's statement on human rights penned by Melville Herskovits in 1947. There has been an enduring concern that rendering the concept of human rights universal represents an ethnocentric imposition of Western cultural values on indigenous and non-Western societies and potentially results in the erasure of the latter's own culturally specific understandings (see Downing and Kushner 1988; Messer 1995; Wilson 1997a; Bell 2000). Globalization intensified this concern for many since, as Sally Merry (1997) points out, the global dissemination of the discourse of human rights represented for some the imperialist extension of Western legal orders to the rest of the world. The critique of universal rights as a form of cultural imperialism remains an earnest one in the anthropological community today (see *Anthropology News* 2006; Goodale 2006a).

Some years ago, Richard Wilson (1997a: 3–4) suggested that anthropologists should move beyond the totalizing conceptualizations of the universalist/relativist dichotomy. He called for detailed studies of human rights directed "not towards foreclosing their ontological status, but instead exploring their meaning and use" in particular contexts. Following Wilson's suggestion, in the late 1990s we each conducted research on several different groups' interpretations and uses of human rights discourse in Chiapas. The groups we analyze here range from Zapatista communities and independent indigenous organizations to San Cristóbal elites, Chol paramilitaries, and even the state. Our research shows that these different groups' understandings of human rights emerge both from the particular historical experiences and political subjectivities of each group and from their dialogic engagement with other social actors, leading to multiple and divergent interpretations and uses of human rights. Their mobilizations of this discourse have a sort of prism effect—refracting it into multiple discourses whose meanings correlate to distinct positionalities in relation to the conflict and to society.

In the context of such extreme diversity, it is difficult to talk of universals, and it is clear that the process at work is not one of the imperialist impositions of ideas on non-Western peoples, at least not in an uncomplicated way. Rather, based on our observation of dynamics in Chiapas, we argue that local understandings of human rights discourse emerge in dialogic interaction with others, including both local and nonlocal actors, and that local usages of the discourse represent rearticulations based on local knowledges, positionalities, and goals.[2]

While emphasizing this interaction, we do not ignore inherent power relations; clearly, indigenous people face far greater challenges in making their voices heard in this metaphorical dialogue than does the state, for example. However, the failure to recognize that they are actively engaged in these dialogic interactions only serves to further silence them. At the same time, we do not wish to imply that the discourse of human rights is inherently emancipatory or even contestatory in the hands of indigenous peoples. Rather, we think a close look at varied local usages reflects the differing relations of power and coercion in which human rights, indigenous people, and nation-states are enmeshed.

Chiapas: The Local Terrain

In the 1980s the emergence of the discourse of human rights in Chiapas was tied to four parallel processes occurring in the state: the pastoral work of the San Cristóbal de Las Casas diocese; the Central American wars, and particularly the scorched-earth campaign in Guatemala that generated a refugee flow into Chiapas; the agrarian struggles of organizations, communities, and indigenous campesinos; and the political-religious expulsions traditionalist communities and indigenous caciques perpetrated against dissident community members. Below we will explore in further detail how these processes arose and how they intertwine.

The discourse of human rights appeared for the first time in many indigenous communities in Chiapas through the work of Bishop Samuel Ruiz García and the catechists of the Catholic diocese of San Cristóbal de Las Casas. Ruiz became the bishop of the diocese in 1960.[3] Arriving in Chiapas a conservative, in a relatively short period of time Ruiz, influenced by the extreme poverty and marginalization in Chiapas, was "converted" to the cause of the poor (qtd. in Womack 1998: 49). By the early 1970s he was training catechists and giving masses strongly influenced by liberation theology, a critical discourse focusing on the structures of domination, exploitation, and political control of the poor. Christine Kovic (2005) suggests that "the option for the poor" was the progressive church's human rights discourse. She argues that liberation theologians purposefully utilized a discourse of "the rights of the poor" rather than of "human rights" to emphasize that the equality assumed in liberal rights theory did not exist, and to highlight the economic structural and institutional violence that kept some people from realizing these rights.

Ruiz recognized that the indigenous people of Chiapas were the poorest of the poor—those most affected by structural and institutional violence—and under his leadership the "option for the poor" soon evolved into the "option for the indigenous" and *teología india* (Indian theology) emerged (Ruiz García 1999: 61). *Teología india* is based on a strong valorization of indigenous culture and, notably, on the understanding that human beings of all cultures are equal before God (whether or not they enjoyed equality on earth) (Kovic 2005; Meyer with Gallardo and Ríos 2000; Ruiz García 1999). As Kovic argues in this volume, the diocese's message to indigenous people regarding human rights largely concerned economic injustice: it was a message that challenged the system of peonage and subordination under which they had lived on haciendas and fincas from the colonial period onward (García de León 1984; Gómez and Ruz 1992; Benjamin 1989; Toledo Tello 2002; Leyva Solano and Ascencio Franco 1996), as well as the racist ideology underpinning that system that had gone largely unchallenged into the present period (Gall Sonabend 1994, 1999).

In the early 1980s, in the context of the arrival of thousands of Guatemalan refugees fleeing the Guatemalan military's scorched-earth campaign, the discourse of human rights began to gain broader prominence in Chiapas (García Aguilar 1998). The actions of the dioceses of San Cristóbal and Tapachula on behalf of the refugees and the formation and consolidation of nongovernmental organizations (NGOs) in this period laid the groundwork for what would become in the following decade the political banner most vigorously waved—and also most contested. The first human rights organization in Chiapas, the Centro de Derechos Humanos Fray Bartolomé (Fray Bartolomé de Las Casas Human Rights Center, CDHFBC), was founded in 1989 (Kovic 2005).[4] The center was a project of the diocese of San Cristóbal, and Bishop Ruiz served as its president.[5] Since its inception, this organization has taken on the task of documenting and denouncing human rights abuses, most of which emerged from agrarian and political conflicts, as well as from abuses committed by the authorities. Other organizations that worked with refugees also often deployed a discourse of human rights, although no other organization specifically devoted to the defense of human rights was formed until the early 1990s.

Genocidal violence and the defense of rights (human, political, indigenous) echoed beyond the pastoral workers and the bishop in Chiapas because during the same period indigenous communities in Chiapas were launching struggles for land against landowners who continued to amass it (Cruz Coutiño 1982; Marión 1984; González Esponda 1989; Luna 1992; Leyva Solano 1995b; Harvey 1998b). These were not isolated and disarticulated demands, but rather ones made by an agrarian campesino movement whose leaders and organizations argued, via different discourses, their "right to land." While this language emerged directly from the Mexican Revolution ("the land belongs to he who works it"), it was also tied to a generalized Mexican and Latin American claim about "the right to have rights" (Jelin 1996; Harvey 1998b).

The response to these demands, claims, and movements were state violence and governmental repression, which reached their climax between 1982 and 1988, the period during which the governor of Chiapas (Absalón Castellanos) was a military professional, aside from being a large landholder himself. The criminalization of the agrarian conflict lead the indigenous communities, their leaders, and their organizations to the systematic national and international denunciation of arbitrary arrests and evictions, thefts of documentation, rapes, kidnappings, torture, disappearances, and assassinations committed by the ruling powers.[6] Thus the local dynamics, accelerated by the arrival of the Guatemalan refugees, favored the expansion of human rights, not only as a discourse but also as a concrete political practice framed within a war of positions waged on both sides of the southern border of Mexico.

By the mid-1980s the human rights discourse had become popular not only in the rural indigenous regions of Chiapas but also in the very heart of the colonial city (San Cristóbal de Las Casas) through the demands raised by the urban organizations of indigenous people expelled from various villages in the highlands. They had decided to leave the traditionalist religion, the official party, and alcohol and had taken on new religions and political parties. The communitarian caciques or local factions in power took this as an affront, and again their immediate response was violent (Rus and Wasserstrom 1981; Robledo Hernández 1987; Sterk 1991; Morquecho 1992; López Maza 1992; Ruíz Ortiz 1996; Rus and Vigil 2007).[7] In fact, the greater the number of aggressions, the greater the number of claims concerning human rights violations against the expelled, who from within their organizations coordinated with the diocese of San Cristóbal, Protestant organizations such as the Consejo de Representantes Indigenas de los Altos de Chiapas (Counsel of Indigenous Representatives of the Chiapas Highlands, CRIACH), and/or with factions of the independent campesino movement. It is through these sometimes parallel, sometimes interconnected processes that the discourse and the practice of human rights attained common usage in Chiapas.

The EZLN, the Zapatista Autonomous Municipalities, and the Independent Campesino Organizations: Local Defense and Empowerment after 1994

As we noted above, many groups' engagement with the discourse of human rights intensified after the beginning of the Zapatista uprising in 1994. The Ejercito Zapatista de Liberación Nacional (Zapatista Army of National Liberation, EZLN) and its supporters form one group that has very effectively mobilized the discourse of human rights in the post-1994 conflict period. The events of February 1995 offer a notable early example. In an attempt to end the uprising, the government extended its military control over the conflict zone of the Lacandon jungle and launched a military incursion to detain the Zapatista leadership. The EZLN sent out communiqués that were quickly picked up by the national and international press and that circulated widely (and almost instantly) on the Internet, informing the group's supporters in Mexico and abroad that the Mexican Army was violating the human rights of people in the newly occupied communities. Protests were quickly organized in cities throughout Mexico and internationally, especially in the United States and in Europe. These protests and other actions put direct pressure on the Mexican government; they also exerted indirect pressure by exhorting other governments to pursue diplomatic channels to stop the human rights violations. The Mexican government found itself obliged to limit its actions in the conflict zone and to release many of the indigenous people detained during the military mobilization (*La Jornada*, February 10–12, 1995).

People in the indigenous Zapatista base support communities quickly understood the power of the human rights discourse. Within a few years, many came to see human rights as their primary line of defense. This became evident when the state government, using the discourse of the "rule of law" (*estado de derecho*), began in 1998 to pursue a policy of dismantling Zapatista autonomous municipalities (see Speed and Collier 2000). The communities and organizations that suffered the massive joint police-army-immigration raids recognized the usefulness—in fact, the necessity—of deploying a human rights discourse. In the community of Nicolás Ruíz, "Ricardo," the newly appointed "human rights defender," said of the raid on the municipal seat: "We never knew anything about human rights, until the [joint raid] of June 1998. . . . It was then that we realized that we had to learn about human rights to defend ourselves from the government, because [the government] doesn't want us around."[8]

The power of this line of defense lies in the evocation of the moral concept and the legal framework of human rights, which permitted the mobilization of networks of activists and organizations using this discourse. In the Lacandon jungle, where Zapatistas lived side by side with members of other independent and government-aligned campesino and indigenous organizations and where militarization was strongly evident, the discourse of human rights became a form of empowerment for independent organizations that have historically confronted local rancher groups and non-Indian (Ladinos) and elite groups in general. These groups have created new alliances and entered social networks that have allowed them to advance their demands more forcefully. For example, in June 1998, the Coalición de Organizaciones Autónomas de Ocosingo (Coalition of Autonomous Organizations of Ocosingo, COAO), a regional umbrella group of independent campesino organizations, demanded the revocation of indictments (*autos de formal prisión*) ordered against sixteen indigenous men detained during the dismantling of the Zapatista autonomous municipality of Ricardo Flores Magón (Taniperlas). The COAO could back its demand with a ruling by the

Inter-American Human Rights Commission of the Organization of American States (OAS), which requested the prisoners' release based on "the existence of serious irregularities in the legal process" (Henríquez 1998).[9] While this might not seem a remarkable occurrence today, only a few years earlier such an undertaking would have been unlikely, if not completely out of the question.

In Chiapas, indigenous peoples' mobilization of human rights has generally passed through the mediation of NGOs, which provide political and legal defense to communities and/or organizations. Thus NGOs function as intermediaries between local communities and the extralocal discourses and practices of human rights.[10] As necessary mediators with the know-how and the resources to carry out human rights defense, NGOs have been helpful to, but also have wielded a good deal of power over, indigenous communities. The dependency relationship created by NGOs providing a service to indigenous communities proves even more problematic in the context of these communities' struggle for autonomy and self-determination: NGOs are beholden to the logics, agendas, and timetables of their international funders, as well as having their own organizational agendas and internal dynamics. All of these concerns may place them at quite a distance from the goals and worries of the communities who must turn to them for help.

However, it is worth noting that from the late 1990s on, indigenous communities have begun to bypass the mediation of these NGOs and to define themselves in their own terms. This process has entailed the emergence of indigenous human rights defenders who have trained intensively to do the work formerly done only by NGOs and private attorneys. For example, in 1999 the Red de Defensores Comunitarios por los Derechos Humanos (Community Human Rights Defenders Network) was formed. The Red is made up of young indigenous people chosen by their communities. They undertake a year and a half of training in international human rights and Mexican law and then become the defenders of their communities' human rights. The fact that their communities considered it important to elect these defenders and allowed young, able-bodied men to dedicate themselves to this task reveals, to some extent, how indigenous communities have come to value knowledge of human rights and the capacity for their defense. Their slogan, "Assuming Our Own Defense," is a statement of indigenous communities' collective interest to not only understand and become familiar with human rights issues but also of their desire to do it for themselves, rather than through intermediary NGOs. It signifies processes of empowerment that took place first through NGOs but that are now moving beyond them. However problematic the relationship with NGOs is, it is also the case that through these interactions local individuals, groups, and communities have strengthened their position in renegotiating their relationship with the state. Furthermore, the contradictory nature of the relationship between indigenous communities and NGOs may diminish as increasingly empowered actors shed these intermediaries.

In short, for the EZLN, their base communities, and independent campesino organizations that align with them in particular political junctures, there is an increasing appropriation of the human rights discourse, which is based on these groups' lived experience of its role in their defense and empowerment. The Zapatistas probably owe their continued survival to the willingness and ability of independent human rights organizations to publicize violations, which has made the Mexican government reluctant to use military force against dissidents. Further, the discourse has proven empowering to organized indigenous peoples who are appropriating it in new ways and using it to support their ongoing struggle for self-determination and autonomy. Not surprisingly, other actors in this conflict also recognize the power of the discourse at this political juncture, but they interpret it in a very different manner, in the light of their particular history and the current associations it holds. In the following sections, we look at two of these groups: San Cristóbal elites and indigenous members of paramilitary groups in the Northern Zone of the state of Chiapas.

Divergent Interpretations: Alternative Engagements with Human Rights

After the Zapatista uprising began, Chiapas became so socially polarized that it often seemed there were only two positions: pro- or anti-Zapatista. There was a widespread perception that everyone was implicated in the larger social conflict in some way. (This has diminished over the past few years, but it has not disappeared altogether.) Human rights, as a master narrative in the conflict, played a significant role in defining how different social actors were understood in relation to the conflict. The social actors who opposed the Zapatistas perceived human rights as a weapon of war. That is, just as Zapatistas and their supporters understood human rights as providing support in their struggle to renegotiate the unequal power relations that placed them at a disadvantage, those who stood to lose authority, legitimacy, control, and political power in this renegotiation viewed human rights quite differently: as an attack against them, and as something they must fight against. For groups as diverse as the Ladino elite of San Cristóbal de Las Casas (*Coletos*),[11] and Chol Indians from the Northern Zone associated with the paramilitary group Desarrollo, Paz y Justicia (Development, Peace, and Justice), human rights represent a threat to the structure of power relations from which they have long benefited. Their interpretation is not ahistorical; it emerges from the particular context of relationships in which the discourse was introduced into the state, particularly through the diocese of San Cristóbal, and in which it has been mobilized to their disadvantage in recent years. Below, we look first at *Coletos* and then turn to the Northern Zone.

THE *COLETOS* OF SAN CRISTÓBAL

San Cristóbal de Las Casas, formerly Ciudad Real, is a colonial city founded in 1528 by the Spanish conquistador Diego de Mazariegos. Originally a Spanish stronghold against the surrounding Indian communities, it was eventually renamed in honor of Fray Bartolomé de Las Casas, the famous defender of the Indians. The city experienced several Indian rebellions in the course of its history, leading to a deeply ingrained fear of Indian invasion. After independence, it served as the state capital until 1892 and was the conservative political rival of the liberal Tuxtla Gutierrez, today's capital (Benjamin 1989).

The relationship between the indigenous communities of the Chiapas highlands and the city of San Cristóbal de Las Casas has been the focus of anthropological attention for many decades (e.g., Pozas 1958; Aguirre Beltrán 1957; Favre 1973; De la Fuente 1968; McQuown and Pitt-Rivers 1970; Pitt-Rivers 1973). The extreme nature of the relations of economic exploitation and the social division and racism between the Ladino residents of San Cristóbal and the Indians of the communities that surround it have made this area a "laboratory for the study of interethnic relations"; one major research project in the 1950s cited among its rationales for choosing the city as its site of study its "notoriously retrograde Mestizo elite" (Hewitt de Alcántara 1984). As recently as the 1950s, San Cristóbal prided itself on being a criollo city of direct Spanish heritage and descent (Paris Pombo 2000). While in the rest of the country the discourse of *mestizaje* posited the emergence of a mestizo nation, in some parts of Chiapas (in particular in the highlands) Ladino remained a social category posited against that of Indian, the purpose of which was to fix social categories of power and domination (Paris Pombo 2000).[12]

In the decades prior to the uprising, *Coletos* had felt pressured by the changing demographics of the city of San Cristóbal. Demographic pressures on the land, and more importantly, religious-political conflicts in highlands communities, contributed to a dramatic influx of tens of thousands of Tzotzils and Tzeltals, who established neighborhoods on the peripheries of the city (CNDH 1995; Kovic 2005). The growth of tourism brought ever larger numbers of foreigners, who were principally drawn to the town because they were interested in local Indian culture (Van Den Berghe 1994). Faced with the influx of foreigners and Indians, a conservative core developed a xenophobic discourse that posited outsiders as "invaders," "criminals," and particularly Indians as "savages" (Paris Pombo 2000).

This understanding was only exacerbated—after the start of the Zapatista uprising in 1994—by the association of foreigners (both from other countries and from other parts of Mexico) and Indians with political opposition.[13] The Zapatistas' incursion into San Cristóbal and the taking of the municipal government building by armed indigenous people stimulated long-held fears of Indian invasion, illegality, and the loss of control. While tourism dropped to near zero levels that year, the notable influx of national and international solidarity and human rights activists after the uprising linked foreigners to political opposition and further fueled xenophobic sentiments. Some *Coletos,* looking for someone to blame for social instability and challenges to their dominance, had traditionally defined enemies at hand: Indians and foreigners. Racism fed their belief that Indians were incapable of planning and launching a rebellion of this scale and that foreigners were behind the revolt.

Many conservative *Coletos,* upset by the challenge to the old system by Indians they had regarded, on the one hand, as childlike and incompetent and, on the other, as a long-standing threat, accused Bishop Ruiz and the Fray Bartolomé de Las Casas Human Rights Center of having fomented the uprising. This attitude was clearly reflected in the comment of a *Coleta* woman to one of the authors in 1997: Shannon Speed was passing the plaza in front of the municipal president's building (adjacent to the cathedral) when she came upon a group of people burning an effigy. Looking closer, she realized the effigy was of the bishop and asked a woman nearby for clarification. The woman's face showed visible annoyance at the question, and she responded, "What you *foreigners* can't understand is that these *Indians* you love so much are silly and ignorant. They can't even pull themselves out of the dirt, so how could they have planned all this [presumably, the uprising]. Everybody knows it was the work of 'the Red Bishop.' "[14]

Coletos and other Ladino local elites have undoubtedly lost power in recent times, though not just because of the uprising. In late-nineteenth-century Chiapas, the axis of social and economic life was the finca, to which Indian subordination was fundamental. In 1993, 52.58 percent of the land in the state of Chiapas was organized into ejidos (Villafuerte Solís et al. 1999: 123), and independent organizations occupied a central place in the political life of the state. This combined with the demographic changes to the city had many *Coletos* feeling defensive.

The fact that in 1995 the CDHFBC began to sponsor many national and international human rights observers through its Civilian Peace Camps program provided those inclined to view human rights workers as leftist agitators with further "proof" of the intimate connections between human rights advocacy, the diocese of San Cristóbal, and indigenous rebellion. Human rights, which became synonymous with the work of the diocese in defense of indigenous peoples and the poor, provided *Coletos* with another outlet for their defensive anger.

It would be hard to deny that many of the international human rights observers who came to Chiapas either arrived or left with a pro-Zapatista stance. Human rights workers argued that this was because it was "clear whose rights were being violated, and who was in need of defense."[15] The visits of foreign diplomatic representatives often ended with the same conclusions. For example, three representatives of the United Nations (UN) have visited Chiapas since the Acteal Massacre of December 1997: Asma Jahangir, the special envoy on extrajudicial executions; Mary Robinson, the high commissioner on human rights; and Erika Daes, the president of the Special Working Group on Indigenous Peoples. All were critical of the government's human rights record, some sharply so.

In this intensely polarized climate, the dramatic support for the Zapatistas from abroad and strong criticisms coming even from distinguished diplomatic sources made foreigners in Chiapas the objects of suspicion by government officials, *Coletos,* and local authorities of the ruling party in indigenous communities. Particularly after the governmental campaign against foreigners began in earnest following the massacre at Acteal, foreigners were reflexively associated with human rights work, and thus with Zapatista support (Global Exchange et al. 1999).[16] In the minds of many, a triangulation of negative association occurred among the diocese of San Cristóbal, the Zapatistas, and human rights, and this was reflected in the words and actions of some *Coletos*.

CHOL PARAMILITARIES IN THE NORTHERN ZONE

This conflation of human rights, the church, and foreign human rights workers also occurred in other politically divided communities and regions, especially those with strong Zapatista contestation. Like the Partido Revolucionario Institucional (Revolutionary Institutional Party, PRI) government and elites in San Cristóbal,[17] these groups feared challenges to the legitimacy of their local power, which they had long held as authorities of the ruling party. In some areas such as the Northern Zone, paramilitary groups emerged. This happened mainly in traditional PRI strongholds in which PRI supporters had become the minority in relation to members of the Partido Revolucionario Democrático (Revolutionary Democratic Party, PRD) and to Zapatista supporters (in the Northern Zone these were often synonymous) and who thus, perhaps reasonably, felt threatened.[18] Paramilitary violence pitted brother against brother in communities and had devastating local effects including hundreds of deaths among both pro- and antigovernment groups, and the generation of tens of thousands of internal refugees and hundreds of political prisoners (CDHFBC 1996).

The emergence of paramilitary groups began in the Northern Zone with groups called the Chinchulines and Desarrollo, Paz y Justicia. Paramilitarization spread to the highlands and later to the jungle with groups like Mascara Roja and the Movimiento Indígena Revolucionario Anti-Zapatista (Anti-Zapatista Indigenous Revolutionary Movement, MIRA) respectively. Because of these groups' shadowy nature, it is difficult to document their relationship with the government and the military. However, their pro–ruling party stance and a few high-profile connections—like a local congressperson who openly formed and directed Paz y Justicia,[19] and an ex-governor who, while still in office, formed the Coordination for State Security, through which money and training were channeled to paramilitary groups—have led a number of analysts to argue that they are state sponsored (CDHFBC 1996; Olivera 1998; Ramírez 1997; Global Exchange, CIEPAC, and CENCOS 2000).

Many in the region understand paramilitarization as part of a campaign of low-intensity warfare, a divide-and-rule strategy designed to exhaust and terrify the rebellious population into submission (Global Exchange et al. 1999; Olivera 1998; Ramírez 1997, Leyva Solano 2003b; López y Rivas 2004; Leyva Solano and Burguete Cal y Mayor 2008).

Because human rights groups saw the paramilitaries as sponsored by the state and as active human rights violators, they regularly engaged in defense work of groups attacked or expelled by paramilitary violence. In 1997, five organizations engaged in different forms of human rights work formed a coalition specifically focused on the paramilitary violence in the Northern Zone.[20] This group, the Estación Norte, sent delegations into conflicted communities and attempted to stem the tide of rights violations—with little impact other than in some cases that actually exacerbated tensions.

This was the case because the local actors involved in paramilitary groups interpreted human rights as sinister and invasive. Paz y Justicia's slogan, for example, was "derechos humanos asesinos" (human rights, murderers).[21] This stigmatization derived from their perception that all human rights workers were linked to the Fray Bartolomé de Las Casas Human Rights Center and thus directly associated with the diocese and Bishop Ruiz. The bishop and the diocese, in turn, were seen as the promoters of the uprising and as EZLN supporters. For the paramilitaries "human rights" was the discourse of the enemy. The book *Ni derechos, ni humanos* (*Neither Rights, Nor Humans*), printed by an anonymous publisher, explicitly elaborates their views on the issues (Desarrollo, Paz y Justicia 1997).

This stance was not simply political posturing, but rather, as with the *Coletos* discussed above, it reflected the particular history and political positionality of the actors involved. Like other indigenous peoples of the region, Chols had long faced exploitation by outsiders. It began with forced relocations and tribute payments to the Crown (Carton de Grammont and Flores 1982), followed by postindependence domination by non-Indian elites who resided in the municipal seats. In 1891 Chol lands were privatized, opening them up to German and American companies that quickly began exploiting the region for coffee production (Benjamin 1989). For the following fifty years, Chols suffered near slavery under the foreign companies, a period known in Chol oral history as *el mosojüntel*, or "the time when we were servants" (Alejos 1988). The harsh treatment they received from foreigners and Ladinos from colonial times into the mid-twentieth century, but particularly during the *mosojüntel*, inculcated a strong aversion to all non-Chols (CDHFBC 1996). José Alejos (1988) argues that they developed a binary understanding of the world, in which Chols were equated with good, and *Kaxlanes*, or non-Chols, with evil. Their oral history—and certainly their current political discourse—reflects this binary understanding, frequently evoking images of evil *Kaxlanes* and good or saintly Chols.

During the 1930s, the regime of Lázaro Cárdenas carried out agrarian reform in Chiapas. As part of a larger postrevolutionary project of national consolidation, the Cardenista agrarian ideology posited the integration of all campesinos into the nation-state through land reform (Benjamin 1989). The Northern Zone benefited, receiving large tracts of communally held farmland known as ejidos. The Cardenistas were surprised when the Chols, rather than integrating themselves into the national economy through coffee production, took their land and withdrew, returning to subsistence agriculture based on corn production. Nevertheless, the agrarian reform embedded the state in the Chol imaginary as an ally against exploitative *Kaxlanes*, and Chols remained strongly affiliated with the ruling party, the PRI, for the following several decades (CDHFBC 1996).[22]

In the 1970s, the liberation theology message of the diocese of San Cristóbal began to have an impact in the region. Franciscans had been active in the zone since the 1950s, training a small number of educated bilingual Chol teachers as catechists. The liberation evangelizing propagated throughout the region by the pastoral agents of the diocese gave Chol communities both a group of trained leaders and a discourse that justified and organized community mobilization against marginalization and exploitation (CDHFBC 1996). As in other areas of the state, when the diocese of San Cristóbal formed the Fray Bartolomé de Las Casas Human Rights Center, human rights became associated in the popular imaginary with the diocese, its bishop, its pastoral agents, and its catechists.

Also in the 1970s, the boom in the world coffee market motivated Chols to begin growing coffee again. However, because agroindustrial processing, as well as the financing and marketing of the coffee industry, lay in the hands of *Kaxlanes*, others reaped the benefits of their labor, and Chols ultimately ended up with social conditions starkly similar to those of the *mosojüntel* (Alejos 1988).

In 1980, the coffee producers of the region formed a cooperative, Pajal Yakatik, in an attempt to strengthen the communities against outside exploitation (Benjamin 1996). The disastrous dissolution of Pajal some years later would establish the lines along which the radical, violent conflicts of the 1990s were drawn. Pajal was the indirect product of the 1970s intellectual movement Política Popular (CHFBLC 1996). One of the most criticized tenets of the Política Popular was their *política de dos caras,* or the two-faced policy of taking advantage of government programs for campesinos while organizing oppositionally, generally around agrarian issues (Harvey 1998). Adopting this pragmatic approach, Pajal engaged in campesino base organizing, while simultaneously involving itself with Instituto Mexicano del Café (Mexican Coffee Institute, INMECAFE), a state organization that promoted the monocultivation of coffee for export. The dependency on coffee cultivation and on INMECAFE left campesinos in the Northern Zone destitute when coffee markets fell in the late 1980s (Harvey 1998).

Pajal dissolved in crisis, and the communities of the Northern Zone divided into two camps that reflected the two "faces" of the organization: those who organized oppositionally and those who allied with the government. Members in one community told Speed that the experience of Pajal radically altered their vision of the state from potential ally to oppressor. They again withdrew, many engaging in passive resistance such as refusing to pay taxes or electric bills. Within a few years, these communities would emerge as bastions of the opposition PRD and as EZLN base supporters. Notably, they were often communities who had strong leaders trained as catechists by the diocese of San Cristóbal. A number of the communities that maintained a strong alliance with the government later emerged as participants in paramilitary organizations. The political division exploded after the Zapatista uprising in 1994, as support for the EZLN increased in the region and PRI party militants increasingly became a minority and faced losing their hold on local power.

It is not hard to understand how these groups' history and recent political experiences shaped their understanding and utilization of the discourse of human rights. Paz y Justicia's extreme understanding of human rights as "murderous" results from their association of human rights with foreigners or *Kaxlanes* (i.e., with evil); with the Fray Bartolomé de Las Casas Human Rights Center, and thus directly with the diocese, Bishop Ruiz, and the catechists leading enemy communities; and with the EZLN. For them, human rights was the discourse and the embodiment of the enemy. Communities allied with the EZLN had a similar set of understandings of human rights, though of course their associations were positive. That they emerged from Pajal with an antigovernment attitude, that their leaders were often trained catechists with strong links to the diocese, and their involvement with the EZLN all brought them to very different interpretations of human rights.

In sum, human rights in Chiapas have been primarily associated with struggles for social and political change that betters the lives of some and threatens the power of others. By historical association, in many parts of the state human rights are understood to mean the Fray Bartolomé de Las Casas Human Rights Center of the Catholic diocese, with whatever positive or negative connotations this might have. The term is also associated with foreign supporters of the Zapatista rebellion, whether such foreigners are regarded as allies or as meddlesome outsiders. In Chiapas, as elsewhere in the world, the discourse of human rights does not play the neutral role that some of its international proponents imagine. Rather, it has taken on the meanings ascribed to it by social groups involved in particular political struggles. The broad range of meanings assigned to human rights in Chiapas reflects the fact that social actors on all sides of the Chiapas conflict understand it through the lens of their own historical experiences and particular subjectivities. Their interpretations emerge in dialogic engagement with outside actors and social processes. In the following section, we look to another important social actor in this interaction: the state.

THE STATE GOVERNMENT: MOBILIZING THE DISCOURSE OF HUMAN RIGHTS

The simultaneous emergence of human rights organizations and state neoliberalization is fairly clear. It was during the administration of Carlos Salinas de Gortari, with its accelerated neoliberalization policies, that the Comisión Nacional de Derechos Humanos (National Human Rights Commission, CNDH) was founded by presidential decree in 1990.[23] A number of state-level organizations were created during the same period, and in the state of Chiapas, the Comisión Estatal de Derechos Humanos (State Human Rights Commission, CEDH) was established in 1990. Constitutional and legal reforms were implemented that integrated human rights standards into Mexican law,[24] and the discourse of public figures increasingly carried human rights language. This was in part because the process of joining the new global order brought with it an increased pressure to conform to the rights standards of other countries (Brysk 2002). But the consolidation of neoliberalism in Mexico also required new forms of rule: the old corporatism of the Mexican state, with its social welfare orientation and its reliance on state intervention in many areas of social life was simply not compatible with neoliberal state downsizing. As the responsibility for the management of social inequality shifted from the state to civil society, human rights had a role to play. Rights in general, and human rights in particular, became the state-approved mode of social struggle. This placed the burden on NGOs to seek to rectify relations of oppression, at the same time reinforcing the legal regimes of the state and leaving unquestioned the state's power to grant or deny rights. For the state, this shift implied an emphasis on specific kinds of human rights, deemphasizing the social rights contained in the 1917 constitution such as the right to land and to collective land holdings.[25]

Thus the state was also a key social actor using the discourse of human rights to its own ends, and it did so prior to the other actors looked at previously. In fact, it was in part the state's appropriation of the discourse of human rights that made it a useful one for oppositional movements like the Zapatistas, who were seeking to renegotiate their relationship with the state in this new political context. Yet such effective mobilizations of the discourse made it a dangerous one for the state. Given the crucial role of human rights discourse in limiting the state's ability to act with impunity and in strengthening indigenous resistance struggles, both the federal and the state governments sought to redeploy it in order to limit this dynamic (Speed and Collier 2000).

One important way this was done was by mobilizing individual human rights against the claims of collective indigenous rights. For example, the language of individual human rights has been used to reduce the parameters of indigenous rights as established in the law. Both national and state-level legislation on indigenous rights contains wording that specifically employs the notion of individual human rights to limit indigenous autonomy. The *Law on Indigenous Rights and Culture*, passed by the Mexican Congress in 2001, states that indigenous peoples can "obtain the recognition of their internal normative systems, to the extent that these are not contrary to constitutional guarantees and human rights." In Chiapas, such wording was adopted in the 1999 law on indigenous rights and culture. Article 10, which opens the section on the administration of justice, reads: "The uses, customs, and ancestral traditions of indigenous communities constitute the fundamental basis for the resolution of their controversies. Such uses, customs and traditions will be applied within the limits of their habitat, as long as they do not constitute violations of human rights."[26] While many find it difficult to oppose the inclusion of such language, it is nevertheless remarkable that these individual rights consistently appear as a limiting factor to indigenous autonomy.[27]

The dynamic of using individual rights to limit indigenous autonomy becomes more menacing when it leaves the realm of legal wording and enters the terrain of political practice. This is especially clear in Chiapas, a primary battleground in the struggle to gain indigenous rights and redefine state power. Here, the state government has regularly harnessed the discourse of human rights to its own ends, playing the individual rights established in the Mexican constitution off against collective indigenous rights to limit indigenous people's pursuit of autonomy (Speed and Collier 2000). During the late 1990s, the state government of Chiapas regularly cited the violation of individuals' rights as the justification for massive raids on autonomous municipalities and for the jailing of autonomous authorities— even when the supposedly violating practices were traditional customs practices in indigenous communities throughout the state.

The state government has used the discourse of human rights to justify its campaign of dismantling Zapatista autonomous municipalities, as well as to justify repression against political opposition from Zapatista communities and authorities more generally (Speed and Collier 2000). For example, a few days before the raid on the community of Nicolás Ruíz in June 1998, the interim governor Albores Guillén declared: "A group of radicals has once again disrupted normal life in Nicolás Ruíz with a highly primitive approach of *usos y costumbres.* But these cannot exist in opposition to the elemental laws and norms of human coexistence, [nor can they] trample individual rights. . . . We will not permit illegality, in Nicolás Ruíz or in any other part of Chiapas. We will make the rule of law prevail and restore constitutionality" (*El Cuarto Poder,* June 2, 1998).

Similarly, there were accusations that the authorities of the Zapatista autonomous municipality of Tierra y Libertad had violated the individual rights of two people detained, in relation to a land dispute, for more than the seventy-two hours allowed by Mexican law for detention without formal charges. The violation of these "individual rights" justified the arrest of fifty-three indigenous people from that community in a raid involving more than a thousand soldiers, police, and immigration agents (*La Jornada*, May 2, 1998).[28] This violent event and the subsequent imprisonment of several key authorities effectively destroyed the autonomous seat of government, which was popularly viewed as the true objective of the raid.

Thus the state government effectively redeployed the discourse of human rights used to challenge it by the Zapatistas and by other political opposition groups to both undermine this political opposition and to make the redeployment very difficult to contest. While it may be entirely appropriate for governments to propagate the discourse of human rights, in Chiapas the PRI government did so most often to serve its own political ends.[29]

But the complexities of that particular mobilization extend beyond the simple boundaries of political affiliation, as another example demonstrates. In the highlands community of Zinacantán in 1999, the indigenous authorities belonged to the PRI, although they enjoyed a good deal of local autonomy in conflict resolution and community governance. In a meeting that year attended by the anthropologist Jane Collier (see Speed and Collier 2000), held to debate the new state law on indigenous rights and culture being introduced by then interim governor Albores Guillén, a judge from the indigenous court stated that it would be impossible for the indigenous judges to apply their customary norms and sanctions if the clause invoking human rights remained in the law, because "when we sentence someone to two weeks of community service, 'human rights' comes along and frees him." In this context, "human rights" referred to human rights organizations, which the Zinacanteco authorities considered to be external agents who impeded the use of their own indigenous traditions. The state legislation would have supported this practice and thus was opposed by the Zinacanteco authorities, even though they were allied with the ruling party.

Here, the tension between individual and collective rights was pressed into service by the state government, sometimes with political success. However, the social actors involved also recognize the contradictions inherent in this type of government mobilization of the discourse of human rights, and they may respond by withholding support for government initiatives, policies, or practices.

Conclusions

The globalization of the discourse of human rights has shaped the way that many social actors involved in the Chiapas conflict express their positions and take their actions. Most are deploying a discourse of human rights in one form or another to defend their political goals. This is true of organized indigenous people who are struggling for greater recognition before the state, as well as of those who seek a broader sociopolitical change. The framing of their demands and their own defense emphasizing the political dimension of their rights struggles allows them to mobilize support from broad networks of actors and organizations and thus strengthens their position vis-à-vis the state. The state and federal governments have recognized this, and in the face of new strategies and pressures exerted by this conjunction of global and local forces, they, too, seek new ways to defend their power. The discourse of human rights has provided the state with a justification for its actions that is difficult to contest. Meanwhile, local elites as unalike as San Cristóbal *Coletos* and Chol paramilitaries have redeployed the discourse of human rights in their struggle to maintain the status quo. The individual groups' particular relations of power were reflected in their distinct uses of the discourse of human rights.

Thus, even though the globalization of human rights has shaped the local elaboration of identities and forms of resistance, by no means has there occurred a process of overt or direct imposition. The diversity of local usages of the discourse by actors in relation to the Chiapas conflict makes this clear. The argument that indigenous people are passive receivers of imperializing global discourses eliminates their history and their agency. As the cases we have discussed demonstrate, indigenous people, like all parties in the Chiapas conflict, have been adopting, rearticulating, and redeploying the discourse based on their own histories, understandings, and political positionalities—and for their own goals.

We do not intend this simply as a reelaboration of the relativist position that there are many different concepts of human rights in different cultural contexts. It is not that indigenous people or others in Chiapas have their own notions of human rights, separate and distinct from Western ones. Rather, we suggest the existence of a *dialogic process* in which differing interpretations of human rights emerge precisely from the intense interactions among globalized discourses, transnational actors, agents of the nation-state, and various local groups in the context of conflict. In other words, the varying discourses of human rights that have emerged during the Chiapas conflict are neither products of the imposition of Western ideas nor of specifically indigenous or local concepts. Rather, they have emerged from their multiple engagements on a highly politicized terrain in which all have much at stake. There is no more a unified indigenous conception of human rights than there is a single Western one. If we understand human rights in this way, it is no longer critical to demonstrate their universality, nor to reject them as cultural impositions. In our view, we can learn more by looking at the varied meanings and sociopolitical uses of the discourse of human rights, and at the ways in which they emerge in different interactions.

Notes

Portions of this chapter appear in the authors' doctoral dissertations (Speed 2001 and Leyva Solano 2001), and some of the material contained herein was published in Speed 2007. Speed's research and writing were supported by the Social Science Research Council–MacArthur Foundation Fellowship on International Peace and Security in a Changing World, the Ford Foundation, and the American Anthropological Association. Leyva Solano's research and writing were supported by the Consejo Nacional de Ciencias y Tecnología (National Counsel on Science and Technology, CONACYT) and the Centro de Investigaciones y Estudios Superiores en Antropología (Center for Research and Higher Education in Social Anthropology, CIESAS). We thank Kathleen Dill, Jennifer Bickham Mendez, and Angela Steusse, as well as the anonymous reviewers at Duke University Press, for their comments, which greatly improved the text. We also thank Jutta Meier Weidenbach for the translation of portions of this text.

1. According to the reports of the secretary of defense (Secretaria de la Defensa Nacional, SEDENA) there were between seventeen and twenty-five thousand Mexican Army troops in Chiapas at the height of military presence in 1998. Organizations monitoring the militarization in Chiapas have placed the figures much higher, between seventy and eighty thousand troops (Global Exchange, CIEPAC, and CENCOS 2000). Also, in mid-1999, there were reportedly twelve paramilitary groups operating in the state. After taking office in 2000, President Vicente Fox withdrew military bases and checkpoints in key communities as part of his administration's efforts to reestablish a dialogue with the EZLN. This reduced the number of troops in Chiapas, though figures on how much the number was diminished are not available, nor is it known how many troops returned to the state after it became clear that the dialogue would not be reopened.

2. We use the concept "dialogic" in the Bakhtinian sense. For M. M. Bakhtin (1981), every speech act implied a dialogic process, a response to others. Our discourse only exists in the context of previous or alternative discourses, and is in dialogue with them. Following Dennis Tedlock and Bruce Mannheim (1995), we believe that cultural systems and practices are constantly produced, reproduced, and revised in dialogues among their members, and in dialogue with other cultures and cultural expressions.

3. The diocese in 1960 covered the entire state of Chiapas. In 1964, the diocese was divided into three (San Cristóbal de Las Casas, Tapachula, and Tuxtla Gutierrez) at the urging of Ruiz, who wanted to devote more of the diocese's work to the indigenous populations of the state, virtually all of which were situated within the area of the diocese of San Cristóbal (Womack 1998). This area, which covers 48 percent of the state, was then subdivided by the diocese into six ethnogeographic zones: the Zona Chol, Zona Sur, Zona Sureste, Zona Centro, Zona Tzotzil, and Zona Tzeltal (Leyva Solano 1995a).

4. According to María del Carmen García Aguilar (1998), the primary antecedent of today's human rights organizations was the Comité Diocesano de Ayuda a Inmigrantes Fronterizos (Diocesan Committee on Aid to Border Immigrants, CODAIF), a project of the Catholic Church registered in 1986 to assist Guatemalan refugees.

5. Ruiz is still the president, although he retired as bishop in 1999.

6. Araceli Burguete Cal y Mayor (1994: 39) asserts that between 1982 and 1987, according to the complaints filed by leftist activists, there were 102 politically motivated murders, 327 forced disappearances, 590 arbitrary detentions, 427 people kidnapped and tortured, 261 injured in political violence, 40 families expelled from their communities, 54 people forcibly removed from lands, 27 threats of forced removal from lands, 12 women raped, 548 threats of expulsion, 18 homes, churches, and schools destroyed, 31 attacks on marches and protests, and 4 attacks on offices of social organizations. For more information, see, for example, the campesino organizations' bulletins (CNPA and FNCR 1981; CLCH 1986; Albores and González 1983), Amnesty International reports from 1985, 1986, and 1987 (e.g., Amnesty International 1986), or the book *Chiapas, Chronology of a Recent Ethnocide: A Brief Account of the Political Violence against the Indians (1974–1987)*, written by a sociologist who received her funding from the recently founded Mexican Academy of Human Rights (Burguete Cal y Mayor 1989).

7. The first large indigenous migration arrived in San Cristóbal in 1976, when a thousand Protestant converts were expelled from San Juan Chamula. By 1980, approximately three thousand indigenous people had arrived and taken up residence in San Cristóbal and had founded four new *colonias*. By the end of the 1980s, the number of indigenous residents in the city had grown by about twenty thousand and there were sixteen new *colonias*. In the year 2000 there were approximately sixty thousand indigenous residents—more than half of them children or minors—living in a city of between 120,000 and 160,000 residents. In comparative demographic terms, the same city in 1970 had only 28,000 residents, principally *mestizos* (Rus and Vigil 2007).

8. Interview with Shannon Speed, July 1999.

9. There was a distinction in the claims of the COAO and the decision of the Inter-American Commission on Human Rights (IACHR): the COAO viewed the violation of the prisoners' rights as having taken place during the illegal raid in which they were apprehended. The court ruled that their rights had been violated during the legal process.

10. Speed has argued elsewhere that there is a close relationship between neoliberal governance practices, NGOization, and human rights discourse (Speed and Reyes this volume; Speed 2007). NGOS—like the discourse of human rights—are compatible with, and in fact their predominance is largely a product of, the state decentralization and divestment of responsibility for the mediation of social inequality to civil society that are basic elements of neoliberalization. The relationship between human rights and NGOS is thus more problematic than the dependency relationships they create. In fact, engaging the state through NGOS may serve to uphold neoliberal forms of rule (García Aguilar 1998), thus supporting a process that has had a negative impact on most local indigenous peoples (certainly this argument can be made for Chiapas).

11. Historically the term *Coletos* refers to the ponytails male Spanish descendants wore. Nowadays the term is polysemous.

12. In Chiapas and in Guatemala, the term *Ladino* is employed for non-Indians. The term *mestizo*, used in much of the rest of the country, has only recently gained currency in Chiapas, as it is increasingly acknowledged that no clear line separates people of Indian and people of Spanish descent, as the Ladino/Indian construct maintained.

13. As is the case in much of the region, "foreigners" refers not only to non-Mexicans but to any non-locals. The term in Spanish, *extranjero*, means both "foreigner" and "stranger."

14. This interpretation, openly expressed here with all its racist content, is argued with only slightly more restraint by the Mexican scholar Enrique Krauze (1999). The woman did not wish to give her name, but she did say that she had been born and had lived all her life in San Cristóbal.

15. This view was expressed by Marina Patricia Jimenez, the executive secretary of the Fray Bartolomé de Las Casas Human Rights Center, when Speed interviewed her on August 3, 2000.

16. This campaign included a public relations campaign in the press and the placing of immigration checkpoints throughout the conflict zones, resulting in the summary expulsion of foreigners found in those areas.

17. The PRI held power in Mexico for seven decades. It was finally defeated by Vicente Fox's Partido de Acción Nacional (National Action Party, PAN) in the presidential elections of 2000. That same year, the PRI lost the governorship of the state of Chiapas to Pablo Salazar Mediguchia, an ex-Priísta who ran on a coalition of opposition parties, including the PAN and the center-left PRD.

18. The PRD has been the most important left-of-center party in Mexico since 1988.

19. Samuel Sánchez Sánchez was imprisoned in 2001 and later released for his participation as a leader of Paz y Justicia.

20. The groups involved were the CDHFBC, Global Exchange, Servicio Internacional para la Paz (International Service for Peace, SIPAZ), Centro de Derechos Indígena, A. C. (Center for Indigenous Rights, CEDIAC), and Coordinación de Organiza-

ciones Nogubernamentales por la Paz (CONPAZ). Speed worked with Estación Norte as part of Global Exchange during this period.

21. This comes from the colloquial use of the Spanish in which members of a group are called by the name of that group. Thus human rights workers or organizations are "human rights" and soldiers are "armies" (*ejércitos*).

22. This was a social process that took place in indigenous communities throughout the state.

23. Prior to the creation of the CNDH, the Dirección General de Derechos Humanos existed for one year under the secretary of the interior (Gobernación). In 1999, a constitutional reform made the CNDH an autonomous entity. Information is available on the commission's Web site (www.cndh.org.mx).

24. For example, torture was outlawed in 1991 by the *Federal Law for the Prevention and Punishment of Torture* (*Ley Federal para Prevenir y Sancionar la Tortura*).

25. The discourse of individual equality and the protection of private property emerged simultaneously with the birth of the state. Prior to 1917, constitutional documents such as the Consitutional Decree of Apatzingán of 1814 and the constitution of 1857 contained a broad range of rights of a liberal-individualist orientation (Terrazas 1996). However, the constitution of 1917, a product of the Mexican Revolution, contained such strong social rights that many considered Mexico a socialist-leaning country during the corporatist period. Many of these social rights were eliminated or reduced in the constitutional reforms of 1992, which prepared the national terrain for the North American Free Trade Agreement (NAFTA) to go into effect January 1, 1994.

26. Gobierno del Estado de Chiapas, *Ley de Derechos y Cultura Indígena del estado de Chiapas* (1999). At the insistence of government representatives, the San Andrés Accords on Indigenous Rights and Culture, signed in 1996 by the EZLN and the government, contained a similar clause. This wording also exists in international agreements, such as the 1989 International Labor Organization Convention Concerning Indigenous and Tribal Peoples in Independent Countries (ILO Convention 169), signed and ratified by Mexico in 1991. Its article 8 states that "[indigenous] peoples shall have the right to retain their own customs and institutions, where these are not incompatible with fundamental rights defined by the national legal system and with internationally recognized human rights."

27. This is what Will Kymlicka (1996: 35) refers to as the "external protections" over "internal restrictions" in minority rights.

28. Human rights are inscribed in the Mexican constitution as "individual guarantees."

29. Since December 2000, when Pablo Salazar took office as governor, the state government has generally adopted a less confrontational approach in its dealings with distinct actors involved in the Chiapas conflict. However, this does not mean that the violation of human rights has disappeared; on the contrary, an ongoing, selective violation of those rights persists.

Breaking the Reign of Silence
Ethnography of a Clandestine Cemetery

> Perhaps all one can really hope for, all I am entitled to, is no more
> than this: to write it down. To report what I know. So that it will not be
> possible for any man ever to say again: I knew nothing about it.
>
> ANDRÉ BRINK, *A DRY WHITE SEASON*

Between the late 1970s and the late 1980s, Guatemala was torn by a time of
mass terror and extreme violence in a genocidal campaign against the
Maya that became known as "La Violencia." In the end, some 626 villages
were massacred by the army, 1.5 million people were displaced, and more
than 200,000 civilians were dead or disappeared. More than 80 percent of
the victims of this violence were Maya. This essay explores the joint efforts
of Maya massacre survivors, forensic anthropologists, the Archbishop's Office for Human Rights, and the Guatemalan truth commission to investigate
the 1978 army massacre in Panzós. Just as the forensic investigation becomes
a framework for revealing evidence of the massacre and of genocide, this
ethnography—based on testimonies of survivors, interviews with perpetrators and archival research—provides an opportunity to understand its
structure and context from the lived experiences of survivors. Indeed, as
was the case in the massacre of Plan de Sánchez, survivor testimony provided both local context and understanding beyond the scientific findings
of the exhumation. This local perspective is critical for understanding the
contemporary transitional justice in which survivors live and seek to re-

build their lives and communities through local mobilizations for truth, justice, and human rights. The very act of giving testimony challenges the official silencing of the past, present, and future. Indeed, as Dominick La-Capra has noted: the mobilization of memory "relates acknowledgement and immanent critique to situational transcendence of the past that is not total but is nonetheless essential for opening up more desirable possibilities in the future" (1998: 16). Exhumations of clandestine cemeteries are the physical and symbolic representations of these contemporary Maya struggles for human rights, as well as their future possibilities (Sanford 2003). Thus in the Maya region of Guatemala, where human rights violations peaked at a horrific rate during La Violencia, indigenous people are currently mobilizing human rights discourse and practice as a mode of empowerment in their struggle to heal and to regain some control over their histories and their futures. John Beverly has pointed out that testimony "is first and foremost an act, a tactic by means of which people engage in the process of self-constitution and survival" (1996: 46). By participating in the exhumation of a clandestine cemetery and giving testimony, massacre survivors reassert their political agency by giving these testimonies for truth commission reports and court cases.

Initial newspaper articles reporting the May 29, 1978, Guatemalan army massacre of Q'eqchi' Maya peasants in the plaza of Panzós gave the official army count of thirty-four casualties. As survivors gave testimony in the capital and journalists were allowed into Panzós, some newspaper articles began to include peasant survivor estimates of more than one hundred dead. Following the June 8, 1978, march commemorating the assassination of Mario López Larrave and protesting the massacre in Panzós, popular organizations and others in the democratic opposition challenged official estimates and asserted that the death toll exceeded a hundred. Between 1978 and 1997, popular, academic, and press accounts of the massacre cited one to two hundred victims (Williams 1994: 148; Watanabe 1992: 250; Levenson-Estrada 1994: 142; Wilson 1995: 218; Aguilera Peralta 1981: 200; Montejo 1999: 40; Zur 1998: 69).[1] By the time the Fundación de Antropología Forense de Guatemala (Guatemalan Forensic Anthropology Foundation, FAFG) prepared for its survey visit to Panzós in July 1997, popular knowledge of the massacre numbered the victims as at least two hundred.[2]

Nineteen years after the massacre, the FAFG and the regional prosecutor from the departmental capital of Coban and his assistant traveled to Panzós to carry out a preliminary site visit to gather information for the forensic investigation and the legal proceedings planned by the prosecutor. We were accompanied by two representatives of the Misión de Naciones Unidad para Guatemala (UN Verification Mission in Guatemala, MINUGUA) and five members of the Fuerzas de Respuesta Inmediata (Immediate Response Forces, FRI). The FRI were clad in their heavy black cotton uniforms with black wool berets—clothing better suited for the cool highlands than the hot, humid lowlands. These young Ladino men from Zacapa and Jutiapa each carried a machine gun, pistol, and other light weapons. The prosecutor had requested FRI presence because of death threats he had received from legal representatives of local plantation owners as he proceeded in a recent case in the murder of a teacher implicating the sons of Flavio Monzon—one of these same owners—in the 1978 massacre.

When we reached Panzós, more than two hundred widows ranging in age from thirty-five to seventy were waiting for us at the entrance to the cemetery. On arrival, we immediately explained that the FRI were with us to help the prosecutor and that no one should be afraid of them. We walked with the mostly older and elderly men and women, the prosecutor, the MINUGUA representatives, and the five FRI up to the site of the mass grave on a hill overlooking the municipal cemetery near the western entrance to Panzós. Initial apprehension of the FRI dissipated, and the widows seemed satisfied that so many "powerful" people were helping them in the exhumation. Accompanying the group of widows were adults and adolescents orphaned in La Violencia, as well as several elderly men who had lost their sons during the violence. The median age was probably about sixty. There was one thirty-five-year-old widow—she had been fifteen and pregnant when her husband was killed in the plaza massacre. Conspicuously absent were forty-five- to sixty-year-old men. They were absent for the same reason that forty-five- to sixty-year-old women and sixty- to eighty-year-old men and women were present: their husbands and sons accounted for the majority of victims of La Violencia. These missing men were the victims of the plaza massacre and the wave of disappearances and assassinations that followed.

At the top of the hill, a whitewashed cross made of railroad ties marked the grave of the massacre victims. Almost immediately, the two hundred widows began to give testimony about the day of the massacre and collectively wept. Though our organizational goal for the day was to locate the grave site and gather basic information about the circumstances of the massacre rather than collect individual testimony, we listened as each widow spoke. We tried to comfort the men and women who sobbed as they recounted surviving the massacre and witnessing army soldiers killing their sons and husbands.

One young woman spoke firmly and wept as she recounted her survival and how, at the age of twelve, she had witnessed the killing of her grandmother, Mama Maquín, in the plaza. "I saw people dying there," María declared. "They were falling. There were some who fell on top of me and bullets flew by my face. I threw myself on the ground. I was face down and pretended to be dead. And there I was mixed in with those who had stopped moving."[3]

Everyone began to step forward wanting to give testimony about the massacre. We explained to the group that we would carefully listen to each of them when we returned to carry out the exhumation because we knew they had much to share with us and that it would require many days to take all the testimonies. We reaffirmed their right to speak and their need to be heard. En masse, we then went to a small, dark community building to explain the exhumation process and to answer any questions the witnesses and survivors might have about the process. Because few in the group spoke Spanish, our entire presentation was conducted through interpreters. We showed a slide presentation of exhumations in other parts of Guatemala that outlined the archaeological and logistical procedures and prepared survivors for what they would witness. Everyone listened with hushed attention. The sense of anticipation grew within the room. At the end of the presentation, rather than asking questions, several dozen people (mostly the elderly mothers and fathers) stood up holding the identification papers of their dead and disappeared loved ones and expressed their desire to begin the identification process right then and there.

Once again, we explained that we would collect the information from each of them when we returned to do the exhumation. When we left, we felt extremely satisfied with the meeting and the level of community participation. More than two hundred widows had come to the meeting, thus reaffirming the reported two hundred killed in the massacre. We believed the grave site was larger than community members indicated to us because the site they outlined was too small to hold so many people. Later that same day in Coban, we met with a religious worker who had been in Panzós the day after the massacre and who had worked there for several years. She smiled on hearing that two hundred widows had gathered to take us to the grave site and to participate in our meeting. She said, "Until recently violence and silence reigned in Panzós."[4]

Testimony and the Excavation of Memory

On our return to Panzós to begin the exhumation, in September of 1997, the same widows were waiting for us. Two translators accompanied us. We set up two private corners within a nearby house where we would conduct interviews. The house sat on a little hill above the cemetery. A thatched roof rested on the walls of wood slabs and bamboolike sticks. The dirt floor was swept clean. The sparse furnishings gave the room a spacious feeling. In one corner was a bed of plywood slats. A hammock hung diagonally across the room. Against the wall facing the door was a small table covered with a piece of floral plastic. Candles, a few flowers in a cola bottle, an image of a saint, and old tin cans blackened by smoke from incense transformed the humble table into an altar. A plain wood slab table and bench became our work-space. We moved the table from the center of the room to the empty corners. Only when the rays of the afternoon sun beat down on us through the bamboo wall did we understand why this side of the room was empty— the heat was more intense where we were working inside the dark house than it was in the direct midday sun outside.

Before beginning our work at the site, and before taking survivor testi-monies, we went to the municipal offices on the plaza to meet with the mayor. I asked for the death registers from 1978 and reviewed them with another team member. The registers revealed that on May 29, 1978, Edeli-berto Asig (police chief then and now) and then mayor Walter Overdick recorded twenty-four deaths with the letters xxx in the spaces provided for the names of the deceased. The time of death was recorded as 9:00 a.m. and the word *balas* (bullets) filled the space for the cause of death (*Registro de Defunciones de Panzós*, 24). We wondered where the other 175 entries were and what had prevented the mayor and police chief from recording the other deaths in the plaza massacre. We noted data about deaths before, during, and after May of 1978.

That same morning when we returned to the humble house near the graveyard where we were to conduct our interviews, I began the day by outlining the interview process in the same way that each individual interview is outlined prior to taping. Through my interpreter, I assured those present that interviews would be private, not public, and that all interview data would be held confidential between the FAFG and the person interviewed. The women nodded in agreement with me and with one another. I explained that we would use the information from the interviews for our report to the Comisión de Clarificación Histórico (Historical Clarification Commission, CEH), but that we would not use their individual names. I also explained that others including myself would most likely use this information to write books and articles about Panzós, but that people's identities would remain anonymous. In individual interviews, from this first day on, the majority of Panzós survivors established their own authority and individual political rights by asserting that they wanted their names used. Men and women would say, "What more can happen to me? They killed my son [or husband]. I have nothing. We want justice. Write my name down."

Although I have used the Widow Cus and María Maquín's real names, there are numerous others whose names I have replaced with pseudonyms despite their requests to the contrary. While the home of the Widow Cus was the public gathering place during the excavation and María Maquín has been featured in national and international news stories following the reburial of the remains, the other individuals are not publicly known figures. Their testimonies have been given in private and often clandestinely. Public knowledge of their testimonies could put these individuals and their families at further risk.

The giving of testimony is an emotionally charged experience. When individuals say, "I have nothing to lose. Write my name down," they are asserting a position of defiance in the present to the pain of the past. Rather than debate the potential risks of using real names (which are in themselves acknowledged by the words "I have nothing left to lose"), I suggest we discuss it later. Sometimes, we talk about it at the end of the interview. Usually, we discuss it within a few days when they seek me out to tell me they have decided they would prefer not to use their real names. More often than not, they have second thoughts about using their real names and express fear of potential harm, not to themselves, but to relatives or neighbors. As I always ask those I interview if they have a name they would prefer for me to use in place of their own, they put great effort into choosing a pseudonym that holds personal meaning for them—many times, it is the name of a relative or friend who died in La Violencia. In the case of those few who asked me to use their real name with whom I had no later contact, I have chosen to err on the side of safety and use a pseudonym.

Finally, although the majority of survivors with whom I have spoken have sooner or later chosen anonymity, not once has a single survivor asked me not to use their testimony. Indeed, when asking for anonymity, survivors emphasize that it is the story that has urgent need to be known. As Doña Juanita explained after changing her mind about the use of her name, "I am afraid of what might happen to my children if I use my name. But if you need my name to give faith to my testimony, I give you my permission" (Panzós Testimony No. 7, September 7, 1997). While survivors come forward and speak for many different reasons, many wish to unburden their pain, to share the content of their lived experience of violence, and to have their experiences validated by those who listen and the wider audience they hope their testimony will reach.

In the early afternoon of our first day of research in Panzós, we returned to the municipal archives with more FAFG team members to help us review and make note of pertinent data from all Panzós death registers from 1978 to 1985, as well as from other municipal records. On our return we were informed that the municipal employee responsible for these records (which we had perused that same morning) was on vacation and would not be returning until the end of October. We would be welcome to return to Panzós in October to review the documents. I requested a meeting with the mayor who directed me to the municipal secretary (who, like the police chief, El Canché Asig, is a permanent employee of the municipality). The municipal secretary glared at me and his face turned red with anger as I explained that the records we were requesting were public documents to which everyone had legal access, regardless of employee vacations. Having asserted the law yet seeking to avoid a confrontation with the secretary and the disappearance of the documents, I then thanked him for his collaboration and offered that it would be embarrassing for both of us if MINUGUA representatives had to come to look for the documents and that perhaps someone else in the municipal office might know where to find them— thereby avoiding embarrassment for both of us. He asked us to wait and said he would try to find someone to help us. Twenty minutes later we were given the same documents we had been viewing earlier that morning. In the *libro de actas* (book of minutes [of local municipal meetings]), the page containing the minutes for the first council meeting held after the massacre had been meticulously marked out with cursive circles in blue ink, completely covering all writing below.

Several FAFG team members stayed at the municipal offices to record data from the death registers and council meeting minutes. I returned to the little house above the graveyard with my research assistant, Leanor, and the translators, Miguel and María,[5] to take testimonies. For nearly three weeks, we interviewed daily from 7:00 a.m. to 6:30 p.m., often without taking a break because there were so many people waiting to be interviewed. The number of survivors waiting to give testimony never seemed to diminish. People would arrive at seven in the morning and wait until three in the afternoon to give their testimony. Don Salvador waited with his sweat-stained hat in hand from 7:00 a.m. to 6:00 p.m. to ensure that his testimony was heard. Each day, as the afternoon approached, I would look out to those waiting for their turn to speak and count more than forty men and women. They had left their work in the fields to wait all day to give their testimony. They would sit patiently in the heat, without food or drink, just waiting for their turn to speak.

Soon, Leanor, Miguel, María, and I were sharing our lunches with the people we were interviewing because we knew that no matter how tired we were, their need to speak was greater than our need to rest. In the end, we greatly counted on each other to make sure that all pertinent facts were covered in the taking of testimonies. The humidity was so great that our clothes were drenched. Our minds were numbed by the heat and the endless testimonies of violence. The skin on our faces became irritated from using tissue to wipe away the sweat. We perspired so much that we dripped onto our notebooks. We learned why the widows carried a hand towel with them. As we wiped the sweat from our faces and necks, fanned our bodies with our damp clothes, and shared cigarettes, Gatorade, and snacks with survivors, the formal relationships that divide researcher, research assistant, interpreter, and informant became blurred. Our days were spent taking testimonies in collective conversations in which we all shared the goal of trying to understand what had happened in Panzós.

In all we interviewed almost two hundred people in Panzós and several more in other parts of the country. The first day we interviewed eighteen people and discovered that most came to give testimony about disappeared husbands, sons, brothers, or fathers, rather than about loved ones murdered in the plaza.

The Survivor Story: Ana, Juana, and Rosario

Doña Ana holds her chin in her hands and looks off to a faraway place beyond the graveyard below: "We suffered so much. My God, how we suffered." She is recounting the violence that selectively destroyed the interdependence of Q'eqchi' families and communities, replacing a social fabric based on collaboration with one of betrayal and mistrust. "In the middle of the night Ladinos and Q'eqchi's came to our house. They were Q'eqchi's from here because they speak like we speak, but they had their faces covered. The Ladinos didn't cover their faces." Partially hidden by the darkness of the night, they quietly moved through the village until they reached the door to Doña Ana's humble home. With a swift kick and a slam of machine gun butts, the door gave way and loudly fell to the floor. Seeking to protect her husband, Doña Ana rose from bed and stood between the armed men and her husband. "They knocked me down on the ground," she says with sadness as she clutches her stomach and rocks forward. "They tied up my husband and kicked him and hit him with their guns." Doña Ana begins to cry as she recounts, "They took him away." Then she pauses for a moment and takes a deep breath. She shifts her gaze and looks directly into my eyes. She is strong. She is afraid. She declares quietly, but firmly, "El Canché was with them" (Panzós Testimony No. 3, September 6, 1997).

Wiping the sweat from her brow with a small hand towel, Doña Juana seats herself at the table. She has been waiting nearly eight hours to give her testimony. Her skin has a gray pallor, accompanied by the thick cough associated with tuberculosis. She immediately begins to speak, "My son was a catechist. He knew how to read. Now in the village, no one knows how to read. My son just disappeared." She is desperate. She is hopeful. "Do you know where he is?" she asks me. I am powerless and feel close to useless as I explain that we are exhuming the victims of the plaza massacre and that we do not know the fate or place of burial of the disappeared. "My son was in the plaza," she tells me. "My God, we have all suffered here" (Panzós Testimony No. 17, September 7, 1997).

In 1978, at fifty-five, Don Manuel was the eldest Maya priest in his village. He was a spiritual leader and a guide respected throughout Panzós. One year after the plaza massacre, he and his wife Doña Rosario were awakened in the middle of the night by the sound of a truck on the dirt road near their home. "It was so dark and we couldn't find our flashlight. I heard my son yelling from his house, 'Oh my God! Papá!' because he could hear the soldiers surrounding our house."

Soldiers broke into the house of the Mayan priest and dragged him out of the house wrapped in the hammock in which he had been sleeping. "They were beating and kicking him with no mercy," remembers Doña Rosario. "That same night, the other priests disappeared too" (Panzós Testimony No. 10, September 7, 1997).

In most cases, Asig, the chief of police (popularly known as El Canché) was implicated in the disappearances. According to twelve testimonies, he participated in the kidnapping of the disappeared from their homes or had threatened them shortly before.[6]

As the days went by, our tabulation of victims based on testimony began to show a rapidly increasing number of disappeared and a slow increase in the number of victims of the plaza massacre. While the number of disappeared increased by twenty to thirty each day, the number of massacre victims increased by only three to six. Each day, an average of forty-three survivors and witnesses waited in the stifling heat for their turn to speak on the impact of the massacre on their lives. Many who had already given testimony returned with a relative *para apoyar* (to support) the widows, victims, and survivors. Often they returned ostensibly to share a new fact they had remembered. In most cases, more than wanting to provide new information, they simply wanted to keep talking. The silence had been broken. Many said, "Ya siento aliviada. Quiero aliviarme un poco más" (I feel relieved, I want to relieve myself a little more).

"A Year of Death": Juanita, Feliciana, and Magdalena

Doña Juanita shares her sadness as she fans herself from the heat, "My husband died in the plaza. I was thirty-five and had six children." She looks off into the distance and rubs her chest, "My baby died because I transmitted my sadness and fear in my milk." She glances toward the dirt floor, vaguely nods in agreement with herself, and declares, "The massacre in the plaza killed my husband and my baby." She raises her head to look at me. Tears fall down her face as she recounts her children's suffering. "Maltiox," she thanks me. As she stands, she squeezes my hand before she walks away (Panzós Testimony No. 7, September 7, 1997).

After Doña Juanita, three women and one man give their testimonies. Doña Feliciana is the eleventh interview on September 7, 1997. She stares at the ground as she sits down in the chair. She begins to cry even before she begins to speak. We try to comfort her, though it seems like an impossibility. I look over to the area where victims and survivors are waiting for their opportunity to give testimony: I count thirty-two people within my field of vision. Mixed in my interview notes, I find I have written, "How can we ever get through this line of people? What can we give them?"

As we gently pat Doña Feliciana's shoulder and back, offer her a soda and some Kleenex, she composes herself. She sits up erectly in the chair. She looks directly at the tape recorder and states, "My father died in the plaza. My husband survived, but not completely. He lost his arm from machine-gun fire. He can't work the land anymore. Ever since then, all he can do is work as a carrier. He carries one hundred pounds, and they pay him eighty centavos to one quetzal to carry it one to three kilometers" (Panzós Testimony No. 11, September 7, 1997).

Doña Magdalena's parents and brothers survived the plaza massacre. Her husband was not so fortunate. "I had ten children when my husband died in the plaza. But that year, many people died," she explains trying to give context to the incomprehensible by making ordinary the extraordinary. She pauses for a moment nodding her chin and rocking her body. Then she says almost matter-of-factly, "It was a year of death" (Panzós Testimony No. 16, September 7, 1997).

In a certain way, regardless of the memories that are shared, each survivor and each witness must suspend his or her own disbelief to believe that the outside listener, whether national or international, human rights worker or academic researcher, might actually be able to comprehend personal representations and memories of terror. Then, in the giving of testimony or in responding to interview questions, the witness seeks to consciously represent the memories of terror that dominate the unconscious and continue to shape daily encounters even absent the public acknowledgment of terror and its memory. As Jorge Luís Borges has noted, "Only one thing does not exist. It is forgetting" (qtd. in Benedetti 1995: 11).

On the third day of our investigation, we decided to interview those who came to give testimony about a relative killed in the plaza massacre before those who sought to testify of relatives sequestered, disappeared, and assassinated following the massacre. We did this because the archaeologists carrying out the excavation of the mass grave needed the information we were gathering and because we were trying to estimate the number of individuals killed in the massacre. Thus we began to organize those who came to give testimony by placing those with a relative who had died in the plaza at the front of the line. Those who came to give testimonies of violence and loss following the massacre agreed to allow the others to go first as long as we promised we would take their testimonies. Each day, they patiently waited until there were no more plaza massacre testimonies so that they could give their own testimonies of survival. Plaza massacre survivors reaffirmed the right of others to give testimony, "Sufrímos igual. Aqui, todos sufrímos" (We suffered equally. Here, we all suffered).

Searching for Facts and Bearing Witness

Despite the reorganization of the testimony-taking process, each day brought only a few plaza testimonies. Yet information about the day of the massacre remained consistent in both what was said and what was not said. While all books and articles written about the Panzós massacre reported Guatemalan army soldiers firing into a large group of peasants protesting for land in the plaza in front of the municipal offices, no one seemed to know who organized the protest, or if indeed there was a protest the day of the massacre. The reported number of people congregating in the plaza was widely inconsistent, ranging from 150 to 2,000.

The next issue that had initially seemed a nonissue became both a critical and an extremely delicate question. While news articles, books, and political propaganda documenting the Panzós massacre consistently outlined the army shooting on a peasant protest over land, this was not the story we were told. By the end of the first day, we no longer asked if the deceased had attended the protest in the plaza; rather we called it a meeting. The next day we referred to it as a reunion. As more people came each day, it became increasingly clear that they wanted to talk about their fear and their pain, which we of course wanted to hear (if only to bear witness), but we also needed facts for our report to the CEH. By the third day, as the FAFG archaeologists continued to prepare the site for the exhumation, I told the archaeologists that I did not believe two hundred people were killed in the massacre or buried in the grave. I estimated the number as low as twenty-five (based on the death register) and as high as sixty-five (somewhat randomly doubling the testimonies we had already taken), but no higher.

By this time, our composite account of the plaza massacre based on survivor and witness testimonies went something like this: Somewhere between two hundred and nine hundred men, women, and children (but mostly men and boys) marched to the plaza with machetes and *palos* (sticks) in their possession, and possibly waving them in the air. Witnesses and survivors reported the mood of the crowd as angry and happy, and therefore unclear. Due to contradictory testimonies, the crowd's intention was unclear as well. The people were organized by an unidentified group of local residents. They went to the plaza expecting to receive land. In fact, some witnesses and survivors reported that the mayor called the meeting promising land to all who arrived.

From the vantage point of investigating the massacre for the FAFG report to the CEH, it was from the flood of individual and community memories that we sought to establish a reasonable and verifiable reconstruction of the massacre by comparing and contrasting consistencies and contradictions within the testimonies and then seeking corroboration from other sources. This required a constant review of testimonies and a nightly dissection and comparison of key moments described by widows and survivors. While the actual excavation of skeletal remains provides material for forensic and archaeological, that is, scientific, analysis to determine facts such as the gender, age, and identity of the victims, as well as the cause of death and methods used to dispose of the remains, the historical reconstruction of the massacre relies on testimonies, interviews, and archival resources—each of which can rightly be described as being subjective and/or biased.

When presenting ethnographic material and sharing testimonies of massacre survivors in academic and policy venues, I have often been asked, "How do you know they are telling you the truth? How do you decide what is true?" While one might believe that these questions reflect the disbelief of the person asking, I have come to believe that these questions (like the popular usage of ¿Saber?) more reflect a desire for an orderly and tangible world—a world that, if it ever existed, was turned upside down and made surreal by the obscenity of war. This is not particular to the Guatemalan genocide. Indeed, in his work on the Holocaust, the philosopher and survivor Bruno Bettleheim has written of how the truth of his first work on trauma and survival (1979) was doubted and the work itself was repeatedly rejected by peer-reviewed psychology journals as not scientific, not replicable, too emotional, not objective, and potentially offensive in its portrayal of the Nazis. Thus memories of survival seem both obscene and surreal to those who have not either experienced or come close to it through its recounting by survivors. Conversely, those who have experienced and survived extreme state violence, regardless of place and time, often comment that the testimonies resonate with their own experiences of survival. In my own experience, Indonesians, South Africans, Rwandans, Israelis, Palestinians, Sri Lankans, Salvadorans, Argentines, and Chileans, among others, have often shared their own stories in public venues to contest those who have asked about the truth of the testimonies I have presented.

In his writing on the Vietnam War, Tim O'Brien offers, "You can tell a true war story by the questions you ask. Somebody tells a story, let's say, and afterward you ask, 'Is it true?' and if the answer matters, you've got your answer" (1990: 89). This is not the glib response it may appear to be. He further explains: "In a true war story, if there's a moral at all, it's like the thread that makes the cloth. You can't tease it out. You can't extract the meaning without unraveling the deeper meaning. . . . It comes down to gut instinct. A true war story, if truly told, makes the stomach believe. . . . a true war story is never about war. . . . It's about love and memory. It's about sorrow. . . . You can tell a true war story by the way it never seems to end. Not then, not ever" (83–91).

The following excerpts from seemingly never-ending testimonies were among those we used to reconstruct events preceding the massacre. They are indicative of the deluge of painful memories shared with us as widows and survivors sought to reconstruct their personal and community histories and, at the same time, communicate the experience and memory of these events to outsiders. It is from this deluge that enveloped us, as well as those giving testimonies, that we sought to dissect and disentangle "facts" and, at the same time, understand and respect the raw memories shared with us. The offering of these fragments is my modest attempt to share both the survivor memories and the challenge they present to the researcher in the field who, while overwhelmed by the sensation of their immediacy and sorrow, seeks to understand the lived experiences of survivors in such a way that this understanding might make sense to survivors, researchers, and readers.

Why the Peasants Went to the Plaza

DOÑA JUANITA

We were soliciting a little piece of land. For this they killed my husband.
(Panzós Testimony No. 7, September 7, 1997)

DOÑA FRANCISCA

We had gone to make Mayejak [Maya ceremony] with the rest of the people. To do this ceremony, we were soliciting land for our children. We made Mayejak with the intention that we would be heard when we went to the plaza. We supplicated God that we would be heard when we reached the plaza. (Panzós Testimony No. 13, September 7, 1997)

DOÑA ROSA

My husband only wanted a small piece of land. He just wanted a little bit of land to grow our maize. He didn't have any problems. He had not done anything wrong. We lived in tranquility. He never thought something like this would happen to us. He never thought our children would be left orphans. (Panzós Testimony No. 2, September 7, 1997)

DOÑA TOMASA

My deceased husband came to the plaza for land. He was interested in getting a little bit of land. (Panzós Testimony No. 14, September 7, 1997)

DOÑA JACINTA

They came for the lands they had solicited. They had just finished a ceremony. They came with the hope that their needs would be met. They never thought they were coming to die. (Panzós Testimony No. 20, September 7, 1997)

DOÑA SOLEDAD

They made a ceremony. They asked for land. They received death. (Panzós Testimony No. 1, September 9, 1997)

DOÑA JULIA

My son died in the plaza. He was a member of the committee. They sent papers and requests for land. The mayor never responded, so they decided to go to the municipality because that is the maximum authority here. (Panzós Testimony No. 6, September 10, 1997)

DOÑA ELENA

In the morning, early in the morning, the mayor sent a message calling us to the plaza. (Panzós Testimony No. 1, September 20, 1997)

DOÑA MANUELA

The army did not want us to dialogue with the mayor. (Panzós Testimony No. 1, October 2, 1997)

DOÑA JOSEFA

A paper came from Guatemala City. The mayor was the one who received the paper. He knew that the people needed lands and so he called everyone, "Everyone who needs land should come." So there was a grand convocation. People arrived from everywhere. (Panzós Testimony No. 1, October 17, 1997)

When the crowd arrived at the plaza around 8 a.m. they saw between twenty to sixty soldiers, most of them perched on the roofs of buildings surrounding the plaza. Trying to make sense of what happened, Doña Dominga cautiously posits, "Maybe they just got bored with us going to the municipality all the time. The mayor got bored with us." Then, with hands grasped tightly together as if to pray, she taps the table firmly and says, "They had this all planned because there were soldiers on the roofs of the municipality, the salon, and the church" (Panzós Testimony No. 6, October 9, 1997).

By this point in our investigation, all testimonies corroborated that those who had gone to the plaza had done so because they needed lands to cultivate their subsistence maize crops. It was also clear that prior to the gathering at the plaza, the participants had celebrated Mayajek in various communities. Perhaps if any of the Maya priests had survived La Violencia, we would have more complete details about the celebration of Mayajek and its relationship to the land organization. But all the Maya priests were killed. So we listened carefully to the representations of history and memory shared by their widows, and from this individual and collective intervention we reconstructed the massacre and the violence that followed.

The Plaza Massacre

Based on survivor and witness testimony, as well as on municipal records, we knew that at 9:00 a.m. on May 29, 1978, there was a burst of gunfire into the crowd gathered in the Panzós plaza and that those who were not shot fled. Nobody disputed that the Guatemalan army opened fire onto a crowd of civilians. Indeed, a striking consistency in the testimonies of and interviews with witnesses and former functionaries was that everyone claimed that the gunfire came from army soldiers and lasted for no more than a few minutes. Though contradictions arise in the testimonies concerning the minutes before, during, and after the massacre, these fragments, like the numerous testimonies from which they were drawn, represent a slow accretion of facts through the reconstruction of community history by way of individual memories and lived experiences.

Minutes That Marked Survivor Memories

DON JACINTO

When they knew that the people were soliciting a little piece of land, they didn't like it. They called the army. They gathered all the people together and asked, "Do you have our papers?" The man asked the question one more time and no one responded. After they had asked for these documents several times and no one responded, they opened fire. (Panzós Testimony No. 8, September 6, 1997)

DOÑA JOSEFA

I saw what happened there. The mayor, Don Walter, received a paper. It was the third time we were going to speak with him. He didn't like that he had received this paper. He extended his arm in the direction of the people on the plaza, and they opened fire on the people. Many people fell there. There in the plaza was a small tree, and I hid myself beneath this. Gunfire passed so close to me. (Panzós Testimony No. 1, October 17, 1997)

DOÑA MANUELA

A campesino tried to snatch a weapon, but didn't know how to use it. (Panzós Testimony No. 1, October 2, 1997)

MARÍA MAQUÍN

With just one burst of gunfire they killed the people. It was only just for a moment and everyone fell there. I was so surprised because we had only arrived just a few moments before. My grandmother was going to ask for a favor. She said she wanted to speak with the mayor. But they didn't respond well to her. They answered asking, "What do you want?" She just wanted to speak with him, ask him a favor. She wanted to ask for help, for a little bit of land. *"For a little bit of land, that's what we came for,"* she said. They responded, *"There are your lands, there in the cemetery."* The soldiers were the ones who said this to her. So then my grandmother said nothing. That's when they opened fire at the count of three. One. Two. Three. They opened fire, and I was in shock as I watched the people die. (Panzós Testimony No. 2, September 6, 1997)

DOÑA MANUELA

The Señora Rosa Maquín [Mama Maquín] with her granddaughters was at the front on the steps of the municipal building. They fell to the ground, the little girls and the old woman. The bullets hit the old woman. It blew off the top of her skull. (Panzós Testimony No. 1, October 2, 1997)

DON JACINTO

Everyone was thrown down on the ground. Some were fleeing. They were injured. They were covered with blood. (Panzós Testimony No. 8, September 6, 1997)

DOÑA FELIPA

My mother-in-law died in the plaza. Only her sons reached the house. Then the injured arrived. Many arrived with fractured arms and legs [from machine-gun fire]. Many came to my house. (Panzós Testimony No. 3, September 7, 1997)

DOÑA FRANCISCA

My husband survived the massacre. He reached the house and said, "Something very painful has just happened. They have just killed the people in the plaza." (Panzós Testimony No. 13, September 7, 1997)

Those who survived the shooting and fled the plaza feared returning to their villages because army helicopters were following crowds of people. The majority of survivors fled to the river to hide. Some spent up to thirty-six hours in the water hiding from soldiers on the shore of the river. Survivor testimony and news articles written by journalists who visited Panzós following the massacre indicate that both the wave of civilian flight and the wave of army occupation and violence radiated throughout the area engulfing everyone.

Conclusion: Time and the Quantification of Genocide

The 1997 exhumation of the clandestine cemetery of 1978 plaza massacre victims recovered the remains of thirty-five people.[7] This number was significantly lower than that expected by the FAFG and the CEH. Indeed, as we began the exhumation, popular opinion placed the death toll between one and two hundred victims (see Barnoya García 1984; Barry 1986; Black 1984; CEIHS 1979; Figueroa Ibarra 1991; Aguilera Peralta 1981). When dealing with an event such as a massacre, how do you define "victim"? While this might seem intuitively obvious, in fact there are a number of distinct ways of defining and counting victims, and the Panzós massacre offers an instructive example of how this process works.

In our forensic investigation, the collection of survivor testimonies revealed numerous deaths and disappearances following the actual massacre. These provided a lens into the community's understanding of the massacre as part of a continuum of violence, rather than as a discrete incident. Moreover, research in the Panzós municipal archives corroborated survivor and widow testimonies of deaths following the massacre. The oral historian Alessandro Portelli's "grammar of time" sheds light on the survivors' understanding of their lived experience of violence. He writes, "Time is a continuum; placing an event in time requires that the continuum be broken down and made discrete" (1991: 69). No doubt, the choices made in the breaking down of moments on the continuum reflect cultural cosmologies. Still one wonders about the source and propagation of the widely held belief of popular organizations, academics, and others that more than one hundred people were killed in the Panzós massacre.

In my review of fifty-five paid advertisements placed in the Guatemalan newspaper *El Gráfico* in 1978 by various popular organizations, I found a June 18 full-page ad that provided a list of sixty-eight named victims of the Panzós massacre. I have cross-checked the names in this ad with the names of victims listed in reports prepared by the FAFG (2000: 57), which named the thirty-five skeletons exhumed; with the *Nunca más* (*Never Again*) report by Archbishop's Office for Human Rights (REMHI 1998: 4:69), which named eight of the massacre victims; and with the CEH's *Memory of Silence* report, which named fifty-three victims (1999: 16:21). Portelli's grammar of time is also important to consider when reviewing these varying numbers because he draws attention to the often overlooked variable of the researcher's timing: the moment in the life of the subject's history in which the researcher makes his or her entrance. This issue of timing can also be extended from the life cycles of individuals to the life cycles of communities.

First, there were thirty-five skeletons in the mass grave of victims—no more, no less. Of the thirty-five skeletons, the FAFG named twenty-five victims based on forensic identification, including the probable identification of twenty-three based on antemortem interviews and two positive identifications based on antemortem interviews in tandem with the laboratory testing of skeletal remains. The possibility of DNA testing was eliminated because all the skeletons displayed an advanced stage of decomposition due to the soil's high acidity level. Insufficient scientific data prohibited the positive identification of the remaining ten skeletons, as well as the scientific confirmation of the additional ten names I collected through testimonies.

The Archbishop's *Nunca más* report, also known as the REMHI (Proyecto Interdiocesano de Recuperación de la Memoria Histórica, the Interdiocesene Project for the Recuperation of Historical Memory) report, most clearly raises the variable of timing in research, as well as that of access to survivors and witnesses. When the REMHI began its far-reaching investigation utilizing the infrastructure of the Catholic Church in municipalities throughout the country, many survivors and witnesses still feared coming forward, and many local REMHI investigators had to be extremely cautious about their own security, as well as that of their witnesses. Unlike us in our forensic investigation of Panzós, REMHI investigators were not able to hold large public gatherings on a daily basis for three months while conducting their research. Nor did they have the benefit of the frequent visits by the prosecutor, MINUGUA and CEH representatives, the human rights ombudsman, national and international press representatives, and human rights observers. No doubt, the forensic team's access to survivors and witnesses was greatly increased by the presence and support of all these individuals and organizations. Indeed, their presence, and our access to local survivors and witnesses, largely resulted from previous investigative work conducted in the area and support given to community members by REMHI and MINUGUA. The willingness of witnesses and survivors to come forward was also increased by the signing of peace accords, the demobilization of civil patrols, and the reinsertion of the guerrillas into civil society—each of which took place prior to our arrival in Panzós. Whereas we were able to collect two hundred testimonies in our investigation, the REMHI report, which named eight victims, was based on four testimonies (1998: 69).

Because the CEH report was written after the commission received our forensic documentation of the exhumation, the CEH list of fifty-three named victims is extremely interesting. In its final report, the CEH noted that the forensic report revealed thirty-five skeletons in the mass grave. The CEH investigation, however, in addition to the thirty-five victims in the grave, included the names of those who were injured in the plaza and died after fleeing the army massacre, of those who drowned in the river fleeing, and of those who were executed by security forces shortly thereafter. Thus the CEH concluded that "the Guatemalan army arbitrarily executed fifty-three people and attempted to kill another forty-seven who were injured in the plaza massacre," resulting in "a grave violation of the right to life" (1999: 6:21). The CEH's methodology, which was legally based in international human rights law and the collection of legal evidence of human rights violations, encompassed violations occurring in the actual massacre and those occurring shortly thereafter that could be tied to the violence meted out by the army in the plaza.

While the REMHI report was affected by timing and access to witnesses and survivors, the forensic report was limited by the parameters of forensic science that define what is and what is not considered positive scientific evidence. The CEH's timing and legal methodology allowed for a more comprehensive analysis of the violence experienced in the Panzós massacre than the forensic or REMHI reports. The ad from 1978 naming sixty-eight victims was based on whatever information the witnesses and survivors to whom the organization had access in the nineteen days following the massacre provided.[8]

Each of these organizations' methodologies in compiling a list of victims was grounded, to some degree, in the collection of survivor testimony. And testimonies, as the theorist John Beverly has noted, are the narrated memories of real people "who continue living and acting in a real social history that also continues" (1996: 37). Both the testimony of the witness and the involvement of the listener and documentor also form part of that real and continuing social history in the making. In this sense, the lists of names can be understood as more than a naming of massacre victims. They can also be regarded as "the real and significant historical fact" that is "memory itself" (Portelli 1991: 26), and this memory is one of genocide. The only certainty we can derive from the study of genocide is that for all that we can learn and document from investigating these types of atrocities, regardless of our methodologies, the very destructive force that is the essence of genocide impedes our ability to ever fully document, know, or understand the totality of the devastation.

Still, despite the limitations we may encounter when attempting to understand such limit events as the Guatemalan army genocide of the Maya, we cannot allow atrocity to "be its own explanation. Violence cannot be allowed to speak for itself, for violence is not its own meaning. To be made thinkable, it needs to be historicized" (Mamdani 2001: 228–29). Panzós massacre survivors have continued to historicize the 1978 massacre and their own cultural history through the building of a local community museum that includes testimonies of massacre survivors. This museum was built to ensure that future generations would know their own history as told by their surviving elders. In this essay, I have demonstrated the key role of Maya survivors in historicizing La Violencia and the importance of local mobilizations for exhumations to national debates about truth, human rights, and justice. This article has called attention to the myriad ways in which rural Maya have created and seized political spaces in Guatemala's nascent democracy, thereby making Maya community human rights organizing a nexus between Maya citizens and the nation (Sanford 2003). Moreover, it points to the absolute necessity of Maya participation in constructing national and community political structures and practices for these projects to truly realize their creative intention of developing a new moral vision of equality and human rights in Guatemala.

Notes

This essay is dedicated to the survivors of Panzós. I draw on field research conducted in September 1997 and May 1998 with the Guatemalan Forensic Anthropology Foundation for their report to the Commission for Historical Clarification. Without the generosity of the forensic team and the trust of the community, this work would not have been possible. Fulbright-Hays, Inter-American Foundation, and MacArthur Consortium grants made the research possible. I especially thank Anna Haughton, Helena Pohlandt-McCormick, and Phyllis Beech for reviewing drafts of this article, and Shannon Speed for including me in this volume. Any errors and all opinions expressed are mine alone.

1. It is interesting to note that recent publications also cite more than one hundred deaths. Most cite between one hundred and two hundred deaths. Judith Zur gives seven hundred.

2. At the request of the FAFG, I developed a research methodology and led the investigation for the historical reconstruction of massacres in Panzós, Alta Verapaz, and Acul, Nebaj, El Quiché (FAFG 2000). The methodology was then repli-

cated in two additional investigations for the CEH in Belen, Sacatepequez and Chel, Chajul, El Quiché. In May and June of 1998, I wrote the historical reconstruction of the massacres in Panzós and Acul and supervised the writings of the reconstructions for Belen and Chel. The report I coauthored was presented to the CEH in a public conference with copies for the public and published by the FAFG in 2000.

3. Interview with the author, Panzós, July 23, 1997.

4. Interview with the author, Coban, July 23, 1997.

5. Both translators requested that their real names not be used.

6. Panzós Testimony Nos. 1, 2, 3, 9, 12, 19—September 6, 1997; 3, 4, 10—September 7, 1997; 8, 13, 18—October 9, 1997.

7. This section builds on previously published pieces on the Panzós massacre. See Sanford 2003, 1999, 2001, 2000, 1997.

8. At the entrance to Panzós shortly after the massacre, soldiers verbally and physically abused journalists trying to cover the massacre. They were denied entry and soldiers took away their cameras and tape recorders at gunpoint. See *El Imparcial,* June 1, 1978.

Rights of the Poor
Progressive Catholicism and Indigenous Resistance in Chiapas

On October 14, 2000, a group of 275 indigenous people of Chiapas began an eight-hundred-mile pilgrimage to Mexico City. The pilgrims, members of the faith-based groups Xi' Nich' (The Ant) and Las Abejas (The Bees), walked on foot carrying white banners for peace, the Mexican flag, and images of the Virgin of Guadalupe. After walking for fifty-seven days, the pilgrims reached the basilica in Mexico City, where they asked for the "maternal intercession" of the Virgin of Guadalupe. Their prayers to the Virgin focused on the need for peace and justice in Chiapas and denounced poverty, racism, the lack of land and social services, and political repression, as well as the political violence that had claimed hundreds of lives and caused thousands of people to flee their homes. The pilgrimage was a religious event, yet it carried a powerful political message. The indigenous pilgrims demanded that their voices be heard as they persisted in their path of nonviolent resistance.

Members of Xi' Nich' and Las Abejas, like thousands of indigenous Catholics in Chiapas, have linked their faith to their struggles for human rights. Time and again in my interviews and conversations with Catholics in the diocese of San Cristóbal de Las Casas people emphasized that all human beings are equal in the eyes of God and that all are sons and daughters of God. They criticized inequalities in Chiapas and reasserted their own right to lead a dignified life, stating that God desired that all live in dignity. While conducting research in Chiapas I heard hundreds of complaints of basic human rights violations—from torture to arbitrary arrest, intimidation, assassination, negligence, and impunity, among many others. Yet indigenous Catholics and others demand more than the protection of basic human rights. They insist on structural change that will ensure the equality of all people living in Chiapas and demand that they and their way of life be respected. This final demand cannot be easily codified in legal terms. In highland indigenous communities, respect refers to carrying out mutual responsibilities toward others within a community and to being treated as equals by those outside the community. Respect also includes the right to speak and to be heard, not only within communities but also by government officials and others.

Pastoral workers of the San Cristóbal diocese, especially under the leadership of Bishop Samuel Ruiz García (1960–2000), served as an ally in indigenous struggles for human rights.[1] In many cases pastoral workers brought the formal concept of human rights to indigenous communities. Yet these workers engaged in dialogue with indigenous peoples, allowing for the development of models of rights that incorporated indigenous perspectives. Central to the Catholic perspective on rights is the concept of human dignity and the right of all humans to live a dignified life. This notion of dignity includes not only individual liberties but also economic, social, and cultural rights. Catholic social teaching provides a powerful validation for rights; it argues that all humans have fundamental dignity and are equal because they are created in the image of God. In Chiapas the concept of dignity strongly resonates with indigenous concepts of respect. Overall, Catholicism gives a powerful language to and justification for indigenous struggles to defend their human rights.

The institutional Catholic Church of the San Cristóbal diocese and indigenous Catholic activists follow an understanding of human rights described by Gustavo Gutiérrez, a Peruvian liberation theologian, as "rights of the poor." Gutiérrez uses the term *rights of the poor* instead of *human rights* to critique a laissez-faire liberal view that presupposes "a social equality that simply does not exist in Latin American societies" (1983: 211) and focuses on political and civil rights rather than on economic and social rights. Gutiérrez cautions that respect for individual liberties will not change the profound social and economic inequalities in Latin America. His caution echoes Leonardo Boff and Clodovis Boff's critiques of reformism, which they note "seeks to improve the situation of the poor, but always within existing social relationships and the basic structuring of society, which rules out greater participation by all and diminution in the privileges enjoyed by the ruling classes" (1987: 5). The criticism of a reformist view of human rights for Latin America is important in a postcolonial context in which neoliberal economic models challenge the right to basic subsistence. The model of rights of the poor demands structural change, and as Gutiérrez contends, the Catholic Church must address institutionalized violence, the cause of the most "blatant forms of repression" (1983).[2]

This essay examines indigenous understandings of human rights in Chiapas and the ways in which these understandings have been supported by the work of the Catholic diocese of San Cristóbal. Following a brief overview of the diocese, this essay explores indigenous Catholics' understandings of rights through two cases: human rights courses given by the diocesan human rights center and several faith-based grass-roots organizations of nonviolent resistance.[3] The article is based on data from interviews, participant observation, and an analysis of documents in the San Cristóbal diocese from 1993 to 2001.

The Catholic Diocese of San Cristóbal de Las Casas and the Rights of the Poor

At the root of all our pastoral orientation is one criterion of the Gospel: to announce and live a faith that leads to life, and life in abundance (John 10, 10).
SAMUEL RUIZ GARCÍA, *EN ESTA HORA DE GRACIA: CARTA PASTORAL*

In his forty years as the bishop of the San Cristóbal diocese, Samuel Ruiz García underwent profound changes in his approach to working with the indigenous and rural poor who comprised the majority of the diocese.[4] He arrived in Chiapas in 1960 at age thirty-five adhering to the model of *indigenismo,* which attempted to address the social needs of indigenous peoples, but focused especially on assimilating indigenous communities into the modern Mexican nation. Hence, in his first pastoral plan of the 1960s, Ruiz set out to improve campesino life by teaching indigenous peoples Spanish, giving them shoes, and teaching them catechism. As Ruiz spent time in rural communities, witnessing oppression and exploitation along with the hope evident in day-to-day struggles for survival, his views began to change. In time Ruiz was, in his words, "converted by the poor." He attended the historic meetings of the Second Vatican Council (1962–65) and the Latin American Bishops' Conference in Medellín, Colombia (1968), which emphasized the structural roots of poverty and called on the church to take concrete actions to end injustice. Ruiz began to recognize indigenous peoples as "subjects of their own history," with his new pastoral goal being to accompany them on their path to liberation. This was a dramatic change from his earlier view in which he saw indigenous peoples as objects to be evangelized and Westernized. His change was consistent with a broader policy change of many Latin American bishops in the 1970s and 1980s "from paternalism to accompaniment" (Cleary and Steigenga 2004: 9). Accompaniment means walking *with* rather than *in front of* indigenous peoples in their struggle; it refers to listening to the demands of indigenous communities rather than speaking for them.

In this context, Ruiz and pastoral workers began to work to promote human rights in the diocese, initially in the broad terms of justice, equality, and liberation, rather than in the language of rights. Two early examples of this work are the Indigenous Congress of 1974 and catechism courses. The diocese played a significant role in organizing the Indigenous Congress of 1974 at which indigenous peoples from throughout the diocese united to speak about their situation in public spaces formerly dominated by mestizos. In San Cristóbal each of the four major Mayan ethnic groups of the diocese—Tzeltals, Tzotzils, Chols, and Tojolabals—prepared a presentation on the themes of the congress: land, commerce, education, and health. Each presentation was full of examples of the oppression indigenous peoples experienced. Presenters spoke of land evictions, corruption, and negligence on the part of agrarian authorities, and of their experiences working long hours for starvation wages on coffee plantations. The slogan of the congress, "Equality in Justice," denounced the poverty and marginality of indigenous peoples as it called for a change in the established social order of Chiapas.

Liberation from the oppressive conditions of working on plantations or as sharecroppers became an important theme of catechism courses in the 1970s. Observing the similarity between the peasants' search for land and the Bible's second book Exodus, Dominican missionaries along with the Marist brother Javier Vargas worked with Tzeltal Catholics in the Ocosingo region to develop a catechism addressing the peasant reality in Chiapas. The result of this collaboration was *Los tzeltales de la selva anuncian la buena nueva* (*Tzeltales of the Jungle Announce the Good News*), a catechism with three sections: "The Thought of God from the Beginning," "How We Live in

Oppression," and "Faith, Hope, and Charity." Of particular interest is the second section on oppression, which contrasts the lack of land and oppressive work in plantations with God's will that all are entitled to a dignified life. One lesson is based on John 10:10, where Jesus says, "I came that they may have life, and have it abundantly." Reflecting on the reading, the Tzeltal catechists noted, "Life in abundance means that there is enough of many things. But, is life in abundance eating only maize and beans? We know that there are other fruits to eat and we don't eat them, we are suffering oppression because our life depends only of maize and beans. . . . Life in abundance means having sufficient land to work; it means having enough food of many types; having money; having good health. . . . To have security for our future is the right of all humans" (qtd. in De Vos 2002: 225–26).[5]

The definition and defense of rights in Chiapas was necessarily linked to the state's political and economic context. The existence of plantations and other large landholdings made land redistribution a central demand in the 1970s.[6] Households lacking potable water, electricity, and sewage systems were (and are) common in rural Chiapas, particularly in indigenous communities, and social services—from schools to health clinics—rare and underfunded. Hence social and economic rights were of extreme importance in the San Cristóbal diocese. When popular resistance to oppressive conditions grew in the 1970s and especially the 1980s, owners of large estates, with the support of the police and the military, violently repressed grass-roots mobilization. The assassination of political leaders, arbitrary arrests, torture, violent land evictions, negligence, and impunity are some of the human rights violations common to this period.

The concerns of the Tzeltal catechists and of the participants of the 1974 Indigenous Congress parallel what Gutiérrez labels "the rights of the poor." The indigenous campesinos demanded a comprehensive view of human rights and insisted that structural change was necessary to address human rights violations.

In 1989, the San Cristóbal diocese and Ruiz formalized their commitment to human rights by establishing the Fray Bartolomé de Las Casas Human Rights Center. The center is named after the first bishop of Chiapas, remembered in the diocese for denouncing the abuses committed by Spaniards against indigenous peoples in the Americas during the early colonial period. The center documents and denounces human rights abuses and provides legal assistance to those experiencing violations. In addition, the center facilitates workshops to support and promote knowledge of human rights. As a result of its educational workshops and other activities, rural and urban communities have established dozens of local human rights committees throughout the diocese. Since the center opened, Ruiz has served as its president, and the institution has been a constant thorn in the side of the Mexican government as it denounces abuses committed by state and federal officials.

Pastoral workers and those working with the center follow Paulo Freire's methodology of popular education and the concept of *conscientizacão* (conscientization) in supporting the awakening of a critical consciousness as the oppressed question the injustices of their reality and begin to work to transform them. For Freire it is critical that the oppressed are actors in this process, with outside facilitators engaging in dialogue with them rather than directing the process. As Gutiérrez states, "in order for this liberation to be authentic and complete, it has to be undertaken by the oppressed themselves and so must stem from the values proper to them" (1983: 57).

For the most part the work of the diocese, both in its human rights workshops and its support of grass-roots organizing efforts, followed Freire's model in accompanying the oppressed on their path toward liberation rather than in walking in front of them. Yet applying Freire's model proves a challenge; change is to come from the oppressed themselves, but outsiders play a central role in conscientization. In the process of learning to walk with the Catholics of the San Cristóbal diocese, of listening to their needs and respecting their path for resistance, pastoral workers certainly faced and reproduced this contradiction. In its relationship with indigenous groups, the diocese supported the organizational process in which people worked toward liberation, yet pastoral workers as individuals carried privilege and power that could reproduce repression. At times they paternalistically spoke for the poor, that is, told them what to do, and decided the path to liberation. Some pastoral workers failed to give sufficient attention to the dramatic differences —particularly those of class and ethnicity—between themselves and the residents of poor communities, leading to a failure to recognize the differences in goals and methods for social change. Another common error was assuming homogeneity among indigenous Catholics, most powerfully evident in the common use of such terms as *los hermanos* (the brothers and sisters) and *los pobres* (the poor) to refer to all residents of rural and poor communities. In sum, the conversion to the poor did not happen overnight but was an ongoing process. And in spite of the many errors that occurred during this process, pastoral workers sacrificed a great deal in supporting indigenous struggles for revolutionary social change. In the long term, members of indigenous communities made the decision to continue working with the diocese because they saw it as a strategic ally for their political resistance.

Defining Rights: A Radical Vision

God wants all humans to live in happiness and to have that which they need for a dignified life. God made us all his sons and daughters.

REFLECTION OF PARTICIPANTS AT HUMAN RIGHTS WORKSHOP, VILLA DE LAS ROSAS,

CHIAPAS 1991

The priests, nuns, and lay people (most of whom are mestizo) who work at the center regularly organize workshops on human rights in different regions of the diocese. The workshops promote dialogue between workshop facilitators (center staff) and participants (residents of indigenous and campesino communities) regarding the meaning of rights and the ways to apply these rights to local contexts. As such, the facilitators work to raise consciousness in Freire's terms. Ideally, facilitators listen to and respect local understandings of rights, local processes, and goals for social change. Yet facilitators are also actors in the process. They share concrete information on laws (primarily the Mexican constitution and the UN Declaration on Human Rights) that protect human rights. Facilitators correct legal misperceptions about human rights, guide discussion, and literally set the agenda for workshops in deciding topics, exercises, and the schedule. Nonetheless, in all my observations facilitators were respectful of local needs and carefully listened to and acknowledged local conceptions of rights, as well as the goals, comments, and criticisms of community members.

Workshops are carried out following the request of a community member, catechist, or pastoral worker. Some workshops provide a general overview of rights, while others focus on a specific topic such as the electoral process, indigenous rights, or the rights of children or women. Workshop participants are primarily peasants and indigenous peoples from rural communities. Often communities select a small number of representatives to travel to workshops in San Cristóbal or in nearby towns; these representatives are expected to share what they have learned with the community. In other cases, all catechists from a community attend workshops, and when workshops are held within a community, a large group of people may attend.

In the following, I analyze the *memorias* (literally, "memories," or reports of the discussion) of workshops facilitated by the center to gain an insight into indigenous Catholics' understandings of human rights. I examined *memorias* from fourteen workshops that took place between 1989 and 1991 and observed an additional five workshops between 1993 and 1995. Overall, the workshops demonstrate the ways in which indigenous peoples and campesinos appropriate the concept of human rights, adapt it to their own historic circumstances, and use it as a tool of resistance. The complex view presented by workshop participants emphasizes economic and social rights, without excluding civil and political rights, and demands human dignity as well as respect for community. The *memorias* are gathered from conversations at the workshops, but they are written and edited by the facilitators, meaning that the workers of the center play a central role in what gets remembered. Particularly difficult discussions or material considered confidential or inappropriate may be edited out of the *memorias*. For example, negative comments about gender equality and criticism or even the rejection of exercises or presentations seldom appear in *memorias*, even though these are voiced in workshops.

The quote at the beginning of this section emphasizes that God desires equality and a dignified life for all. In the context of extreme racism in Chiapas and in a highly stratified global context, this makes for a radical view. The notion that everyone has the right to a dignified life demands structural change. In his analysis of the use of human rights in liberation theology, Mark Engler (2000) summarizes the critiques of the Western-European idea of individual rights: they overlook economic rights and basic human needs, support reform rather than systematic change, and support the basis of capitalism through private property and other bourgeois concerns. Most relevant for the case at hand, Engler notes that this individual conception of rights can deny the poor agency because the definition and defense of rights are managed by those with access to the legal system (2000: 349). Engler suggests that the concept of the rights of the poor brings a historicization to human rights. It "draws attention to other uses of 'rights' that better allow the poor to become agents in the making of history. Human rights can function as utopian norms at the root of a vision of just relations and as a set of demands that mandate immediate historical action by many persons and groups working with the poor for a better society" (2000: 358).

The workshops described in this section contain such utopian norms, although these are articulated as the necessary elements to build a just society. For example, in one workshop given in San Cristóbal de Las Casas (October 18–21, 1989), participants made lists of the rights of people (or individuals) and of communities. In a brainstorming session, participants noted that individuals "have the right to live, be equal, be free, work, be paid a just salary, enjoy the fruits of our work, be doctors or professionals, eat, talk, think, sleep, and rest; have dignity, education, a home; marry freely and have the children that we want; have religion; have a car and go up in a plane; go to other countries; advise others; live in the country or city; enjoy protection of the law, justice; organize in our homes; travel in the street, and work for the betterment of our family."

In reflecting on their rights in communities, participants at the same workshop noted: "We have the right to have land, request land; grow fruit trees; have cattle; form collectives; have sports facilities, roads, electricity, potable water, health clinics, schools; buy goods cheaply; receive a just price for our harvest; cooperate in the community; speak our own language; receive respect for our culture; have fiestas in the community; organize ourselves; participate in solving problems in the municipality; elect our authorities; hold demonstrations; get rid of our municipal president if he doesn't work; have a political opinion, and occupy political positions."

These two lists begin with what are commonly defined as rights: the right to life, equality, freedom, work, a just salary, freedom of religion, political participation, and education. However, the lists go well beyond traditional definitions of rights; they include cultural rights specific to indigenous communities such as the right to "speak our own language." Inclusion of the "rights" to "be doctors or professionals" and to "have a car and go up in a plane" show a keen awareness of the existing inequalities between mestizos and indigenous people, as well as of inequality in the global system. According to course participants, indigenous people have the right to do these things just as mestizos do. Some rights, such as the right to "cooperate in the community" or "participate in solving problems" are obligations (or reciprocal responsibilities) rather than entitlements traditionally included in the category of rights.

The human rights workshops commonly begin with the question, "Why do we have rights?" The answers given in distinct communities are similar: people state that rights are given by God, not by the government, a powerful contention in a nation that has continually violated the rights of indigenous and poor peasants. People note that they have rights because "we are human beings," "we are created in the image of God," and "we are sons and daughters of God."

At each workshop, participants discuss problems that exist—in the terms used in workshops, "that cause suffering"—at three different levels: family, community, and township. Problems commonly mentioned at the family level include illness, poverty, alcohol abuse, lack of work, lack of respect for children, and inequality between men and women. At the community level, participants name the problem of a lack of teachers, of medical attention, roads, potable water, and organization among community members. At the township level corrupt authorities, divisions between communities, and a lack of markets for products are listed.

After naming these problems, workshop participants are asked to reflect on the causes of the suffering. Their responses emphasize structural factors: corrupt authorities, electoral fraud, unjust laws, capitalism, and the unequal distribution of land, among others. To give one powerful example of a critique of structural violence in Chiapas, one group of participants in a workshop held in Huistán in 1990 described the root of their suffering as fundamental inequalities in society. "Society is very divided between the rich and the poor. The rich are few and the poor are many. The rich know the laws, put authorities in place, eat well, and see doctors while the poor eat badly, don't have money to go to doctors. The rich appropriate [from the poor]. They are the owners of the work of others."

Another theme in the courses is the history of the struggle for the protection of human rights. The revolutions of France, the United States, Russia, and Mexico, as well as the resulting laws, are discussed. Specific documents, most important Mexico's constitution and the United Nations (UN) Universal Declaration of Human Rights are discussed in depth. The notion of equality among all human beings in Mexican law is emphasized. On paper, rich and poor, men and women, indigenous and mestizos are equal, yet as participants point out, equality does not exist in practice. Workshop participants give examples of this inequality at both the national level, where indigenous people are not granted the same rights as mestizos, and within rural communities, where people work to promote the participation of women in public life and to limit the use of alcohol.

As part of the workshops, participants commonly read and reflect on the Bible from a social justice perspective. This follows the model of see (a reflection on oppression and on why it exists), judge (an examination of what the word of God states about oppression), and act (work for justice and the transformation of society inspired by faith) (Boff and Boff 1987). To give an example, at a workshop held in 1991 in Ocosingo, participants read Isaiah 65:17–25, which says, "Lo, I am about to create new heavens and a new earth. . . . They shall live in the houses they build, and eat the fruit of the vineyards they plant; They shall not build houses for others to live in, or plant for others to eat." Participants discussed the reading by linking it to their own lives. "God spoke of a peace based in justice and authentic reconciliation, a peace where there is health, work with justice, and happiness. Humans have the right to a long life. The peace that God wants is that we are united and help ourselves and each other. We must fight to achieve the peace with justice that God wants. We see that now there is much injustice." The model of see, judge, act is put in practice with participants reflecting on the injustice in the current sociopolitical context of Chiapas and describing the need to take action to achieve a just peace.

At the various workshops, participants discuss violations of both civil and political rights and economic and social rights, yet the latter and their violations are emphasized more strongly. Two important examples are the right to health and the right to work. Regarding health, workshop participants criticize the lack of adequate food and drinking water in their communities, as well as the lack of clinics, medical supplies, and medicine. They note that illness is "not a punishment from God," but a result of structural factors such as poverty. In a workshop held in Villa de Las Rosas in 1991, participants noted that "God does not want us to be sick. . . . But the authorities see to it that we have [only] the right to die." Regarding work, participants criticize low pay and unemployment. To quote from the same Villa Las Rosas workshop: "The powerful do not value our work and pay us less than what we deserve." At a later workshop held in the same community, participants affirmed the right to request land, cultivate land, receive a just price for their harvest, stating, "Work gives dignity to humans." At a workshop in Ocosingo, participants linked land to their agency, saying, "God gave us all land to live so that we can defend ourselves." Land is emphasized not only as essential to economic rights—access to land is paramount to campesino survival—but also for its role in promoting human dignity. The workshop participants noted that work can "give dignity" when people have access to land for cultivation so that they do not have to work for others in oppressive conditions.

The comprehensive view of human rights discussed at these workshops is thus not about fixing a few injustices in the judicial system, but about creating a new social order in which all can live with dignity and in which community is valued. The pastoral teams of the diocese implemented the courses as part of a specific organizing strategy. The extensive diocesan structure, with its well-developed networks within and among different geographic regions, allows participants to share their experiences and coordinate their actions. In concluding the workshops, participants commonly agree to put what they have learned into practice by defending their rights. For example, in the agreements reached at the end of a 1990 workshop held in Simojovel, participants noted that they would work with others in their communities to discuss rights and to unite for social change to obtain land for themselves and for future generations; sell their products at a better price; obtain release of political prisoners; and demand access to electricity, water, and schools.

Defending Rights: Faith-Based Nonviolent Resistance

The comprehensive understanding of human rights among the indigenous Catholics of Chiapas is evident in the actions and visions of faith-based grass-roots organizations. Members of Xi' Nich' and of several other groups in the township of Amatán are engaged in acts of nonviolent resistance to demand respect for human rights. These groups grew out of concerns about injustices in their communities; in each case, a specific human rights violation or community crisis pushed people to organize to defend their rights, and in time the groups' goals extended well beyond the initial crisis.

Xi' Nich' and the other groups in Amatán are some of the many organizations in the San Cristóbal diocese motivated by their faith and supported by the diocese in their struggles for a dignified life. Other groups include Pueblo Creyente (People of Faith), a group of diocesan Catholics who work through their faith to build unity and to address issues of poverty and political repression, and hundreds of women's groups linked through the Coordinación Diocesana de Mujeres (Diocesan Coordination of Women, CODIMUJ).[7] In the highland municipality of Chenalho,' Las Abejas formed in 1992 when Catholics joined together during a violent agrarian crisis.[8]

This section examines the struggles of Xi' Nich' and the groups in Amatán to illustrate the ways in which comprehensive understandings of human rights motivate their struggles, as well as the link between faith and politics. Members of the groups demand a broad range of human rights from political rights (democratic elections and the release of political prisoners) to economic rights (access to land and social services) and cultural rights (respect for indigenous languages, customs, and traditions). Members of these groups have walked hundreds of miles in pilgrimages and marches; occupied public plazas, town halls, and government offices for days and weeks; and held prayer vigils and fasts. In addition, members of these groups resist poverty by forming cooperatives to purchase external goods and to sell their own goods at a fair price, among other projects. For example, the cooperative Flor de Amatán (Flower of Amatán) operates a local store, a veterinary clinic, a *tortillería,* and a barbershop, and it commercializes organic coffee. Xi' Nich' has established dozens of cooperatives that open small stores, engage in small-scale subsistence projects such as cultivating fruit or raising chickens, and sell local products such as honey. In the context of extreme poverty, these cooperatives, however small, have the potential to make a significant difference in the daily life of community members. For example, buying staples such as cooking oil and sugar in bulk allows communities to receive a better price and economize transportation costs. In addition, as people work together in the tasks of building and maintaining the cooperatives, they commonly begin to recognize their strength in numbers and may be empowered to become involved in political mobilizations.

Through its evangelization process, human rights courses, and other types of institutional support, the diocese of San Cristóbal has contributed to the formation of these groups. The Catholic clergy served as a "movement catalyst," to use the words of Alison Brysk (2000: 63), who also notes that "the most important sources for external mobilization [for indigenous movements] were the Catholic Church, aid programs, and professional networks." The term *catalyst* suggests that while the church was important in supporting such movements, it did not control or manipulate the actions of indigenous peoples. Regarding the activism of the Chiapas groups, the Mexican government regularly accused priests of inciting violence and stirring things up. For example, the parish priest of Amatán, Felipe Iñiguez, was accused of leading all protests in the region, and a formal legal complaint was filed against him.[9] Government claims that campesinos are manipulated by outsiders constitute an attempt to silence indigenous protesters by discrediting their demands. The accusations carry the racist assumption that indigenous peoples are incapable of taking action on their own accord.

To give one example of diocesan support, when residents of Amatán were arrested in October 1992 for protesting the corrupt township president Nicolás Muñoz López, of the Partido Revolucionario Institucional (Revolutionary Institutional Party, PRI), the Fray Bartolomé de Las Casas Human Rights Center played an important role in helping obtain the prisoners' release. Doña Victoria, one of the detainees, remembers what happened when she was imprisoned in Cerro Hueco and members of the center called the jail: "Around midnight the Human Rights [Center] called. Perhaps they [the police] intended to harm us, because I had heard them say that the elders who had arrived with us weren't going to be able to stand the beating that they were going to give us at four in the morning . . . I heard the police talking among themselves. But, I repeat, around midnight the Human Rights [Center] called, and they [the police] said: "*Chingue a su madre*, now we've got ourselves in a big mess because these annoying, old, unruly people, they've called Human Rights!" (qtd. in SERPAJ 1996: 33–34).

The story of the formation of Xi' Nich' illustrates the repression of the period of Governor Patrocinio González (1988–92), as well as the campesinos' insistence that they be treated with dignity. In December of 1991, the Comité de Defensa de la Libertad Indígena (Committee for the Defense of Indigenous Liberty, CDLI) together with two other campesino groups organized a peaceful demonstration of two hundred people in the city of Palenque, with broad demands for economic rights (potable water, roads, and other services, as well as support for agricultural production) and political rights (democratic elections, an end to corruption, interpreters in government offices, etc.). The protest took place in the context of President Carlos Salinas de Gortari's implementation of neoliberal reforms, which protesters viewed as a threat to their way of life as small-scale rural producers. The protesters remained in the central plaza for days, insisting that the government take notice of them and respond to their demands.

Police stormed the plaza on the third day of the protest, hitting and handcuffing the protesters and pushing them into trucks. According to one witness, some three hundred police filled the plaza. In total 103 people were arrested, some covered with blood from beatings. The detained were held for two days in the state attorney general's office without adequate food or access to legal representation, and on the third day 93 of the prisoners were released. The remaining protesters were charged with committing crimes against peace, the illegal possession of firearms, sedition, and mutiny, among other crimes, and were taken to the state jail Cerro Hueco. A month later these remaining protesters were finally released.

But the story of Xi' Nich' had only just begun after the massive arrest. The state authorities had attempted to humiliate, intimidate, and silence the campesinos, but the strategy did not work. The Xi' Nich' member Sebastián González explains with a metaphor that refers to the origins of the group's name: "The anthill seems small on the surface, but there are many more underneath. If we compare this with our protests, at first there were few ants, in the second a few more, but when the government squashed the anthill, they all came out" (qtd. in SERPAJ 1996: 59). Even in the face of repression, resistance and the assertion of dignity continued. Rather than give up, the protesters decided to take their demands to federal authorities in Mexico City. On March 7, 1992, seven hundred indigenous people from over one hundred communities began the Xi' Nich' March for Peace and Human Rights of the Indigenous Peoples. Members of the Frente Cívico (Civic Front) of Amatán joined the march, protesting political corruption in their township. Together they marched for fifty days from Palenque to Mexico City, where they convened at the basilica to ask the Virgin of Guadalupe to accompany them in their struggle. Representatives of the federal government met with Xi' Nich' marchers just outside Mexico City and agreed to comply with their demands, although in many cases these proved empty promises (Harvey 1998b). Yet members of Xi' Nich' continued to press for their rights. For example, in 1996 some communities refused to pay for electricity (or insisted on only paying a just fee), arguing that government-controlled prices were too high.

In Amatán decades-long struggles to gain access to land and to counter political corruption gathered force in the 1980s because of support from the local Catholic parish. The history of the agrarian struggles in this region share much with other regions of Chiapas, namely, the slowness and negligence of government authorities in addressing agrarian reform. Amatán is primarily an agricultural township in which many residents identify as Zoque Indians, although few speak the Zoque language. In the early twentieth century peasants from Amatán were displaced from their land when German families established the coffee plantation El Escalón; the peasants worked the land as hired hands. In 1956 the peasants made a formal request to the federal government for ejidal (or communally held) lands, which they were finally granted in 1963. In 1966 community members inhabiting the two ejidos attempted to increase their landholdings so that they could continue subsistence cultivation.[10] Residents listed as a possible property the two hundred hectares of fallow lands of El Escalón, the very plantation where their ancestors had worked. Because of their ancestral link to the land, the residents of Amatán insisted that they had a historic right to it. After a thirteen-year delay, the Secretaría de Reforma Agraría (Department of Agrarian Reform) responded negatively to the request. In 1984 community members again requested that their ejidal lands be expanded, and in 1989 they attempted to buy the land without any success. On March 27, 1990, seeing no possibility of gaining access to the land of El Escalón, a group of sixty campesinos began to work the abandoned lands of the ex-finca, hoping that by establishing residence on the land they could gain legal access to it. Just a week later over three hundred police evicted the campesinos, arrested twenty-two people (including eight minors), destroyed the simple housing that people had begun to build, and confiscated work tools.

In the face of repression, community members came together to demand their rights. Domingo, a member of Flor de Amatán, states: "Our most recent struggles as Zoque Indians are from 1984 and 1992, precisely because our human rights were violated. Our pueblo has suffered severe repression for many years, but it has organized to defend its rights, justice, and democracy, all that is necessary for true peace" (qtd. in SERPAJ 1996: 39).

As noted, the struggles in Amatán had been ongoing for decades, but support from the local church served as an important catalyst in the community decision to take more dramatic action. Don Goyo, a resident involved in the struggles, explains, "In the experience of Amatán the word of Lord Jesus presented itself with force, it was able to make the mute speak, the blind see, the deaf hear, and the pueblo walk. And the people of Amatán saw, spoke, listened, and walked very little before" (qtd. in SERPAJ 1996: 17). Don Goyo argues that the word of God motivated the struggle against injustice. Faith played an important role in the tools used by Amatán residents to demand social change. "The people protested with peaceful means. . . . The tools we used were peaceful ones: first, peaceful actions before the Congress (never violent means); second, days of prayer to the deaf ears of the authorities; and third, the organization of the people. Above all, I believe the weapon of the poor is the word of and faith in God. In our communities we still keep our faith and trust that our Lord is our liberator. I believe God has heard the cry of the poor" (qtd. in SERPAJ 1996: 17).

When the residents of Amatán were arrested for working the land of the ex-finca, they carried out acts with religious significance such as prayer vigils taking place alongside sit-ins and hunger strikes. Of particular importance was a period of prayer and fasting led by the wives of the detained. The prisoners were released after being in jail for over a month. As a condition of their release, the governor Patrocinio González demanded that the wives sign a document recognizing the guilt of their spouses.

The actions in Amatán are linked to a comprehensive view of rights. In an interview conducted in November 1993, one member of the community expressed the importance of access to land for campesinos. "The land is like our mother. From this we support ourselves, we eat, and everything, everything is there." He reflected on land as a right: "I believe that human rights are also about the land. We have the right to work."

Overall, the members of Xi' Nich' and the other groups in Amatán demand the right to live a dignified life, a demand difficult to codify in legal terms. I first learned of these grass-roots groups in 1993 when my colleague Patricia Gómez and I traveled to a number of communities to conduct interviews on the issue of land and human rights.[11] We heard about assassinations, arbitrary detentions, physical and psychological abuse, corruption, and negligence, among other violations that can be denounced nationally and internationally through the formal language of human rights. But the indigenous campesinos were telling us something more; they were discussing a broader view of human rights, one tied to community, dignity, and respect. Their way of life as indigenous campesinos is embedded in their call for respect from government officials who refuse to listen.

Sebastián, one of the Xi' Nich' protesters arrested in December 1991 while at the sit-in in the public plaza, describes his experience of being in jail without any water or food:

What we felt there was humiliation, we were living what they were doing to us. Two people [government officials] arrived and told us: stop doing this nonsense because we have our people here. If you gather 500 people, we will send 1,000, if you gather 2,000 we'll send 5,000, so you should stop doing what you are doing.

> After two days, . . . we thought that we should return home and erase [*borrar*] the organization because we felt such humiliating abuse that we didn't have the right to speak. (interview, San Cristóbal de Las Casas, December 1993)

Later in his narrative, Sebastián tells of another protester who was badly beaten and had been dragged for ten meters by the police and "left half dead." He comments that "we felt very humiliated." In this case the formal, legal language of human rights emphasizes the series of abuses: arbitrary arrest, mistreatment, and threats. Yet rather than describe the violations of his legal rights, Sebastián emphasizes humiliation, that is, the way authorities treated him and the others without any respect, as if they were not human. In talking about his own understanding of human rights, Sebastián stresses that all human beings have the right to be respected. "The right to speak" (and to be heard) carries the demand that authorities respect indigenous and poor campesinos and respond to their demands.

Members of Xi' Nich' often describe the importance of receiving respect for their own way of life. For example, they affirm the importance of using their own words, as well as their own way of speaking, as a tool of resistance. Doña Clemencia, a Tzeltal member of Xi' Nich', states, "We have already demonstrated to them that yes we can. God [*Diosito*] gave us our language, and just as the mestizos use Spanish to communicate, we all use our language, and with it we speak and gain strength. Our language is a peaceful path for fighting when we know well what we want to say" (qtd. in SERPAJ 1996: 78). Juan Hernández of Xi' Nich' describes the value of his own way of thinking, his own way of life as an indigenous campesino: "They [government officials] think that with their money they are already intelligent, and they do not accept our way of thinking. For us life is community, food, that which the land gives us, that which we produce" (qtd. in SERPAJ 1996: 85). The diocese has been an ally in this process by providing a public and political space for acknowledging, celebrating, and affirming indigenous culture.

In these and other organizations, peasants demand that they be treated with respect, and they demand that their voices be heard. They request equality, insisting that all—indigenous and mestizo, men and women, rich and poor—are equal. This seemingly simple statement has radical consequences, for it means that the inequality in Chiapas goes against God's will. This cry for equality is supported by diocese's evangelization in both words and actions. For example, a resident of Amatán explains that all are equal under the law and that rights are for everyone, not only for the wealthy. He says, "The people with power think the law isn't for everyone. They think that the law is only for the powerful. . . . But I think that the law exists for everyone. Not only for the people with money, but for all." To reinforce his words, he adds, "I believe that we are all children of God" (interview, November 1993, Amatán Town Center).

Final Considerations

When we began to struggle for our rights we were threatened and persecuted. . . . Our fight is for the future, for our children, and even if they kill us, we hope that our descendants will not live as we live and they will walk freely on the lands of our ancestors. Because of this we have decided to work for change.

FRANCISCO GONZÁLEZ OF XI' NICH'

Liberation theology, a theology from the grass roots, is built on the necessity of listening to the voices of the poor. Regarding human rights in Chiapas, this means hearing their experiences of human rights violations, examining their work to defend their rights, and attempting to understand their complex definition of rights. The understandings of rights discussed in workshops and promoted by members of Xi' Nich' and other groups in Amatán counter the overwhelming lack of respect for humanity that indigenous and campesino poor encounter in daily life. Indigenous Catholics describe a complex notion of human rights that challenges the exclusive address of individual rights. Violations of civil and political rights such as arbitrary arrest, torture, and negligence are denounced, but indigenous campesinos include much more than individual liberties in their understanding of rights. Ongoing abuses of economic and social rights such as racism, poverty, and the lack of land, health clinics, and schools are also criticized. In other words, the normalcy of suffering—including extraordinary events such as the evictions and detentions in Palenque and Amatán— is challenged as people fight for the right to a dignified life. Participants in human rights workshops and members of faith-based organizations demand that they be treated with respect—they demand a right to land for their daily survival and they demand that their voices be heard. The Catholic Church, despite its past as a colonial oppressor of indigenous peoples, has served as an ally in the contemporary indigenous struggle for rights in Chiapas.

What is the outcome of these nonviolent movements? Some might view these movements as a failure because there are no great signs of success from a traditional political perspective. Members of Xi' Nich' and the other groups in Amatán continue their protests and their efforts to improve their members' livelihood through cooperatives and protests. Yet structural inequalities continue to exist in Chiapas, particularly with the implementation of neoliberal economic policies in response to global integration, which reverse Mexico's postrevolutionary promise of social and economic rights. In some ways, the religious dimension of the struggle changes its conditions. For people living in an oppression that denies their dignity, their very humanity, resistance is not only about obtaining material benefits but also about continually reaffirming their own dignity. Workshop participants come away with a different view of themselves; they have been empowered by the struggle. They are in this struggle for the long haul, as Doña Clemencia of Xi' Nich' says: "If we have resisted 503 years, one more day doesn't matter" (qtd. in SERPAJ 1996: 78).

Notes

The author thanks Susan Fitzpatrick Behrens, Jan Rus, and Francisco Argüelles for their valuable comments, and Patricia Gómez and the workers of the Fray Bartolomé de Las Casas Human Rights Center for their ongoing support. An early version of this essay was presented at the "Religion and Identity in the Americas" conference at the University of Florida, Gainesville, on April 11, 2003, and participants provided useful comments. This essay contains material from Kovic 2005 and is used with permission.

1. The Catholic Church has been responsible for the repression of indigenous peoples and the destruction of their culture, especially in the colonial period. Yet in contemporary Latin America, sectors of the church have played an important role in the promotion of indigenous rights.

2. Gutiérrez's criticism of liberal models of rights resonates with arguments made by secular scholars. Wendy Brown notes that a focus on individual political rights can counter needs linked to economic rights. She states, "Rights and needs are constitutive and productive of each other in liberalism. The domain of rights produces a domain of need in a literal sense (as property rights produce a class of tenants and of the homeless); moreover, rights are presumed independent of need *and* are invoked to triumph over need claims" (1995: 159).

3. The religious arena of Chiapas is extremely complex. It includes traditionalists, Catholics, and many Protestant churches. This essay focuses specifically on diocesan Catholics, or those following the progressive Catholicism of the diocese of San Cristóbal de Las Casas.

4. Samuel Ruiz formally retired as bishop at the age of seventy-five in 1999 in accordance with canonical law. He remained bishop until March 31, 2000, when

the Vatican named Felipe Arizmendi as his successor. Enrique Díaz Díaz was consecrated auxiliary bishop in July 2003.

5. See Leyva Solano 1995a and Coello Castro 1991 for detailed descriptions of consciousness raising or empowerment in the catechist courses of the Tzeltal region.

6. In 1960, over 50 percent of the land was held in just 2.4 percent of the properties (qtd. in Gómez Cruz and Kovic 1994: 43).

7. A description of Pueblo Creyente can be found in Kovic 2005, chap. 8. The work of CODIMUJ is described in Kovic 2003a.

8. For a detailed description of Las Abejas, see Kovic 2003b and Moksnes 2003.

9. In the case of Xi' Nich,' the Jesuit priest Geronimo Hernández was arrested in a 1991 protest. On March 3, 1996, Hernández, along with the Jesuit Gonzalo Rosas Morales, was arrested again without any warrant and accused of participating in an ambush in which two police officers were killed. On March 13, 1996, the priests were released due to lack of evidence against them.

10. The history of the conflict over land in Amatán is detailed in Gómez and Kovic 1994.

11. The results of this research are published in Gómez and Kovic 1994.

"Asumiendo Nuestra Propia Defensa"
Resistance and the Red de Defensores Comunitarios in Chiapas

> Rights save neither men nor a philosophy that is reterritorialized on the
> democratic state. Human rights will not make us bless capitalism.
> GILLES DELEUZE AND FÉLIX GUATTARI, *WHAT IS PHILOSOPHY?*

> Positive law is not our law, in our communities we have a different way.
> But it is very useful for us to understand it, in order to defend ourselves
> from the government.
> COMMUNITY *DEFENSOR*

Some analysts have suggested that we must pay attention to the "social life" of rights, meaning the ways in which they are "materialized, appropriated, resisted and transformed" in particular contexts (Wilson 1997a: 23). In the Mexican context, it is perhaps more appropriate to call this their "political life." That is, the exercise and enforcement of human rights, as enshrined in national and international laws and mobilized by various social actors, are highly political matters. In Mexico, as in most states, laws regarding the rights of citizens are selectively applied or enforced based on a gamut of political exigencies of maintaining power. Thus, even though individual Mexican citizens have many rights established in the Mexican constitution and its derivative laws and penal codes, their ability to exercise them is limited, in some cases severely.

One fundamental aspect of the limitation of the exercise of rights is certain individuals' and groups' access to the judicial system, which thereby eliminates their recourse to the law. This is particularly the case for women, indigenous people, and political dissidents (CNDH 1995; Azaola 1996; HRW 1997). Access is denied in a number of ways: inadequate public defense, failure to provide translators (or inadequate translation), bureaucratic stonewalling,[1] and outright political bias on the part of judges in their decisions (i.e., lack of an independent judicial branch) (HRW 1997; AI 1999). This problem is so widespread that on a recent visit to Mexico, the United Nations (UN) special rapporteur on the independence of judges and lawyers stated that Mexico suffers from 95 to 98 percent impunity and that Mexican citizens "do not believe in the possibility of justice" (*La Jornada,* May 15, 2001).

It is therefore interesting and somewhat paradoxical that the very groups most disenfranchised and alienated from the legal system have increasingly over the past two decades framed their struggles in terms of "rights" (Collier 2000). Some theorists, looking at the potentially positive aspects of such processes, have argued that the appropriation of the concepts and structures of law convert national legal systems and law itself into "site[s] of contestation" (Hernandez 2002) or "space[s] of resistance" (Merry 1997). Yet as Sally Merry and others have pointed out, such forms of contestation and resistance also serve to "reinforce the centrality of law as a mode of protest" (1997) and risk reinscribing the very forms and logics of power and domination they are struggling against (Gledhill 1997).

In this article, we explore this process, taking as a case in point the experience of the Chiapas Community Human Rights Defenders Network (Red de Defensores Comunitarios por los Derechos Humanos). We are particularly interested in considering the possibilities for forms of resistance that, while rights based and tied to legal practice, have the potential to do more than simply convert the law into a site of resistance, with the inherent dangers of reinforcing oppressive power relations. We will argue that because of its particular structure and its relationship to the Zapatista autonomous communities it serves, the Defenders Network, in its merging of direct action on the legal terrain of the state with the community-based project of autonomy and indigenous rights, in fact inherently challenges the forms of sovereign power and rule that "the law" serves to uphold. We begin with a discussion of ideas about law and its relation to sovereignty.

Law, the Contract, and the State

To understand both the complicity and effectiveness of rights-based claims in our era, it is first necessary to define law, to locate its position in the architecture of power, and to establish its relationship to rights. In doing so, it is not enough to examine law as a semiotic or aesthetic system, or even as a cultural artifact. While certainly such an analysis could be applied to law, it would not truly map the essence of the law, that is, none would adequately analyze the law as a particular form and structure for the exercise and circulation of power.

Throughout the history of modern Western juridical thought from Hobbes to Hegel law has meant nothing other than the exercise of a sovereign power—the enforcement of a command-obedience relationship between ruler and ruled. (This despite the fact that the site for the exercise of sovereignty has shifted from the monarch to the nation and in its more radical forms to the people.) This does not mean to imply, however, that law is the naked use of force, but rather, as Merry writes, it is "a form of violence endowed with the legitimacy of formally constituted authority" (1992: 360). It is an authority that throughout the history of jurisprudence has been most effectively justified through the philosophical fiction of the contract. This fiction posits that individuals in the state of nature give up their unlimited rights to a sovereign due to a fear of others. This sovereign, through the collection of these rights, holds absolute power within a society and is in turn charged with the task of mediating among competing individual interests with the goal of creating social unity and peace.[2]

Within this contractarian philosophy, the rights that we exercise as subjects of a sovereign are the absolute limits beyond which the sovereign is not allowed to act on its subjects. But how is it possible to limit the actions of a sovereign if, as Hobbes posited, any force that is to limit the sovereign must be greater than the sovereign, and if there is a force greater than the sovereign, the sovereign by definition ceases to exist? This paradox has vexed both natural and positivist legal philosophers, the great majority of whom have been unable to escape the philosophical hegemony of the contractarian theses within legal thought. The natural law solution to this puzzle has been to appeal for rights from a sovereign above and beyond that of the state (i.e., God), whereas the positivist legal solution has been to ask the sovereign itself to create a system of checks and balances on its own power through the recognition and pronouncement of its subjects' rights and the stabilization of the actual processual functions of state bodies (i.e., courts, legislatures, and the executive). Despite the disparities of these viewpoints, both natural and positivist legal philosophies accept in whole the thesis that all power within a state society necessarily emanates from, and is circulated by, the sovereign (see Foucault 1980).

The power of the law is, in thought and in action, the power to produce and reproduce daily practices and subjectivities within society that continually reinforce the founding myth of sovereign power, that is, the power to create subjects that act as if all power emanated from the sovereign. This mystifying, or "normalizing," power of the law, and the unparalleled legitimacy it gives the sovereign and the command-obedience relationship it maintains with its citizens, becomes particularly dangerous in our current global juncture.

On the Local Terrain: Three Conceptual Trajectories of Human Rights in Chiapas

The concept of human rights has three trajectories in Chiapas, one with a religious orientation disseminated through the Catholic Church, another with a positivist legal orientation propagated by the agencies of the state and by nongovernmental organizations (NGOs), and a third centered around the derivative human rights discourse of indigenous rights, promoted most prominently in Mexico by the National Indigenous Congress and the Zapatista Army of National Liberation (Ejercito Zapatista de Liberación Nacional, EZLN).

Although there is a good deal of blurring and overlap in the practice of human rights defense, the first two lines of legal thought correspond to two distinct conceptual frameworks and justifications for the existence of human rights: one that views rights as innate, natural, and prior to any judicial normativity; and a second that posits that rights do not and cannot exist previous to their establishment in law.

THE CATHOLIC CHURCH AND THE NATURAL LAW TRADITION

In Chiapas, the interweaving of strands of natural and positive law largely results from the fundamental role the Catholic Church has played in the development of human rights discourse and practice. The church began its defense of the indigenous peoples of Chiapas as early as the sixteenth century with Bartolomé de Las Casas's famous theses on the humanity of the indigenous subjects of the Spanish crown. However, activists and academics working in the region over the past several decades all seem to agree that the modern discourse and practice of human rights did not appear in contemporary Chiapas until the mid-1980s, and that it was first introduced through the Catholic diocese of San Cristóbal de Las Casas, under the leadership of Bishop Samuel Ruiz García (García Aguilar 1998; Collier 2000).[3]

Ruiz became the bishop of the diocese in 1960.[4] After a process of his own "conversion" from his former conservative views, by the early 1970s he was training catechists and giving masses with a strong liberation theology bent. Of this process he has said, "I came to Chiapas to convert the poor, but they are the ones who have converted me" (qtd. in Womack 1998: 49). Liberation theology gave the church's discourse a strong element of criticism of the structures of domination, exploitation, and political control of the poor. Christina Kovic (2005) suggests that "the option for the poor" was the progressive church's human rights discourse. She notes that liberation theologians purposefully utilized a discourse of "the rights of the poor," rather than of "human rights," to emphasize that the equality assumed in liberal rights theory did not exist, and to highlight the economic structural and institutional violence that kept it from existing. Because the indigenous people of Chiapas were clearly "the poorest of the poor," the "option for the poor" soon evolved into the "option for the indigenous" and *teología india* (Indian theology) emerged (Ruiz García 1999: 61). *Teología india* is based on a strong valorization of indigenous culture and, notably, on the understanding that human beings of all cultures are equal before God (whether or not they enjoyed equality on earth) (Kovic 2005; Meyer with Gallardo and Ríos 2000; Ruiz García 1999).

Throughout the centuries, the conceptualization of human rights that evolved in the Catholic Church has varied little in its affinity with natural law. The discourse currently disseminated through the church in Chiapas had its earliest formulation in the writings of Las Casas in the first half of the sixteenth century, and it can be summarized with his famous statement that "the nature of men is the same and all are called by Christ in the same way" (1974). All men are equal in the eyes of God. By situating God as the highest authority, rather than the sovereign or the state, it follows that the rights of human beings always already exist, regardless of their establishment in the legal regimes of the state. Ruiz affirmed this position on the human rights of indigenous peoples by citing Pope John Paul II, "the rights of your peoples are *prior to any right established in human laws*" ("Discourse in Latacunga II," qtd. in Ruiz García 1999: 69; emphasis added).

The Catholic Church was responsible for the establishment of the earliest human rights organizations in Chiapas, which were formed in the early 1980s in the context of the arrival of thousands of Guatemalan refugees fleeing their country's scorched-earth campaign. In 1988, the Fray Bartolomé de Las Casas Human Rights Center (CDHFBC) was founded. The center, the first organization specifically dedicated to human rights work, was a project of the diocese of San Cristóbal, and Bishop Ruiz served as its president (García Aguilar 1998).[5] This organization, and the other church-based human rights organizations that followed it,[6] had a clear mandate to pursue human rights cases through the legal norms established in national and international law. Thus, as is the case with most organizations that found their conceptions of rights on the authority of God, the Catholic Church in Chiapas has had little choice but to seek the recognition of those rights through the positivist practice of attorneys, courts, and legislatures.

HUMAN RIGHTS NGOS: POSITIVE LAW AND THE GLOBAL ORDER

In the 1990s human rights organizations flourished in Chiapas. Particularly after the Zapatista uprising began in 1994, the number of NGOs increased dramatically as national and international organizations also started to have a presence in the region. By the late 1990s, there were ten independent human rights NGOs (García Aguilar 1998),[7] four national human rights NGOs,[8] and at least nine international human rights organizations with a permanent or periodic presence in Chiapas.[9] The state and federal governments had also established their own human rights agencies in the region.[10]

Several simultaneous and related processes—global, national, and local—contributed to this flourishing of human rights organizations (and of NGOs more generally). At the global level, a number of analysts have argued convincingly that the growth of NGO networks is closely tied to the emergence of a new global order (e.g., Keck and Sikkink 1998). Without a doubt the downfall of the socialist bloc and the subsequent emergence of neoliberal capitalism as the discourse and practice of the new global order have contributed strongly to this dynamic by effectively eliminating political discourses that posit alternative forms of social organization and replacing them with discourses more compatible with neoliberal capitalism itself, notably rights discourses (see Brown 1995; Gledhill 1997). The emergence of this neoliberal global order also signaled a shift in the ways many states related to their populations: they began eliminating their commitment to "oversee processes of redistribution that would bring about greater social justice and equity through reallocation of resources" (Frankovitz 2002), which in turn gave rise to a need for the disenfranchised to pursue new forms of social solidarity to seek redress for inequalities.

We can observe how this process played out at the national level in Mexico. Long characterized by a corporatist state that managed internal dissent through co-optation (turning to coercion and repression when co-optation failed), Mexico found itself increasingly limited in its capacity to finance hegemonic social pacting after the debt crisis of the mid-1980s (Collier 2000). The neoliberal restructuring accelerated during the regime of Carlos Salinas de Gortari in the late 1980s and early 1990s brought Mexico into the emergent global order and ended decades of corporatist rule. For many this meant the end of any hope of balancing out social inequalities through a direct petitioning of the state (through agrarian reform, etc.). Thus the relations between the state and civil society have been fundamentally altered, opening up a space for the flourishing of civil society's activism and organization. Many of these organizations grew up around the issues of specific groups, which tended to be focused on, or composed of, a particular unifying identity and whose claims were strongly rights based. In other words, as globalization has created the conditions in Mexico in which rights-based discourses seem to have the most social salience, it has simultaneously eroded the ability of the state—through a neoliberal economic restructuring that has put an end to redistributive practices and undermined the powers of formal democratic institutions—to respond to these claims, making the creation of intermediary private bodies (i.e., private international foundations and NGOs) increasingly necessary.

Yet many of the resulting nonstate organizations tend to depoliticize the problems that they would like to solve by attempting to sidestep the impossibility of implementing a holistic and coherent political project within the neoliberal state, and they instead settle for managing a series of immediate and seemingly unending crises (Guehnno 1995; Hardt and Negri 2000). Thus, as Gilles Deleuze (1994) posited, the end of corporatist rule does not mean the end of state or sovereign-like mediation of social conflict. Rather, the state and its mediating function have now escaped the confines of formal public institutions to permeate society as a whole (see also Hardt 1998). This has significant implications for the possibilities and pitfalls of NGOs because it suggests that these sites for action and social struggle can easily reproduce the logic of neoliberal sovereign rule in a fashion that effectively outdoes the normative power of the state by involving the entire social body in the circulation and maintenance of the status quo.

Further, the fact that in the current context NGOS fill a necessary mediating role between states and their populations leaves groups attempting to contest state power significantly handicapped. This is the case in part because the marginalized and disenfranchised remain in a vulnerable position in relation to the NGOS themselves, the form and content of their claims being subject to the whims of funding institutions and the internal politics and power moves of NGOS. In channeling their contestatory politics through NGOS, these groups are also forced into complicity with the role NGOS inevitably play in the diffusion of the logic of neoliberal sovereign rule throughout society. That is, indigenous communities in Chiapas may eventually gain access to the judicial system by way of NGOS, but they are then caught in a power imbalance with the NGOS themselves, a power imbalance that is particularly dangerous if we take into consideration this critique of NGOS. Thus, for groups pursuing autonomy and self-determination, a more direct confrontation with the logic of the state—and a clearer consideration of, and disentanglement from, the law as a function of the state—is not only desirable but also absolutely necessary.

THE EMERGENCE OF INDIGENOUS RIGHTS IN CHIAPAS

Parallel to the Catholic Church's natural law defense and the NGOS' positive law defense of indigenous people, there has been an ongoing evolution in the thought and practice of rights within the indigenous communities of Chiapas themselves. One expression of this evolution was the 1994 uprising of the EZLN, which began its first public communiqué by highlighting its indigenous composition and the centuries-long series of abuses against the indigenous people of Mexico with statements like "We are the product of 500 years of struggle" ("Declaration of War of the Zapatista National Liberation Army," *La Jornada,* January 6, 1994).

Twelve days after the EZLN declared war on the Mexican government, and under much national and international pressure, then president Salinas de Gortari (1988–94) decided to declare a unilateral cease-fire that effectively ended open hostilities in Chiapas and began a series of negotiations with the EZLN that have spanned some eight years and three presidencies. The high point of the negotiations was the signing of the San Andrés Accords on Indigenous Rights and Culture by the EZLN and the government of President Ernesto Zedillo (1994–2000). However, shortly after the signing it became evident that the Zedillo administration did not intend to implement the accords. The legislative body that had participated in the negotiations at San Andrés, called the Comisión de Concordia y Pacificación (Peace and Harmony Commission, COCOPA), prepared legislation to comply with the accords and forwarded it to the executive.[11] However, Zedillo refused to submit the legislation, known as the "COCOPA initiative," and finally admitted that he had been unaware of the content of the agreements signed by his own secretary of the interior (*La Jornada*, January 1997).[12]

The Mexican government's failure to comply with the San Andrés Accords—especially its failure to fulfill the commitment to make constitutional reform recognizing indigenous rights and autonomy—signaled its unwillingness to address the indigenous population on the terrain of rights. But governmental inaction had the effect of strongly propelling the Zapatista movement toward precisely that terrain, and the Zapatistas increasingly defined their movement as one for indigenous rights and autonomy. This dynamic had several implications: First, the governmental withdrawal from the San Andrés Accords gave the Zapatistas the moral high ground; they had negotiated in good faith, and the Mexican government had failed to honor its own agreement. Not surprisingly, they increasingly placed this deception at the forefront of their public discourse. Also, the national indigenous movement, which had begun to coalesce out of diverse and previously unrelated organizations and autonomy projects after the Zapatista uprising and particularly after the negotiations at San Andrés, provided a strong national base of support for the EZLN (see Hernández Navarro 1998). But perhaps most important, by closing the door on the possibility of pursuing indigenous self-determination through negotiations and legal reform, the government compelled Zapatista base communities to pursue autonomy unilaterally (see *Fuerte es su corazón* 1998). Although the Zapatistas established thirty-eight "municipalities in rebellion" in 1994, it was from 1997 onward—after the failure of the San Andrés Accords—that these municipalities emerged as a principal space for the organization of resistance and as a strategy for indigenous political participation (González Hernández and Quintanar Quintana 1999). Thus the San Andrés Accords and the Mexican government's failure to implement them contributed to important shifts in Zapatista discourse and practice. The movement for national liberation became a movement for indigenous rights. Even more significant, these rights were no longer elaborated as a demand before the state. By unilaterally pursuing their autonomy projects, people in Zapatista base areas made a fundamental discursive shift: indigenous peoples' right to self-determination was being asserted as prior to, and regardless of, their establishment in the legal regimes of the state.

Autonomy and the Innovations of an
Indigenous Rights Practice in Chiapas

In international law it is commonly accepted that indigenous rights have developed as a derivative discourse of the more general human rights movement institutionalized by the UN and through its Universal Declaration of Human Rights. That is, soon after the initiatives within the UN to decolonize Africa and Asia were recognized, indigenous peoples around the world began to demand that international legal bodies recognize their right to varying forms of autonomy and self-determination. The concrete results of these demands have been several: (1) the adoption of two International Labor Organization (ILO) Conventions, numbers 107 and 169, the latter of which implicitly recognizes the aim of promoting indigenous autonomy and self-determination and is considered the most complete in force summary of indigenous rights in international law; (2) the establishment of a Permanent Indigenous Working Group within the UN, which has drawn up the Draft United Nations Declaration on Indigenous Rights;[13] and (3) the completion of a Draft American Declaration of Indigenous Rights, as well as a growing body of pertinent jurisprudence within the Inter-American Commission on Human Rights and the Inter-American Court of Human Rights (Anaya 2004).

Just as with natural law claims, with which it shares the demand for human equality, the global indigenous movement has had to concede to the positivist practice of existing legal institutions for the recognition and promotion of its rights. But despite the similarities that indigenous rights share with the natural and positivist legal traditions, they also contain normative elements that do not belong to, and that cannot be assimilated into, either of these traditions. As Paul Patton (2000) argues, "indigenous rights" is a bridge concept that attempts to unite the Western legal tradition with the customary normative practices of indigenous peoples that have until recently been unrecognizable as juridical institutions within Western law.

Since the colonization of the Americas, courts around the world, with only a few exceptions (notably the Supreme Court of the United States), have refused to recognize that the internal decision-making structures of indigenous communities rise to the level of normative institutions and as such should be respected. This perspective, and its expression in courts and legislatures around the world, is inextricably tied to the view of indigenous people as "primitives" and "barbarians" incapable of reasoned thought and thus "law."

Yet not only does the recognition of indigenous juridical structures within Western law signal the beginning of the end for the use of law as an instrument of openly racist colonization but it also marks a radical difference between indigenous rights claims made in Chiapas and other identity-based claims made against the state. The Zapatista movement, and the indigenous rights movement in Mexico more broadly, demands autonomy and self-determination—expressed not as the capacity to build another state under a new sovereign, but as the capacity to function unimpeded so as to affect the daily lives and future of its members.[14] The San Andrés Accords attempted to reformulate the relationship between the state and indigenous peoples in several important ways: one was the right of indigenous peoples to choose their authorities through their internal selection mechanisms; another was the right of those authorities to exercise their power to make the political, legal, and economic decisions that directly affect their communities, or at a minimum to be consulted regarding decisions that will affect them. In other words, the San Andrés Accords demanded the recognition of indigenous peoples' right to a relationship with the state based on the principle of consensus rather than that of command-obedience. Thus these indigenous rights claims not only demand that the institutions of sovereignty within a nation recognize indigenous peoples for who they are—human beings with the right to equal treatment—but they also demand that those same institutions not impede the functioning of an existing and parallel power structure (internal indigenous political and judicial mechanisms) to allow the indigenous peoples themselves to decide who they are and who they want to become.[15]

There is a difference between this form of identity-based rights movement and other struggles caught in the positivist and natural law legal traditions, and within the logic of neoliberal capitalist global order. First, in contrast to many ethnic or so-called minority-based struggles, it does not look to the construction of a new sovereign, or of even a limited sovereignty, as its final goal, as is the case, for example, in certain regions of Spain and the former Yugoslavia. Second, it is not satisfied with the recognition of its objectives within state laws and practices; it is not placated by the protection that similarities with the dominant society may provide it. That is, its demands have not been based on the natural law impulse to search for safety in similarity, nor on the positive legal tradition of equality before the law. Rather, this movement has asserted the right to be different. Third, these rights-based claims demand nothing less than a reformulation in the exercise of sovereignty to include and protect a relationship between the sovereign and its subjects based on consensus rather than the command-obedience structure that has otherwise characterized sovereignty in Western legal thought from Hobbes and Locke to Kant and Hegel. The discussion of the Red de Defensores Comunitarios below highlights not only the unique nature of such rights-based claims but also their significance for the conception and practice of other such struggles within the contemporary global order.

Situating the Red de Defensores Comunitarios

The Community Human Rights Defenders' Network (referred to herein as the Red de Defensores) was begun in 1999 by the Chiapas human rights attorney Miguel Angel de los Santos. The objectives were to bring together a group of young indigenous people from various conflicted regions of the state to train them in national and international human rights law, as well as in the fundamental practice of legal defense in the Mexican justice system. Because the conflicts in their regions are largely tied to the struggle for greater rights and autonomy for indigenous people, a significant portion of the training was dedicated to national and international agreements on indigenous rights.

The *defensores* all come from Zapatista base support areas and were chosen by their authorities through the particular *usos y costumbres* (customs and traditions) of their regions in response to letters of invitation sent to the five *aguascalientes* (Zapatista regional points of public contact). The course took shape with fourteen participants: two from Nicolás Ruiz (Central Zone), two from San Miguel (Palenque), two from Cuauhtemoc Chancalá (Palenque), four from the Northern Zone municipality of Tila (Misopá Chinal, Emiliano Zapata, and Petalcingo), two from Morelia

(Altamirano), one from San Jeronimo Tulijá (Chilón), and one Guatemalan refugee representing the communities of Frontera Comalapa (see map). These representatives are from Tzeltal, Chol, Tojolobal, and Mam speaking zones. In 2001, a second generation of *defensores* was invited to join the Red de Defensores from the Zapatista regions Montaña, Maya, Trabajo, and San Pedro Michoacán.

Over the course of two years, the *defensores* participated in monthly training seminars. Their training had four components, two conceptual and two practical. In the conceptual component, they studied international human and indigenous rights laws and treaties (particularly the UN Declaration on Human Rights and ILO Convention 169) and human rights in the Mexican framework (essentially the rights and guarantees contained in the Mexican constitution). In the practical component, they studied and practiced legal defense work within the Mexican legal system (including criminal law and the everyday practice of law in the jails, courts, and the Ministerio Público of the state),[16] as well as the political practice of human rights defense (e.g., writing press releases, public denouncements, and handling negotiations and other interactions with public officials). In addition, a significant portion of the training was dedicated to technical instruction in the use of video cameras for human rights documentation and in the use of computers, word-processing programs, and printers.

The *defensores* work in coordination with a team of several advisors who coordinate training workshops, facilitate the centralization of information, and give input and technical support on issues ranging from legal practice to raising and managing funds to long-range planning and organization. Both of the authors have worked on the advisory team: Speed since its inception; Reyes between 2000 and 2002. We have also been involved with the Red de Defensores in other personal and professional capacities: Speed is married to the Red de Defensores founder De los Santos, and the organization was one of the principal subjects of her doctoral research (Speed 2001). Reyes coordinates Project 169, an independent project of the Red de Defensores involving work around ILO Convention 169. These diverse roles and forms of interaction with the organization and its *defensores* did more than just enable our access to the *defensores* and ensure their trust. It also allowed us to listen to them and learn from them in ways that fundamentally shaped our ideas about the potential of the Red de Defensores and of law as resistance, as we shall elaborate below.

The Work of the *Defensores*

Human rights violations are by no means a new phenomenon in Chiapas (HRW 1991). In fact, arbitrary violence by state and federal police, as well as by landholders' private security forces (so-called white guards) were one aspect of the injustice that gave rise to the Zapatista uprising. However, since the uprising began, communities located in base support areas have suffered new types of rights violations at unprecedented levels. Militarization and military occupation (an estimated seventy thousand Mexican Army troops were stationed in Chiapas at the height of military presence) have made everyday life difficult for people in many areas: soldiers impede their travel to agricultural fields; they occupy lands, cut down fences retaining livestock, harass women, and create a general climate of fear and surveillance (Global Exchange et al. 1999; Global Exchange, CIEPAC, and CENCOS 2000). Notable cases of military human rights violations are the murder of three men in the community of Morelia by soldiers in 1994 (now before the Inter-American Commission on Human Rights), and the rape of three Tzeltal women at a military checkpoint in 1995. More insidious, and with a much higher human toll, has been the paramilitarization of the conflict. The emergence of pro–ruling party paramilitary groups after 1995 has resulted in hundreds killed, tens of thousands of internally displaced, and hundreds of political prisoners (CDHFBC 1996; HRW 1997). Furthermore, all of these aspects of the conflict contribute to the disruption of traditional forms of social organization, production, and worship and thus constitute violations of social, economic, and cultural rights including the right for people to maintain their cultures.

"ASSUMING OUR OWN DEFENSE"

All of the regions covered by the Red de Defensores have suffered violent conflict in recent years. Because of the microregionalization of conflict (in which the conflict takes on local dynamics in different microregions), the types of problems faced by the *defensores* and the communities of their regions vary. Some suffer more problems with militarization, while others face paramilitary violence. Still others are occupied by state police forces, and many have suffered the politically motivated imprisonment of community members.

The *defensores'* work thus entails a range of activities that depend on the needs of their region. The principal activities are taking declarations and testimonies from victims and witnesses regarding rights abuses, video-taping and photographing for evidence, presenting complaints before the *ministerio público* (the official charged with investigating crimes and gather-ing evidence for the state), sending information regarding rights violations to the press and the human rights community at large, and seeking the release or pursuing the defense of people who have been unjustly detained. The most high-profile human rights case they are engaged in is the one mentioned above of the three Zapatista base supporters killed by the Mexi-can Army in Morelia in January 1994. The Red de Defensores is working in collaboration with the Comisión Mexicana de Defensa y Promoción de los Derechos Humanos (Mexican Commission for the Defense and Promotion of Human Rights), which has consultative status before the Inter-American Commission on Human Rights, to seek redress for the widows of the vic-tims. Also, through Project 169, the organization prepared a complaint charging the Mexican government of violating convention 169 by passing the federal legislation on indigenous rights and culture in 2001.[17]

Thus the work of the *defensores* is varied, involves interactions with a variety of actors across social fields, and reflects a significant level of prepa-ration. Prior to coming to the Red, some *defensores* had little or no experi-ence with the concept of human rights. In the words of Ricardo from Nicolás Ruiz, "Before, no one talked about 'human rights.' It had no mean-ing for us."[18] Miguel, from the Northern Zone, notes the transition they have made as part of the Red de Defensores: "We indigenous people do not know what our rights are. They say we have rights, but we don't know what those rights are, for example [in relation to] the taxes imposed on us by the government through its institutions. Indigenous *priístas* don't know their rights. The government helps them, in order to get their votes, but they still don't know what their rights are. We as human rights *defensores* are learning what our rights are, and we are reclaiming them."[19]

But the Red de Defensores is not simply an organization designed to tell indigenous people what their rights are. There are several aspects of the organization that distinguish its work from that of others functioning in the educational or legal realms around rights-based claims. First, in its concep-tualization, the Red de Defensores has parted significantly from the numer-ous existing projects for teaching indigenous people about their human rights. Often these have focused on the training of human rights *promotores* (promoters) to recognize and document human rights violations and then proceed to the nearest human rights organization (usually the one that provided them the training). From there, the NGO takes the information and makes decisions about the appropriate course of action. Once the information has been taken, the *promotores* are often sent on their way, while the organization undertakes the work of preparing the complaints; contacting the police, government human rights agencies, the press, and/or the international community; preparing the documentation; and when necessary providing follow-up on the case. In contrast, the Red de Defensores was conceived and designed to prepare the *defensores* (loosely "defenders"; however, in Spanish, defense attorneys and public defenders are also called *defensores,* thus the term carries the connotation of the legal defense of human rights, not just of their promotion) to make the decisions and proceed with the actions on their own, thereby eliminating dependence on attorneys and NGOs that have their own agendas, potentially quite distinct from those of the communities. A basic purpose of the Red de Defensores, then, is to eliminate the NGO middlemen and allow the communities to "assume their own defense" (which is, in fact, the slogan of the organization).

Some of the *defensores* have had previous experience or training as *promotores.* For example, Manolo, from Altamirano, had been a human rights *promotor* and a regional coordinator for three years before coming to the Red de Defensores. Because of this previous experience he was chosen by his community authorities to participate in the training and later in the Red de Defensores when it became a formal organization: "When the invitation from Lic. Miguel Angel came, the authorities of my community told me, 'You should go because you already know something about law and you will quickly learn how to do this work.'"

Rafael had also had several years of training as a *promotor* provided by the local Catholic parish in Tila, which ended when the 1994 uprising began. He was clear about the difference between the training he received as a *promotor* and what he has received with the Red de Defensores: "They taught us what human rights are . . . and if we saw violations, they told us, we should go to the Fray Bartolomé [Human Rights Center]. . . . [With the Red] it is more practical—we are learning how to handle the MP [*ministerio público*], write documents, defend rights with the articles [of the Mexican Constitution], the penal codes, the ILO 169."

Like Rafael, Manolo distinguished his training as a *promotor* from that as a *defensor* and pointed to some of the reasons why training is important in his region:

> In our communities, we don't have a lot of economic resources, and we don't have any way to go quickly to San Cristóbal. Even if we [do], by the time we arrive in San Cristóbal and go to an organization to explain, it is too late to make the denouncement—those who committed the violations are long gone. The journalists and human rights observers also arrive to the community too late to gather information and make the denouncement. *We* are *in* our communities. That's why we are taking this course to learn how to take testimony and elaborate a denouncement. This is very important, because one never knows when [human rights violations] will happen. When the Federal Army comes or Federal Police or state police are entering the communities, we are ready.

The ability to act directly from the community is important to the victims of rights violations and facilitates human rights work. For this reason, the *defensores* are based in their regions, rather than in San Cristóbal or in another town. Pablo, also from the Northern Zone, notes the value of coming from a shared language, culture, and experience: "An attorney from the city doesn't speak our language. We *defensores* understand more clearly what [victims and witnesses] are trying to say and express. This is much better because we think the same, talk the same, and we have suffered the same repressions. They trust us."

There are thus some clear practical reasons why *defensores* based in the community may work more effectively without intermediary NGOs. But beyond eliminating the intermediary, their effectiveness can also be understood as a result of strengthening autonomous practice in the nascent Zapatista autonomous municipalities. Indigenous communities in Zapatista autonomous regions have often substituted NGO support for the support previously received from the government in its corporatist moment (Van der Haar 2005). While NGOs have no doubt provided valuable assistance and reinforcement to communities pursuing autonomy, we have already pointed to the problematic nature of the community-NGO relationship. Shifting reliance on governmental assistance to reliance on NGOs can still prevent communities from being able to act autonomously.

This brings us to a second important aspect of the Red de Defensores: its base in the communities of Zapatista autonomous municipalities.

The defensores *seated around the meeting table in the San Cristóbal office smiled broadly when the topic of the recent workshop they had attended in Hue-huetenango, Guatemala, was raised. Ricardo spoke excitedly: "It went very well," he said. "Everyone [there] was very impressed with the* Red. *There was an exercise in which they asked us to draw a picture of the structure of our organiza- tion, and when we showed ours with the three circles and the community in the center, everyone was silent for a minute, surprised, then they all started asking, 'Can you explain it again? How does it work?' They were very impressed."*

After the initial two years of training, the Red de Defensores became a formal organization, made up of the participants of the training workshops. Its unique structure, which Ricardo refers to above, was devised by the *defensores* and resembles conceptualizations of power relations in the com- munities. It is notably distinct from the structures often seen in NGOs, which have traditionally been conceived as pyramids with the officials at the top (coordinator, director, president, executive secretary, etc.), the attorneys, project directors, public relations and press coordinators, and fund-raisers in the middle, and the *promotores* from indigenous communities at the base. The Red de Defensores, by contrast, is conceptualized in concentric circles, with the communities at the center, the *defensores* in the second ring, and an advisory council in the outer ring. Perhaps the obvious difference lies in not having outsiders at the top, and in the elimination of the top-down mode of operation. This structure emphasizes that the indigenous communities form the heart of the project.

The work of the Red de Defensores begins with, is directed by, and is answerable to the communities themselves, as well as to the authorities of the Zapatista autonomous regions to which they pertain. This fundamental principle underlies the original election of the *defensores* by the authority structures of the communities, the *defensores*' work, which is based in the community, and the organizational structure that keeps the community as the center.

"TO ORGANIZE OURSELVES IN THE WAY THAT WE CHOOSE"

It was a sunny afternoon in June of 2000 when Abelardo Mendez Arcos made some casual comments that would later contribute to a shift in our thinking on the work of legal defense from the community in Chiapas. "It's simple," he said,

"I began doing legal work to help the compañeros *[Zapatistas]. It is all part of the struggle, the struggle for autonomy." Mendez, a Chol from the Northern Zone of the state, was a Zapatista political prisoner from 1996–97 and on his release became the external representative of the political prisoners group La Voz de Cerro Hueco. He is in a sense the proto-*defensor, *having worked with and learned from the attorney De los Santos on the cases of dozens of prisoners over several years. Given to lengthy political monologues, he repeated the simple premise several times in different ways before flashing a suddenly self-conscious smile and concluding: "That's what the* Red *is for: to defend our rights, our autonomy."*[20]

At the time, Mendez's comments seemed like straightforward political rhetoric about "the struggle." But in the course of our dialogue with the *defensores,* we began to interpret this conceptual linkage of the organization's work in legal defense and the broader project of Zapatista autonomy for the communities that constitute its support base. That is, there is more to "defense from the community" than simply eliminating the intermediary or than even creating local empowerment by appropriating the legal terrain of the state. Carrying out legal defense from the community is important, as we see it (and more important, as the *defensores* see it), primarily because it allows community members to "defend their autonomy," as Mendez put it, and because it is in itself an extension of autonomous practices.

As the opening quote suggests, the *defensores* recognize positive law, and the Mexican legal system specifically, as alien to their forms of organization and conflict resolution, but nevertheless as an important tool to use precisely in defending their communities' ability to do things "their way." They understand the political nature of rights as a tool of power wielded against them by the government, and one that they can use to fight back. In Manolo's words: "We, as human rights *defensores,* . . . are getting to know what our rights are and we are demanding them. But the government is playing a political game. For example, for the government, "civil resistance" is a violation of the law, but they do not take into account all the laws that have already been established, the international laws that they themselves signed, [because] they don't want to recognize that we have the right to organize ourselves in the way that we choose. . . . We know how to defend ourselves with the law, because the government is not going to do it for us— it is not in their interest."[21] In statements such as this one, the unique and politically sophisticated view of law held by the *defensores* comes into view.

In our multilayered interactions with the *defensores*—as activists, as advisors to the Red de Defensores, and as researchers—it has become clear to us that they do not wish only to protect or expand their own ability to present cases in courts or with state officials, even though this constitutes their daily work. That is, their end goal is not a just, or even an adequate, state mediation of local problems. Rather, they tend to view their work as the subproject of a much larger undertaking, one that Manolo refers to as "civil resistance" above. This resistance is practiced through using the legal system to protect communities from general violations of law including assassination, torture, disappearance, arbitrary detention, and military occupation. But the rights violated by these sorts of actions are not viewed as a priori rights; rather, they are viewed as derivative of a more central demand and right: the right "to organize ourselves in the ways that we choose." Thus the *defensores* not only recognize the political nature of law and the political motivations for the abuses directed against their communities but they also identify their source of strength in a larger social architecture of power and its ultimate political difference with the law, a difference that lies in their self-organization.

The autonomy and self-determination that the indigenous rights movement seeks will not be provided by organizations such as the Red de Defensores. However, the practices of legitimizing the internal decision-making structures of indigenous communities, and of disseminating at a grass-roots level the knowledge and tools necessary for the communities to deal with adequately intrusive state structures, do tendentially strengthen those communities prior to and regardless of the recognition provided by NGOs or the state and its laws. This in turn allows the participating indigenous communities of Chiapas to accumulate the space necessary to further expand their internal autonomy projects (such as building schools, hospitals, and water systems, as well as forming a generation of health promoters, teachers, and community-trained engineers) and thus improves their position in the national and global structure of power, making violations of human rights less likely and state mediation of local problems less and less necessary.

Conclusion

Earlier we noted two characteristics of globalization that highlight the dangers of law. First, the onset of neoliberal restructuring has emptied the state of its redistributive capacity, making adequate mediation among the competing forces within its territory impossible. Second, the rise of global sources of power (i.e., multinational corporations and global financial markets) to a dominant position within the current world system forces many states to accept subordinate roles often limited to furthering the empowerment of the global actors just mentioned. Thus when combined with these characteristics of neoliberal rule, the law and its founding myth of sovereign power can create the trap through which oppositional groups are assimilated into a system in which legal process becomes an empty signifier for the resolution of immediate conflicts while leaving the architecture of power that created those conflicts unquestioned. Similarly, the law's illusion that organized power can only be exercised through the sovereign is combined with the desperation created by the social decay that accompanies the downsizing of the corporatist state, resulting in marginalized groups making claims to a sclerotic neoliberal state whose capacity to resolve social conflict is increasingly limited to its police function. Thus, although immediate conflict and violence may be temporarily resolved, this "resolution" comes at an increasing cost to the most basic individual liberties (Agamben 1998: 126–35; Hardt and Negri 2000: 311–14; and Guehénno 1995: 96).

Thus, with the tendential abandonment by the state of its mediating role among competing subjects, it would seem that a critique of law and sovereign power would be the order of the day for disenfranchised groups in Mexico and elsewhere. Ironically, it is exactly at this juncture that most disenfranchised identity groups and the NGOs that support them have adopted the discourse of rights and the practice of law to further their struggles. It is as if at the moment at which the state is capable of doing the least to positively transform society, its capacity for self-legitimation through the dissemination of its legal discourse and subsequent creation of normalized subjects is at its apex. Yet as we hope our discussion thus far has made clear, not all rights-based claims must fall prey to the power and mystification of the law and thus not all rights-based movements are simply reproducing the structure of power that maintains neoliberal global rule.

Most rights-based movements and NGOs in Mexico and around the world are undoubtedly caught within the power of law. That is, they are trapped waiting for the sovereign to recognize their rights while leaving the power and myth of the sovereign unquestioned. Thus these movements waste valuable energy and resources on actions that further legitimate institutions and empty forms functioning to guarantee their ultimate subordination. In mobilizing the discourse of law, they reinscribe the very relations of power they are resisting. In this article we have focused on the Red de Defensores because we believe that it represents a form of political resistance through the use of identity-based rights claims and a direct exercise of unmediated power that has implications for these questions. We offer the experience of the Red de Defensores as one example of potential alternatives that break with the normalizing characteristics of legal discourse and practice and offer us a glimpse of possible alternatives.

The Red de Defensores' appropriation of the concept and structures of law as a "site of contestation" or a "space of resistance" does not necessarily "reinforce the centrality of law as a mode of protest" (Merry 1997). The nature and power of the Red de Defensores goes beyond the strategic use of rights discourses and of the Mexican legal system to the larger political project that this tool is wielded to defend. Its power is that of the Zapatista communities its defenders come from and respond to, and whose movement asserts the right to autonomy and self-determination—expressed as the capacity to control and affect their daily lives—that inevitably puts sovereignty (state or global) and its power of absolute command in question.

This challenge takes place on both the philosophical and the material terrains. The direct exercise of rights by the *defensores* is an exercise of power, one free of intermediaries who in fact serve to limit their power and the power of the communities they represent. More important, in the unilateral exercise of their right to self-determination, they disengage from both natural and positive law and redefine rights as existing in their exercise, not as designations from God/the church or the state or sovereign. Writing in the 1600s, Benedict de Spinoza argued, "Nature's right and its order . . . forbids only those things that no one desires and no one can do." That is, for Spinoza, a body's right was coextensive with what it could do (qtd. in Deleuze 1990: 126).[22] From this perspective, rights exist in their exercise, not in law or in nature. At a philosophical level, this conceptualization is radically distinct from, and thus presents a challenge to, the legal discourses that underpin the power relations in the current global order.

On the material terrain, the challenge comes through the assertion of parallel power structures. That is, indigenous communities function on the knowledge that law and its sovereignty are a myth, and their communiqués and antineoliberal rhetoric signal that they are well aware of the sclerotic nature of the current state. Their actions and the shape their political project has taken expose the myth of sovereign power and escape the dangers of the normalizing force of the state by directing their resistance toward a project of self-organization, thus enlivening a parallel power structure. This parallel power might engage with the state and even ask it to recognize a series of rights, as is the case with the San Andrés Accords. But this engagement with state structures thrives on the knowledge that such rights and their protection will arise only as a result of a struggle of social forces in which they must engage, and not because of the will or decision of the sovereign. The idea that rights struggles form part of the play of social forces while counteracting the notion of a sovereign power is central to the EZLN's perspective of its struggle, and it is expressed by its spokesperson Subcomandante Marcos when he states, "We the Zapatistas want to *exercise power*, not take it."[23]

The Red de Defensores allows this powerful political understanding of the indigenous movement in Chiapas to be expressed fully because its purpose is to eliminate the need for intermediaries between the indigenous communities and the state. Besides participating in the strengthening of the communities' internal organization, the Red de Defensores allows indigenous people themselves to engage the state to halt repression without having to give up their ultimate political goals. In this sense the Red de Defensores signals the reemergence of a truly politicized legal defense. Without this defense the indigenous communities of Chiapas would be left vulnerable to intermediaries who conceptualize rights in a different manner and inadvertently contribute to putting indigenous communities at the mercy of law and its myth of sovereign power. Thus the Red de Defensores, and the larger movement for autonomy of which it forms a part, is redeploying globalizing discourses in ways that ultimately challenge the material structure of the global order, as well as the discourses of law that sustain it.

Notes

Shannon Speed's research was supported by a Social Science Research Council–MacArthur Foundation Fellowship on International Peace and Security, and writing was supported by the Ford Foundation and the American Anthropological Association. We would like to thank Miguel Angel de los Santos, Kathleen Dill, Mara Kaufman, Lisa Glowacki, and the anonymous reviewers for their comments. An earlier version of this text was published as " 'In Our Own Defence': Rights and Resistance in Chiapas," in *PoLAR: Political and Legal Anthropology Review* 25 (1): 69–89, 2002. Portions were also published in Speed 2007.

1. Refusal to take a rape complaint from a woman, for example, or to accept complaints of rights violations that are handwritten and / or in nonlegal language. It is also common to make the process of making a complaint so lengthy, arduous, and costly that it is no longer viable to the victim.

2. For the paradigmatic expression of the function of the sovereign in contractarian philosophy, see Hobbes 1996: 114; and, generally, Bobbio 1995. For the latest popular variant of this tradition, see John Rawls's notions of "the orignal position" and "the veil of ignorance" in *A Theory of Justice* (1971).

3. Interviews by Shannon Speed with Mercedes Olivera (July 2000), Marta Figueroa (May 1999 and June 2000), Miguel Angel de los Santos (June 1998), and Marina Patricia Jímenez (June 2000), San Cristóbal de Las Casas, Chiapas.

4. The diocese in 1960 covered the entire state of Chiapas. In 1964, the diocese was divided into three (San Cristóbal de Las Casas, Tapachula, and Tuxtla Gutiérrez) at the urging of Ruiz, who wanted to be able to devote more of the diocese's work to the indigenous populations of the state, virtually all of which were situated within the area of the diocese of San Cristóbal (Womack 1998). This area, which covers 48 percent of the state, was then subdivided by the diocese into six ethnogeographic zones: the Zona Chol, Zona Sur, Zona Sureste, Zona Centro, Zona Tzotzil, and Zona Tzeltal (Leyva Solano 1995b).

5. Ruiz is still the president, though he retired as bishop in 1999.

6. Notably the Centro de Derechos Indígenas, AC (Center for Indigenous Rights, CEDIAC) in Bachajón and the Fray Pedro Lorenzo del la Nada Human Rights Center (Centro de Derechos Humanos Fray Pedro Lorenzo de la Nada) in Ocosingo.

7. Collier 2000 cites at least ten more, though we were not able to verify their existence.

8. These included the Mexican Commission for the Defence and Promotion of Human Rights (Comisión Mexicana de Defensa y Promoción de los Derechos Humanos, CMDPDH), the Mexican Academy of Human Rights (Academia Mexicana de Derechos Humanos), the Agustín Pro Human Rights Center (Centro de Derechos Humanos Miguel Agustín Pro), and the All Rights for All Network (Red Todos los Derechos para Todos).

9. International organizations with offices in Chiapas were International Service for Peace (Servicio Internacional por la Paz, SIPAZ) and Global Exchange. Others had a periodic presence through commissions or delegations; these included Human Rights Watch, Amnesty International, the Minnesota Advocates for Human Rights, the Humanitarian Law Project, the Inter-American Commission on Human Rights (IACHR), the International Federation for the Rights of Man (Federación Internaciónal de los Derechos del Hombre, FIDH), and the Inter-American Institute of Human Rights (Instituto Interamericano de Derechos Humanos, IIDH) (drawn in part from Collier 2000).

10. The state government formed the Comisión Estatal de Derechos Humanos (State Human Rights Commission, CEDH) in 1990, and the federal government's human

rights agency, the Comisión Nacional de Derechos Humanos (National Human Rights Commission, CNDH), was formed in 1990 and opened offices in Chiapas in 1994.

11. In Mexico, the vast majority of legislation is submitted to Congress by the executive branch.

12. Legislation at that time in Mexico was virtually always submitted to Congress by the executive, rather than by the lawmakers themselves.

13. After taking more than twenty years to draft and reach agreement on, the UN Draft Declaration on the Rights of Indigenous Peoples was adopted by the United Nations Human Rights Council on June 29, 2006.

14. The consideration of nationhood varies from indigenous group to indigenous group, but for the purposes of this essay we have attempted to concentrate on the express goals and principles of the indigenous movement in southern Mexico and, more specifically, in Chiapas.

15. See, for example, Principle 2 of the Declaration of Principles on the Rights of Indigenous Peoples and Article 7 of the International Labor Organization's Convention number 169 Concerning Indigenous and Tribal Peoples in Independent Countries.

16. Because the majority of political prisoners in Chiapas are accused of common crimes rather than of political ones, knowledge of criminal law is fundamental to their defense. The Ministerio Público is the institution that receives complaints, assigns detectives to investigate crimes, and presents evidence on behalf of the state against a suspect at a preliminary hearing and during trial.

17. In 2000, Vicente Fox of the Partido de Acción Nacional (National Action Party, PAN) was elected, ending seven decades of Partido Revolucionario Institucional (Revolutionary Institutional Party, PRI) party rule. In an attempt to eliminate the Chiapas conflict quickly, he complied with several key Zapatista demands, including submitting the years-old COCOPA law to Congress. Thousands of Zapatistas and their supporters marched to Mexico City to express their support for the bill. They were met by a crowd of sixty thousand supporters in Mexico City. Tzeltal Comandante Esther gave a moving speech in a historic special session of congress, for which she received a standing ovation. Nevertheless, in April 2001, the Mexican Congress passed a greatly watered down version of the original accords, so watered down it was considered by most to actually set indigenous rights back from the standard marked by Mexico's ratification of ILO 169 in 1990. The law was rejected unanimously by indigenous peoples throughout Mexico; the Zapatistas issued a communiqué calling it a "legislative joke" (Subcomandante Marcos "Communiqué from the Clandestine Revolutionary Indigenous Committee—General Command of the Zapatista Army of National Liberation," April 29, 2001). In the weeks and months following the vote and its ratification by a majority of states, more than three hundred challenges to its constitutionality were filed before the supreme court. The court eventually refused to hear the cases, claiming

they were not within its jurisdiction.

18. We have given pseudonyms to the *defensores* we quote (with the exception of one public figure) out of concern for their personal security. Our use of pseudonyms is a reminder that the discourses we discuss are grounded in very real political dynamics for the local people the names represent, and that accountability is an issue not just for those involved in these dynamics but also for those of us who enter into critically engaged studies of them.

19. *Priístas* are followers of the PRI party, which ruled Mexico and the state of Chiapas for more than seventy years until 2000. This and all quotes by *defensores* come from unstructured interviews with them by one or both of the authors in San Cristóbal de Las Casas between late 1999 and early 2001. Notes in possession of the authors.

20. In this case we have used Mendez's real name. Because he is a public figure, his security is not likely to be (further) jeopardized by the publication of his name here. His comments were made to Shannon Speed in June 2000. Recording and notes in possession of Speed.

21. Interview with "Manolo," February 2000, San Cristóbal de Las Casas. Notes in possession of the Red de Defensores.

22. For an extended discussion of the unique and radical nature of Spinoza's discourse on rights, see Negri 1990; Deleuze 1990; and Montag 1999.

23. This notion of rights as the product of factors purely immanent to society, or as the product of particular relations of force, is not exclusive to the indigenous rights movement in southern Mexico. In addition to the striking similarity between Subcomandante Marcos's statements and those made by Michel Foucault (1980) in his famous "Two Lectures," evidence of a practice of rights outside of law and the state within the Western philosophical tradition date as far back as the 1600s when Spinoza wrote that "Nature's right and its order . . . forbids only those things that no one desires and no one can do" (qtd. in Montag 1999: 65). That is, for Spinoza a body's right was coextensive with what it could do.

Making Rights Meaningful for Mayas
Reflections on Culture, Rights, and Power

This volume makes a valuable contribution to the debate on human rights in the Maya region, especially in its inclusion of a variety of perspectives on how human rights are appropriated, resisted, or just plain ignored within Maya communities, and in the empirical detail it presents on how Mayas strategize politically within broader relations of state power and the international human rights framework. Uniquely, it combines the discussion of human rights among Mayas in both Chiapas and Guatemala, whereas in the past these constituted two separate conversations. This is an extremely important development that could change the field of Maya studies as we know it. Evaluating the impact of human rights across the Mayan region allows deeper insights than focusing on one set of experiences alone, especially given the historic exchanges of political ideas between Mexican and Guatemalan Maya groups. The fact that social analysts have come to think in this way is a result of the concrete political interactions in the 1980s and 1990s between Mayas in Chiapas and tens of thousands of displaced Mayas from the war in Guatemala. It is also a consequence of the similarities in the more long-term experiences of marginality and social exclusion of Mayas in both Mexico and Guatemala.

The volume contains an admirable historical depth in its analysis of thirty years of human rights movements, from their origins in the teachings of the liberation theology of the 1970s, to the quest for democratization and accountability in the 1980s, to the language of indigenous rights in the

1990s. Such a historical perspective is essential when trying to fathom the long-term implications of a broad, seemingly all-encompassing metanarrative. Human rights is the latest in a long line of Western sociopolitical narratives to shape the politics and culture of the Maya region. Christianity, for one, came to exert a profound and long-term influence on the minds of Mayas. Others such as Marxism were pervasive once but have now fallen into obscurity. Modernization theory and nationalism have had more uneven and varied results, and their influence has ebbed and flowed, but they have retained a stubborn salience over time.

What kind of outcome will human rights have as an overarching political discourse—that of Marxism, of nationalism, or of Christianity? In trying to answer this question, the contributors have generally not taken the view that human rights are bound to fail simply because they are Western or foreign or new. Instead, they have sought to identify the elective affinities between human rights and particular social constituencies, and they have situated rights talk within the sociocultural contexts and political framework in which it is found. They have asked: What opportunities exist for local activists to pursue political autonomy through rights talk? Conversely, how does rights talk facilitate cooptation by states? What are the unintended consequences of making claims in the idiom of human rights?

These questions have elicited a range of responses from contributors which may or may not be fully compatible. For instance, it is possible to discern two distinct positions with regard to the relationship between human rights and culture: one set of articles portrays Maya cultural practices and beliefs as largely incompatible with human rights, while the other understands them as at least potentially complementary. Different positions also emerge regarding human rights and the projects of the state: either human rights undermine state projects of domination and repression, or human rights facilitate the neoliberal projects of the state. I examine these divergent portrayals in turn, beginning with the question of the compatibility of Maya culture and rights.

Culture and Rights

The essays in this volume direct our attention to the different empirical instances in which Maya culture encounters rights politics. This is productive insofar as it avoids the sterile debate between abstracted universalist and relativist philosophical positions.[1] Nonetheless divergences of analysis do crop up, and we can perceive two discrete positions on the introduction of rights into Maya communities: one that sees Mayan culture and human rights as contradictory and another that believes Mayan culture can be the basis for human rights claims.

MAYAN CULTURE AS AN OBSTACLE TO HUMAN RIGHTS

One set of contributors emphasizes the philosophical chasm between the Western rights tradition and Mayan conceptions of sociality and authority. For instance, Robert Carmack observes that human rights originated in a unique tradition of Western culture and welfare-state liberalism that has little relevance to the Guatemalan context. As such, he avers that human rights may be "dangerously idealistic, even ethnocentric."

Pedro Pitarch's essay on the translation of the United Nations (UN) Declaration of Human Rights into Tzeltal in Chiapas provides a more specific instantiation of this view. In their translation, indigenous translators intended to associate human rights with the Tzeltal idea of *mantal*, a set of rules and norms relating to material correctness, referring both to human bodies and the natural world. Despite attempts to translate human rights in a way that makes them "conceptually indigenous," Pitarch judges the translation to be deeply flawed, and even confusing for locals, with the end result that human rights remain alien to Tzeltal norms and practices. Although Pitarch invokes the linguistic theory of Benjamin Whorf, he stops short of asserting utter incommensurability between Western rights documents and Tzeltal translations. While much meaning is inevitably lost in the translation process, translations might make more sense if they were accompanied by a profound intercultural dialogue, thus underlining a point made some time ago by R. Pannikar (1992).

In a similar fashion, Julian López García writes that human rights are an external set of ideas imposed by culturally insensitive UN human rights training programs on the Ch'orti' of Guatemala. As a result, Ch'orti's respond to UN representatives by declaring, "Here it is different."[2] López García locates human rights within a much longer trajectory of failed modernization projects, from ones involving sanitation to those proffering sewing machines. He sees few reasons for the human rights project to be any different. Echoing Pitarch, López García asserts that unless the top-down training model gives way to meaningful cultural exchange (which seldom, if ever, occurs), the history of failure and deafness is condemned to repeat itself.

Intriguingly, this view of a potential "cultural clash" between Mayan conceptions and human rights does not appear in each and every discussion of human rights in the Maya region but seems to crop up most often in discussions of civil-political rights.[3] Perhaps this is not surprising, given the historically impoverished institutions of formal liberal democracy among Mayas in both Mexico and Guatemala. Nor does the cultural clash model appear everywhere in the Mayan region, but tends to be most pronounced in Mayan communities (such as Totonicapán or eastern Guatemala where López García worked) where human rights violations have been least widespread and where questions of accountability for mass atrocities are least pressing. Few Mayas who have experienced violent military repression in highland Guatemala or Chiapas are reported as stating that human rights have no relevance. Thus local Mayan views on culture and rights are closely related to historical experiences of political violence.

MAYAN CULTURE AS THE BASIS FOR HUMAN RIGHTS CLAIMS

Claims made in the language of indigenous rights, themselves a subset of human rights, rely on the idea that local indigenous culture is shared, distinctive, and so essential for the construction of the self and the community that such claims are compelling and well-nigh undeniable. Rodolfo Stavenhagen's vision of multicultural citizenship is philosophically grounded in Charles Taylor's "politics of recognition," which is in turn inspired by Jean-Jacques Rousseau's early critique of liberal individualism (see Taylor 1994). In this tradition, equality is achieved not through the equal rights of atomized individuals, but through the collective recognition of group identity. The right to difference is the fundamental universal right, as our essential humanity only becomes apparent in the unfettered expression of our particular cultural identity. In the hands of cultural rights theorists such as Stavenhagen, then, multicultural citizenship begins with the recognition that indigenous peoples are peoples, with an undeniable right to self-determination. It moves on to assert that Maya groups, as distinctive cultural groups with collective rights, require not only the recognition of their negative rights (as in the 1948 Genocide Convention) but also a whole set of positive rights. States are obliged, for instance, to promote indigenous institutions of education and health care and law.

This normative argument is supported by Shannon Speed and Xochitl Leyva Solano's empirical research in Mexico. They assert, much more emphatically than Carmack, López García, or Pitarch, that "rights discourses contain a moral grammar that resonates with indigenous experience." Speed and Leyva Solano observe that human rights can enter Maya communities without erasing local cultural forms, and that they can be approached through a more dialogical process of cultural translation. Indigenous rights, if implemented properly, can create a bridge between Western law and customary law and lead to the recognition of the internal decision-making structures of Maya communities. Indigenous rights frameworks can help create a parallel power structure based on the normative practices of indigenous peoples and thereby advance the cause of self-determination.

Both of the above formulations of culture and rights have a number of merits, especially insofar as they recognize that there are long-standing, distinctive cultural practices within Maya communities and that these shape how rights are perceived and manifested. Religious practices (such as those dedicated to saints, ancestors, or landscape gods), economic practices (such as reciprocal labor), and political institutions (community-based decision making) have been an important part of communal identities for hundreds of years. In the new political context, such established features of community life can serve as a resource that may be drawn on—either as a counterweight to external ideologies and institutions or as a bridge to a new politics where Mayas can exercise more autonomy and independence in the national sphere.[4] Although these strategies appear fundamentally opposed to one another, in fact both are strategies of local autonomy, albeit constructed in different ways. Both establish continuity with a time-honored principle of protecting and enhancing local independence. In both cases, state and community authority are mutually constitutive, rather than isolated and autonomous social fields.

The Perils of Cultural Analysis

There are clear problems with basing one's analysis too much on the idea of a "Mayan culture" as a whole, integrated packet. Deducing the consequences for politics from the inner logic of cultural or religious discourse is problematical given the heterogeneity of actual beliefs and practices within and among Maya communities. Some Mayas believe in animal spirits, others do not; some believe in ancestor spirits, others do not; some have customary legal institutions, others do not; and finally, some Mayas are evangelical Protestants, while others are Catholics, and still others urban secularists. Given this cultural complexity, according a single valence to a putative Maya culture elides the complexity of what Mayas actually do. If we accept this, then we might also have to accept that there is not any single answer to the question, "What is the relationship between 'Maya culture' and human rights?"

A number of things follow from this proposition. Clearly the concept of Maya culture is prevalent in political discourse, and it is a very powerful and persuasive political discourse for many Mayas, but it should remain the subject of our investigations and not serve as the analytical frame itself. We might be better advised to identify the social conditions that generate specific ideas about culture and to examine how such ideas come to have a salience due to their propagation by particular actors, who often share identifiable material and political interests. These interests will not be determinant in every instance, but we still need to understand human rights in relation to systems of hierarchy and contestation, of gender, and of class and status within Maya communities that both go back generations and that have been transformed by armed conflicts in Chiapas and Guatemala.[5] Without this sociological grounding, analyses can run the risk of an idealized cultural determinism, especially if they focus exclusively on the semantics of cultural translation and provide wholly cultural answers to what are fundamentally political questions.

This point may be illustrated with an empirical example taken from my own fieldwork on human rights among Maya-Q'eqchi' speakers in Alta Verapaz, Guatemala. In August 1996, I attended a two-day workshop coorganized by the Misión de Naciones Unidad para Guatemala (UN Verification Mission in Guatemala, MINUGUA) and the Catholic Church, which took place in a marquee alongside the Calvary Catholic church overlooking the departmental capital of Cobán. The workshop was opened in grand fashion by the MINUGUA departmental director, Goran Dejiæ. The subject of the workshop was the Global Human Rights Declaration signed between the Guatemalan government and the Revolutionary National Unity of Guatemala (Unidad Revolucionaría Nacional Guatemalteca, URNG) guerrillas. This document had been translated into Q'eqchi' by urban Maya professionals associated with the national Academy of Mayan Languages. The leaders of this exercise in human rights public education were Q'eqchi'-speaking Catholic lay catechists and former catechists. The 150 or so workshop participants were Q'eqchi' men and women from rural villages in Alta Verapaz.

It was fascinating to see what kinds of choices the translators had made in their rendition of the declaration. As in the Tzeltal case described by Pitarch, declaration was translated as *chakrab,*' which literally means "law." In the minds of the catechist-trained Maya-Q'eqchi participants, this term has clear echoes of the New Testament, which is the Ak' Chakrab' (or literally, the "New Law").[6] As in Tzeltal, there is no word or phrase in Q'eqchi' that remotely corresponds to a government accord or international convention or declaration. Human rights specifically were translated as *xk'ulub'em li poyanam.* Without getting too technical, *xk'ulub'em* (sing. *k'ulub'*) derives from the verb *k'uluk,* which means "to receive" or "to happen to," so *xk'ulub'em li poyanam* could be literally translated as "what all people receive." Rather less literally, it could be translated as "what all people are worthy to receive" or as "what all people deserve," as in actual usage *k'ulub'* can refer to ideas of worth, just desserts, and dignity. Why do all people have dignity? The workshop leaders drew again on Christian images, "Because each of us is sacred."[7] Whether one opts for the literal or the more interpretative reading of *k'ulub',* what is clear is that the translators chose a fairly inactive term to describe rights, one that emphasizes what individuals passively receive, rather than what they actively claim.

More vigorous and dynamic possibilities do exist in Q'eqchi' such as *patz'om* ("that which is petitioned for") or *titz'om* ("that which is demanded"), but these were rejected by the translators. What the Q'eqchi' participants got was a new set of rules that approached the status of law and carried strong Christian overtones about what they might passively deserve or receive. If we only stayed within the discourse of the translation, human rights education among Q'eqchi's would engender political passivity and a resigned, perhaps even fatalistic attitude to making demands before state and other political authorities. However, when analyzing actual politics in Alta Verapaz in the late 1990s, the actions of Q'eqchi's after receiving human rights training have been far from passive. Many of the participants at the workshop returned to their villages and rededicated themselves to petitioning the state to title their lands and to build roads, bridges, and schools in their communities. They set about documenting past human rights violations for both the Catholic Church's Recuperation of Historical Memory project and for the official Historical Clarification Commission. They saw the language of rights as assisting them in the pursuit of these various undertakings.

Their political agency also took them beyond the language of rights, demonstrating that rights talk neither exists in a political vacuum nor totally dominates the political landscape. A number of the workshop leaders were individuals who had spent between five and seven years in the 1980s in the mountains of Alta Verapaz, in areas for a time controlled by the Guerrilla Army of the Poor (EGP).[8] In the 1990s, their views were considered too radical for the Catholic Church, and they resigned as catechists and espoused a millenarian Maya religious ethic that sought to expel supposedly foreign ideas and retain only that which was "purely Maya," or, in Q'eqchi,' that which pertains to *ral ch'och'* (the "sons of the earth"). They drew up plans for Q'eqchi's to take power from Ladinos by winning elections in local municipal councils. Further, they set up their own nongovernmental organization to bypass international intermediaries and liaise directly with MINUGUA and external aid donors on development initiatives in Q'eqchi' villages. Despite the fact that the Catholic Church–MINUGUA discourse of rights was quietist and bland, Q'eqchi' actors integrated rights into an already existing political strategy that emphasized purposive political agency to engage the state and the international community to improve their conditions of life. Indeed, for these Q'eqchi's human rights were a reassuring expression that they were now working within the law, with a hope for all the safety and protection from persecution that staying within the law entailed.

To see what impact ideas such as human rights will have on a cultural context, we must complement our analysis of the semantics and logic of the ideas with an understanding of their actual usage in specific political and economic contexts. Rights are embedded in patterns of authority and processes of contestation among Mayas, between Mayas and separate state institutions, and between Mayas and international institutions such as the Catholic Church and the UN. Some parts of that contestation are new (the presence of the UN), other parts are two hundred years old (the Guatemalan or Mexican state), and still other elements are five hundred years old (the Catholic Church). Any inquiry into the culture of rights therefore needs to be complemented by a thorough account of the power relations within communities, among communities, and between communities and state institutions and intergovernmental organizations such as the UN.

Human Rights in Neoliberal States

A number of essays in this book analyze rights in the context of state power and examine the political outcomes of rights talk and rights movements. Usefully, they examine how rights function within neoliberal states and thereby provide insights into how rights operate in the present political environment in Mexico and Guatemala. Perhaps inevitably, they come up against the complexity of political usages and consequences of the rights regime, and as a result, clear oppositions in interpretation and analysis become apparent. In particular, two contradictory positions on rights and neoliberal state regulation emerge in the accounts: one that sees rights as undermining and potentially challenging state power, and another that sees rights as an extension of a state project of domination.

HUMAN RIGHTS AS A CENTRAL PART OF THE PROJECT OF THE NEOLIBERAL STATE

Human rights have discernible affinities with flexible global capitalism and the neoliberal restructuring of the state in Latin America and elsewhere. In their article on Mexico, Speed and Leyva Solano argue that indigenous rights and customary law coincide with the neoliberal Mexican state's project of privatizing and fragmenting normal state functions, and more specifically with those of cutting back on social programs, privatizing law and security, and allowing NGOs and private organizations to take over state functions. Alvaro Reyes and Speed push this argument one step further. Human rights are an assimilationist trap in the context of a state that seeks to slough off normal state services, to shirk its basic responsibilities to the citizenry, and to disengage from any socioeconomic redistributive measures. They are a form of deception that raises expectations but that transforms neither state nor society. Worse, by directing popular aspirations toward the legal process, they "normalize" and legitimize an unequal structure of power and authority.

This view also finds echoes in the studies of Guatemala, although Rachel Sieder qualifies her analysis by saying that human rights coincide with neoliberalism with regard to indigenous rights, but not with regard to classic civil-political rights. Sieder counsels us that creating a parallel system of customary law in some indigenous communities may only exacerbate a cycle of vengeance in Maya communities and reinforce existing tendencies to pursue mob justice. Guatemala has been afflicted by a wave of lynchings since 1996, 415 in the five year period up to 2001, resulting in 215 killings and hundreds of serious injuries. A number of things are going on here. Genocidal violence has been documented by the Recuperation of Historical Memory project and by the Commission of Historical Clarification, but the main perpetrators have gone unpunished. Mayas traumatized by state-sponsored political violence continually reenact that violence in an ostensibly nonpolitical context of everyday criminality. The present Guatemalan state is either unable, or worse, unwilling, to contain the massive wave of societal criminality. The criminologist Stan Cohen (2002) demonstrates how states benefit from constructing categories of social deviancy and fomenting a generalized moral panic around them since this inhibits rational debate about solutions to the social problems. In this situation, the kind of legal decentralization (and some say, fragmentation) espoused by indigenous rights activists may well lead to the "illegal pluralism" of widespread criminality and mob justice, which is surely detrimental to the human rights of Mayas in the long run.

HUMAN RIGHTS AS A POLITICAL LANGUAGE OF RESISTANCE TO THE STATE

While Sieder is cautious about the consequences of indigenous rights, she sees civil-political rights as a challenge to widespread impunity in Guatemala. She reminds us how the rule of law became a goal of the left in the 1980s and 1990s after the macabre deformations of law under authoritarian regimes; one need only think of General Ríos Montt's secret special tribunals that executed fifteen individuals by firing squad in 1982–83 without proper legal representation or any semblance of due process (see Schirmer 1997, 1998). After a history of flagrant violations of basic legal rights, procedural fairness and the rule of law are not to be lightly dismissed. In the Guatemalan context, even the partial realization of basic legal rights would require a quite different type of criminal justice system and, while we are at it, of the Guatemalan state.

Several of the articles on Guatemala reinforce this more emancipatory view of rights. Victoria Sanford's account of the ethics and political implications of truth finding illustrates how documenting human rights abuses allows Mayas to lift a state-sponsored regime of denial. This enables local actors to open up a public space for political discussion and organizing and to pursue accountability and democratization. Several of the essays on human rights in Chiapas, including those by Christine Kovic and by Speed and Reyes, also uphold the analysis of human rights as a tool of resistance to violent government incursions in Maya communities. The capacity for human rights organizations to mobilize international sympathy and to shame the national government can provide significant protection for local Maya activists.

Finally, we must recognize that engaging the state in the language of rights with a view to reforming state institutions has both positive and negative consequences. Positively, it can undermine state attempts at repression and force the state to democratize, and with a more democratic state comes a new "praxis of citizenship," to use Jürgen Habermas's (1992) phrase. Yet forging a closer nexus between citizens and states that have acted cynically in the past, even within a language of resistance, can establish a relationship susceptible to co-optation or manipulation in the future.

Theorizing Human Rights and the State

While the above efforts to theorize the relationship between rights and Maya culture, on the one hand, and rights and the state, on the other, seem contradictory and mutually incompatible, each speaks to one feature of the complexity of the situation on the ground and illuminates one facet of the multiplicity of distinctive political strategies advocated in the language of rights. This is perhaps not too surprising. After all, a persuasive explanation of the global rise of human rights is their capacity to appeal to radically dissimilar political projects. So at least in part, the success of rights talk is a result of its ideological promiscuity and of its ability to embrace reformists and revolutionaries, Christians and secularists, liberal individualists and indigenous rights activists. This makes neatly categorizing and authoritatively analyzing human rights highly problematic, since different groups both inside and outside the state promote distinct political programs within the same discursive framework. To add to the mixture, different state institutions (the military, the educational system, the criminal justice system) all have their own discourse on rights, and their own political motivations for employing rights talk.

If we accept this view we are prevented from choosing, once and for all, any of the above analytical formulations of rights over any of the others. Perhaps another way of thinking about the problem is to identify the political processes constitutive of each of the formulations of state and culture outlined above. Four such cross-cutting processes come to mind: legalization, verticalization, and the centralizing and pluralizing practices of both state and nonstate actors. The salience of these processes varies according to place and historical moment.

Rights are a way of articulating aspirations and claims, but such articulations must ultimately be directed at becoming legally enforceable in a court of law if they are to endure. Therefore human rights have an inherent tendency to channel discord in civil society into the legal process, and thereby to turn political contention into legal contention. Conflicts, say, regarding land, must be expressed in such a way that the law can hear them; that is, they must conform to legal convention and precedent. What are the consequences of this? A number of our contributors have argued that legalizing a conflict is depoliticizing insofar as it turns political problems into technical, legal ones. The legalization of rights is mystifying in the materialist sense in that it raises expectations that the state can solve social and economic problems, and normalizing, in that it employs the legal-bureaucratic system without challenging it.

Yet legalization is not always to be decried.[9] By concentrating on the actual functioning of the legal process, indigenous rights activists have managed to pry open new legal avenues and to make courts more accessible to indigenous communities (for instance, by pressing for the right to simultaneous translation into Mayan languages as part of a wider set of language rights). Since state institutions are a significant (although not the only) source of resources in both Guatemala and Mexico, some claims will have to be legalized to make them durable and enforceable. Furthermore, holding the Guatemalan military accountable for past human rights violations requires recourse to legal institutions, both within Guatemala and at the Interamerican Commission and Court of Human Rights.

THE VERTICALIZATION OF CONFLICT

Appealing to human rights verticalizes local conflicts, that is, it lifts the question of conflict resolution out of a community context and raises it to a higher level. Here, Mayas may enlist the power and authority of the state on their behalf, usually in a struggle over land with neighboring communities. Human rights talk not only verticalizes conflict to the nation-state level but also internationalizes the conflict. Appeal for the involvement of international actors means bypassing state institutions and forging alliances with international NGOs, departments of the UN, and powerful private institutions such as the Ford Foundation. This may allow local Mayas to realize goals that they have been struggling to achieve for centuries. But the verticalization of rights is also a double-edged sword. It can bring international aid to beleaguered local actors, and it can also, as David Stoll (1997) has been telling us for some time, pit one group of poor people against another and ratchet up the stakes and the potential for violent conflict. Stoll's account in this volume of the changing economic relations in postconflict Ixil country, where finca owners have steadily sold their landholdings to Ixils as a result of the conflict, is highly informative. This allowed Ixils to aspire to wield greater authority than before the violence, and Ixil professionals have come to exercise authority within the municipalities. Overall, the economic and political transformations have coincided with a kind of ethnic détente in Ixil country. Where there is an ongoing transfer of property and political power from Ladinos to Ixils at the municipal and regional level, the verticalization of land conflicts and the involvement of international actors may be counterproductive.

THE CENTRALIZATION VERSUS THE DECENTRALIZATION OF THE STATE

State legal and bureaucratic institutions are simultaneously subjected to centralizing and pluralizing forms of political action and knowledge production. Modern states continually attempt to rationalize and institutionalize their legal dominion, and at times that is achieved through centralization (think of the resurgent French state during the nineteenth century Bourbon Restoration), while at other times domination is pursued through a set of pluralizing strategies (think of British indirect colonial rule in Africa). States may have their plans, but of course the locals are not always quiescent. Max Weber noted in his analysis of the emergence of legal authority that the character of national law is "structured by the competition between central rulers trying to maintain the maximum of power over their subjects and the local power-holders trying to carve out their own domains of arbitrary power over their dependants and limit the central government's claims on them" (qtd. in Humphreys 1985: 246). At times, Mayas have reinforced the centralizing strategies of state officials, and in the present, seeking to reform state law along classic civil-political human rights lines may be part of this historical trajectory. However, insofar as they do not exert a complete monopoly over judicial practices, states encounter resistance in the form of local legal practices and institutions. Legal pluralism in the Maya region has recently taken the form of indigenous rights, but it is part of a much older power struggle between communities and the state (Smith 1990).

Conclusions

At the beginning of this essay I noted that it can be useful to highlight the similarities in human rights practices among the Mayas of both Guatemala and Mexico. Yet it is also instructive to note the differences that surface, particularly with regard to state practice. In her article, Sieder thoughtfully reminds us that in our study of both Guatemala and Mexico, we are dealing with very different kinds of states and that therefore legal pluralism has different kinds of consequences in each context. Apart from the military, the Guatemalan state has historically had a feeble infrastructure, and it has especially lacked the kind of legal infrastructure that could make rights meaningful. Historically, it has been able to deliver very little in the way of services and resources and instead has been highly repressive toward its Maya population. The Mexican state is a more developed and disciplinary state, with a manifestly greater redistributive capacity. For most of the twentieth century, the governing Partido Revolucionario Institucional (Revolutionary Institutional Party, PRI) party was able to maintain power through corporatist strategies, which did involve delivering real goods and services to rural communities. While the Mexican state has been violent and repressive at times, the extent of the violence has been nothing like the systematic program of genocide carried out by the Guatemalan state in the early 1980s.

While my essay initially applauded the pan-Maya focus of this book, a comparative approach to human rights in Mexico and Guatemala requires further qualification and discussion insofar as we are dealing with dissimilar polities with often unrelated histories. If we take this point seriously, then we might have to accept that there is no single solution to human rights problems that applies across the Maya region, and we might come to the view that the circumstances of two countries necessitate different political strategies. For instance, indigenous rights may be more compatible with the political context of Mexico insofar as these rights decentralize an already strong, even if neoliberalizing, central state. Despite the last fifteen or so years of privatization and liberalization, the Mexican state still exhibits elements of a corporatist infrastructure, and the state retains the (albeit diminished) capacity to redistribute social and economic resources. The pluralizing processes promoted by the indigenous rights movement may represent a means of both pressuring the state to deliver resources to indigenous communities and of pursuing greater autonomy within those communities, especially in regard to negotiating with international development agencies.

In Guatemala, massive levels of human rights violations over several decades present a much more pressing challenge. Justice is, at least for now, less a question of redistributive justice (though that matters too) than it is an issue of retributive justice and accountability. The overall thrust of the Guatemalan human rights movement over the past thirty years has been to counter societal criminality and arbitrary state violence by building up the rule of law and creating a legal infrastructure that is swift and fair. While the theorization that law is solely an instrument of regulation and discipline may still hold sway among some neo-Foucauldian academics, segments of the Latin American left abandoned such a view in the 1980s and sought instead to recover the rule of law as a left project to challenge the impunity of the military and to confront the enclaves of authoritarianism within state and society. The idea of the rule of law was wrested from its conservative, Hobbesian moorings and integrated into a more social democratic vision.

In the context of such a weak state that lacks both infrastructure and legitimacy, it might be sensible to approach human rights through their classic civil-political manifestation, as a means to democratize state institutions, so they can begin to address both state repression and the criminalization of society. It does not seem to make sense to engage in strategies that pluralize and decentralize state law until after the foundations of a system of accountability are secure and until after the state can administer justice in a manner that is more efficient and fair. As others such as Michael Ignatieff (1999) have noted, disintegrating and fragmenting states are precisely the kind that massively violate the human rights of their citizens. Protecting human rights requires states with genuine legal competence and a vibrant civil society that continually badgers the state to prioritize human rights concerns.

Whether we are speaking of Guatemala or Mexico, it is clear that human rights in the Maya region and elsewhere have become the political language of choice for Mayas pursuing an enormous range of interests, from economic claims to land and resources, to improved government educational and health services, to claims for cultural autonomy, to basic legal rights ensuring protection against extrajudicial detainment or murder. They are also part of a dramatic set of transformations of citizens' relationships to the state over the past twenty years. Not only have participants in human rights movements come to see themselves as political actors with purposive agency but a new dynamic has also been introduced into the citizen-state nexus with the arrival of a host of international and transnational intermediaries.

It is too early to tell what the ultimate outcome of all this will be. The attention paid to human rights may produce democratizing reforms and more participatory state institutions. Or it may, if state officials negotiate in bad faith, lead to a dead end and the eventual abandonment of human rights in favor of another master narrative, likely a return to political authoritarianism or religious revivalism. Yet a few things are reasonably clear. While human rights may assist Mayas in pressuring the state and winning some real concessions, they also demonstrate significant limitations and therefore should not displace all other types of political organization and discourse. Indeed, the realization of human rights ideals requires social movements with a broader political view, as we saw in the case of the Community Human Rights Defenders in Chiapas who both work in legal defense and have an abiding interest in the broader project of regional Maya autonomy.

While claims in the language of human rights are limited and politically reformist, their civic humanism might actually be a pragmatic asset, given that Mayas in both Guatemala and Mexico have engaged in armed rebellion against the state at distinct points in the past two decades and have been met with a systematic repression that has often reversed previous political gains. Given the disposition of both the Guatemalan and Mexican states to respond with overwhelming force to perceived threats from Mayas, we might recommend, for now, the continued capacity of human rights to establish a common medium through which Mayas communicate difference, cooperate across ethnic boundaries, and compete for the resources of both the state and the international community.

Notes

1. See Cowan, Dembour, and Wilson 2001 for a specific discussion of culture and rights.
2. A number of articles claim that the advent of human rights in Guatemala began with MINUGUA. While MINUGUA certainly extended the scope of rights talk, we

need to recognize that a number of human rights organizations in the 1980s counted on a significant Mayan presence, including the Grupo de Apoyo Mutuo (Mutual Support Group, GAM), Coordinadora Nacional de Viudas de Guatemala (National Committee of Guatemalan Widows, CONAVIGUA), and Consejo de Comunidades Étnicas Runujel Junam (Runujel Junam Counsel of Ethnic Communities, CERJ). Before that, in the 1970s, human rights concerns formed part of the discourses of both the heavily Mayan Catholic catechist movement and of revolutionary peasant organizations such as the Comité Unidad Campesina (Committee for Peasant Unity, CUC). In Chiapas, Bishop Samuel Ruiz García was also introducing human rights ideas at that time.

3. It also appears in discussions of gender in rural Maya communities.

4. Greg Grandin (2000) documents how Mayas at various historical periods have sought to identify closely with state modernization projects.

5. See the classic works on intercommunal tensions by Douglas Brintnall (1979), Frank Cancian (1965), and Waldemar Smith (1977).

6. At the time, only the New Testament had been translated, and this was the only book commonly available for Q'eqchi' speakers in their own language.

7. Sacred was parsed as *waan xloq'al.*

8. This fact, while still dangerous for the individuals concerned, is not a secret to anyone.

9. For an expansion of this argument in the context of the Guatemalan Historical Clarification Commission, see Wilson 2006.

References

Abell, John. 1999. "The Neoliberal World Order: The View from the Highlands of Guatemala." *NACLA Report on the Americas* 33 (1): 37–41.

Acuerdo sobre identidad y derechos de los pueblos indígenas. 1995. Guatemala City: Coordinación de Organizaciones del Pueblo Maya de Guatemala.

Adams, Richard, and Santiago Bastos. 2003. *Las relaciones étnicas en Guatemala, 1944–2000.* Antigua, Guatemala: Centro de Investigaciones Regionales de Mesoamérica.

Agamben, Giorgio. 1998. *Homo Sacer: Sovereign Power and Bare Life.* Trans. Daniel Heller-Roazen. Stanford, CA: Stanford University Press.

Aguilera Peralta, Gabriel. 1981. *Dialéctica del terror en Guatemala.* San José, Costa Rica: Editorial Universitaria Centroamericana.

Aguirre Beltrán, Gonzalo. 1957. *El proceso de aculturación y el cambio sociocultural en México.* Mexico City: Universidad Nacional Autónoma de Mexico.

Alarcón Osorio, Daniel. n.d. "La costumbre jurídica comunal de la étnia kaqchikel." Paper presented at the Dirección General de Investigación, Universidad de San Carlos de Guatemala and Llerena, Guatemala City.

Albores, Arturo, and Marisela González. 1983. "La vinculación popular y el encuentro con la realidad." Unpublished Manuscript.

Alejos, José. 1988. "Lak Oñel: Praxis y discurso en el agrarismo Chol." MA thesis, Instituto Nacional de Antropologia e Historia.

———. 1992–94. "GAM: Indígenas y derechos humanos en Guatemala." In *Memorias del Primer Congreso Internacional de Mayistas.* 3 vols. Mexico City: Universidad Nacional Autónoma de Mexico. 1:450–67.

Alvarez, Sonia E., Evelina Dagnino, and Arturo Escobar, eds. 1998. *Cultures of Politics/Politics of Cultures: Revisioning Latin American Social Movements.* Boulder, CO: Westview.

Amadiume, Ife, and Abdullahi A. An-Na'im. 2000. *The Politics of Memory: Truth, Healing and Social Justice.* London: Zed.

American Anthropological Association (AAA). 1947. "Statement on Human Rights." *American Anthropologist* 49 (4): 539–43.

Amnesty International (AI). 1986. *Mexico: Human Rights in Rural Areas; An Exchange of Documents with the Mexican Government on Human Rights in Oaxaca and Chiapas.* London: Amnesty International.

———. 1999. *Systemic Injustice: Torture, "Disappearance," and Extrajudicial Executions in Mexico.* London: Amnesty International.

Amnistía Internacional (AI). 1998. *Declaración Universal de los Derechos Humanos, versión traducida a tzotzil, tzeltal, tojolabal, ch'ol, popoluca y náhuatl.* Trans. Roberto Santiz Gómez and Felipa Pérez López. Mexico City: Amnistía Internacional.

Anaya, James. 2004. *Indigenous People in International Law.* 2nd ed. Oxford: Oxford University Press.

Anderson, Benedict. 1983. *Imagined Communities: Reflections on the Origin and Spread of Nationalism.* London: Verso.

An'Naím, Abdullahi Ahmed. 1992. *Human Rights in Cross-cultural Perspective: A Quest for Consensus.* Philadelphia: University of Pennsylvania Press.

Anthropology News. 2006, July.

Appelbaum, Richard P., William L. F. Felstiner, and Volkmar Gessner, eds. 2001. *Rules and Networks: The Legal Culture of Global Business Transactions.* Oxford: Hart.

Ara, Domingo de. 1986. *Vocabulario de lengua tzeldal según el orden de Copanabastla.* Ed. Mario H. Ruz. Mexico City: Universidad Nacional Autónoma de Mexico.

Assies, Willem, Gemma van der Haar, and André Hoekema, eds. 1999. *El reto de la diversidad. Zamora, Mexico:* El Colegio de Michoacán.

———. 2000. *The Challenge of Diversity: Indigenous Peoples and Reform of the State in Latin America.* Amsterdam: Thela Thesis.

Ávila, Hugo. n.d. *Manual de educación en derechos humanos.* Guatemala City: Missión de Naciones Unidas para la Verificación de los Derechos Humanos en Guatemala.

Azaola, Elena. 1996. *El delito de ser mujer.* Mexico City: Plaza y Valdes.

Baeza Martínez, Luis Felipe. 2005. "Los derechos humanos de las personas con capacidades diferentes en el estado de Yucatán en la actualidad: Mérida, Yucatán." Undergraduate thesis, Facultad de Derecho de la Universidad Autónoma de Yucatán.

Bakhtin, M. M. 1981. *The Dialogic Imagination: Four Essays.* Trans. Caryl Emerson and Michael Holquist. Austin: University of Texas Press.

Ball, Patrick, Paul Kobrak, and Herbert Spirer. 1999. *State Violence in Guatemala, 1960–1996: A Quantitative Reflection.* New York: American Association for the Advancement of Science.

Baloyra, Enrique. 1983. "Reactionary Despotism in Central America." *Journal of Latin American Studies* 15:295–319.

Barnoya García, José. 1984. *Panzós y unas historias.* Guatemala City: Editorial Universitaria.

Barry, Tom. 1986. *Guatemala: The Politics of Counterinsurgency.* Albuquerque: Inter-Hemispheric Education Resource Center.

——. 1992. *Inside Guatemala.* Albuquerque: Inter-Hemispheric Education Resource Center.

Barth, Fredrik, ed. 1969. *Ethnic Groups and Boundaries: The Social Organization of Culture Difference.* Bergen, Norway: Universitetsforlaget.

Bastos, Santiago. 1997. "¿En busca de la ciudadanía étnica? Reflexiones en torno al movimiento maya y al acuerdo de identidad y derechos de los pueblos indígenas." Paper presented at the Congreso de Estudios Mayas, Universidad Rafael Landívar, Guatemala City, August 6–8.

——. 2001. "De la nación estado a la nación multicultural: Una reflexión histórica y crítica." *Revista Trayectorias* 3 (4–5): 106–17.

Bastos, Santiago, and Manuela Camus. 2003. *Entre el mecapal y el cielo: Desarrollo del movimiento maya en Guatemala.* Guatemala City: Facultad Latinoamericana de Ciencias Sociales.

——. 2004. "Multiculturalismo y pueblos indígenas: Reflexiones a partir del caso de Guatemala." *Revista Centroamericana de Ciencias Sociales* 1:106–17.

Bastos, Santiago, Domingo Hernández, and Leopoldo Méndez. In press. "Resarcimiento y reconstitución del pueblo maya en Guatemala: Entre la acción autónoma y el reconocimiento estatal." In *Gobernar (en) la diversidad: Experiencias indígenas desde América Latina; Hacia una investigación descolonizada,* ed. Jorge Ramón, González-Ponciano. Mexico City: Centro de Investigaciones y Estudios Superiores en Antropología Social.

Bastos, Santiago, and Aura Cumes, eds. In press. *Mayanización y vida cotidiana: La ideología multicultural en la sociedad guatemalteca.* 2 vols. Guatemala City: Facultad Latinoamericana de Ciencias Sociales.

Bauer, Alfonso, et al. 1992. "El derecho al refugio." In *Una década de refugio en México: Los refugiados guatemaltecos y los derechos humanos,* ed. Graciela Freyermuth and R. Aída Hernández Castillo. Mexico City: Centro de Investigaciones y Estudios Superiores en Antropología Social. 59–67.

Beibersheimer, Christina. 2001. "Justice Reform in Latin America and the Caribbean: The IDB Perspective." In *Rule of Law in Latin America: The International Promotion of Judicial Reform,* ed. Pilar Domingo and Rachel Sieder. London: Institute of Latin American Studies. 99–121.

Bell, Daniel. 2000. *East Meets West: Human Rights and Democracy in East Asia.* Princeton: Princeton University Press.

Benda-Beckmann, Franz. 1997. "Citizens, Strangers and Indigenous Peoples: Conceptual Politics and Legal Pluralism." *Law and Anthropology* 9:1–42.

Benedetti, Mario. 1995. "The Triumph of Memory." *NACLA Report on the Americas* 29 (3): 10–12.

Bengoa, José. 2000. *La emergencia indígena en América Latina.* Mexico City: FCE.

Benjamin, Thomas. 1989. *A Rich Land, a Poor People: Politics and Society in Modern Chiapas.* Albuquerque: University of New Mexico Press.

Berger, Susan. 2006. *Guatemaltecas: The Women's Movement 1986–2003.* Austin: University of Texas Press.

Bettelheim, Bruno. 1979. *Surviving and other essays.* Knopf: New York.

Beverly, John. 1996. "The Margin at the Center." In *The Real Thing: Testimonial Discourse and Latin America,* ed. Georg Gugelberger. Durham, NC: Duke University Press. 23–41.

Bhabha, Homi K. 1994. *The Location of Culture.* London: Routledge.

Bickham Mendez, Jennifer. 2005. *From the Revolution to the Maquiladoras: Gender, Labor, and Globalization in Nicaragua.* Durham, NC: Duke University Press.

Black, George. 1984. *Garrison Guatemala.* London: Zed.

Bloch, Anne-Christine. 1995. "Minorities and Indigenous Peoples." In *Economic, Social and Cultural Rights: A Textbook,* ed. Asbjørn Eide, Catarina Krause, and Allan Rosas. Dordrecht, Netherlands: Martinus Nijhoff.

Bloque campesino del Estado de Chiapas. n.d. "La política agraria del régimen y la respuesta del movimiento chiapaneco." Unpublished manuscript.

Bobbio, Norberto. 1995. *Thomas Hobbes and the Natural Law Tradition.* Chicago: University of Chicago Press.

Bobrow-Strain, Aaron. 2007. *Intimate Enemies: Landowners, Power and Violence in Chiapas.* Durham: Duke University Press.

Boff, Leonardo, and Clodovis Boff. 1987. *Introducing Liberation Theology.* Trans. Paul Burns. Maryknoll, NY: Orbis.

Booth, John. 1998. *Costa Rica: Quest for Democracy.* Boulder, CO: Westview.

——. 2000. "Globalization and Democratization in Guatemala." *Journal of Interamerican Studies and World Affairs* 42:4–19.

Boremanse, Didier. 1998. "Máquinas de coser y la espiritualidad maya q'eqchi': La vitalidad de la cultura q'eqchi' expresada en el rito wa'tesink." *Estudios Sociales* 59:239–45.

Bracamonte y Sosa, Pedro. 1994. *La memoria enclaustrada: Historia indígena de Yucatán, 1750–1915.* Mexico City: Centro de Investigaciones y Estudios Superiores en Antropología Social.

Breton, Alain, and Jaques Arnauld, with Marie Charlotte Arnaud and Mario Humberto Ruz, eds. 1994. *Los mayas: La pasión por los antepasados, el deseo de perdurar.* Trans. Hélène Lévesques Dion. Mexico City: Editorial Grijalbo.

Brintnall, Douglas. 1979. *Revolt against the Dead: The Modernization of a Mayan Community in the Highlands of Guatemala.* New York: Gordon and Breach.

Brölmann, Catherine, et al., eds. 1993. *Peoples and Minorities in International Law.* Dordrecht, Netherlands: Martinus Nijhoff Publishers.

Brown, Wendy. 1995. *States of Injury: Power and Freedom in Late Modernity.* Princeton: Princeton University Press.

Brown, Wendy, and Janet Halley, eds. 2002. *Left Legalism/Left Critique.* Durham, NC: Duke University Press.

Brownlie, Ian. 1988. "The Rights of Peoples in Modern International Law." In *The Rights of Peoples,* ed. James Crawford. Oxford: Clarendon. 1–16.

Brysk, Alison. 1993. "From Above and Below: Social Movements, the International

System, and Human Rights in Argentina." *Comparative Political Studies* 26 (3): 259–285.

———. 1996. "Turning Weakness into Strength: The Internationalization of Indian Rights." *Latin American Perspectives* 23 (2): 38–57.

———. 2000. *From Tribal Village to Global Village: Indian Rights and International Relations in Latin America.* Stanford, CA: Stanford University Press.

———. 2002. *Globalization and Human Rights.* Berkeley: University of California Press.

Buenrostro, Manuel. 2006. "La justicia indígena de Quintana Roo dentro de un contexto global." Paper presented at the Red Latinoamerico de Antropología Jurídica Conference V, Oaxtepec, Morelos, October.

Buergenthal, Thomas. 1988. *International Human Rights in a Nutshell.* St. Paul, MN: West.

Burchell, Graham. 1996. "Liberal Government and Techniques of the Self." In *Foucault and Political Reason: Liberalism, Neo-liberalism, and Rationalities of Government,* ed. Andrew Barry, Thomas Osburne, and Nikolas Rose. London: University College London. 19–36.

Burgers, J. Herman. 1990a. "The Function of Human Rights as Individual and Collective Rights." In *Human Rights in a Pluralist World: Individuals and Collectivities,* ed. Burgers et al. London: Meckler. 63–74.

———. 1990b. "The Right to Cultural Identity." In *Human Rights in a Pluralist World: Individuals and Collectivities,* ed. Burgers et al. London: Meckler. 251–53.

Burguete Cal y Mayor, Araceli. 1989. *Cronología de un etnocidio reciente: Breve recuento de la violencia política a los indios, 1974–1987.* Mexico City: Claves Latinoamericanas.

———. 1994. "Las cuentas pendientes: Absalón y Ernesto Castellanos Domínguez." *CEMOS Memoria* 63:33–40.

Burguete Cal y Mayor, Araceli, and Miguel Gómez. In press. "Gobernar en la diversidad en San Juan Cancuc, Chiapas, México." In *Gobernar (en) la diversidad: experiencias indígenas desde América Latina: Hacia una investigación descolonizada,* ed. Jorge Ramón, González-Ponciano. Mexico City: Centro de Investigaciones y Estudios Superiores en Antropología Social.

Burkhart, Louise M. 1989. *The Slippery Earth: Nahua-Christian Moral Dialogue in Sixteenth-Century Mexico.* Tucson: University of Arizona Press.

Cabanas Díaz, Andrés. 1999. *Los sueños perseguidos: Memoria de las Comunidades de Población en Resistencia de la Sierra.* Vol. 1. Guatemala City: Magna Terra.

Cabrera, María Luisa. 1995. *Otra historia por contar: Promotores de salud en Guatemala.* Guatemala City: ASECSA.

Caldeira, Teresa. 2000. *City of Walls: Crime, Segregation, and Citizenship in São Paulo.* Berkeley: University of California Press.

Call, Charles T. 2000. "Sustainable Development in Central America: The Challenges of Violence, Injustice and Insecurity." Hamburg, Central America 2020 Working Paper.

Camey Rodríguez, Carmen. 1992. "Relaciones entre derechos humanos, refugiados y retorno." In *Una década de refugio en México: Los refugiados guatemaltecos y los derechos humanos,* ed. Graciela Freyermuth and R. Aída Hernández Castillo. Mexico City: Centro de Investigaciones y Estudios Superiores en Antropología Social. 345–61.

Camus, Manuela. 2002. "Mujeres mayas: Sus distintas expresiones." In "Nuevas tendencias de los movimientos indígenas en las países andinos y Guatemala a comienzos del nuevo milenio," ed. Juliana Ströbele-Gregor. Special issue, *Indiana* 17–18:31–56.

Cancian, Frank. 1965. *Economics and Prestige in a Maya Community: The Religious Cargo System in Zinacantán.* Stanford, CA: Stanford University Press.

Cantón Osalde, Sandra Lorena. 2001. "Eficacia de la comisión de derechos humanos." Undergraduate thesis, Facultad de Derecho de la Universidad Autónoma de Yucatán, Mérida.

Carlsen, Robert S. 1997. *The War for the Heart and Soul of a Highland Maya Town.* Austin: University of Texas Press.

Carmack, Robert M. 1973. *Quichean Civilization: The Ethnohistoric, Ethnographic, and Archaeological Sources.* Berkeley: University of California Press.

——. 1979a. *La evolución del reino quiché.* Guatemala City: Editorial Piedra Santa.

——. 1979b. Historia social de los quichés. Seminario de Integración Social Guatemalteca No. 38. Guatemala: Ministerio de Educación.

——. 1988. *Harvest of Violence: The Maya Indians and the Guatemalan Crisis.* Norman: University of Oklahoma Press.

——. 1995. *Rebels of Highland Guatemala: The Quiché-Mayas of Momostenango.* Norman: University of Oklahoma Press.

Carmack, Robert M., and James L. Mondloch, eds. and trans. 1983. *El Título de Totonicapán: Su texto, traducción y comentario.* Mexico City: Universidad Nacional Autónoma de Mexico, Centro de Estudios Mayas.

Carothers, Thomas. 1999. *Aiding Democracy Abroad: The Learning Curve.* Washington: Carnegie Endowment for International Peace.

——. 2001. "The Many Agendas of Rule-of-Law Reform in Latin America." In *Rule of Law in Latin America: The International Promotion of Judicial Reform,* ed. Pilar Domingo and Rachel Sieder. London: Institute of Latin American Studies, 4–16.

Carrithers, Michael. 1985. "An Alternative Social History of the Self." In *The Category of the Person: Anthropology, Philosophy, History,* ed. Carrithers, Steven Collins, and Steven Lukes. Cambridge: Cambridge University Press. 234–56.

Carton de Grammont, Humberto, and Sara Lara Flores. 1982. "Argunas ideas acerca der la interpación de un grupo indígina a la economía nacional: El caso de los Choles de Chiapas." *Revista Texual* 9:53–76.

Castañeda, Mario. 1992. "El derecho al retorno." In *México: Los refugiados guatemaltecos y los derechos humanos,* ed. R. Aída Hernández Castillo. Mexico City: Centro de Investigaciones y Estudios Superiores en Antropología Social. 392–97.

Castells, Manuel. 1997. *The Power of Identity.* Vol. 2 of *The Information Age: Economy, Society and Culture.* Oxford: Blackwell.

Castro Soto, Gustavo Enrique. 1994. "Guatemala y sus refugiados en el conflicto armado de Chiapas." In *Pensar Chiapas, repensar México: Reflexiones de las ONGS mexicanas sobre el conflicto,* ed. Mario B. Monroy. Mexico City: Convergencia de Organismos Civiles por la Democracia. 179–88.

Ce Acatl. 1996. "Los primeros Acuerdos de Sacam Ch'en: Compromisos propuestas y pronunciamientos de la mesa de trabajo 1, 'Derechos y cultura indígena.'" Special issue, *Ce Acatl* 78–79 (March–April).

Centro de Derechos Humanos Fray Bartolomé de Las Casas (CDHFBC). 1996. *Ni paz, ni justicia: Informe amplio acerca de la guerra civil que sufren los ch'oles en la zona norte de Chiapas.* San Cristóbal de Las Casas: Centro de Derechos Humanos Fray Bartolomé de Las Casas.

Centró de Investigaciones de Historia Social (CEIHS). 1979. *Panzós: Testimonio.* Guatemala City: Centró de Investigaciones de Historia Social.

Chirix García, Emma Delfina. 2003. *Alas y raíces: Afectividad de las mujeres mayas.* Guatemala City: Kaqla Nawal Wuj.

Cleary, Edward, and Timothy Steigenga, eds. 2004. *Resurgent Voices in Latin America: Indigenous Peoples, Political Mobilization, and Religious Change.* New Brunswick, NJ: Rutgers University Press.

Clifford, James. 2005. "Mixed Feelings." In *Cosmopolitics: Thinking and Feeling Beyond the Nation,* ed. Pheag Cheah and Bruce Bobbins. Minneapolis: University of Minnesota Press. 362–70.

Coello Castro, Reyna Matilde. 1991. "Proceso catequistico en la Zona Tzeltal y desarrollo social." Undergraduate thesis, Universidad Autónoma de Tlaxcala.

Cohen, Stanley. 2002. *Folk Devils and Moral Panics: The Creation of the Mods and Rockers.* 3rd ed. London: Routledge.

Cojtí Cuxil, Demetrio. 1989. "Sistemas colonialistas de identificación del indio y atribución de su nacionalidad." *Tradiciones de Guatemala* 32:67–100.

——. 1994. *Políticas para la reivindicación de los Mayas de hoy.* Guatemala City: Cholsamaj.

——. 1996. "The Politics of Maya Revindication." In *Maya Cultural Activism in Guatemala,* ed. E. Fischer and R. Mckenna Brown. Austin: University of Texas Press. 19–50.

——. 1997. *Ri maya' moloj pa iximulew/El movimiento maya (en Guatemala).* Guatemala City: Cholsamaj.

Collí Ek, Víctor Manuel. 2004. "Compilación de los usos y costumbres y sistemas normativos que los jueces de conciliación en las comunidades indígenas en el estado de Campeche, aplican al momento de conciliar y resolver un asunto dentro de su competencia." Comisión Nacional para el Desarrollo de los Pueblos Indígenas, Universidad Autónoma de Campeche, Poder Judicial del estado de Campeche. Unpublished manuscript.

Collier, George. 2000. "Emergent Identities in Chiapas: 1986–1993." Paper presented at the annual meeting of the Latin American Studies Association, Miami, March.

Colom, Yolanda. 1998. *Mujeres en la alborada: Guerrilla y participación femenina en Guatemala*. Guatemala City: Editorial Artemis y Edinter.

Comisión de Fortalecimiento de la Justicia. 1998. *Una nueva justicia para la paz: Informe final*. Guatemala City: Comisión de Fortalecimiento de la Justicia.

Comisión Nacional de Derechos Humanos (CNDH). 1995. *El problema de las expulsiones en las comunidades indígenas de los Altos de Chiapas y los derechos humanos*. Mexico City: Comisión Nacional de Derechos Humanos.

Comisión para el Esclarecimiento Histórico de Guatemala (CEH). 1999. *Guatemala: Memoria del silencio*. Vols. 1–12. Guatemala City: Comisión para el Esclarecimiento Histórico de Guatemala.

Connor, Walker. 1972. "Nation Building or Nation Destroying." *World Politics* 24 (3): 319–55.

Constitución Política de los Estados Unidos Mexicanos. 2000. Mexico City: Instituto Federal Electoral.

Coordinadora de Luchas de Chiapas (CLCH). 1986. *Veintidós días de la movilización de la Coordinadora de Luchas de Chiapas*. Pamphlet.

Coordinadora Nacional Plan de Ayala (CNPA) and Frente Nacional Contra la Represión (FNCR). 1981. *¡Alto a la represión en Chiapas!* Pamphlet.

Couture, Eduardo. 1953. *Vocabulario jurídico*. Mexico City: Publicaciones Jurídicas.

Cowan, Jane, Marie-Bénédicte Dembour, and Richard A. Wilson, eds. 2001. *Culture and Rights: Anthropological Perspectives*. Cambridge: Cambridge University Press.

Cruz Coutiño, José Antonio. 1982. *Absalón Castellanos Domínguez y terratenientes: Un análisis coyuntural*. San Cristóbal de Las Casas: Universidad Autónoma de Chiapas.

Dary, Claudia. 1997. *Derecho internacional humanitario y el órden jurídico maya*. Guatemala City: Facultad Latinoamericana de Ciencias Sociales–Comité Internacional de la Cruz Roja.

Dary, Claudia, et al., eds. 1998. *Estrategias de sobrevivencia campesina en ecosistemas frágiles: Los Ch'orti' en las laderas secas del oriente de Guatemala*. Guatemala City: Facultad Latinoamericana de Ciencias Sociales.

Defensoría de la Mujer Indígena (DEMI). 2003. *First Report on the Rights and Status of Indigenous Women in Guatemala*. Guatemala City: Defensoría de la Mujer Indígena.

Defensoría Maya. 1999. *Experiencias de justicia maya, experiencias de Defensoría Maya*. Guatemala City: Serviprensa.

De La Cruz Montoya, Martín, and Flor María Pérez Robledo. 1993. "Conflicto social y derechos Humanos en Chiapas." Undergraduate Thesis, Universidad Autónoma de Chiapas, San Cristóbal de Las Casas.

De la Fuente, Julio. 1968 [1952]. "Ethnic and Comunal Relations." In *Heritage of Conquest*, ed. Sol Tax. New York: Copper Square Publishers. 76–96.

De la Garza, Mercedes. 1987. "Palabras de inauguración." In *Memorias del Primer Coloquio Internacional de Mayistas (5 al 10 de agosto de 1985)*. Mexico City: Universidad Autónoma de Mexico, Instituto de Investigaciones Filológicas y Centro de Estudios Mayas. 7–10.

———. 1992. "Discurso de inauguración." In *Memorias del Primer Congreso Internacional de Mayistas*. 3 vols. Mexico City: Universidad Nacional Autónoma de Mexico. 1:5–9.

De la Peña, Guillermo. 1995. "Notas preliminares sobre ciudadanía étnica (el caso de México)." In *La sociedad civil: De la teoría a la realidad*, ed. Alberto J. Olvera. Mexico City: El Colegio de México. 283–304.

———. 1998. "Etnicidad, ciudadanía y cambio agrario: Apuntes comparativos sobre tres países latinoamericanos." In *La construcción de la nación y la representación ciudadana en México, Guatemala, Perú, Ecuador y Bolivia*, ed. Claudia Dary. Guatemala City: Facultad Latinoamericana de Ciencias Sociales. 27–86.

Deleuze, Gilles. 1990. *Expressionism in Philosophy: Spinoza*. Trans. Martin Joughin. London: Zone.

———. 1994. "Postscript on Societies of Control." In *Negotiations, 1972–1995*. New York: Columbia University Press. 177–82.

Deleuze, Gilles, and Félix Guattari. 1991. *What Is Philosophy?* New York: Columbia University Press.

Dembour, Marie-Bénédicte. 1996. "Human Rights Talks and Anthropological Ambivalence: The Particular Context of Universal Claims." In *Inside and Outside the Law: Anthropological Studies of Authority and Ambiguity*, ed. Olivia Harris. London: Routledge. 19–40.

Desarrollo, Paz y Justicia. 1997. *Ni derechos ni humanos en la Zona Norte de Chiapas: La otra verdad de los sucesos en la zona ch'ol, como respuesta a la versión difundida por el Centro de Derechos Humanos Fray Bartolomé de Las Casas*. Tila, Mexico: Desarrollo, Paz y Justicia.

De Souza Santos, Boaventura. 1998. *Por una concepción multicultural de los derechos humanos*. Mexico City: Universidad Nacional Autónoma de Mexico.

De Vos, Jan. 1993. *Las fronteras de la frontera sur*. Villahermosa: Universidad Juárez Autónoma de Tabasco.

———. 2002. *Una tierra para sembrar sueños: Historia reciente de la Selva Lacandona, 1950–2000*. Mexico City: Centro de Investigaciones y Estudios Superiores en Antropología Social.

Dezalay, Yves, and Bryant G. Garth. 2002a. *The Internationalization of Palace Wars: Lawyers, Economists, and the Contest to Transform Latin American States*. Chicago: University of Chicago Press.

———, eds. 2002b. *Global Prescriptions: The Production, Exportation and Importation of a New Legal Orthodoxy*. Ann Arbor: University of Michigan Press.

Diamond, Larry. 1994. "The Global Imperative: Building a Democratic World Order." *Current History* 93:1–6.

Diani, Mario, and Doug McAdam, eds. 2003. *Social Movements and Networks: Relational Approaches to Collective Action*. New York: Oxford University Press.

Díaz-Polanco, Héctor. 1996. *Autonomía regional: La autodeterminación de los pueblos indios*. Mexico City: Siglo XXI.

———. 1997. *La rebellion zapatista y la autonomía*. Mexico City: Siglo XXI.

———. 2006. *Elogio de la diversidad: Globalización, multiculturalismo y etnofagia*. Mexico City: Siglo XXI.

Domingo, Pilar, and Rachel Sieder, eds. 2001. *Rule of Law in Latin America: The International Promotion of Judicial Reform*. London: Institute of Latin American Studies.

Donnelly, Jack. 1989. *Universal Human Rights in Theory and Practice*. 1st ed. Ithaca: Cornell University Press.

Donnelly, Jack. 2003. *Universal Human Rights in Theory and Practice*. 2nd ed. Ithaca: Cornell University Press.

Downing, Theodore E., and Gilbert Kushner, with Jennifer Schirmer, Alison Dundes Renteln, and Laurie Wiseberg, eds. 1988. *Human Rights and Anthropology*. Cambridge, MA: Cultural Survival.

Dunkerely, James. 1988. *Power in the Isthmus: A Political History of Modern Central America*. London: Verso.

———. 1994. *The Pacification of Central America: Political Change in the Isthmus, 1987–1993*. London: Verso.

Dworkin, Ronald. 1978. *Taking Rights Seriously*. Cambridge: Harvard University Press.

Eckstein, Susan. 1989. *Power and Popular Protest: Latin American Social Movements*. Berkeley: University of California Press.

Eide, Asbjørn. 1994. *Peaceful and Constructive Resolution of Situations Involving Minorities*. Oslo: Norwegian Institute of Human Rights.

Eide, Asbjørn, et al., eds. 1995. *Economic, Social and Cultural Rights*. Dordrecht, Netherlands: Martinus Nijhoff Publishers.

Ejercito Zapatista de Liberación Nacional (EZLN). 1994. *Documentos y Comunicados*. Mexico City: Editorial Era.

Ekern, Stener. 1997. "Institutional Development among Mayan Organizations in Guatemala." In *Institutional Development in an Indigenous Context*. Oslo: Norwegian Programme for Indigenous Peoples, for Applied Social Science. 35–47.

———. 2006. "Making Government: Community and Leadership in Mayan Guatemala." PhD diss., University of Oslo.

Engler, Mark. 2000. "Toward the Rights of the Poor: Human Rights in Liberation Theology." *Journal of Religious Ethics* 28 (3): 339–65.

Equipo de Anthropología Forense de Guatemala. 1995. *Las masacres en Rabinal: Estudio histórico antropológico de las masacres de Plan de Sánchez, Chichupac y Río Negro*. Guatemala City: Cholsamaj.

Equipo Indignación, Promoción y Defensa de los Derechos Humanos. 2001. *Medio katún: Diez años de (documentar la) indignación*. Mérida, Mexico: Equipo Indignación.

Ermacora, Felix. 1964. *Der Minderheitenschutz in der Arbeit der Vereinten Nationen*. Vienna: Wilhelm Braumüller.

———. 1984. "The Protection of Minorities before the United Nations." In *Recueil des Cours: Collected Courses of the Hague Academy of International Law,* Vol. 182. The Hague: Martinus Nijhoff Publishers.

Escobar, Arturo. 2000. "Notes on Networks and Anti-globalization Social Movements." Paper presented at the American Anthropological Association annual meeting, San Francisco, November 15–19.

———. 2004. "Beyond the Third World: Imperial Globality, Global Coloniality, and Anti-globalization Social Movements." *Third World Quarterly* 25 (1): 207–30.

Escobar, Arturo. Forthcoming. *Places and Regions in the Age of Globality: Social Movements and Biodiversity Conservation in the Colombian Pacific.* Durham, NC: Duke University Press.

Escobar, Arturo, and Sonia E. Alvarez, eds. 1992. *The Making of Social Movements in Latin America: Identity, Strategy, and Democracy.* Boulder, CO: Westview.

Esquit Choy, Edgar, and Carlos Ochoa García, eds. 1995. *Yiqalil q'anej: Kunimaaj tziij; Niman tzij/El respeto a la palabra: El orden jurídico del pueblo maya.* Guatemala City: Centro de Estudios de la Cultura Maya.

Estrada, Erin, Eduardo Bello, and María Eugenia García. 2006. "Derecho consuetudinario en tierras mayas de Quintana Roo, México." Paper presented at the Red Latinoamerico de Antropología Jurídica Conference V, Oaxtepec, Morelos, October.

Fábregas Puig, Andrés. 2000. "Mesoamérica: Pasado y presente de un concepto." In *Anuario 1999 del CESMECA.* Tuxtla Gutiérrez, Mexico: Universidad de Ciencias y Artes de Chiapas. 142–47.

Fagen, P. W., and M. A. Garreton, eds. 1993. *Fear at the Edge: State Terror and Resistance in Latin America.* Berkeley: University of California Press.

Farmer, Paul. 2003. *Pathologies of Power: Health, Human Rights, and the New War on the Poor.* Berkeley: University of California Press.

Favre, Henri. 1973. *Cambio y continuidad entre los Mayas de México.* Mexico City: Siglo XXI.

Fernández Lira, Carlos. 1995. "Identidad y razón en Chiapas: Algunas reflexiones sobre la cuestión de los derechos humanos." In Anuario del Instituto de Estudios Indígenas V, 91–110.

Ferrajoli, Luigi. 2001. *Los fundamentos de los derechos fundamentales.* Madrid: Trotta.

Figueroa Ibarra, Carlos. 1991. *El recurso del miedo: Ensayo sobre el estado y el terror en Guatemala.* San José, Costa Rica: Editorial Universitaria Centroamericana.

Flores, William V., and Rina Benmayor. 1997. "Constructing Cultural Citizenship." In *Latino Cultural Citizenship: Claiming Identity, Space and Rights,* ed. Flores and Benmayor. Boston: Beacon. 255–77.

Foro de Reflexión. 1990. *Los refugiados guatemaltecos y los derechos humanos: El derecho al refugio.* Tuxtla Gutiérrez: Centro de Investigaciones y Estudios Superiores en Antropología Social.

Foro Nacional de la Mujer. 2002. *Avances en la participación de las mujeres guatemal-*

tecas 1997–2001. Guatemala City: Misión Dinamarca, Programa de Dinamarca Pro Derechos Humanos Para Centroamérica.

Forsythe, David. 1989. *Human Rights and World Politics.* Lincoln: University of Nebraska Press.

Foucault, Michel. 1980. "Two Lectures." In *Power/Knowledge: Selected Interviews and Other Writings, 1972–1977.* Ed. Colin Gordon. New York: Random House. 78–109.

Frankovitz, André. 2002. "Rules to Live By: The Human Rights Approach to Development." *Praxis* 8:9–18.

Frente Zapatista de Liberacíon Nacional. 1998. *Fuerte es su corazón: Los municipios rebeldes Zapatistas.* Mexico City: Frente Zapatista de Liberacíon Nacional.

Freyermuth, Graciela, and Rosalva Aída Hernández, eds. 1992. *Una década de refugio en México: Los refugiados guatemaltecos y los derechos humanos.* Mexico City: Centro de Investigaciones y Estudios Superiores en Antropología Social.

Fuentes, Carlos. 1985. *Latin America: At War with the Past.* Montreal: CBC Enterprises.

Fuller, Chris. 1994. "Legal Anthropology: Legal Pluralism and Legal Thought." *Anthropology Today* 10 (3): 9–12.

Fundación de Antropología Forense de Guatemala (FAFG). 2000. *Informe de la fundación de antropología forense de Guatemala: Cuatro casos paradigmáticos solicitados por la Comisión para el Esclarecimiento Histórico de Guatemala.* Guatemala City: Fundación de Antropología Forense de Guatemala.

Gabbert, Wolfgang. 2006. "Los juzgados indígenas en el sur de México." Paper presented at the Red Latinoamerico de Antropología Jurídica Conference V, Oaxtepec, Morelos, October.

Gall Sonabend, Olivia. 1994. "Oligarquía, ideología y racismo en Chiapas: 1876–1994." Unpublished manuscript.

——. 1999. "Racismo, modernidad y legalidad en Chiapas." *Dimensión Antropológica* 6 (15): 55–85.

Garaiz, Esteban. 1992. "COMAR y los derechos humanos de los refugiados." In *Una década de refugio en México: Los refugiados guatemaltecos y los derechos humanos,* ed. Graciela Freyermuth and R. Aída Hernández Castillo. Mexico City: Centro de Investigaciones y Estudios Superiores en Antropología Social. 37–42.

García Aguilar, María del Carmen. 1998. "Las organizaciones no gubernamentales en los espacios rurales de Chiapas: Reflexiones en turno a su actuación política." In *Espacios disputados: Transformaciones rurales en Chiapas,* ed. María Eugenia Reyes, Reyna Moguel Viveros, and Gemma van der Haar. Mexico City: *Universidad Autonoma Metropolitana Xochimilco* and El Colegio de la Frontera Sur. 311–40.

Garcia de León, Antonio. 1984. *Resistencia y Utopía.* Mexico City: Editiones Era.

Garza, Anna María. 2002. *Género, interlegalidad y conflicto en San Pedro Chenalhó.* Mexico City: Universidad Nacional Autónoma de Mexico, Programa de Investigaciones Multidisciplinarias sobre Mesoamerica y Sureste.

Giddens, Anthony. 1981. *A Contemporary Critique of Historical Materialism.* 2 vols. Berkeley: University of California Press.

———. 1990. *The Consequences of Modernity.* Stanford, CA: Stanford University Press.

Gill, Lesley. 2000. *Teetering on the Rim: Global Restructuring, Daily Life, and the Armed Retreat of the Bolivian State.* New York: Columbia University Press.

Girard, Rafael. 1949. *Los Chortís ante el problema maya.* Mexico City: Editorial Cultura.

Glassman, Ronald. 1989. *Democracy and Equality: Theories and Programs for the Modern World.* New York: Praeger.

Gledhill, John. 1997. "Liberalism, Socio-economic Rights, and the Politics of Identity: From Moral Economy to Indigenous Rights." In *Human Rights, Culture and Context: Anthropological Perspectives,* ed. Richard Wilson. London: Pluto. 70–110.

Global Exchange, Centro de Investigaciones Económicas y Políticas de Acción Communitaria (CIEPAC), and Centro Nacional de Comunicación Social (CENCOS). 2000. "Las Fuerzas Armadas de Mexico City: Siempre cerca, siempre lejos." Internal report.

Global Exchange et al. 1999. "On the Offensive: Intensified Military Occupation in Chiapas Six Months since the Massacre at Acteal." International report.

Gobierno del Estado de Chiapas. 1997. *Yak'el ta Na'el ta Stojol Spamal Balumilal te Yich'el ta Muk' Kirsanuetik/Declaración Universal de los Derechos Humanos.* Trans. Miguel Gómez Gómez and Juan Santiz Cruz. San Cristóbal de Las Casas: Gobierno del Estado de Chiapas.

———. 1999. *Ley de Derechos y Cultura Indígena del estado de Chiapas.* Tuxtla Gutiérrez, Mexico: Gobierno del Estado de Chiapas.

———. 2003. *Desarrollo social en cifras.* Tuxtla Gutiérrez, Mexico: Secretaría de Desarrollo Social.

Godoy, Angelina Snodgrass. 2002. "Lynchings and the Democratization of Terror in Postwar Guatemala: Implications for Human Rights." *Human Rights Quarterly* 24 (3): 640–61.

Goldin, Liliana. 1998. "Fabricando identidades: Mayas y ladinos en la producción industrial." *Estudios Sociales* 59:57–65.

Goldman, Francisco. 2002. "Victory in Guatemala." *New York Review of Books,* May 23.

Gómez, Antonio, and Mario Humberto Ruz. 1992. *Memoria baldía: Los tojolabales y las fincas; Testimonios.* Mexico City: Universidad Nacional Autónoma de Mexico, Centro de Estudios Mayas.

Gómez Cruz, Patricia Jovita, and Christina María Kovic. 1994. *Con un pueblo vivo, en tierra negada: Un esayo sobre los derechos humanos y el conflicto agrario en Chiapas, 1989–1993.* San Cristóbal de Las Casas: Centro de Derechos Humanos Fray Bartolomé de Las Casas.

González Esponda, Juan, 1989. "Movimiento campesino chiapaneco, 1974–84." Undergraduate thesis, Universidad Autónoma de Chiapas, San Cristóbal de las Casas.

González Hernández, Miguel, and Elvia Quintanar Quintana. 1999. "La reconstrucción de la región autónoma norte y el ejercicio del gobierno municipal." In *Mexico*

City: Experiencias de autonomía indígena, ed. Araceli Burguete Cal y Mayor. Copenhagen: International Work Group for Indigenous Affairs. 210–33.

González-Ponciano, Jorge Ramón. 1992–94. "Guatemala, el estado y los indígenas." In *Memorias del Primer Congreso Internacional de Mayistas.* 3 vols. Mexico City: Universidad Nacional Autónoma de Mexico. 1:468–80.

——. 1998. "Esas sangres no están limpias: El racismo, el estado y la nación en Guatemala (1994–1997)." *Separata Anuario 1997.* Centro de Estudios Superiores de México y Centroamérica. San Cristóbal de Las Casas: Universidad de Ciencias y Artes del Estado de Chiapas.

González-Ponciano, Jorge Ramón, and Miguel Lisbona, eds. Forthcoming. *Estado y ciudadanía en México y Guatemala.* Mexico City: Universidad Nacional Autónoma de Mexico, Programa de Investigaciones Multidisciplinarias sobre Mesoamerica y Sureste.

Goodale, Mark. 2006a. "Ethical Theory as Social Practice." *American Anthropologist* 108 (1): 25–37.

——. 2006b. "Reclaiming Modernity: Indigenous Cosmopolitanism and the Coming of the Second Revolution in Bolivia." *American Ethnologist* 33 (4): 634–49.

——. 2007. "Locating Rights, Envisioning Law between the Global and the Local." In *The Practice of Human Rights: Tracking Law between the Global and the Local,* ed. Goodale and Sally Engle Merry. Cambridge: Cambridge University Press.

Gossen, H. Gary. 1974. *The Chamulas in the World of the Sun: Time and Space in a Maya Oral Tradition.* Prospect Heights: Waveland.

Grandin, Greg. 2000. *The Blood of Guatemala: A History of Race and Nation.* Durham, NC: Duke University Press.

——. 2006. *The Last Colonial Massacre: Latin America in the Cold War.* Chicago: University of Chicago Press.

Griffiths, John. 1986. "What Is Legal Pluralism?" *Journal of Legal Pluralism and Unofficial Law* 24:1–55.

Guehénno, Jean-Marie. 1995. *The End of the Nation-State.* Trans. Victoria Elliott. Minneapolis: University of Minnesota Press.

Guiteras Holmes, Calixta. 1986 [1961]. *Los peligros del alma: Visión del mundo de un Tzotzil.* Mexico City: Fondo de Cultura Económica.

Gustafson, Bret. 2002. "Paradoxes of Liberal Indigenism: Indigenous Movements, State Processes, and Intercultural Reform in Bolivia." In *The Politics of Ethnicity: Indigenous Peoples in Latin American States,* ed. David Maybury-Lewis. Cambridge: Harvard University Press. 267–306.

Gutiérrez, Gustavo. 1983. *The Power of the Poor in History.* Maryknoll, NY: Orbis.

Gutiérrez, Marta, and Paul Kobrak. 2001. *Los linchamientos: Pos conflicto y violencia colectiva en Huehuetenango, Guatemala.* Huehuetenango: Centro de Estudios y Desarrollo de la Frontera Occidental de Guatemala.

Gutiérrez Rivero, Dea María. 2001. "Los juzgados de conciliación en el estado de Campeche." In *Aproximaciones a la antropología jurídica de los mayas peninsulares,* ed. Esteban Krotz. Mérida, Mexico: Universidad Autónoma de Yucatán. 99–105.

Habermas, Jürgen. 1992. "Citizenship and National Identity: Some Reflections on the Future of Europe." *Praxis International* 12 (2): 1–19.

——. 1994. "Struggles for Recognition in the Democratic Constitutional State." In *Multiculturalism and "The politics of recognition": an essay,* by Charles Taylor, ed. Amy Gutmann. Princeton: Princeton University Press. 112–23.

Hale, Charles R. 2001. "What Is Activist Research?" *Items* 2 (1–2): 13–15.

——. 2002. "Does Multiculturalism Menace? Governance, Cultural Rights and the Politics of Identity in Guatemala." *Journal of Latin American Studies* 34:481–524.

——. 2003. *Ciudadanía e identidad en Chimaltenango.* Guatemala City: Centro de Investigaciones Regionales de Mesoamérica.

——. 2004. "Reflexiones hacia la práctica de una investigación descolonizada." Paper presented at the second International Gathering of the Project Governing in Diversity, Encuentro Internacional del Proyecto Gobernar en la Diversidad, Quito, October.

——. 2005. "Mistados, Cholos, y la negación de la identidad en el Altiplano Guatemalteco." In *Memorias del mestizaje: Cultura política en Centroamerica de 1920 al presente,* ed. Dario A. Euraque, Jeffrey L. Gould, and Hale. Guatemala City: Centro de Investigaciones Regionales de Mesoamérica. 113–65.

——. 2006a. "¿En contra del reconocimiento? Gobierno plural y análisis social ante la diferencia cultural." Paper presented at the Red Latinoamerico de Antropología Jurídica Conference V, Oaxtepec, Morelos, October.

——. 2006b. *Más que un Indio: Racial Ambivalence and Neoliberal Multiculturalism in Guatemala.* Santa Fe: School of American Research.

Hall, Stuart, and Paul du Gay, eds. 1996. *Questions of Cultural Identity.* London: Sage.

Handy, Jim. 1994. *Revolution in the Countryside: Community, Land, and Reform in Guatemala.* Chapel Hill: University of North Carolina Press.

Hannum, Hurst. 1992. *Autonomy, Sovereignty, and Self-Determination: The Accommodation of Conflicting Rights.* Philadelphia: University of Pennsylvania Press.

Haraway, Donna J. 1988. "Situated Knowledge: The Science Question in Feminism and the Privilege of Partial Studies." *Feminist Studies* 14 (3): 575–99.

Hardt, Michael. 1998. "The Withering of Civil Society." In *Deleuze and Guattari: New Mappings in Politics and Philosophy,* ed. Eleanor Kaufman and Kevin Jon Heller. Minneapolis: University of Minnesota Press. 23–39.

Hardt, Michael, and Negri, Antonio. 2000. *Empire.* Cambridge: Harvard University Press.

Harris, Olivia. 1996. "Introduction: Inside and Outside the Law." In *Inside and Outside the Law: Anthropological Studies of Authority and Ambiguity,* ed. Harris. London: Routledge. 1–19.

Harvey, Neil. 1998a. "La autonomía indígena y ciudadanía étnica en Chiapas." *Boletín de Antropología Americana* 32:97–110.

——. 1998b. *The Chiapas Rebellion: The Struggle for Land and Democracy.* Durham, NC: Duke University Press.

Hatch, Elvin. 1983. *Culture and Morality: The Relativity of Values in Anthropology.* New York: Columbia University Press.

Hayner, Priscilla B. 2001. *Unspeakable Truths: Confronting State Terror and Atrocity.* New York: Routledge.

Hendrix, Steven E. 2000. "Guatemalan 'Justice Centers': The Centerpiece for Advancing Transparency, Efficiency, Due Process, and Access to Justice." *American University International Law Review* 15 (4): 813–68.

Henríquez, Elio. 1998. "Detectó la CIDH serias anomalías en el juicio a 16 detenidos en Taniperla." *La Jornada,* June 29.

Hernández Castillo, R. Aída. 2002a. "Distintas maneras de ser mujer: Ante la construcción de un nuevo feminismo indígena." Unpublished manuscript.

——. 2002b. "Indigenous Law and Identity Politics in Mexico: Indigenous Women Recreate Multiculturalism." *PoLAR: Political and Legal Anthropology Review* 25 (1): 90–109.

Hernández Navarro, Luis. 1998. "Ciudadanos iguales, ciudadanos diferentes." In *Los Acuerdos de San Andrés,* ed. Hernández Navarro and Ramón Vera Herrera. Mexico City: Ediciones Era. 15–22.

Hernández Navarro, Luis, and Ramón Vera Herrera, eds. 1998. *Los Acuerdos de San Andrés.* Mexico City: Ediciones Era.

Hewitt de Alcántara, Cynthia. 1984. *Anthropological Perspectives on Rural Mexico.* London: Routledge and Kegan Paul.

Hobbes, Thomas. 1996 [1651]. *Leviathan.* Ed. J. C. A. Gaskin. Oxford: Oxford University Press.

Hobsbawm, Eric, and Terence Ranger, eds. 1983. *The Invention of Tradition.* Cambridge: Cambridge University Press.

Human Rights Watch (HRW). 1991. *Unceasing Abuses: Human Rights in Mexico One Year after the Introduction of Reform.* New York: Human Rights Watch.

——. 1997. *Implausible Deniability: State Responsibility for Rural Violence in Mexico.* New York: Human Rights Watch.

——. 2001. *World Report 2001: Guatemala,* www.hrw.org/wr2k1/americas/guatemala.html.

Humphreys, Sally. 1985. "Law as Discourse." *History and Anthropology* 1:241–64.

Huntington, Samuel P. 1997. *El choque de civilizaciones y la reconfiguración del orden mundial.* Barcelona: Paidós.

Ignatieff, Michael. 1999. *The Warrior's Honor: Ethnic War and the Modern Conscience.* London: Vintage.

——. 2003. *Human Rights as Politics and Idolatry.* Princeton: Princeton University Press.

Instituto de Investigaciones Económicas y Sociales (IDIES). 1999. El sistema jurídico K'iche': Una aproximación. Ed. Juán de Dios González. Guatemala City: Instituto de Investigaciones Económicas y Sociales.

Instituto Nacional de Estadística, Geografía e Informática (INEGI). 2001. *Anuario de estadísticas por entidad federativa.* Aguascalientes, Mexico: Instituto Nacional de Estadística, Geografía e Informática.

——. 2002. Chiapas: Perfil sociodemocráfico; XII Censo de población y vivienda 2000. Aguascalientes, Mexico: Instituto Nacional de Estadística, Geografía e Informática.

Interamerican Development Bank (IDB). 2001. Desarrollo: Más allá de la economía; Progreso económico y social en América Latina; Informe 2000. Washington: Interamerican Development Bank.

International Indigenous Women's Forum (FEMI). 2005. "Visiones del feminismo desde las mujeres indígenas." Panel in the Association for Women's Rights in Development Forum (AWID), Bangkok, October 27–30.

Izquierdo, Ana Luisa. 2002. "Palabras de Ana Luisa Izquierdo, coordinadora del Centro de Estudios Mayas." In *Memoria del Tercer Congreso Internacional de Mayistas (9 al 15 de julio de 1995).* Mexico City: Universidad Autónoma de Mexico, Instituto de Investigaciones Filológicas y Centro de Estudios Mayas. 5–8.

——. 2003. "Discurso de inauguración Ana Luisa Izquierdo, coordinadora del Centro de Estudios Mayas." *Memoria del Cuarto Congreso Internacional de Mayistas (2 al 8 de agosto de 1998).* Mexico City: Universidad Autónoma de México, Instituto de Investigaciones Filológicas y Centro de Estudios Mayas. 7–9.

Jackson, Jean, and Kay Warren. 2005. "Indigenous Movements in Latin America, 1992–2004: Controversies, Ironies, New Directions." *Annual Review of Anthropology* 34:549–73.

Jameson, Fredric. 1983. "Postmodernism and Consumer Society." In *The Anti-aesthetic: Essays on Postmodern Culture,* ed. Hal Foster. Port Townsend, WA: Bay.

——. 1991. *Postmodernism; or, The Cultural Logic of Late Capitalism.* Durham, NC: Duke University Press.

——. 1999. "Notes on Globalization as a Philosophical Issue." In *The Cultures of Globalization,* ed. Jameson and Masao Miyoshi. Durham, NC: Duke University Press.

Jameson, Fredric, and Masao Miyoshi, eds. 1998. *The Cultures of Globalization.* Durham, NC: Duke University Press.

Jelin, Elizabeth. 1996. "Citizenship Revisited: Solidarity, Responsibility and Rights." In *Constructing Democracy, Human Rights, Citizenship, and Society in Latin America,* ed. Jelin and Eric Hershberg. Boulder, CO: Westview, 101–19.

——. 2002. *La política de la memoria: El movimiento de los derechos humanos y la transición a la democracia.* Madrid: Siglo XXI.

Jelin, Elizabeth, and Eric Hershberg, eds. 1996. *Constructing Democracy: Human Rights, Citizenship, and Society in Latin America.* Boulder, CO: Westview.

Jonas, Suzanne. 2000. *Of Centaurs and Doves: Guatemala's Peace Process.* Boulder, CO: Westview.

Joseph, Gilbert, and Daniel Nugent, eds. 1994. *Everyday Forms of State Formation:*

Revolution and the Negotiation of Modern Rule in Mexico. Durham, NC: Duke University Press.

Joyce, Rosemary A. 2000. *Gender and Power in Prehispanic Mesoamerica.* Austin: University of Texas Press.

Kagan, Robert. 2003. *Of Paradise and Power: America and Europe in the New World Order.* New York: Knopf.

Kauffer Michel, Edith. 1998. "Los refugiados guatemaltecos en Chiapas y los derechos humanos: De la búsqueda de la seguridad a la organización política." In *Anuario de Estudios Indígenas VII.* Tuxtla Gutiérrez, Mexico: Universidad Autónoma de Chiapas, Instituto de Estudios Indígenas. 283–306.

Keck, Margaret E., and Kathryn Sikkink. 1998. *Activists beyond Borders: Advocacy Networks in International Politics.* Ithaca: Cornell University Press.

Kellogg, Susan. 2005. *A History of Latin America's Indigenous Women from the Prehispanic to the Present.* Oxford: Oxford University Press.

Keynes, John. 1935. *The General Theory.* New York: Harcourt, Brace and World.

Kirchhoff, Paul. 1960. *Mesoamérica: Sus límites geográficos, composición étnica y caracteres culturales.* Mexico City: Escuela Nacional de Antropología e Historia–Sociedad de Alumnos.

Kobrak, Paul. 1997. "Village Troubles: The Civil Patrols in Aguacatán, Guatemala." PhD diss., University of Michigan.

Kovic, María Christine. 1995. " 'Con un solo corazón': La Iglesia católica, la identidad indígena y los derechos humanos en Chiapas." In *La explosión de comunidades en Chiapas,* ed. June Nash et al. Copenhagen: International Work Group for Indigenous Affairs. 109–20.

——. 2003a. "Demanding Their Dignity as Daughters of God: Catholic Women and Human Rights." In *Women of Chiapas: Making History in Times of Struggle and Hope,* ed. Christine Eber and Kovic. New York: Routledge. 131–46.

——. 2003b. "The Struggle for Liberation and Reconciliation in Chiapas, Mexico: Las Abejas and the Path of Non-violent Resistance." *Latin American Perspectives* 30 (3): 58–79.

——. 2005. *Mayan Voices for Human Rights: Displaced Catholics in Highland Chiapas.* Austin: University of Texas Press.

——. Forthcoming. *Walking with One Heart: Human Rights and the Catholic Church among the Maya of Highland Chiapas.* Austin: University of Texas Press.

Krauze, Enrique. 1999. "Chiapas: The Indians' Prophet." *New York Review of Books,* December 16, 65–73.

Kritz, Neil J., ed. 1995. *Transitional Justice: How Emerging Democracies Reckon with Former Regimes.* 3 vols. Washington: U.S. Institute of Peace Press.

Krotz, Esteban. 2000a. "La formulación de los derechos humanos como proceso de aprendizaje intercultural." *Devenires* 3 (5): 81–95.

——. 2000b. "Sociedades, conflictos, cultura y derecho desde una perspectiva antropológica." In *Antropología jurídica: Perspectivas socioculturales en el estudio del derecho,* ed. Esteban Krotz. Barcelona: Anthropos y Universidad Autónoma Metropolitana. 13–50.

——. 2004a. "Los derechos humanos hoy: De la aculturación al diálogo intercultural. In *Los desafíos de la interculturalidad: Identidad, política y derecho,* ed. Milka Castro-Lucic. Santiago: Universidad de Chile. 151–71.

——. 2004b. "Rodolfo Stavenhagen: La situación de los derechos humanos las libertades fundamentales de los indígenas." *Revista de la Universidad Autónoma de Yucatán* 19 (31): 70–76.

——, ed. 1997. *Aspectos de la cultura jurídica en Yucatán.* Mérida, Mexico: Universidad Autónoma de Yucatán.

——. 2001. *Aproximaciones a la antropología jurídica de los mayas peninsulares.* Mérida, Mexico: Universidad Autónoma de Yucatán.

Kymlicka, Will. 1995. *Multicultural Citizenship.* Oxford: Clarendon.

——. 1996 *Ciudadanía multicultural.* Trans. Joaquin Sanz. Barcelona: Paidós.

——. 2001. *Politics in the Vernacular: Nationalism, Multiculturalism, and Citizenship.* Oxford: Oxford University Press.

LaCapra, Dominick. 1998. *History and Memory after Auschwitz.* Ithaca: Cornell University Press.

Laclau, Ernesto. 1990. *New Reflections on the Revolution of Our Time.* London. Verso.

Las Casas, Fray Bartolomé de. 1974 [1542]. *In Defense of the Indians.* Ed. Stafford Poole. DeKalb: Northern Illinois University Press.

Laughlin, Robert M. 1975. *The Great Tzotzil Dictionary of San Lorenzo Zinacantán.* Washington: Smithsonian Institution Press.

Le Bot, Yvon. 1996. *La guerra en tierra maya: Comunidad, violencia y modernidad en Guatemala.* Mexico City: Fondo de Cultura Económica.

——. 1997. *Subcomandante Marcos: El sueño zapatista.* Mexico City: Plaza y Janés.

Levenson-Estrada, Deborah. 1994. *Trade Unionists against Terror: Guatemala City, 1954–1985.* Chapel Hill: University of North Carolina Press.

Levine, Daniel. 1992. *Popular Voices in Latin American Catholicism.* Princeton: Princeton University Press.

Levy, Jacob T. 2000. *The Multiculturalism of Fear.* Oxford: Oxford University Press.

Leyva Solano, Xochitl. 1995a. "Catequistas, misioneros y tradiciones en las Cañadas." In *Chiapas: Los rumbos de otra historia,* ed. Juan Pedro Viqueira and Mario Humberto Ruz. Mexico City: Universidad Nacional Autónoma de Mexico. 375–406.

——. 1995b. "Militancia político-religiosa e identidad en la Lacandona." *Espiral* 1 (2): 59–88.

——. 1998. "The New Zapatista Movement: Political Levels, Actors, and Political Discourse in Contemporary Mexico." In *Encuentros Antropológicos: Politics, Identity and Mobility in Mexican Society,* ed. Valentina Napolitano and Leyva Solano. London: Institute of Latin American Studies. 35–55.

——. 2001. "Neo-zapatismo: Networks of Power and War." PhD diss., University of Manchester.

———. 2003a. "Regional, Communal, and Organizational Transformations in Las Cañadas." In *Mayan Lives, Mayan Utopias: The Indigenous Peoples of Chiapas and the Zapatista Rebellion,* ed. Jan Rus, Rosalva Aída Hernández Castillo, and Shannan L. Mattiace. Lanham, MD: Rowman and Littlefield. 161–84.

———. 2003b. "Violence raciale, racisme et relations interethniques en contexte de guerre: Un regard sur le Chiapas et un coup d'aeil sur le Guatemala." *Ateliers* 26:171–96.

———. 2005. "Indigenismo, Indianismo, and 'Ethnic Citizenship' in Chiapas." In "Rural Chiapas Ten Years after the Zapatista Uprising," ed. Sarah Washbrook. Special issue, *Journal of Peasant Studies* 32 (3–4): 555–83.

———. 2006a. "Acerca de la metodología colaborativa." Paper presented at the Fifth International Seminary Governing in Diversity, Mexico City, March 31–April 2.

———. 2006b. "Zapatista Movement Networks Respond to Globalization." LASA *Forum* 37 (1): 37–39.

———. 2007. "¿Antropología de la ciudadanía . . . ? étnica . . . en construcción desde América Latina." *Revista Liminar* 5 (5): 87–91.

Leyva Solano, Xochitl, and Gabriel Ascencio Franco. 1996. *Lacandonia al filo del agua.* Mexico City: Centro de Investigaciones y Estudios Superiores en Antropología Social.

Leyva Solano, Xochitl, Araceli Burguete Cal y Mayor, and Shannon Speed. In press. *Gobernar (en) la diversidad: Experiencias indígenas desde América Latina; Hacia una investigación descolonizada.* Mexico City: Centro de Investigaciones y Estudios Superiores en Antropología Social.

Leyva Solano, Xochitl, and Araceli Burguete Cal y Mayor, eds. 2008. *La re-municipalización en Chiapas: La política y lo político en tiempos de contrainsurgencia.* Mexico City: Centro de Investigaciones y Estudios Superiores en Antropología Social.

Libro de Actas de Panzós. 1978. Panzós, Guatemala.

Lima-Soto, Ricardo E. 1995. *Aproximación a la cosmovisión Maya.* Guatemala City: Universidad Rafael Landívar.

Little, Walter E., and Timothy J. Smith. n.d. "Mayan Postwar Guatemala: Harvest of Violence Revisited." Unpublished manuscript.

López García, Julián. 1995. "La sangre y las categorías culinarias entre los Chortís del oriente de Guatemala." *Tradiciones de Guatemala* 44:17–45.

———. 1998. "El mundo al revés: Sobre ladinos que quieren ser Mayas-Ch'orti's." Paper presented at the Ninety-Seventh Annual Meeting of the American Anthropological Association, Philadelphia, November.

———. 2001. *Alimentación y Sociedad en Iberoaamérica y España: Cinco Étnografías de la Comida y la Cocina.* Cáceres, Spain: Universidad de Extremadura.

López Maza, Ángel. 1992. "Sistema religioso político y las expulsiones en Chamula, Chiapas." Undergraduate thesis, Universidad Autónoma de Chiapas, San Cristóbal de Las Casas.

López y Rivas, Gilberto. 2004. *Autonomías: Democracia o contrainsurgencia*. Mexico: Ediciones Era.

Luna, Jorge Arturo. 1992. "El movimiento campesino indígena chiapaneco: Una interpretación de sus tendencias principales." Paper presented at the "Chiapas en el Umbral del siglo XXI" conference, San Cristóbal de Las Casas.

Lux de Cotí, Otilia. 1995. "Educación Maya: Perspectiva para Guatemala." In *Educación maya: Experiencias y expectativas en Guatemala*. Guatemala City: Cholsamaj, 104–5.

Malamud-Goti, Jaime. 1996. *Game without End: State Terror and the Politics of Justice*. Norman: University of Oklahoma Press.

Mallón, Florencia. 1995. *Peasant and Nation: The Making of Postcolonial Mexico and Peru*. Berkeley: University of California Press.

Mamdani, Mahmood. 2001. *When Victims Become Killers: Colonialism, Nativism, and the Genocide in Rwanda*. Princeton: Princeton University Press.

Marión, Marie Odile. 1984. *El movimiento campesino en Chiapas*. Mexico City: Centro de Estudios Históricos del Agrarismo en México.

Mauss, Marcel. 1971. "Sobre una categoría del espíritu humano: La noción de persona y la noción del 'yo.'" In *Sociología y antropología*, ed. Mauss. Madrid: Editorial Tecnos, 309–37.

Mayén, Guisela. 1995. "Derecho consuetudinario indígena en Guatemala." *ASIES Guatemala* 4:41.

McQuown, Norman, and Julian Pitt-Rivers. 1970. *Ensayos de antropología en la Zona Central de Chiapas*. Mexico City: Instituto Nacional Indigenista.

Memoria del Cuarto Congreso Internacional de Mayistas (2 al 8 de agosto de 1998). 2003. Mexico City: Universidad Autónoma de México, Instituto de Investigaciones Filológicas y Centro de Estudios Mayas.

Memoria de los conversatorios ¿Existe movimiento maya? 2006. Guatemala City: Programa Educativo Pop Noj Moloj.

Memoria del Segundo Congreso Internacional de Mayistas. 1995. Mexico City: Universidad Autónoma de México, Instituto de Investigaciones Filológicas y Centro de Estudios Mayas.

Memoria del Tercer Congreso Internacional de Mayistas (9 al 15 de julio de 1995). 2002. Mexico City: Universidad Autónoma de México, Instituto de Investigaciones Filológicas y Centro de Estudios Mayas.

Memorias del Primer Coloquio Internacional de Mayistas (5 al 10 de agosto de 1985). 1987. Mexico City: Universidad Autónoma de México, Instituto de Investigaciones Filológicas y Centro de Estudios Mayas.

Memorias del II Coloquio Internacional de Mayistas (17 al 21 de agosto de 1987). 1989. Vols. 1–2. Mexico City: Universidad Nacional Autónoma de Mexico.

Mendizábal, Sergio. 2007. "Dinámicas de mayanización en las políticas de transformación estructural de la sociedad guatemalteca." Unpublished manuscript.

Mendoza, Freya. 2003. "Análisis jurídico de los artículos 15 y 17 de la Ley de la

Comisión de Derechos Humanos del Estado de Yucatán." Undergraduate thesis, Universidad Autónoma de Yucatán, Mérida.

Menon, Nivedita. 2004. *Recovering Subversion: Feminist Politics beyond the Law*. Chicago: University of Chicago Press.

Merry, Sally Engle. 1988. "Legal Pluralism." *Law and Society Review* 22 (5): 869–96.

———. 1992. "Anthropology, Law and Transnational Processes." *Annual Review of Anthropology* 21:357–79.

———.1997. "Legal Pluralism and Transnational Culture: The Ka Ho'okolokolonui Kanaka Maoli Tribunal, Hawai'i, 1993." In *Human Rights, Culture and Context: Anthropological Perspectives on Human Rights*, ed. Richard Wilson. London: Pluto. 28–48.

———. 2001. "Rights, Religion and Community: Approaches to Violence against Women in the Context of Globalisation." *Law and Society Review* 35 (1): 39–88.

———. 2003. "Human Rights Law and the Demonization of Culture (and Anthropology Along the Way)." *PoLAR: Political and Legal Anthropology Review* 26 (1): 55–77.

———. 2006. *Human Rights and Gender Violence: Translating International Law into Local Justice*. Chicago: University of Chicago Press.

Mesa Redonda XVII de la Sociedad Mexicana de Antropología en San Cristóbal de Las Casas. 1984. *Investigaciones recientes en el área maya*. 4 vols. San Cristóbal de Las Casas: Universidad Autónoma de Chiapas.

Messer, Ellen. 1993. "Anthropology and Human Rights." *Annual Review of Anthropology* 221:224–25.

———. 1995. "Anthropology and Human Rights in Latin America." *Journal of Latin American Anthropology* 1 (1): 48–97.

Metz, Brent E. 1995. "Experiencing Conquest: The Political Economic Roots and Cultural Expression of Ch'orti'-Maya Ethos." PhD diss., State University of New York, Albany.

Meyer, Jean, with Federico Anaya Gallardo and Julio Ríos. 2000. *Samuel Ruiz en San Cristóbal, 1960–2000*. Mexico City: Tusquets Editores.

Minnow, Martha. 1998. *Between Vengeance and Forgiveness: Facing History after Genocide and Mass Violence*. Boston: Beacon.

Minority Rights Group. 1994. *The Maya of Guatemala*. London: Minority Rights Group.

Misión de Naciones Unidad para Guatemala (MINUGUA). 1999. *Ninth Report on Human Rights of the UN Verification Mission in Guatemala, 1 April 1998 to 31 December 1998*. Guatemala City: United Nations.

———. 2002. "Los linchamientos: Un flagelo que persiste." August, www.minugua.guate.net.

Moksnes, Heidi. 2003. "Mayan Suffering, Mayan Rights: Faith and Citizenship among Catholic Tzotziles in Highland Chiapas, Mexico." PhD diss., Goteborg University, Sweden.

Montag, Warren. 1999. *Bodies, Masses, Power: Spinoza and his Contemporaries*. London: Verso.

Montejo, Victor. 1999. *Voices from Exile: Violence and Survival in Modern Maya History.* Norman: University of Oklahoma Press.

Montoya, Rodrigo. 1996. "La ciudadanía étnica como un nuevo fragmento en la utopía de la libertad." In *Democracia y estado multiétnico en América Latina,* ed. Pablo González Casanova and Marcos Roitman Rosenmann. Mexico City: Universidad Nacional Autónoma de Mexico. 107–27.

Moore, Sally Falk. 1986. *Social Facts and Fabrications: Customary Law on Kilimanjaro, 1880–1980.* New York: Cambridge University Press.

Morquecho, Gaspar. 1992. "Los indios en un proceso de organización: La Organización Indígena de los Altos de Chiapas (ORIACH)." Undergraduate thesis, Universidad Autónoma de Chiapas, San Cristóbal de Las Casas.

Murphy, Robert Francis. 1971. *The Dialectics of Social Life: Alarms and Excursions in Anthropological Theory.* New York: Basic Books.

Nagengast, Carol, and Terence Turner. 1997. "Introduction: Universal Human Rights versus Cultural Relativity." *Journal of Anthropological Research* 53 (3): 269–72.

Naples, Nancy. 2003. *Feminism and Method: Ethnography, Discourse Analysis, and Activist Research.* New York: Routledge.

National Coordinating Office on Refugees and Displaced of Guatemala. 1995. NCOORD *Newsletter* 3 (5): 7

Neçak-Lük, Albina. 1995. "The Linguistic Aspect of Ethnic Conflict in Yugoslavia." In *Yugoslavia, the Former and Future: Reflections by Scholars from the Region,* ed. Payam Akhavan and Robert Howse. Geneva: United Nations Research Institute for Social Development.

Negri, Antonio. 1990. *The Savage Anomaly.* Minneapolis: University of Minnesota Press.

Nieç, Halina, ed. 1998. *Cultural Rights and Wrongs.* Paris: UNESCO Publishing.

O'Brien, Tim. 1990. *The Things They Carried.* New York: Penguin.

O'Dogherty, Laura. 1989. "Mayas en el exilio: Los refugiados guatemaltecos en México." In *Memorias del II Coloquio Internacional de Mayistas (17 al 21 de agosto de 1987).* Mexico City: Universidad Nacional Autónoma de Mexico. 1:213–17.

Office of the High Commissioner for Human Rights. 2003. *Report of the Special Rapporteur on the Situation of Human Rights and Fundamental Liberties of Indigenous Peoples.* Guatemala: Office of the High Commissioner for Human Rights.

Olivera, Mercedes. 1998. "Acteal: Los efectos de la guerra de baja intensidad." In *La otra palabra: Mujeres y violencia en Chiapas; Antes y después de Acteal,* ed. Rosalva Aída Hernández Castillo. Mexico City: Centro de Investigaciones y Estudios Superiores en Antropología Social. 30–49.

Ordóñez Cifuentes, José. 1992–94. "Constitución y derechos étnicos México-Centroamérica: Especificidades." In *Memorias del Primer Congreso Internacional de Mayistas.* 3 vols. Mexico City: Universidad Nacional Autónoma de Mexico. 1:434–49.

——. 2000. *Dos ensayos en torno al derecho social en Mesoamérica: México-Guatemala.* Mexico City: Universidad Nacional Autónoma de Mexico.

Pagden, Anthony. 1995. *Lords of All the World*. New Haven: Yale University Press.

Palencia Prado, Tania. 1999. *Género y sosmovisión Maya*. Guatemala: Editorial Saquil Tzij.

Pannikar, R. 1992. "Is the Notion of Human Rights a Western Concept?" *Law and Anthropology*, ed. Peter Sack and Jonathan Aleck. Aldershot, UK: Dartmouth.

Paris Pombo, María Dolores. 2000. *Los Coletos de San Cristóbal de Las Casas*. Mexico: Facultad Latinoamericana de Ciencias Sociales.

———. 2001. *Oligarquia, tradicion y ruptura en el centro de Chiapas*. Mexico City: La Jornada Publications.

Pásara, Luis. 2002. "Reforma judicial: El caso de Guatemala." Unpublished manuscript.

Pateman, Carol. 1989. *The Sexual Contract*. Stanford, CA: Stanford University Press.

Patton, Paul. 2000. *Deleuze and the Political*. London: Routledge.

Physicians for Human Rights (PHR). 1994. *Waiting for Justice in Chiapas*. Boston: Physicians for Human Rights.

Pineda, Luz Olivia 1999. Introduction to *Descripción Geográfica del Departamento de Chiapas y Soconusco*, by Emeterio Pineda. Mexico City: Fondo de Cultura Económica. 7–10.

Pitarch, Pedro. 1996. *Ch'ulel: Una étnografía de las almas tzeltales*. Mexico City: Fondo de Cultura Económica.

———. 2003. "Infidelidades indígenas." *Revista de Occidente* 269:60–76.

———. 2004a. "La conversión de los cuerpos: Singularidades de las identificaciones religiosas indígenas." *Liminar* 2 (2): 6–19.

———. 2004b. "The Zapatistas and the Art of Ventriloquism." *Journal of Human Rights* 3 (3): 35–63.

Pitarch, Pedro, and Julián López. 2001. *Los derechos humanos en tierras mayas: Política, representaciones y moralidad*. Madrid: Sociedad Española de Estudios Mayas.

Pitt-Rivers, Julian. 1973. "Race in Latin America." *Archives of European Sociology* 19:3–31.

Pohl, Karl-Heinz. n.d. "Beyond Universalism and Relativism: Reflections on an East-West Intercultural Dialogue." Unpublished manuscript.

Pollis, Adamantia. 1996. "Cultural Relativism Revisited: Through a State Prism." *Human Rights Quarterly* 18 (2): 316–44.

Portelli, Alessandro. 1991. *The Death of Luigi Trastulli and Other Stories: Form and Meaning in Oral History*. Albany: State University of New York Press.

Postero, Nancy Grey. 2001. "Constructing Indigenous Citizens in Multicultural Bolivia." Unpublished manuscript.

———. 2007. *Now We Are Citizens: Indigenous Politics in Postmulticultural Bolivia*. Stanford, CA: Stanford University Press.

Pozas, Ricardo. 1958. *Chamula: Un pueblo indio de los altos de Chiapas*. Mexico City: Instituto Nacional Indígena.

Preis, Ann-Belinda S. 1996. "Human Rights as Cultural Practice: An Anthropological Critique." *Human Rights Quarterly* (18) 2: 286–315.

Programa de Naciones Unidas para el Desarrollo (PNUD). 2001a. *Acceso a la justicia en Centroamérica: Seguridad jurídica e inversión.* 2nd ed. San José, Costa Rica: Programa de las Naciones Unidas para el Desarrollo.

———. 2001b. *Guatemala: Informe del desarrollo humano 2000.* Guatemala City: Programa de las Naciones Unidas para el Desarrollo.

———. 2005. *Informe nacional de desarrollo humano: Diversidad étnico-cultural; La ciudadanía en un estado plural.* Guatemala City: Programa de las Naciones Unidas para el Desarrollo.

Prott, Lyndel V. 1988. "Cultural Rights as Peoples' Rights in International Law." In *The Rights of Peoples,* ed. James Crawford. Oxford: Clarendon. 92–106.

Ramírez, Jesús. 1997. "Mapa de contra-insurgencia." *Masiosare,* January 13, 8–10.

Rawls, John. 1971. *A Theory of Justice.* Cambridge: Harvard University Press.

Recuperación de la Memoria Histórica, Informe del Proyecto Interdiocesano para la (REMHI). 1998. *Guatemala: Nunca más.* 4 vols. Guatemala City: Oficina de Derechos Humanos del Arzobispado de Guatemala.

Red Nacional de Organismos Civiles de los Derechos Humanos. 1998. "Informe sobre los sucesos de Acteal." January. Internal report.

Registro de Defunciones de Panzós. 1978. Panzós, Guatemala.

Renteln, Alison Dundes. 1990. *International Human Rights: Universalism versus Relativism.* Newbury Park, CA: Sage.

Reyes, Javier, and Pedro Ek Cituk. 2001. "Solución de controversias de acuerdo con la Ley de Justicia Indígena del estado de Quintana Roo." In *Aproximaciones a la antropología jurídica de los mayas peninsulares,* ed. Esteban Krotz. Mérida, Mexico: Universidad Autónoma de Yucatán. 87–98.

Reygadas, Rafael. 1998. *Abriendo veredas: Iniciativas públicas y sociales de las redes de organizaciones civiles.* Mexico City: Convergencia de Organizaciones Civiles por la Democracia.

Robinson, William. 1996. *Promoting Polyarchy: Globalization, U.S. Intervention and Hegemony.* Cambridge: Cambridge University Press.

Robledo Hernández, Gabriela P. 1987. "Disidencia y religión de los expulsados de San Juan Chamula." Undergraduate thesis, Escuela Nacional de Antropología e Historia, Mexico City.

Rodríguez y Rodríguez, Jesús. 1989. "Los derechos humanos de los refugiados guatemaltecos en México." *Memorias del II Coloquio Internacional de Mayistas (17 al 21 de agosto de 1987).* 4 vols. Mexico City: Universidad Nacional Autónoma de Mexico 1:193–204.

Rosaldo, Renato. 1997. "Cultural Citizenship, Inequality and Multiculturalism." *Latino Cultural Citizenship: Claiming Identity, Space and Rights,* ed. William Flores and Rina Benmayor. Boston: Beacon. 27–38.

Rose, Nikolas. 1999. *Powers of Freedom: Reframing Political Thought.* Cambridge: Cambridge University Press.

Rousseau, Jean Jacques. 2003 [1762]. *On the Social Contract.* Trans. G. D. H. Cole. Mineola, NY: Dover.

Ruiz García, Samuel. 1992. "Los refugiados y los derechos humanos." In *Una década de refugio en México: Los refugiados guatemaltecos y los derechos humanos,* ed. Graciela Freyermuth and R. Aída Hernández Castillo. Mexico City: Centro de Investigaciones y Estudios Superiores en Antropología Social. 59–67.

——. 1993. *En esta hora de gracia: Carta pastoral.* Mexico City: Ediciones Dabar.

——. 1999. *Mi trabajo pastoral en la diocesis de San Cristóbal de Las Casas: Principios teológicos.* Mexico City: Ediciones Paulinas.

Ruíz Ortiz, Juana María. 1996. "Los primeros pobladores de Nich'ix, la colonia La Hormiga." In *Anuario de estudios indígenas VI.* San Cristóbal de Las Casas: Universidad Autónoma de Chiapas, Instituto de Estudios Indígenas. 11–24.

Rus, Jan. 1995. "Local Adaptation to Global Change: The Reordering of Native Society in Highland Chiapas, 1974–1994." *European Review of Latin American and Caribbean Studies* 58:71–89.

Rus, Jan, Rosalva Aída Hernández Castillo, and Shannan L. Mattiace, eds. 2003. *Mayan Lives, Mayan Utopias: The Indigenous Peoples of Chiapas and the Zapatista Rebellion.* Lanham, MD: Rowman and Littlefield.

Rus, Jan, and James Diego Vigil. 2007. "Rapid Urbanization and Migrant Indigenous Youth in San Cristóbal, Chiapas, Mexico." In *Gangs in the Global City,* ed. John M. Hagedorn. Urbana: University of Illinois Press.

Rus, Jan, and Robert W. Wasserstrom. 1981. "Evangelization and Political Control in Mexico." In *Is God an American?* ed. Søren Hvalkof and Peter Aaby. Copenhagen: International Working Group for Indigenous Affairs. 163–72.

Ruz, Mario Humberto. 1989. "Derechos humanos." In *Memorias del II Coloquio Internacional de Mayistas (17 al 21 de agosto de 1987).* 4 vols. Mexico City: Universidad Nacional Autónoma de Mexico. 1:191–92.

Salas, Luis. 2001. "From Law and Development to Rule of Law: New and Old Issues in Justice Reform in Latin America." In *Rule of Law in Latin America: The International Promotion of Judicial Reform,* ed. Pilar Domingo and Rachel Sieder. London: Institute of Latin American Studies. 17–46.

Salazar Tetzaguic, Manuel, and Vicenta Telón Sajcabún. 1998. *Valores Mayas.* Guatemala City: Cholsamaj and Nawal Wuj.

Sandoval Palacios, Juan Manuel. 1992. "Los refugiados centroamericanos en la frontera México-Estados Unidos ¿Problemas de seguridad nacional o de derechos humanos?" In *Una década de refugio en México: Los refugiados guatemaltecos y los derechos humanos,* ed. Graciela Freyermuth and R. Aída Hernández Castillo. Mexico City: Centro de Investigaciones y Estudios Superiores en Antropología Social. 270–92.

Sanford, Victoria. 1997. *Mothers, Widows and Guerrilleras: Anonymous Conversations with Survivors of State Terror.* Uppsala: Life and Peace Institute.

——. 1999. "Between Rigoberta Menchú and La Violencia: Deconstructing David Stoll's History of Guatemala." *Latin American Perspectives* 126 (6): 38–46.

——. 2000. "The Silencing of Maya Women from Mamá Maquín to Rigoberta Menchú." *Social Justice* 27 (1): 128–56.

———. 2001. "From I, Rigoberta to the Commissioning of Truth: Maya Women and the Reshaping of Guatemalan History." *Cultural Critique* 47:16–53.

———. 2003. *Buried Secrets: Truth and Human Rights in Guatemala*. New York: Palgrave Macmillan.

Sanford, Victoria and Asale Angel-Ajani eds. 2006. *Engaged Observer: Anthropology, Advocacy and Activism*. New Brunswick: Rutgers University Press.

Santos, Boaventura de Souza. 1987. "Law: A Map of Misreading; Toward a Post-modern Conception of Law." *Journal of Law and Society* 14 (3): 279–302.

———. 1995. *Towards a New Commonsense: Law, Science and Politics in the Paradigmatic Transition*. New York: Routledge.

———. 1998. *La globalización del derecho: Los nuevos caminos de la regulación y la emancipación*. Bogotá: Instituto Latinoamericano de Servicios Legales Alternativos.

Saqb'ichil-Copmagua. 2000. *Investigaciones en derecho consuetudinario y poder local*. Guatemala City: Serviprensa.

Schackt, Jon 2000. "Los mayas: El origen del término y la creación del pueblo." In "De indígenas a Mayas: Identidades indígenas en Guatemala y Chiapas," ed. Schackt. Special issue, *Revista Estudios Interétnicos* 10 (16): 7–26.

Schild, Veronica. 1998. "New Subjects of Rights? Women's Movements and the Construction of Citizenship in the 'New Democracies.'" In Cultures of Politics/Politics of Culture: Revisioning Latin American Social Movements, ed. Sonia E. Alvarez, Evelina Dagnino, and Arturo Escobar. Boulder, CO: Westview. 93–117.

Schirmer, Jennifer. 1997. "Universal and Sustainable Human Rights? Special Tribunals in Guatemala." In *Human Rights, Culture and Context: Anthropological Perspectives*, ed. Richard Wilson. London: Pluto. 161–86.

———. 1998. *The Guatemalan Military Project: A Violence Called Democracy*. Philadelphia: University of Pennsylvania Press.

———. 2001. *Intimidades del proyecto político de los militares en Guatemala*. Guatemala City: Facultad Latinoamericana de Ciencias Sociales.

Schoultz, Lars. 1981. *Human Rights and United States Policy toward Latin America*. Princeton: Princeton University Press.

Scupin, Raymond. 1995. *Cultural Anthropology: A Global Perspective*. Englewood Cliffs, NJ: Prentice Hall.

Se, Teruhisa and Karatsu Rie. 2004. "A Conception of Human Rights Based on Japanese Culture: Promoting Cross-cultural Debates." *Journal of Human Rights* 3 (3): 269–290.

Secretaria General de Planificación. 2000. *Informe de gestión gobierno*. Guatemala City: Secretaria General de Planificación.

Secretariado de Jueces para la Democracia. 1997. "Sobre la masacre de campesinos en Chiapas y la situación de los derechos humanos en México," December, www.derechos.org/nizkor/jueces/doc/chiapas.html.

Servico Paz y Justicia (SERPAJ). 1996. *Amatán y Xi'Nich: La lucha no violenta continúa por la paz con justicia*. Mexico City: Editorial Jus.

Shute, Stephen, and Susan Hurley, eds. 1993. *On Human Rights*. New York: Basic Books.

Sieder, Rachel. 1998. "Reinterpretando la ciudadanía: Los derechos indígenas, el poder local y el proceso de paz en Guatemala." In *Anuario 1997*. San Cristóbal de Las Casas: Universidad de Ciencias y Artes del Estado de Chiapas. 313–36.

———. 2001. "War, Peace and the Politics of Memory in Guatemala." In *Burying the Past: Making Peace and Doing Justice after Civil Conflict*, ed. Nigel Biggar. Washington: Georgetown University Press. 184–206.

———, ed. 2002. *Multiculturalism in Latin America: Indigenous Rights, Diversity and Democracy*. Houndmills, Basingstoke: Macmillan.

Sieder, Rachel, and Jessica Witchell. 2001. "Advancing Indigenous Claims through the Law: Reflections on the Guatemalan Peace Process." In *Culture and Rights: Anthropological Perspectives*, ed. Jane Cowan, Marie Dembour, and Richard Ashby Wilson. Cambridge: Cambridge University Press. 201–25.

Sierra, María Teresa. 2001. "Human Rights, Gender and Ethnicity: Legal Claims and Anthropological Challenges in Mexico." *PoLAR: Political and Legal Anthropology Review* 23 (2): 76–92.

Sikkink, Kathryn. 1993. "Human Rights, Principled Issue-Networks, and Sovereignty in Latin America." *International Organization* 47 (3): 411–41.

———. 2005. "The Transnational Dimension of the Judicialization of Politics in Latin America." In *The Judicialization of Politics in Latin America*, ed. Rachel Sieder, Line Schjolden, and Alan Angell. New York: Palgrave Macmillan. 263–92.

Slocum, Mariana, and Florencia Gerdel. 1981. *Vocabulario Tzeltal de Bachajón*. Mexico City: Instituto Lingüístico de Verano.

Sluka, Jeffrey A., ed. 1999. *Death Squad: The Anthropology of State Terror*. Philadelphia: University of Pennsylvania Press.

Smith, Carol A. 1984. "Local History in Global Context: Social and Economic Transitions in Western Guatemala." *Comparative Studies in Society and History* 26 (2): 193–228.

———, with Marilyn M. Moors, ed. 1990. *Guatemalan Indians and the State, 1540–1988*. Austin, Texas: University of Texas Press.

Smith, Waldemar. 1977. *The Fiesta System and Economic Change*. New York: Columbia University Press.

Solórzano Fonseca, Juan Carlos. 1993. "Los años finales de la dominación española (1750–1821)." In *Historia general de Centroamérica: De la ilustración al liberalismo*, ed. Hector Pérez Brignoli. 7 vols. Madrid: Sociedad Estatal Quinto Centenario. 3:13–71.

Son, Benjamín. 2000. "Socio-economic Consequences of the War and a Proposal from a Community Organisation to Build Peace." In *Guatemala: Dilemmas in Democratisation: Seminar Proceedings*, ed. Trygve Bendiksby and Stener Ekern. Oslo: Norwegian Institute of Human Rights, University of Oslo.

Soysal, Yasemin Nuhoglu. 1994. *Limits of Citizenship: Migrants and Postnational Membership in Europe*. Chicago: University of Chicago Press.

Speed, Shannon. 2001. "Global Discourses on the Local Terrain: Grounding Human Rights in Chiapas, Mexico." PhD diss., University of California, Davis.

———. 2006. "At the Crossroads of Human Rights and Anthropology: Toward a Critically Engaged Activist Research." *American Anthropologist* 108 (1): 66–76.

———. 2007. *Rights in Rebellion: Indigenous Struggle and Human Rights in Chiapas.* Stanford: Stanford University Press.

Speed, Shannon, and Jane F. Collier. 2000. "Limiting Indigenous Autonomy in Chiapas, Mexico: The State Government's Use of Human Rights." *Human Rights Quarterly* 22 (4): 877–905.

Speed, Shannon, and Teresa Sierra, eds. 2005. "Dangerous Discourses: Human Rights and Multiculturalism in Mexico." Special issue, *PoLAR: Political and Legal Anthropology Review* 28 (1): 29–51.

Spinner, Jeff. 1994. *The Boundaries of Citizenship: Race, Ethnicity, and Nationality in the Liberal State.* Baltimore: Johns Hopkins University Press.

Starr, June, and Jane Collier, eds. 1989. *History and Power in the Study of Law: New Directions in Legal Anthropology.* Ithaca: Cornell University Press.

State Government of Chiapas. 1999. *Ley de Derechos y Cultura Indígena del Estado de Chiapas.* Tuxtla Gutiérrez, Mexico: State of Chiapas.

Stavenhagen, Rodolfo. 1990a. *The Ethnic Question: Conflicts, Development and Human Rights.* Tokyo: United Nations University Press.

———. 1990b. "The Right to Cultural Identity." In *Human Rights in a Pluralist World: Individuals and Collectivities,* ed. Jon Berting et al. London: Meckler. 255–58.

———. 1993. "Self-Determination, Right or Demon?" *Stanford Journal of International Affairs* 2:1–12.

———. 1995. "Indigenous Peoples: Emerging Actors in Latin America." In *Ethnic Conflict and Governance in Comparative Perspective.* Washington: Woodrow Wilson International Center for Scholars. 112–53.

———. 1996. "Indigenous Rights: Some Conceptual Problems." In *Constructing Democracy: Human Rights, Citizenship and Society in Latin America,* ed. Elizabeth Jelin and Eric Hershberg. Boulder, CO: Westview. 141–59.

Stephen, Lynn. 1999. "The Construction of Indigenous Suspects: Militarization and the Gendered and Ethnic Dynamics of Human Rights Abuses in Southern Mexico." *American Ethnologist* 26 (4): 822–42.

Stepputat, Finn. 1999. "Repatriation and Everyday Forms of State Formation in Guatemala." In *The End of the Refugee Cycle? Refugee Repatriation and Reconstruction,* ed. Richard Black and Khalid Khoser. New York: Berghahn. 210–26.

Sterk, Vern 1991. "The Dynamics of Persecution." Doctorate of Missionology diss., Fuller Theological Seminary, Pasadena.

Stoll, David. 1993. *Between Two Armies in the Ixil Towns of Guatemala.* New York: Columbia University Press.

———. 1995. "Guatemala: Solidarity Activists Head for Trouble." *Christian Century* 112 (1): 17–21.

———. 1997. "To Whom Should We Listen? Human Rights Activism in Two Guatemalan Land Disputes." In *Human Rights, Culture and Context: Anthropological Perspectives,* ed. Richard Wilson. London: Pluto. 187–215.

———. 1999a. *Entre dos fuegos en los pueblos ixiles de Guatemala*. Quito: Abya-yala.

———. 1999b. *Rigoberta Menchú and the Story of All Poor Guatemalans*. Boulder, CO: Westview.

Taracena Arriola, Arturo. 2002. *Etnicidad, estado y nación en Guatemala, 1808–1944*. Guatemala City: Centro de Investigaciones Regionales de Mesoamérica.

Tax, Susan. 1966. "Actividad de desplazamiento en Zinacantán." In *Los Zinacantecos: Un pueblo tzotzil de los altos de Chiapas*, ed. Evon Z. Vogt. Mexico City: Instituto Nacional Indigenista. 369–411.

Taylor, Charles. 1994. "The Politics of Recognition." In *Multiculturalism and "The politics of recognition": An essay*, by Charles Taylor, ed. Amy Gutmann. Princeton: Princeton University Press. 25–73.

Tedlock, Dennis, and Bruce Mannheim. 1995. *The Dialogic Emergence of Culture*. Urbana: University of Illinois Press.

Terrazas, Carlos R. 1996. *Los derechos humanos en las constituciones políticas de México*. Mexico City: Miguel Angel Porrua Editorial.

Teubner, Gunther, ed. 1996. *Global Law without a State*. Aldershot, UK: Dartmouth.

Theidon, Kimberly. 2004. *Entre prójimos: El conflicto armado interno y la política de la reconciliación en el Perú*. Lima: Instituto de Estudios Peruanos.

Thompson, Michael, Richard Ellis, and Aaron Wildavsky. 1990. *Cultural Theory*. Boulder, CO: Westview.

Toledo Tello, Sonia. 1989. "Atraso y violencia en Chiapas: El caso de Simojovel." In *Memorias del II Coloquio Internacional de Mayistas (17 al 21 de agosto de 1987)*. 4 vols. Mexico City: Universidad Nacional Autónoma de Mexico. 1:205–11.

———. 2002. *Fincas, poder y cultura en Simojovel, Chiapas*. Mexico City: Universidad Nacional Autónoma de Mexico, Programa de Investigaciones Multidisciplinarias sobre Mesoamerica y Sureste.

Tomuschat, Christian, ed. 1993. *Modern Law of Self-Determination*. Dordrecht, Netherlands: Martinus Nijhoff Publishers.

Tranfo, Luigi. 1975. *Vida y magia en un pueblo otomí del Mezquital*. Mexico City: Instituto Nacional Indigenista.

Trinh, T. Minh-ha. 1989. *Woman, Native, Other: Writing Postcoloniality and Feminism*. Bloomington: Indiana University Press.

Trubek, David M., et al. 1994. "Global Restructuring and the Law: Studies of the Internationalization of Legal Fields and the Creation of Transnational Arenas." *Case Western Reserve Law Review* 44:407–98.

United Nations (UN), Department of Public Information. 1984. *The United Nations and Human Rights*. New York: United Nations.

———. 1986. *Is Universality in Jeopardy?* New York: United Nations.

United Nations Educational, Scientific and Cultural Organization (UNESCO). 1982. *World Conference on Cultural Policies: Final Report*. Paris: UNESCO Publishing.

———. 1995. *Our Creative Diversity: Report of the World Commission on Culture and Development*. Paris: UNESCO Publishing.

———. 1996. *Learning: The Treasure Within; Report to UNESCO of the International Commission on Education for the Twenty-First Century.* Paris. UNESCO Publishing.

———. 2000. *World Culture Report 2000: Cultural Diversity, Conflict and Pluralism.* Paris. UNESCO Publishing.

Universidad Rafael Landívar. 1998. *El sistema jurídico maya: Una aproximación.* Guatemala City: Universidad Rafael Landívar.

Valdés, Juan Antonio. 2003. "Lo maya, los mayas y los mayistas." *Memoria del Cuarto Congreso Internacional de Mayistas: (2 al 8 de agosto de 1998).* Mexico City: Universidad Nacional Autónoma de Mexico. 15–24.

Van Cott, Donna Lee. 2000. *The Friendly Liquidation of the Past: The Politics of Diversity in Latin America.* Pittsburgh: University of Pittsburgh Press.

Van Den Berghe, Pierre L. 1994. *The Quest for the Other: Ethnic Tourism in San Cristóbal, Mexico.* Seattle: University of Washington Press.

Van der Haar, Gemma. 2005. "Autonomía zapatista a ras de tierra: Algunas implicaciones y dilemas de la autonomia zapatista en la práctica." In *Tejiendo historias: Tierra, genero y poder en Chiapas,* ed. Maya Lorena Perez Ruíz. Mexico City: Instituto Nacional de Antropología e Historia. 119–42.

Vasconcelos, Jose. 1997 [1948]. *The Cosmic Race: A Bilingual Edition.* Ed. and trans. Didier T. Jaén. Baltimore: Johns Hopkins University Press.

Vela, Manolo, Alexander Sequén-Mónchez, and Hugo Antonio Solares. 2001. *El lado oscuro de la Eterna Primavera: Violencia, criminalidad y delincuencia en la postguerra.* Guatemala City: Facultad Latinoamericana de Ciencias Sociales.

Vilas, Carlos. 2001. "(In)justicia por mano propia: Linchamientos en el México contemporáneo." *Revista Mexicana de Sociología* 1 (63): 131–60.

Villafuerte Solís, Daniel. 2001. *Integraciones comerciales en la frontera sur: Chiapas frente al Tratado de Libre Comercio México-Centroamérica.* Mexico City: Universidad Nacional Autónoma de Mexico.

Villafuerte Solís, Daniel, et al. 1999. *La tierra en Chiapas: Viejos problemas nuevos.* Mexico City: Centro de Estudios Superiores de Mexico y Centroamérica.

Villoro, Luis. 2002. "Ciudadanía y estado plural." In *Democracia, ciudadanía y diversidad: El debate político,* ed. Diego Iturralde. Quetzaltenango, Guatemala: Programa de Naciones Unidas Sede. 25–47.

Viqueira, Juan Pedro, and Mario Humberto Ruz. 2002. *Chiapas: Los rumbos de otra historia.* Mexico City: Universidad Nacional Autónoma de Mexico, Centro de Estudios Mayas.

Wagley, Charles. 1957. *Santiago chimaltenango: Estudio antropológico-social de una comunidad indígena de Huehuetenango.* Trans. Joaquín Noval. Guatemala City: Seminario de Integración Social Guatemalteca.

Wallerstein, Immanuel. 2002. "The Eagle Has Landed." *Foreign Policy* 136:60–68.

———, ed. 2006. *Abrir las ciencias sociales.* Mexico City: Siglo XXI.

Warren, Kay. 1998. *Indigenous Movements and Their Critics: Pan-Maya Activism in Guatemala.* Princeton: Princeton University Press.

Warren, Kay and Jean Jackson. 2002. *Indigenous Movements, Self-Representation, and the State in Latin America.* Austin: University of Texas.

Watanabe, John M. 1990. "From Saints to Shibboleths: Image, Structure, and Identity in Mayan Religious Syncretism." *American Ethnologist* 17 (1): 131–50.

——. 1992. *Maya Saints and Souls in a Changing World.* Austin: University of Texas Press.

Waterman, Peter. 1998. *Globalization, Social Movements and the New Internationalism.* London: Mansell.

Whorf, Benjamin Lee. 1956. *Language, Thought and Reality: Selected Writings by Benjamin Lee Whorf.* Ed. John Carroll. Cambridge: MIT Press.

Williams, Roger G. 1994. *States and Social Evolution: Coffee and the Rise of National Governments in Central America.* Chapel Hill: University of North Carolina Press.

Wilson, Richard. 1995. *Maya Resurgence in Guatemala.* Norman: University of Oklahoma Press.

——. 1997a. *Human Rights, Culture and Context: Anthropological Perspectives.* London: Pluto.

——. 1997b. "Human Rights, Culture and Context: An Introduction and 'Representing Human Rights Violations: Social Contexts and Subjectivities.'" In *Human Rights, Culture and Context: Anthropological Perspectives,* ed. Wilson. London: Pluto. 7–27.

——. 1999. *Resurgimiento maya en Guatemala (Experiencias q'eqchi'es).* Guatemala City: Centro de Investigaciones Regionales de Mesoamérica/Plumsock Mesoamerican Studies.

——. 2000. *The Politics of Truth and Reconciliation in South Africa: Legitimizing the Post-apartheid State.* Cambridge: Cambridge University Press.

——. 2006. "Is the Legalization of Human Rights Really the Problem? Genocide in the Guatemalan Historical Clarification Commission." In *The Legalization of Human Rights: Multidisciplinary Perspectives on Human Rights and Human Rights Law,* ed. Saladin Meckled-Garcia and Başak Çali. New York: Routledge. 81–98.

Womack, John, Jr. 1998. *Chiapas: El obispo de San Cristóbal y la revuelta zapatista.* Mexico City: Cal y Arena.

——. 1999. *Rebellion in Chiapas: An Historical Reader.* New York: New Press.

Yashar, Deborah. 1999. "Democracy, Indigenous Movements, and the Postliberal Challenge in Latin America." *World Politics* 52:76–104.

Yoldi, Pilar. 1996. *Don Juan Coc: Principe q'eqchi' (1945–1995).* Guatemala City: Centro Impresor Piedra Santa.

Young, Crawford. 1976. *The Politics of Cultural Pluralism.* Madison: University of Wisconsin Press.

Yrigoyen Fajardo, Raquel. 1999. *Pautas de coordinación entre el derecho indígena y el derecho estatal.* Guatemala City: Fundación Myrna Mack.

Zapeta, Estuardo. 1999. *Las huellas de B'alam, 1994–96.* Guatemala City: Cholsamaj.

Zapeta García, José Angel. 2005. *El movimiento maya: Sus tendencias y transformaciones, 1980–2005.* Guatemala City: Asociación Maya Uk'u'x B'e.

Zárate, Eduardo J. 2002. "Ciudadanía, comunidad y modernidades étnicas." In *Ciudadanía, cultura, política y reforma del estado en América Latina,* ed. Marco A. Calderón Molgora, Willem Assies, and Ton Salman. Zamora, Mexico: Instituto Federal Electoral and Colegio de Michoacán. 407–27.

Zur, Judith. 1998. *Violent Memories: Mayan War Widows in Guatemala.* Boulder, CO: Westview.

Contributors

ROBERT M. CARMACK is professor emeritus at the State University of New York. His fields of specialization include political anthropology, ethnohistory, Mesoamerican studies, and anthropological theory. He has authored or edited numerous books and articles including *Legacy of Mesoamerica*; *The Quiché Mayas of Utatlán*; *Harvest of Violence*; *The Rebels of Highland Guatemala*; *Political Economy and Ecology in Costa Rica: The Buenos Aires Case*; and *Sociocultural Anthropology: A World History Approach* (in press). He is currently preparing a comparative political history of three Central American Indian communities (Buenos Aires, Argentina; Masaya, Nicaragua; and Momostenango, Guatemala).

STENER EKERN is an associate professor at the Norwegian Centre for Human Rights at the University of Oslo. He has done fieldwork in Nicaragua (1984–85) and Guatemala (2000–2003) and specializes in political anthropology, human rights, Central America, and indigenous peoples. He has also worked in Norwegian development cooperation and at the United Nations.

CHRISTINE KOVIC, an associate professor of anthropology at the University of Houston, Clear Lake, conducted research on indigenous rights and religion in highland Chiapas from 1993 to 2001. She is the author of *Mayan Voices for Human Rights: Displaced Catholics in Highland Chiapas* and the coeditor of *Women of Chiapas: Making History in Times of Struggle and Hope*. Her most recent research project examines the human rights of Central Americans crossing Mexico's southern border en route to the United States.

XOCHITL LEYVA SOLANO is a researcher and a professor at the Centro de Investigaciones e Estudios Superiores en Antropología Social, CIESAS-Sureste in Chiapas. She is a member of neo-Zapatista and antisystemic networks, as well as of those promoting decolonized, activist research. Among her books are *Power and Regional Development*; *Lancandonia al filo del agua* (coauthored with Gabriel Ascencio); and *Encuentros Antropológicos: Politics, Identity and Mobility in Mexican Society* (edited with Valentina Napolitano).

JULIÁN LÓPEZ GARCÍA is a professor at the University of Córdoba (Spain). He researches notions of food, hunger, and suffering, as well as the politics and practices of identity and violence in the indigenous regions of the Americas (generally the Maya-Ch'orti' of Guatemala). Recent publications include the book *Símbolos en la comida indígena guatemalteca* and the volumes *Lugares indígenas de la violencia en Iberoamérica* and *Derechos humanos en tierras mayas* (edited with Pedro Pitarch).

IRMA OTZOY is a Maya-Kaqchikel woman from Guatemala. She received her doctorate in social anthropology from the University of California, Davis, in 1999. She is currently a member of the Fundación para Estudios y Profesionalización (FEPMaya) and an independent consultant.

PEDRO PITARCH is a professor of anthropology at the Complutense University in Madrid. He has carried out fieldwork in Spain and, for the past eighteen years, in Chiapas, where he has focused on native concepts of personhood. His books include: *Ch'ulel: Una etnografía de las almas tzeltales*; *Antropología de los sentidos: La vista*; *Los derechos humanos en tierras mayas: Política, representaciones y moralidad* (edited with Julián López García); and, as an editor, *Lugares indígenas de la violencia en Iberoamérica*.

ALVARO REYES holds a JD from the University of Pennsylvania Law School and is a student in the Graduate Program in Literature at Duke University. He currently researches sovereignty at the intersection of globalization and comparative ethnic studies. He is a founding member of El Kilombo collective in Durham, North Carolina, and is the former executive director of Project 169, an indigenous rights initiative formed in conjunction with the Chiapas Community Defenders' Network.

VICTORIA SANFORD is an associate professor of anthropology at Lehman College of the City University of New York. She holds a PhD in anthropology from Stanford University (2000), where she also received training in international human rights law at Stanford Law School. She is the author of *Buried Secrets: Truth and Human Rights in Guatemala*; *Violencia y genocidio en Guatemala*; and *La masacre de Panzós*. She is the coeditor (with Asale Angel-Ajani) of *Engaged Observer: Anthropology, Advocacy and Activism*.

RACHEL SIEDER teaches at the Institute for the Study of the Americas, School of Advanced Studies, University of London. Her books include, as an editor, *Multiculturalism in Latin America: Indigenous Rights, Diversity and Democracy*; and *The Judicialization of Politics in Latin America* (edited with Line Schjolden and Alan Angell). She is one of the editors of the *Journal of Latin American Studies*.

SHANNON SPEED is an assistant professor of anthropology at the University of Texas, Austin. Her research interests include human rights, indigenous rights, globalization, gender, social justice and resistance movements, and activist research methods. For the past thirteen years, she has done research in Chiapas, where she worked with Global Exchange and the Red de Defensores Comunitarios por los Derechos Humanos. She is the author of *Rights in Rebellion: Indigenous Struggle and Human Rights in Chiapas* (2007), and *Bajo la lanza: Lucha por la tierra y identidad comunitaria en Nicolás Ruiz* (2006). She is the coeditor of *Dissident Women: Gender and Cultural Politics in Chiapas* (2006), and *Gobernar en la diversidad: Experiencias indígenas desde América Latina* (2008).

RODOLFO STAVENHAGEN, a professor emeritus at El Colegio de México, has written on human rights, indigenous peoples, agrarian problems, and social development in Latin America and elsewhere, on ethnic conflicts, and on nation building. He has been a visiting professor at Harvard and Stanford universities, among others. He was assistant director for social sciences at UNESCO in Paris and since 2001 is the United Nations special rapporteur for the human rights of indigenous peoples.

DAVID STOLL is a professor of anthropology at Middlebury College. His books include *Is Latin America Turning Protestant?*; *Between Two Armies in the Ixil Towns of Guatemala*; and *Rigoberta Menchú and the Story of All Poor Guatemalans*.

RICHARD ASHBY WILSON is the Gladstein Distinguished Chair of Human Rights, a professor of anthropology, and the director of the Human Rights Institute at the University of Connecticut. He is the author of *Maya Resurgence in Guatemala* and *The Politics of Truth and Reconciliation in South Africa: Legitimizing the Post-apartheid State*, and the editor of *Human Rights, Culture, and Context: Anthropological Perspectives* and *Human Rights in the "War on Terror."* He is also a coeditor of *Low Intensity Democracy: Political Power in the New World Order*; *Culture and Rights: Anthropological Perspectives*; and *Human Rights in Global Perspective*. Presently he is writing a comparative study of the historical accounts of international criminal tribunals.

Index

Arzú, Alvaro, 75, 150

communitarianism, 6, 56

Communities of Population in Resistance (CPRS), 190–91, 194, 198–99

Community Human Rights Defenders Network. *See* Red de Defensores Comunitarios por los Derechos Humanos

CONAVIGUA (National Committee of Guatemalan Widows; Coordinadora Nacional de Viudas de Guatemala), 74, 194, 320–21 n. 2

conciliation courts, 22 n. 14

CONIC (National Indigenous and Campesino Coalition), 196

Connor, Walker, 38

CONPAZ (Coordination of Nongovernmental Organizations for Peace; Coordinación de Organizaciones Nogubernamentales por la Paz), 230–31 n. 20

conscientizacão (conscientization), 262–63

conservatism, 56, 58, 62

constitution (1857), 231 n. 25

constitution (1917), 231 n. 25, 266

Constitutional Decree of Apatzingán (1814), 231 n. 25

Convention on the Elimination of All Forms of Discrimination against Women, 175

cooperatives, 269

Coordination for State Security, 219

Coordination of Nongovernmental Organizations for Peace (Coordinación de Organizaciones Nogubernamentales por la Paz; CONPAZ), 230–31 n. 20

corporativist social pacting, 14, 285

cosmic race, 6

Council of the Indies, 4–5

CPP (Penal Procedures Code; Códego Procesal Penal), 73, 75, 87 n. 12

CPRS (Communities of Population in Resistance), 190–91, 194, 198–99

creativity, 30–31

CRIACH (Counsel of Indigenous Representatives of the Chiapas Highlands; Consejo de Representantes Indigenas de los Altos de Chiapas), 212

Criminal Procedures Act (1994), 142 n. 3

Croatian language, 33

CUC (Committee for Peasant Unity; Comité Unidad Campesina), 321 n. 2

cultural relativism, 55, 57–58

culture, cultural rights, 27, 49 n. 5; African values and, 37; as capital, 29–30; collective rights and, 34–35, 308; as creativity, 30–31; cultural diversity and, 35–40, 49 nn. 10–11, 49 n. 13, 49 n. 16, 208; cultural genocide and, 39, 44, 49 n. 11; cultural hegemons vs. other cultures, 38–39, 49 n. 10; cultural minorities' rights, 40–41; culture wars, 33; high vs. low, 31; indigenous rights and, 42–46; international standards and, 40–43; multicultural citizenship and, 46–48, 50 n. 20; national cultures and, 30, 32, 38, 40; problems and meanings of, 27–29, 48 n. 1, 49 n. 3; right to cultural identity and, 28, 34, 37–40, 308; state policies and, 43

Cus, Widow, 238

customary (Mayan) law: ancestors' role in, 128, 141; autonomy of, 139–40; balance and harmony in, 128; community and human rights in, 123–24, 135–40, 142–43 nn. 7–8; community in, 128–30, 133, 141–42; cycle of fiestas in, 127–28; divorce in, 131; ethics and, 120–21 n. 8; evolutionary perspective on, 125; Guatemalan law vs., 127, 129; hierarchies in, 127–30, 133; human rights vs., 125–26, 133–34; land rights under, 132; *makaj* in, 128–29; marriage in, 132–33; Mayan self-rule and, 130,

140–41, 142 n. 2; in practice, 129–32, 142 nn. 2–3; priests and elders in, 130–34, 140; promoting human rights and, 129, 139–42; right of indigenous people to, 77–79, 87 n. 11, 87 n. 13; the sacred in, 128; state expansion and, 124–25; vice mayors in, 130–31, 133; Western law and, 133, 288, 309

Daes, Erika, 218
Dary, Claudia, 166, 178
Declaration on Cultural Policies (UNESCO), 49 n. 3
Defensoría Maya, 87 n. 13
Dejiae, Goran, 310
de León Carpio, Ramiro, 60
Deleuze, Gilles, 285
de los Santos, Miguel Angel, 290–91, 294, 297
de Mazariegos, Diego, 216
Dembour, Marie-Bénédicte, 140
DEMI (Office for the Defense of Indigenous Women; Defensoría de la Mujer Indígena), 175–78, 180, 184–85 nn. 4–5
Department of Agrarian Reform (Secretaría de Reforma Agraría), 272
Department of Education (MINEDUC), 148
derecho maya, el (Mayan law), 78–79
Desarrollo, Paz y Justicia (Development, Peace, and Justice), 216, 219–20, 222, 230 n. 19
Dezaley, Yves, 69
dialogic interactions, 209, 227, 228 n. 2
Diamond, Larry, 57
Díaz Díaz, Enrique, 277 n. 4
difference, 48 n. 1, 308
dignity, 52, 257–58, 261, 264, 267–68, 273–74
Diocesan Coordination of Women (Coordinación Diocesana de Mujeres; CODIMUJ), 268
Domingo de Ara, Friar, 121 n. 9

Dominican missionaries, 260
Donnelly, Jack, 52, 63
Draft American Declaration of Indigenous Rights (2006), 288

Earth Tree Water (Ulew Che' Ja'; UCJ), 135–36, 142–43 n. 7
Ecuador, 45–46
Education Manual in Human Rights (Ávila), 155, 157, 160–61, 163–64
EGP (Guerrilla Army of the Poor), 190–91, 194–96, 199, 201–2, 203–4 n. 2, 312, 321 n. 8
Eide, Asbjørn, 27–28, 41–42
Ejercito Zapatista de Liberación Nacional. See Zapatistas
ejidos (communal lands), 5, 132
Ekern, Stener, 154, 189
El Salvador, 83
Engler, Mark, 264
Enlightenment, 53, 134
equality, 231 n. 25, 257–58, 274–75, 283, 308
Escalón, El (Amatán, Chiapas), 271–73
Esquit Choy, Edgar, 127–28, 133, 140, 176
Estación Norte, 220, 231 n. 20
ethnic citizenship, 47–48
European Union (EU), 191
Exodus, Book of, 260
external protection, 231 n. 27
EZLN. See Zapatistas

FAFG (Guatemalan Forensic Anthropology Foundation; Fundación de Antropología Forense de Guatemala), 234–35, 238–40, 244–45, 251–52, 254–55 n. 2
faith-based nonviolent resistance, 257, 268–76, 277 n. 9
Federal Law for the Prevention and Punishment of Torture (Ley Federal para Prevenir y Sancionar la Tortura), 231 n. 24

human rights (*cont.*)

given, 266, 281, 283; human being as focus of, 125–26; individual vs. collective, 224–26, 231 n. 26, 231 n. 28, 308; as legal framework of treaties and conventions, 67–68; legalization of, 315–16; liberal models of, 258–59, 276 n. 2; limitations on exercise of, 279–80; Maya-Ch'orti' culture and, 154–58, 160–63, 169 n. 17; Mayan culture and, 307–9, 321 nn. 3–4; modernization and, 145, 148–53, 168 n. 8, 168 n. 10; natural law view of, 281–83, 288; neoliberal states and, 8–9, 13–17, 312–15; political vs. economic, 276 n. 2; as political language of resistance, 314–15; political life of, 279; positive law view of, 281–82, 284–86, 288; reformist view of, 258–59; social reciprocity and, 118; training in, 151–52, 168 nn. 7–8; verticalization of conflict and, 315–17; violations in 1970s and 1980s of, 261; of women, 163–67, 169 n. 19. *See also* rights of the poor

human rights and the Maya region: conceptualizations of the region, 2–4, 20 nn. 2–3; discourses on human rights, 1–2, 4, 6–7, 9–14, 16–19, 22 n. 14; historical perspective on, 305–6; human and indigenous rights in Chiapas and Guatemala, 3–8, 22 n. 14; local autonomy vs. human rights, 12, 14–15, 22–23 n. 15; local culture and, 10–13; neoliberalism and, 1, 8–17; resistance movements and networks, 15–17; Western concept of human rights, 9–11, 307

Human Rights Commission of Yucatán (Comisión de Derechos Humanos del Estado de Yucátan; CODHEY), 22 n. 14

human rights discourse in Chiapas, 207, 217, 226–28, 231; CDHFBC and, 211, 218, 220–23, 230 n. 20; cultural imperialism and, 208–9; neoliberalism and, 223–24; NGOS and, 210–11, 214–15, 284; popularity of, 211–12; poverty and, 210; San Cristóbal diocese and, 209–12, 216, 218–22; following scorched-earth campaign, 209–11; state mobilization of, 223–26, 231 n. 29, 231 nn. 25–26; state violence and, 211–12, 229 n. 6; Zapatistas and, 207–8, 212–13, 215–16, 222–23

Human Rights Ombudsman (Procuraduría de Derechos Humanos; PDH), 135, 137, 193–94

Human Rights Watch, 302 n. 9

humiliation, 273–74

ich'el ta muk (respect), 97

IDB (Inter-American Development Bank), 16–17, 74, 78, 82

identity-based rights claims, 289–90, 300

IDIES (Institute of Economic and Social Research; Instituto de Investigaciones Ecónomicas y Sociales), 130

IFAD (International Fund for Agricultural Development), 154

IIDH (Inter-American Institute of Human Rights; Instituto Interamericano de Derechos Humanos), 302 n. 9

ILO (International Labor Organization), 42–44, 63, 68, 87 nn. 10–11, 129, 168 n. 8, 174, 231 n. 26, 288

Immediate Response Forces (Fuerzas de Respuesta Inmediata; FRI), 235

INAB (National Forestry Agency; Instituto Nacional de Bosques), 135–36

indigenismo, 259

Indigenous Congress (1974), 260–61

indigenous law, 174–78, 181–84, 185 nn. 6–7, 185 n. 10, 185 n. 13

indigenous people: autonomy of, 76;

cosmopolitanism of, 16; cultural rights of, 42–46; defined, 42–44; discrimination against, 4, 42, 172; history of, 172, 178–84; insensitivity toward, 173, 184 n. 3; literacy rate among, 21 n. 6, 172; marginalization of, 4, 20–21 n. 6, 42; Mayan ethnolinguistic groups among, 20 n. 6; poverty of, 20–21 n. 6, 172; rights of, 3–8, 22 n. 14, 42–46, 76, 87 nn. 10–11, 173–74, 176, 308–9; self-identifications of, 2–3; worldwide population of, 49 n. 17. *See also* human and indigenous rights in Chiapas

individual human rights, 264–65, 275. *See also* cultural rights and human rights

individualism, 308

INGUAT (Guatemalan Institute of Tourism), 148

Iñiguez, Felipe, 269

INMECAFE (Mexican Coffee Institute; Instituto Mexicano del Café), 222

Institute of Economic and Social Research (Instituto de Investigaciones Ecónomicas y Sociales; IDIES), 130

Instituto de Defensa Penal Público, 86 n. 7

Inter-American Court of Human Rights, 75, 197, 288, 316

Inter-American Development Bank (IDB), 16–17, 74, 78, 82

Inter-American Human Rights Commission, 213–14, 229 n. 9

Inter-American Institute of Human Rights (Instituto Interamericano de Derechos Humanos; IIDH), 302 n. 9

Interdiocesene Project for the Recuperation of Historical Memory (REMHI) report, 252–53

International Commission on Education for the Twenty-First Century, 33

International Covenant on Civil and Po-

litical Rights (1976), 28, 34, 40–41, 56, 67–68

International Covenant on Economic, Social and Cultural Rights (1966), 27, 67–68

International Covenant on International and Civil Rights, 76

International Federation for the Rights of Man (Federación Internaciónal de los Derechos del Hombre; FIDH), 302 n. 9

International Fund for Agricultural Development (IFAD), 154

International Indigenous Women's Forum, 173–74

International Labor Organization (ILO), 42–44, 63, 68, 87 nn. 10–11, 129, 168 n. 8, 174, 231 n. 26, 288

International Service for Peace (Servicio Internacional para la Paz; SIPAZ), 230 n. 20, 302 n. 9

International Women's Day, 172–73

Isaiah, Book of, 267

Iturbide, Agustín de, 5

Ixchíu, Pedro, 140

Ixil country (Quiché, Guatemala), 187–90, 197–99; Chacalté exhumation in, 201–2; demilitarization and insecurity in, 187–88, 192–95; Finca La Perla vs. Sotzil and Ilom, 195–97; highway robbery in, 187–88, 194–95; indigenous/Ladino solidarity in, 193; international aid to, 191–92; land conflict and historical memory, 200–203

Jahangir, Asma, 218

Jesus, 261, 272

John, Book of, 261

John Paul II, Pope, 283

Jonas, Susanne, 60–61, 63–64

Joyce, Rosemary, 179

Judicial Organization's Modernization Unit, 148

Pedro Pitarch is a professor of American anthropology at the Universidad Complutense de Madrid, Spain. He is the author of *Ch'ulel: Una etnografía de las almas tzeltales* (1996). His edited collections include (with Julián López García) *Los derechos humanos en tierras mayas: Política, representaciones y moralidad* (2001).

Shannon Speed is an assistant professor in the Department of Anthropology at the University of Texas, Austin. She is the editor (with R. Aída Hernández Castillo and Lynn M. Stephen) of *Dissident Women: Gender and Cultural Politics in Chiapas* (2006), and author of *Rights in Rebellion: Indigenous Struggles and Human Rights in Chiapas* (2007).

Xochitl Leyva Solano is a professor and researcher with the Centro de Investigaciones e Estudios Superiores en Antropología Social, CIESAS–Sureste in Chiapas. Her authored books include *Lacandonia al filo del agua* (1996) and (with Andrés Fábregas Puig) *La antropologia del sur: Contribucion testimonial* (2005). Her edited books include (with Valentina Napolitano) *Encuentros Anthropológicos: Politics, Identity and Mobility in Mexican Society* (1998).

Library of Congress Cataloging-in-Publication Data
Human rights in the Maya region : global politics, cultural contentions, and moral engagements / edited by Pedro Pitarch, Shannon Speed, and Xochitl Leyva Solano.
p. cm.
Includes bibliographical references and index.
ISBN 978-0-8223-4296-0 (cloth : alk. paper)
ISBN 978-0-8223-4313-4 (pbk. : alk. paper)
I. Mayas—Government relations. 2. Mayas—Legal status, laws, etc. 3. Human rights—Mexico—Chiapas. 4. Human rights—Guatemala. 5. Chiapas (Mexico)—Ethnic relations. 6. Guatemala—Ethnic relations. I. Pitarch, Pedro. II. Speed, Shannon, 1964– III. Leyva Solano, Xochitl.
F1435.3.P7.H86 2008
323.1197'42—dc22   2008028483

www.ingramcontent.com/pod-product-compliance
Lightning Source LLC
Chambersburg PA
CBHW051948270326
41929CB00015B/2577